NOVEL
NOSTALGIAS

NOVEL NOSTALGIAS

THE AESTHETICS OF ANTAGONISM IN NINETEENTH-CENTURY U.S. LITERATURE

JOHN FUNCHION

THE OHIO STATE UNIVERSITY PRESS
COLUMBUS

Copyright © 2015 by The Ohio State University.
All rights reserved.

Library of Congress Cataloging-in-Publication Data
Funchion, John, author.
 Novel nostalgias : the aesthetics of antagonism in nineteenth-century U.S. literature / John Funchion.
  pages cm
 Includes bibliographical references and index.
 ISBN 978-0-8142-1287-5 (cloth : alk. paper)
 1. Nostalgia in literature. 2. American fiction—19th century—History and criticism. 3. Nostalgia—United States—19th century. I. Title.
 PS377.F86 2015
 813'.409—dc23
                              2015013286

Cover design by James A. Baumann
Text design by James A. Baumann and Juliet Williams
Type set in Goudy Old Style
Printed by Sheridan Books

∞ The paper used in this publication meets the minimum requirements of the American National Standard for Information Sciences—Permanence of Paper for Printed Library Materials. ANSI Z39.48–1992.

9 8 7 6 5 4 3 2 1

For Melanie

Only other men's nostalgias offend.
—Raymond Williams

CONTENTS

Acknowledgments • ix

INTRODUCTION
There's No Place Like Home • 1

CHAPTER 1
Bad Romances:
Homesick Nationalisms in the Antebellum United States • 27

CHAPTER 2
Confederate Narratives and the Problem of Reconstruction • 61

CHAPTER 3
Longing for a People:
Hamlin Garland's and Pauline Hopkins's Populist Fictions • 96

CHAPTER 4
Left Nostalgia:
Revolutionary Aesthetics in the Radical Novel • 134

CHAPTER 5
Cosmopolitan Nostalgia in L. Frank Baum's Oz and
Henry James's America • 173

EPILOGUE
"Taking the Country Back" in the Twenty-First Century • 211

Bibliography • 217

Index • 241

ACKNOWLEDGMENTS

LET ME FIRST thank the anonymous readers of my manuscript whose extensive, constructive, and incisive comments greatly improved the quality of this book. I also wish to express my gratitude to my unflinchingly supportive editor Lindsay Martin, the press's former director Malcolm Litchfield, and the members of the Editorial Board of The Ohio State University Press. For their work on the production and marketing of *Novel Nostalgias*, Tara Cyphers, Laurie Avery, Linda Patterson Blackwell, and the rest of the OSUP staff all merit my sincerest thanks. I also greatly appreciate the care both OSUP's copyeditor, Rebecca S. Bender, and my graduate student fact-checker, Spencer Tricker, devoted to improving the quality of my manuscript. Portions of chapter 3 previously appeared in a different form as "Putting the Past Out to Pasture: Nostalgia, Regional Aesthetics and the Mutualist Imagination in the 1890s," *Modernist Cultures*, 3.2 (2008): 171–91 and are used by permission of the journal and Edinburgh University Press. A part of chapter 5 also appeared as "When Dorothy Became History: L. Frank Baum's Enduring Fantasy of Cosmopolitan Nostalgia," *Modern Language Quarterly*, 71.4 (2010): 429–51, and is reprinted with the permission of MLQ and Duke University Press.

This book first began to take shape as a dissertation at Brown University. Phil Gould proved to be my ideal director and a loyal mentor. He gave my own inchoate ideas room to breathe but rigorously helped me shape them into a literary argument with an ample archive. Stuart

Burrows tirelessly assisted me with refining my prose and always knew when to offer brilliant criticism or needed encouragement. Deak Nabers displayed a rare ability to get inside the thinking behind my project and always found ways to make it sharper. He also played an indispensable role in getting my manuscript to the capable editors at OSUP. Other faculty members at Brown also helped me develop professionally; Nancy Armstrong, Jim Egan, Laura Hess, William Keach, Kevin McLaughlin, Barbara Herrnstein Smith, and Len Tennenhouse all made my teaching and scholarship stronger. I have a great affection for my graduate cohort, especially David Babcock, Tad Davies, Jonna Iacono, John Melson, Laurel Rayburn, Bethany Shepherd, Steve Satterfield, and Rebecca Summerhays. I owe intellectual and emotional debts too numerous to enumerate to my fellow Americanists Brian Sweeney and Siân Silyn Roberts. Keri Holt continues to be my close and trusted academic sidekick, and she graciously read and commented upon every page of this book.

Before I entered the doctoral program at Brown, I received expert instruction from faculty members at the University of Minnesota and Creighton University. At Minnesota, Tom Augst, Andy Elfenbein, Qadri Ismail, and Richard Leppert all left their mark on my thinking. Pat Crain and Ed Griffin deserve to be singled out for being enthusiastic supporters of my scholarship and for continuing to offer me their invaluable insights whenever I need them. At Creighton, my undergraduate advisers, Bridget Keegan and Greg Zacharias, transformed the way I thought about literature. Their friendship and mentorship has sustained me over the years. Getting to the place in my career where I could compose this book would not have been possible without them.

This manuscript matured into a book thanks to the intellectual verve of the many scholars that I have gotten to know at SEA and C19 conferences and as reviewers of my writing. I thank Duncan Faherty for championing my work through thick and thin and for being a model colleague in every imaginable way. For commenting on early versions of various chapters in *Novel Nostalgias*, I want to recognize especially Marshall Brown, Daniel Moore, Catherine Jurca, Jessica Burstein, David Luis-Brown, Hsuan Hsu, Lori Merish, and Elizabeth Maddock Dillon. For their intellectual insights and camaraderie, I thank Gabe Cervantes, Andy Doolen, Michael Drexler, Robert Gunn, James Lilley, Gretchen Murphy, Steve Thomas, and Ed White. I have learned a great deal from Ned Watts, and his intellectual generosity knows no bounds.

I have found myself surrounded by a warm circle of friends and colleagues in Miami that span two institutions and many departments, and I deeply regret not being able to list them all here. Junior faculty members depend on the support, patience, and wisdom of their department chairs. I could not have asked for two better chairs in this regard than Pam Hammons and Pat McCarthy. I am indebted to the Center for the Humanities at the University of Miami for supporting my research by releasing me from my teaching commitments and for giving me the opportunity to present early drafts of this book to the other fellows. I also received summer research and travel support in the form of three Provost Research Awards from UM that played crucial roles in expanding my book's breadth of archival materials. Funds from the UM Department of English also made it possible for me to hire the graduate research assistant who helped with the final stages of production. I am grateful to those who mentored and supported me in crucial ways in the Department of English, especially Joe Alkana, Tom Goodman, Tassie Gwilliam, Brenna Munro, Ranen Omer-Sherman, and Jeffrey Shoulson. I also cannot imagine navigating my early academic career without being able to depend on Tim Watson's guidance and friendship; this book benefited from his attentive readings of it. I have relished the conversations on matters academic and not-so-academic with Brad Cokelet, Jason Pearl, Nathaniel Cadle, and Jaswinder Bolina. Discussions with Mike Bernath also strengthened this book's engagement with U.S. historical scholarship. In addition to being a stalwart friend and an expert snorkeler, Joel Nickels always reinvigorates my research pursuits and political commitments. Renée Fox has proven to be a great partner in crime when it comes to all things nineteenth century and 1990s.

During and before my professional career, I have relied greatly on family and longtime friends. My sister Maura's visits and her contagious laugh over the years always have provided me with much-needed respites from my work. My in-laws, Marie and Edward, deserve thanks for kindly welcoming us into their home for extended periods of time when we needed to escape the Miami heat. Dave Wake and Norah Bringer are friends who are always there when you most need them. My childhood compatriots from South Dakota remain an important part of my life and are something of an institution. I am grateful for the support offered by my parents, Michael and Margaret, and my mother-in-law, Elizabeth.

I would have never completed this book without the support, humor, intelligence, and love of Melanie Spencer. She found time to read and comment on many versions of this project even while successfully pursuing first a career in publishing and then in the law. I have never ceased marveling over how lucky I was to meet the person who first introduced herself to me in college by poking fun at my last name. And as this book neared completion, our wonderful daughter Dorothy Day became part of our lives. Her determination to fix anything she thinks is broken in the world gives me great hope. Around her it is hard to feel nostalgic; I can only eagerly anticipate the future.

INTRODUCTION

THERE'S NO PLACE LIKE HOME

No OTHER POEM written by a U.S. author embodies nineteenth-century nostalgia better than John Howard Payne's "Home, Sweet Home." Originally appearing in his drama *Clari; or, the Maid of Milan*, which first debuted in London in 1823, this ballad is sung by the eponymous character as she reflects upon the Italian village she left behind. Exiled from her fellow country dwellers, she declaims that "though we may roam, / Be it ever so humble, there's no place like home."[1] Her yearning to return to the familiar charms of her home becomes so overpowering that it severely impairs her enjoyment of the surrounding "pleasures and palaces" of the city.[2] These lines cast her as someone suffering from nostalgia, which her nineteenth-century audience would have understood as synonymous with homesickness or the irrepressible longing to return home.

With startling emotional efficiency, Payne captures three intersecting characterizations of this mental condition. As an individual sentiment, nostalgia encompasses Clari's personal desire to return to the home of her childhood. As a potential illness, it sends her into a state of depression by making her wish for "present death."[3] And as a socially circulating experience, it is as much an expression of Clari's own plight as it is

---

1. Payne, "Home, Sweet Home," lines 1–2.
2. Ibid., line 1.
3. Payne, *Clari*, 1.1. References are to act and scene.

the attachment that binds everyone together in her natal community, as we are told this song "of [her] native village . . . dwells upon every lip there."⁴ Her homesickness is initially debilitating, but Payne displays its potential power when it rescues her from the seductive advances of the play's libertine. She preserves her virtue not by appealing to the sympathy of others but by remaining committed to returning home. She is restored to her village, and the play concludes triumphantly with the chorus proclaiming, "Welcome home! Welcome home!"⁵

While few would later remember the name of Payne's drama set and performed overseas, generations of nineteenth-century Americans would come to know intimately the words to "Home, Sweet Home" as their national song for "homesick wanderers" and "the *Ranz des Vaches* of the nations."⁶ Newspapers and periodicals widely reprinted it several thousand times over the course of the century.⁷ It achieved its greatest notoriety during the years of the Civil War when it became banned on the frontlines, because Union and Confederate doctors feared it would afflict soldiers with bouts of potentially deadly nostalgia.⁸ "Home, Sweet Home" nevertheless emerged as the favored ballad in both sections, as everyone found comfort in a song describing the estrangement they felt from a nation now rendered unfamiliar by the ravages of war. Its restorative promise also proved malleable when wed specifically to either the Union or the Confederate cause. It could conjure up images of a reunited nation or an independent Southern state. Even after the cessation of hostilities, the song sustained its hold on the American imagination. It surfaced in whole or in part in Western dime novels, imperial romances, and eventually in L. Frank Baum's *The Wonderful Wizard of Oz* (1900). Its circulation and citation was so pervasive that in 1889, the prominent journalist and periodical editor B. O. Flower could confidently declare Payne's ballad to be "the great heart song of this century."⁹

---

4. Ibid., 1.1.

5. Ibid., 3.2.

6. Payne, "Home, Sweet Home," 1. The effect of the "Ranz des Vaches on the Swiss" was frequently noted in the nineteenth century as one "creating an irresistible nostalgia, or home sickness." "Zaragoza," 353.

7. A search of the Archive of Americana, for instance, yields well over nine thousand separate citations or republications of Payne's ballad in nineteenth-century books, newspapers, and periodicals. Nineteenth-century biographers who completed studies of Payne's life also insisted the song was universally circulated and noted that its original publisher printed "upwards of one hundred thousand copies" just a year after it first appeared in *Clari*. Harrison, *John Howard Payne, Dramatist, Poet, Actor, and Author of Home, Sweet Home!*, 107.

8. See Matt, *Homesickness*, 5 and 86–87.

9. Flower, *Lessons Learned from Other Lives*, 97.

The enormous popularity of "Home, Sweet Home" offers us an important window into the social psychology of the nineteenth-century United States. The song and its appropriation by others instructively establish that nostalgia had the capacity to forge social bonds though longing instead of belonging. This form of yearning can bind people together through their shared psychical exile from a space or a time to which they long to return. This longing might seem to conform to a Freudian understanding of melancholy, but as "Home, Sweet Home" makes clear, nostalgia differs from melancholy in two crucial ways. First, its object of emotional investment always assumes the form of a home or an important point of origin, whereas the object of melancholy is categorically promiscuous. To be sure, our contemporary understanding of nostalgia may extend to objects that do not seem particularly homelike, but in the nineteenth century nostalgia and homesickness were one and the same. The longing to return home could manifest itself temporally as the wish to return to a particular past, as even Clari associates her homesickness with her "earliest and tenderest recollections."[10] Later, expanded editions of "Home, Sweet Home" further illustrated this modal variation in the added lines, "To us, in spite of the absence of years, / How sweet the remembrance of home still appears!"[11] Second, even though both the melancholic and the nostalgic process loss as exclusion, the affective logic of nostalgia operates as the mirror opposite to melancholia. In the case of the melancholic, as Anne Anlin Cheng reminds us, the loss of the absent object must be denied "in order to sustain the fiction of possession," and this object must never return because it would imperil this "form of possession" by terminating the melancholic's perpetual self-denial.[12] The nostalgic, by contrast, insists upon the loss of an object that may never have been present in the first place in order to demand its return. The underlying fiction of homesickness, then, is not principally one of possession but one of loss, as it conceals acts of imagination as ones of restoration. For this reason, historians and literary critics often chide nostalgic representations of the past for profaning history with anachronisms. "There is no place like home" until the nostalgic participates in its creation.

---

10. Payne, *Clari*, 1.1.
11. Payne, "Home, Sweet Home," lines 29–30.
12. Cheng, *The Melancholy of Race*, 9. Cheng succinctly distills Freud's understanding of melancholy as a mental state contrasted with mourning. As "a healthy response to loss," mourning "is finite in character and accepts substitution (that is, the lost object can be relinquished and eventually replaced)." Cheng, 7. Also see Freud, "Mourning and Melancholia."

Novel Nostalgias argues that nineteenth-century writers imagined new affiliations among people through forms of nostalgic longing instead of national belonging. Whether imagining this psychical exile in temporal or spatial terms, writers used nostalgia to marshal this invented sense of community to advance an array of different political possibilities, especially when they gave it a narrative structure, as many novels did. As a narrative and psychical phenomenon capable of being tied to a multiplicity of ideologies, nostalgia could be used by Southern slave owners and their slaves or by industrial magnates and their impoverished laborers alike to assert their rival visions of the nation as the one sanctioned by a lost precedent awaiting recovery. In nineteenth- and early-twentieth-century novels imbued with nostalgia, we can find a long queue of protagonists—runaway slaves, impressed sailors, drafted soldiers, orphaned children, Confederate sympathizers, dispossessed farmers, besieged radicals, and disaffected Brahmins—waiting to reclaim estranged images of a place, a past, or a people that may have never existed. These narratives, along with a complementary repository of poems, essays, treatises, and orations, served as the conduits for imagining rival nationalisms and antagonistic political movements in the long nineteenth century.

By demonstrating how novels from William Wells Brown's *Clotel* (1853) to Upton Sinclair's *The Jungle* (1906) nostalgically intensified rather than mollified political antagonisms, this book participates in the turn to affect, aesthetics, and politics in nineteenth-century U.S. literary and cultural studies.[13] *Novel Nostalgias* departs from accounts of the nineteenth-century novel characterizing it as a consensus-generating form complicit with disciplinary culture and "the incorporation of America," or "the emergence of a changed, more tightly structured society with new hierarchies of control, and also changed conceptions of that society, of America itself."[14] My book instead examines how the content and form of the nation remained uncertain and contested from the antebellum era until the rise of the Progressive state. Even as American literary realism "acquired a repertory of uses as a result of its

---

13. See, for example, the following for representative examples of this scholarship: Cahill, *Liberty of the Imagination*; Castiglia, *Interior States*; Castronovo, *Beautiful Democracy*; Fleissner, *Women, Compulsion, Modernity*; Gilmore, *Aesthetic Materialism*; Hendler, *Public Sentiments*; Murison, *The Politics of Anxiety in Nineteenth-Century American Literature*; Thrailkill, *Affecting Fictions*; and Ivy Wilson, *Specters of Democracy*.

14. Trachtenberg, *The Incorporation of America*, 3–4. This work encompasses a wide range of scholarship, from Warner Berthoff's consensus-driven celebration of liberalism in *The Ferment of Realism* to later Foucaldian studies, such as Kaplan, *The Social Construction of American Realism*, and Seltzer, *Henry James and the Art of Power*.

competing appropriations," as Nancy Glazener persuasively maintains, *Atlantic*-group periodicals cast realism as "a uniquely democratic and modern form," in contrast to other genres of fiction.[15] By attending to the ways many of these competing genres challenged the *Atlantic* group's ideal of realist democratic consensus, my own work partly takes its cue from Glazener's magisterial study by reading for nostalgia rather than for realism. My book also questions the truism that Americans habitually forget their past, as expressed in Gore Vidal's memorable phrase, "the United States of Amnesia."[16] Nineteenth-century literature and politics suffered less from amnesia than from *hypomnesia*: a selective forgetting and recollection of places and pasts that violently depose rival nationalisms and histories.[17] These nostalgic narratives competed for cultural dominance: many Southerners became more vehemently sectionalist after the Civil War, Populists imagined a classless nation indebted to the tradition of Jeffersonian democracy, and African-American writers unearthed subterranean histories of the U.S. Revolution to imagine a racially inclusive republic. The culture wars of this era, in other words, were a series of battles among contending nostalgias.

In the literary works analyzed in *Novel Nostalgias*, the appearance of this sentiment formally undermines the consensual logic of the historical romance or William Dean Howells's vision of American literary realism. Formally, nostalgia initially figures as a psychologically and generically disruptive force in the narratives that enlist it. It is at these moments when it assumes an aesthetic character. As explained in greater detail later in the introduction, I maintain throughout this book that we can best apprehend nostalgia's aesthetic qualities by turning to Jacques Rancière's characterization of the aesthetic as a regime of art. Art in the aesthetic regime belongs to "a specific sensorium" that can upend established genres of fiction and canons of taste that structure our perception of the world.[18] Art that participates in the aesthetic regime makes the distributions of power and the divisions among people visible in order to imagine new political possibilities. In the narratives examined in this book,

---

15. Glazener, *Reading for Realism*, 13.
16. Vidal, *Imperial America*, 7.
17. For his theory of *hypomnēsis*, see Derrida, *Archive Fever*, 7–31 and *Dissemination*, 91 and 95–117. Here nostalgia can work in tandem with the creation of new nationalisms through a process of forgetting that Ernest Renan saw as essential to the vitality of modern national movements. See Renan, "What Is a Nation?"
18. Rancière, *Aesthetics and Its Discontents*, 29.

the moments of generic estrangement and political awareness Rancière attributes to the aesthetic set into motion a nostalgic narrative logic. The longing for a lost time, place, or community becomes the grounds for insisting upon its restoration in the here and now.

Nostalgia's affective and aesthetic qualities are intrinsic to its longer history as a deviant sentiment that physicians believed took root in the brain's common sense. Its perceived tendency to afflict this part of the mind was significant because the common sense was seen as the brain's cognitive command center and where philosophers located aesthetic judgment. Nostalgia's legacy as an illness is a long one, and the medical discourse on this feeling elucidates its ability both to exact turmoil on the senses and to generate new imaginative possibilities. By surveying both the history of nostalgia before the nineteenth century and its place in contemporary discussions of affect and aesthetics, we can better grasp the way nostalgia unsettles the divisions between the empirical and the fantastic, between the universal and the particular, and between history and art. I lay this foundation in the two sections that follow before outlining how I examine the literary, cultural, and political significance of nostalgia in U.S. novels of the long nineteenth century.

DIAGNOSING HOMESICKNESS: THE PATHOLOGY OF A SENTIMENT

Nostalgia's early medical history sheds light on its evolving psychological and aesthetic dynamism from the seventeenth to the nineteenth century. When nostalgia eventually worked its way into the Anglophone world, it displayed four characteristics that laid the groundwork for the cultural and aesthetic role it would play in nineteenth-century U.S. literature. It remained categorically elusive and intellectually threatening; it was inextricably bound to the imagination and the faculty of common sense; it served as the basis for national, subnational, and supranational communal bonds; and it became a more democratic disease than the larger genus of melancholic ailments to which it originally belonged.

This story begins in 1688 with what could have easily been just one of many forgotten early-modern medical dissertations. To complete the requirements for his degree at the University of Basel, Johannes Hofer investigated what the Swiss commonly called "the Wasting Disease," a grave form of homesickness or a "grief for the lost charm of the Native Land" that afflicted young girls, university students, sailors, and conscripted soldiers.[19] Symptoms of this mental illness, which also went by the names *das Heimweh* and *la Maladie du Pays* in the multilingual vernaculars of the Old Swiss Confederacy, consisted of "lability of emotion, including profound bouts of weeping, anorexia, a generalized 'wasting way,' and, not infrequently, attempts at suicide."[20] Producing the first thorough medical account of this affliction, Hofer gave the disease a new name: *nostalgia*, from the Greek words for home (*nostos*) and longing or suffering (*algia*). His account of it created problems for seventeenth-century conceptions of the nervous system and psychology. As the study of the brain was undergoing a series of revolutionary shifts, nostalgia upended these categories as it would continue to thwart subsequent disciplinary endeavors to categorize it in the nineteenth century.

Nostalgia fostered conceptual dissonance by collapsing three separate internal senses—imagination, cognition, and memory—into an indeterminate diseased one. By affecting the internal senses, it also corrupted the common sense. Its perceived ability to compromise the common sense meant that its sufferers would process external sensory data in radically—even if in maligned—new ways. Hofer propounded that "the strength of the imagination alone" could wreak such devastating effects on the body.[21] By tying nostalgia to the imagination and the common sense, Hofer provided the basis for its close association with aesthetics. Indeed, all of his patients deliriously recollected altered versions of their homes, so that these memories supplanted the places themselves. He accentuates this point by ending his dissertation with a series of excerpts from poems about homesickness. Through a comingling of memory, imagination, and common sense, nostalgia allowed people to dream of a different kind of home before this mania killed them.

Nostalgia's etiological connection to the imagination explains both its dubious status as a maladaptive disorder and its prominent place in Anglophone literary and popular culture in the decades and centuries after Hofer completed his study. In the eighteenth century, Erasmus Darwin argued the voluntary exercise of the imagination could trigger an irrepressible yearning to return home. Identifying it as one of the "diseases of volition," Darwin reported that some physicians saw a connection between reverie, which usually "consists of violent voluntary exertions of ideas to relieve pain," and "particular insanities . . . like

---

19. Hofer, *Medical Dissertation on Nostalgia*, 380.
20. Fred Davis, *Yearning for Yesterday*, 1–2.
21. Hofer, *Medical Dissertation*, 388.

nostalgia."[22] Nostalgia's inextricable link to the imagination and its corruption of memory made it relevant to the discourse of empiricist and associationist psychology in the eighteenth and early nineteenth centuries. Associationism traced its roots back to John Locke, who argued in *An Essay Concerning Human Understanding* (1693) that "some of our ideas have a natural correspondence and connexion one with another."[23] Both external stimuli and other internal ideas forged these associations, which could be voluntary or accidental. When passionately dwelled upon, memories could create new associations among ideas, as "our affections" can introduce "ideas to our memory which had otherwise lain quiet and unregarded."[24] Locke feared that associations of this kind could muddle both the intellect and memory.[25]

Associationists and Scottish Enlightenment thinkers rarely broached the subject of nostalgia outright, but it indirectly surfaces in their work. Dugald Stewart, who significantly developed Locke's theories, alluded to nostalgia when discussing "the influence of perceptible objects in reviving former thoughts and former feelings."[26] He noted how "the well-known effect of a particular tune on Swiss regiments, when at a distance from home, furnishes a very striking illustration of the peculiar power of a perception, or of an impression on the senses, to awaken associated thoughts and feelings."[27] He never refers to this phenomenon as a disease, and instead this allusion to homesickness serves as a poignant example of how association works by correlating external perceptions to previous ideas. Stewart expressed concerns, however, that the associations fostered by nostalgia could unravel his theory of the mind, as evidenced in his understanding of the imagination. He insisted that "the tendency in the human mind to associate or connect its thoughts together" should not be called the imagination.[28] And yet nostalgia appeared to have precisely this cognitive effect, filtering and altering memories and external perceptions though the faculty of the imagination.

---

22. Darwin, *Zoonomia*, 361. For an excellent summation of nostalgia's place in eighteenth-century European medical literature, see Rosen, "Nostalgia," 33–39.
23. Locke, *An Essay Concerning Human Understanding*, 316.
24. Ibid., 99.
25. Given the way nostalgia compromised memory through this associative process, Linda Austin aptly expounds upon the various ways nostalgia behaved "as an associative disorder of the cerebral kind." Austin, *Nostalgia in Transition*, 16.
26. Stewart, *Elements of the Philosophy of the Human Mind*, 253.
27. Ibid., 253–54.
28. Ibid., 259.

Eighteenth-century thinkers' belief that nostalgia could manipulate sensory information and recollection through the imagination became especially clear in discussions surrounding the common sense. Crucially important to Scottish Enlightenment intellectuals and Immanuel Kant, the common sense, or the *sensus communis*, generally referred to a governing internal sense that rendered information from the external and other internal senses intelligible. As Thomas Reid explained, it describes a "degree of reason" used "to judge of things self-evident."[29] Kant altered the concept to define it more precisely as the mechanism that synthesizes our cognitive apprehension of an aesthetic object with our subjective feeling (i.e., judgments of taste) about it. Since this synthetic understanding of the object must "be capable of being universally communicated," the existence of a common sense must be presupposed, otherwise "the subjective condition of cognizing . . . could not arise."[30] This sense produces a "common human understanding" of the world that "takes account (*a priori*) of everyone else's way of representing in thought" a given object.[31]

Nostalgia could interfere with the proper functioning of the common sense by universalizing a particular understanding of an external place; the yearning for this object could render it falsely beautiful. In his late writing, Kant directly acknowledged this feature of the disorder when he noted that "the Swiss . . . are overcome by *homesickness*."[32] Yet he observed that "when they revisit these places, they are greatly disappointed."[33] Cases such as this one demonstrate, for Kant, that the imagination can manufacture illusions of what "we think we see and feel outside us" but "what is only in our mind."[34] As a nineteenth-century magazine writer would succinctly put it, nostalgia "silences the judgment" of the perceptible world.[35] And later the British writer George Sala would speculate that nostalgia could become a kind of "form-sickness," especially in the United States, where one could experience an "unsatisfied yearning for those broken lines, irregular forms, and infinite gradations of colour—reacting as those conditions of form invariably do on the man-

---

29. Reid, *Essays on the Intellectual Powers of Man*, 433.
30. Kant, *Critique of the Power of Judgment*, 122–23.
31. Ibid., 173.
32. Kant, *Anthropology from a Pragmatic Point of View*, 53.
33. Ibid., 53–54.
34. Ibid., 53.
35. "Home Sickness," 223.

ners and characteristics of the people—which are only to be met with in very old countries."[36]

Nostalgia haunted Scottish Enlightenment philosophy and faculty psychology as a renegade sentiment and as a human passion essential to national feeling. British philosophers from Locke to Francis Hutcheson associated the benevolent bonds of filial love with national feeling, which generated social and political cohesion. Hutcheson never uses the word *nostalgia* in his writings, but he underscores the importance of "national Love" in *An Inquiry into the Original of Our Ideas of Beauty and Virtue in Two Treatises*.[37] What makes his discussion of "national love" germane to nostalgia in particular as opposed to the formation of nationalism in general is how he frames it. Discussing the link between self-love and social benevolence, Hutcheson examines the basis of "publick affections."[38] He invites his readers to consider whether "a Person, for Trade, had left his native Country, and with all his Kindred had settled his Fortunes abroad, without any View of returning; and only imagine he had receiv'd no Injurys from his Country: ask such a Man, would it give him no Pleasure to hear of the Prosperity of his Country?"[39] The power of this national sentiment is thus most felt not at home but when abroad.[40] One can "acquire a national Love" for "another Country," but the recollection of one's native country will always function as the original conduit through which "Associations, Friendships, Familys, natural Affections of human Nature, and other human Sentiments" were first fostered and later remembered.[41] These bonds did not always engender benevolence. Born out of estrangement, they easily could drive rival nationalisms. Refining the work of Hutcheson, Adam Smith described how "the animosity of hostile factions" had the capacity to sweep everyone up by the "general contagion" of violent feeling.[42] Nostalgia frequently would be described as an unrestrained desire "to revisit [one's] native land" that could spread

---

36. Sala, "Form-Sickness," 28.
37. Hutcheson, *An Inquiry into the Original of Our Ideas of Beauty and Virtue in Two Treatises*, 115.
38. Ibid., 114.
39. Ibid.
40. Hutcheson describes how the benevolence one feels for one's native land can serve as the basis for a cosmopolitan sensibility or universal benevolence "extended to all Mankind." Hutcheson, *Inquiry*, 114.
41. Ibid., 115.
42. Adam Smith, *The Theory of Moral Sentiments*, 155. For more on the relationship between feeling and contagion, see Silyn Roberts, *Gothic Subjects*, 45–50, and Murison, *Politics*, 107–35.

"rapidly and frightfully" as a "contagion."[43] Though in its strict pathological incarnation nostalgia afflicted only individuals, it transformed into a social emotion later in the nineteenth century to express those political antagonisms examined in *Novel Nostalgias*.

Eighteenth-century thinkers underscored the democratic character of nostalgia when they distinguished it from melancholy. Melancholy became a condition closely associated with the educated and affluent.[44] It was a vaunted condition because it stemmed from a contemplation of mortality. Conversely, everyone could experience nostalgia. Some essayists speculated that "the *Jews*, whilst not yet forsaken and quite abandon'd, were more than any people" inclined to become nostalgic.[45] The English physician William Falconer, who wrote more extensively than many of his peers on nostalgia, stressed that "the lowest ranks are not exempted from this disease."[46] Expressing another widely held view, a letter published in *The Lounger* determined that "Ladies in particular are extremely liable" to fall ill with the most diminutive manifestation of it, "the *Maladie de la ville*."[47] For this reason soldiers of lower rank, or conscripts, proved more vulnerable to bouts of homesickness. And doctors widely contended that outbreaks of nostalgia occurred when "press gangs were especially active in ports" in order to bolster the ranks of the Royal Navy during times of war.[48] By the end of the eighteenth century, doctors associated nostalgia with what they termed *Cachexia Africana*: "a disease to which the negroes, and particularly those lately imported [as slaves to the West Indies], are much subject," which visibly manifested itself as "*dirt-eating*."[49] The eighteenth-century literature on the subject established nostalgia as a democratic illness, one to which commoners especially fell victim but one exhibited by "men of every nation, who, in foreign countries, feel the want of those delights and enjoyments they would meet with among their friends at home."[50]

---

43. "Proceedings of Public Societies," 338.
44. See Burton, *The Anatomy of Melancholy*, 192–93. For the relationship between the learned and melancholy, see Ficino, "Learned People and Melancholy."
45. Harle, *An Historical Essay on the State of Physick in the Old and New Testament, and the Apocryphal Interval*, 70.
46. Falconer, *A Dissertation on the Influence of the Passions upon Disorders of the Body*, 91.
47. "To the Author of the *Lounger*," 308.
48. Rosen, "Nostalgia," 38.
49. "An Account of the *Cachexia Africana*," 171. See also Fleissner, "Earth-Eating, Addiction, Nostalgia."
50. Hamilton, *The Duties of a Regimental Surgeon Considered*, 128.

In Great Britain and throughout the rest of Europe, the number of publications on nostalgia began waning by the late eighteenth century. In North America, on the other hand, Revolutionary War doctors found "nostalgia . . . or the homesickness was a frequent disease in the American army."[51] These cases appeared in the most important American psychological treatise of the first half of the nineteenth century: Benjamin Rush's *Medical Inquiries and Observations upon the Diseases of the Mind* (1812). His study of homesickness leaves its nosology unaltered. He expressed relief that "the disease . . . has passed away with the events of the American Revolution."[52] Little mention of the disease can be found, except in the form of retrospective accounts of the Revolution, until the era of the Mexican-American War. Once again U.S. soldiers fell victim to nostalgia, and this time the idea of homesickness entered into wider circulation. African-American slaves, women, students, immigrants, and Western settlers all emerged as groups especially vulnerable to this ailment. American newspapers and periodicals continued to publicize the features that preceding physicians and philosophers attributed to it. These characteristics—its elision of disciplinary forms of knowledge, its aesthetic volatility, and its ability to ignite the political imagination—all became features of the novels and narratives examined in *Novel Nostalgias* that broke with the forms and genres that participated in the generation of social cohesion.

AFFECTED ANTAGONISM AND REVOLUTIONARY AESTHETICS

Having followed nostalgia's vexed career through early-modern and eighteenth-century psychology, my book embarks upon a path that sets it apart from previous work on this subject. I argue that fictional narratives, the novel especially, mobilized nostalgia as a social affect to stoke U.S. political antagonisms in the long nineteenth century. Existing scholarship, by contrast, chronicles nostalgia's ongoing psychoaffective metamorphosis against the backdrop of psychology. Nicholas Dames examines

---

51. Benjamin Rush, "Extract from an Account of the Influence of the Military & Political Events of the American Revolution upon the Human Body," *Salem Mercury* (Salem, MA), February 10, 1789. Extracted from one of his medical reports on the American Revolution, Rush's account of nostalgia was reprinted widely in major newspapers throughout the United States.

52. Rush, *Medical Inquiries and Observations upon the Diseases of the Mind*, 115.

how Victorian psychologists and novelists consciously dispensed with memory to embrace a nostalgic forgetting, giving rise to a particular subject that he calls the *amnesic self*.[53] Revisiting noncognitive theories of recollection, Linda M. Austin tracks nostalgia's transformation in Victorian culture from a disease into a depathologized aesthetics that celebrated the pleasure of artistic reproduction more so than originality.[54] Susan J. Matt insists that from the eighteenth century to the present, Americans constantly wrestled with homesickness to fashion their sense of individualism and to adapt to a highly mobile capitalist society.[55] Each of these scholars cast the nineteenth century as a moment when nostalgia ceased to be a disease and became instead a mechanism for coping with but not retreating from modernity. I maintain that nostalgia never fully shed its pathologized connotation. For generations of nineteenth-century and twentieth-century intellectuals, nostalgia remained a blight—a social disease synonymous with anti-intellectualism. Although I establish nostalgia's place in medical and psychological history here in the introduction and again in the first chapter, *Novel Nostalgias* principally attends to how its pathological attributes—its overstimulation of the imagination, amplification of nationalist feelings, and capacity to afflict everyone irrespective of rank or race—became aesthetically and affectively translated into broader cultural terms as a set of rival political antagonisms in nineteenth-century U.S. literature.

Nostalgia has an estranged relationship with affect studies and academic inquiry more broadly. We are constantly encouraged to keep it at arm's length. It intermittently surfaces in this body of work as a form of resignation or as "an objectless mood" that has "a de-animating effect on those affected" by it.[56] Defined as an essentially reactionary sentiment, it sometimes appears as a "depleted" or "defensive aesthetics."[57] This enervated nostalgia clashes with the perception of it as a dangerous sensation. Ideologically, it conceals political and economic fissures, creating the illusion of a subject and society devoid of fragmentation.[58] Histo-

---

53. See Dames, *Amnesiac Selves*, 8–10.
54. See Austin, *Nostalgia*, 2–4.
55. See Matt, *Homesickness*, 5–11.
56. Ngai, *Ugly Feelings*, 31. Lacan fleetingly casts nostalgia as an objectless desire when he likens it to the yearning for the experience of "not-having" that produces a longing for the phallus associated with the castration complex. Lacan, *Écrits*, 582. Philip Fisher partially anticipates Ngai's view of nostalgia's de-animating effects when he deems it a comparatively "less vehement" passion. Philip Fisher, *The Vehement Passions*, 25.
57. Castronovo, *Beautiful Democracy*, 3.
58. Žižek maintains that "the function of nostalgic fascination is thus to conceal" the

rians vigorously reject it as a flawed affection for "a warped or wasted past," depriving history of its content.⁵⁹ Nostalgia, in these instances, is a facile reaction to modernity or the yearning for a "charming simplicity" that evokes a "lifeless and undifferentiated sense of the past."⁶⁰ Even worse, it can be used as a tool for mass manipulation or propaganda. The work of U.S. Cold War intellectuals is peppered with invectives directed at this image of nostalgia, following Hannah Arendt's association of it with the rise of fascism and totalitarianism in 1930s Germany.⁶¹ After the Cold War, New Americanist and cultural studies scholars chided their intellectual predecessors for engaging in what Bruce Robbins describes as "retreats to the Arnoldian humanist position, with its immense nostalgia for Europe's lost cultural splendors."⁶² Fredric Jameson performed one of the most trenchant critiques of what he referred to as "nostalgia for the present."⁶³ Nostalgia, specifically the postmodern variety, operates as "some ultimate 'false consciousness'" that deprives the present of historicity or a relation to real historical time with a past and a future.⁶⁴ In the films saturated with this type of nostalgia, the present becomes perpetual and bereft of historical content, with the past evoked only through previous styles and fashions.⁶⁵

---

antimony between the eye and gaze to create the illusion of Cartesian subjectivity, yet my survey of nostalgia's medical genealogy reveals that it pathologically threatens the integrity of the Cartesian subject. Žižek, *Looking Awry*, 115.

59. Kammen, *Mystic Chords of Memory*, 296.

60. Lasch, *The True and Only Heaven*, 118. Also see Lears, *No Place of Grace*, 3–58. Agacinski also insists that, with the advent of modernity, nostalgia "has lost its meaning in everyday life" and become supplanted by alternative, more ontologically complex forms of displacement. Agacinski, *Time Passing*, 17.

61. Arendt attributed the rise of totalitarianism that spread across Europe in the 1930s partially to the emergence of political parities "more and more apologetic and nostalgic in their political approach." Arendt, *The Origins of Totalitarianism*, 315. Arendt's association of totalitarianism with nostalgia thrived in the intellectual climate of U.S. postwar consensus liberalism. When differentiating liberalism from Bolshevism and Nazism, Schlesinger asserts "it is a question of distinguishing between nostalgia and actuality—or rather of holding fast to what one believes to be sane and true." Schlesinger, *The Vital Center*, 147. Even radical New York Intellectuals, such as Irving Howe, cautioned against succumbing to "*the lure of an earlier America, or the corruptions of nostalgia.*" Howe, "Reganism," 414. Richard Hofstadter expounded upon the dangers of nostalgia by aligning it with the anti-intellectualism that plagued American culture and politics since Calvinism first washed ashore in New England. See Hofstadter, *Anti-Intellectualism in American Life*, 301 and 414–19.

62. Robbins, "Espionage as Vocation," 276.

63. Jameson, *Postmodernism*, 279.

64. Ibid., 282.

65. He distinguishes this nostalgia for the present, which he sees as a postmodern condition tied to the emergence of the nostalgia film, from modernist nostalgia, or a painful

Nostalgia is thus usually characterized as a state of deprivation: a de-animating affect, a depleted aesthetics, a lifeless past, or an empty history. These characterizations echo its seventeenth-century designation as a "Wasting Disease."[66] Its effect ranges widely, from the trivial consumption of retro fashions to the terrifying mobilization of fascist desire.[67] Due to its mutable and rebarbative properties, Svetlana Boym separates *reflective* from *restorative* nostalgia. The former denotes a contemplative state tied to individual memory; it can be melancholic or ironic. Restorative nostalgia animates collective and violent forms of recovery; it describes the effort to reconstitute a lost time or homeland. Yet Boym concedes the two senses "overlap in their frames of reference," reaffirming nostalgia's inherent capacity for eliding categorization.[68] Jameson registers its fluctuations when he notes that its "content seems somehow to contaminate the form."[69]

As a sensational, cognitive, and imaginative phenomenon, nostalgia straddles what many see as the divisions among affect, emotion, and feeling. Affect is a presubjective and prelinguistic phenomenon, while emotions and feelings are generally deemed linguistically representable experiences.[70] While emotions and feelings are also couched as communal and individual experiences, respectively, affects manifest them-

---

longing for a past that can be retrieved only aesthetically. See Jameson, *Postmodernism*, 19–21 and 279–96.

66. Hofer, *Medical Dissertation*, 380.

67. Anthropologists and postcolonial scholars also closely associated nostalgia with imperialism. This imperialist nostalgia is attached to the very cultures and peoples displaced by the colonial process. See Rosaldo, *Culture and Truth*, 68–89.

68. Boym, *The Future of Nostalgia*, 49.

69. Jameson, *Postmodernism*, 280. Nostalgia's formal instability is also manifested as synesthesia. Adorno, for example, remarks that Franz Schreker's music "arouses nostalgia, like the nostalgia that attaches itself to the traces of smells which involuntarily recall happiness in childhood." Adorno, *Quasi una Fantasia*, 134. As a concept entwined with the experience of synesthesia (the sound of music conjures up smells associated with memories of childhood), nostalgia mangles forms of perception with their content. Notoriously confounding early psychologists and their neuroscientist successors, synesthesia produces hypermnesis, or felt memories vividly recalled through a cross-wiring of the senses. The objects of synesthesia appear at first to recall themselves through involuntary memory, but their relation to a particular moment in time requires a conscious recollection of a sensation with an idea.

70. For various accounts of this conceptual division, see Teresa Brennan, *The Transmission of Affect*, 6; Deleuze, *The Logic of Sense*, 101; Massumi, *Parables for the Virtual*, 28; Ngai, *Ugly*, 26–27; and Thrailkill, *Affecting*, 32–36. It should be noted, though, that Ruth Leys questions the wisdom of making such distinctions in the first place. Surveying the scientific literature on emotions and affect, she maintains that Massumi and others fundamentally misunderstand this work and inadvertently reproduce the kind of Cartesian dualism they purport to oppose. See Leys, "The Turn to Affect," 468–72.

selves somatically and circulate among an aggregate of bodies and create psychical atmospheres.[71] The nineteenth-century nosology of nostalgia attests to its immediate somatic effects: those suffering from it were said to experience "heat of head; increased rapidity of circulation; constipation; gastro-intestinal disorders of various kinds."[72] Afflicted subjects would also weep uncontrollably and experience vivid hallucinations. Sometimes labeled a form of "crowd poisoning," doctors believed this mental disease was communicable.[73] Recent studies of its affective signatures attribute a wide variety of sensory triggers to the onset of nostalgia, including conversations with childhood friends and encountering familiar smells.[74] Threatening to deprive patients of their volition, these immediate bodily symptoms and their transmissibility reflect nostalgia's affective qualities, but it could be considered an emotional state insofar as writers could willfully direct their nostalgia toward reconstituting a lost object of desire. Nostalgia's cognitive properties spring from involuntary and voluntary recollections that can be amplified, mollified, or sustained by design.[75] It is a social affect and an individual emotion, bolstering the range of its psychic and somatic power. For these reasons, I use the words *affect*, *emotion*, *feeling*, and *sentiment* interchangeably when referring to nostalgia throughout this book. My fluid deployment of these terms should underscore nostalgia's intermodal properties rather than suggest these concepts lack meaningful differences in other contexts.

Belonging to the realm of sensation and feeling, aesthetics as a field of inquiry intersects with studies on affect. While I employ a looser understanding of affect to accommodate nostalgia's multimodality, I use the term *aesthetics* with great specificity. Aesthetics can encompass appraisals of the beautiful and the sublime (Burke, Kant, and Hegel), examinations of the relationship between art and human psychology (Santayana and Dewey), and sociological critiques of taste and the reproduction of class distinctions (Bourdieu and Guillory). The resurgent interest in aesthetics within the field of U.S. literary and cultural studies develops

---

71. Lauren Berlant explains, "Affective atmospheres are shared, not solitary, and . . . bodies are continuously busy judging their environments and responding to the atmospheres in which they find themselves." Berlant, *Cruel Optimism*, 15. As atmospheres and events, affects are thus socially and historically embedded phenomena that impart limited agency to the bodies that inhabit them.

72. Bartholow, "Chapter First," 21.

73. Anderson and Anderson, "Nostalgia and Malingering in the Military During the Civil War," 158.

74. See Wildschut et al., "Nostalgia," 982–85.

75. See Werman, "Normal and Pathological Nostalgia," 392–93.

a different approach to this subject, indebted to Friedrich Schiller and his pithy dictum: "If man is ever to solve that problem of politics in practice he will have to approach it through the problem of the aesthetic, because it is only through Beauty that man makes his way to Freedom."[76] Put less romantically, aesthetics in the Schillerian tradition is interested in how artworks create and respond to a shared perception of the world. For Schiller and Kant, aesthetic contemplation assumed a communal form—the *sensus communis*—that provided opportunities for collective agency.[77] Although common aesthetic experience can facilitate new bonds of social cohesion, it does so through a logic of exclusion. Kant chillingly stipulates that anyone who does not exhibit the common sense can scarcely lay "claim to the name of a human being."[78] The shared sensory reception and cognitive evaluation of art can establish a virtual community predicated on human consensus, but this community of sense also determines what counts as art and who can be counted as part of this community.

Rancière uses the phrase "distribution of the sensible" to describe this seemingly self-evident system that organizes and governs our sensory apprehension of the world. The distribution of the sensible encompasses hierarchies of taste, enshrines rules of representation, and determines the proper subjects of art.[79] The phrase has added political significance, as it defines how subjects are classified into individual types and ultimately aggregated into a larger population. We may see subjects as laborers, citizens, or entrepreneurs, and each of these groups has a particular role in maintaining the state.[80] It determines what we cannot see, such as the subjects that populate many of the literary works examined in *Novel Nostalgias*, including slaves and immigrants, who maintain the state but have no right to participate in its governance. They do not just lack rights; they cannot be seen as subjects, receding into the background. Their plight is positional, not ontological: they are "the part of those who have no part" in the state.[81] The distribution of the sensible, along with

---

76. Schiller, *On the Aesthetic Education of Man*, 9. Austin notes that Schiller as a physician encountered cases of nostalgia that may have affected his aesthetic philosophy, making him a figure that directly conjoins the study of aesthetics to nostalgia. See Austin, 4–15.
77. See Schiller, *Aesthetic*, 97–121, and Dillon, "Sentimental Aesthetics."
78. Kant, *Critique of the Power of Judgment*, 173.
79. See Rancière, *The Politics of Aesthetics*, 12–13.
80. See Rancière, *Disagreement*, 58–59.
81. Ibid., 30. Here he differentiates his thought from Giorgio Agamben's work on the inhuman and the state of exception. Rancière fears that the turn to ethics supplants a

disciplinary power, generates a consensus that commits the fundamental wrong of casting groups of people outside the *polis*.[82]

We cannot redress this wrong before first becoming aware of it, and this revelation is brought about by aesthetics. The *aesthetic regime of art* "is ascribed to a specific form of sensory apprehension."[83] The aesthetic regime works by undermining any rules that govern subject matter, styles, or genres. It harnesses the power of literariness that resides within a "zone of indeterminacy" where individuals are no longer fixed to assigned identities and then aggregated into a consensual whole.[84] Art operating within the aesthetic regime rejects mimetic fidelity and any pretensions of perfection. The aesthetic regime is also heteronomous, not autonomous: its singular capacity to imagine new ways of doing and seeing remains contingent upon the particular distribution of the sensible it revolts against. Here we are not just talking about what usually goes by the name of *context* (e.g., culture, episteme) but also the established forms and genres that the aesthetic regime engages.[85] This regime "restages the past" to incite a revolution rather than to invent a tradition.[86] This new way of relating to the past emphasizes what art and a communal life *"would have been"* and explores how this counterfactual history might be realized in the present.[87] Art belonging to the aesthetic

---

politics that could overturn the order of things by treating the state of exception as "an ontological destiny" that forecloses "the advent of an improbably ontological revolution." Rancière, *Dissensus*, 192–93.

82. Drawing on Foucault, he associates any cultural or institutional mechanisms engineered to legitimate the order of things with what he calls *the police*. Many actions that we might have previously seen as political, like elections, are complicit with *the police*, as they protect the state from any activity posing a threat to it. See Rancière, *Disagreement*, 26–33, and *Dissensus*, 188–89.

83. Rancière, *Aesthetics and Its Discontents*, 29.

84. Rancière, *The Flesh of Words*, 149.

85. See Rancière, *Dissensus*, 115–17, and *Politics*, 23–24.

86. Rancière, *Politics*, 24. The way the aesthetic regime restages the past ought to be distinguished from what Eric Hobsbawm and Terence Ranger termed "the invention of tradition" to describe "a set of practices, normally governed by overtly or tacitly accepted rules and of a ritual or symbolic nature, which seek to inculcate certain values and norms of behaviour by repetition, which automatically implies continuity with the past." Hobsbawm, "Introduction," 1. Nostalgia works on the premise of discontinuity—the notion that either a lost past or place must be resuscitated. Events of the past are not repeated but recovered; this process of recovery actively restages the past in ways that do not belong to the established "fund of knowledge or the ideology of nation, state, or movement." Hobsbawm, "Introduction," 13.

87. Rancière, *Politics*, 25.

regime plays with heterogeneous temporalities to undo consensus and foster disagreement.[88]

Rancière gives us a language to describe nostalgia's affective indeterminacy as coextensive with the regime of aesthetics. In the literary works studied in *Novel Nostalgias*, the appearance of this affect formally disrupts genres, such as the historical romance or works aligned with American literary realism, aimed at producing liberal and republican forms of consensus or reproducing forms of cultural authority. Nostalgia redistributes the sensible through a sense of estrangement that is immediately followed by the longing to recover this loss. It also embodies the threat of democracy that Rancière so closely aligns with his aesthetic inquiries. Nostalgia, or homesickness, was a common feeling that could become a dangerous affliction when suffered by blacks, women, impressed sailors, laborers, or immigrants. In the literary materials I examine, nostalgic estrangement can sometimes spur visions of a new kind of national or international community of equals.

Let me stress two key ways where my understanding of aesthetics and politics departs from Rancière's conceptualization of them. First, his theory of aesthetics is teleological, as the aesthetic regime succeeds the representative regime (where genres and their subjects must conform to a set of proper rules), which arose after the decline of the ethical regime of images (where the image must be worthy of its object of representation and have a virtuous effect upon those who observe it). The aesthetic regime of art is consequently closely associated with the advent of modernism, but I find the idea of the aesthetic regime of art more useful when elastically applied to art that defies ethical norms and mimetic or generic expectations in novels and other literary forms that predate modernism. Second, I use *antagonism* instead of strictly deploying one of Rancière's related notions of politics, *disagreement*, or *dissensus* in order to recast the aesthetic regime as one that enables a wider range of political rivalries. From the revolutionary to the reactionary, the aesthetic regime, like nostalgia, affectively activates a diffuse array of political projects.

Nostalgia, in other words, is not an affect or an aesthetics that belongs solely to a politics of resistance; it instead could be harnessed by imperialists and sectionalists as much as it could be used by abolitionists and anarchists. By using the term *antagonism*, I also situate my work within a broader intellectual context to embrace not just Rancière's work but

---

88. See Rancière, *Aesthetics and Its Discontents*, 100–101.

the thought of a variety of other contemporary political theorists.[89] Art's agency generally and the nostalgic literary works I examine specifically then lie in their ability to transform our common perception of the world. Aesthetic work can only occasionally be politically efficacious; art cannot bring about a revolution on its own, but it can make it imaginable.

NOVEL NOSTALGIAS IN THE LONG NINETEENTH CENTURY

Throughout *Novel Nostalgias* I attend to a wide and deep archive of historical materials. As these poems, treatises, plays, and newspaper articles demonstrate, nostalgia underwent a slow conceptual metamorphosis from denoting a pathological homesickness to becoming a pervasive sense of dislocation to eventually signifying a longing to return to a past time. These different manifestations of the term did not unfold sequentially, but instead nostalgia encompassed all three of these meanings throughout the nineteenth and early twentieth centuries. This is what made it a potent political affect operating within the regime of aesthetics. My book is principally concerned with nostalgia's recurrent role in shaping the political imagination of an array of often incompatible ideological projects, from Southern nationalism to anarchism. Nostalgia could be evoked in a variety of literary and narrative forms, but novels enlisted the affect in the most dynamic ways because they could use sensations of spatial and temporal dislocation to situate individuals, local communities, and nations within sprawling political narratives. Poems and speeches could draw out nostalgic feelings and moor them to certain political sentiments, but they could not dramatically imagine new social orders with the scope that novels could.

Each chapter of my book then pays particular attention to how novels or, in some instances, short stories mobilized the psychodynamics of nostalgia to envision new political possibilities in the nineteenth

---

89. I borrow the notion of *antagonism* directly from Chantal Mouffe, who insists that "forms of agreement . . . are always partial and provisional," because "antagonistic forces will never disappear and politics is characterized by conflict and division." Mouffe, *The Return of the Political*, 69. Badiou similarly claims that "the essence of politics is not the plurality of opinions." Badiou, *Metapolitics*, 24. Instead, the political signals the introduction of an intolerable and previously unthinkable possibility; a political event is one that antagonizes the state and "reveals its excess of power, its repressive dimension." Badiou, *Metapolitics*, 145. Like Rancière, I see the aesthetic as playing a constitutive role in articulating these divisions by undermining the illusion of consensus.

and early-twentieth centuries. These texts consistently introduce us to nostalgic characters who first register their sense of dislocation from a community or nation they inhabit. These feelings of exclusion become expressed as the loss of a home. While some of them experience physical exile, the loss is predominantly a psychical one and one that can shift modally from spatial to temporal estrangement. A cathetic narrative logic then emerges, as the home imagined becomes an object of longing. These "homes" become invested with a set of characteristics that they may never have possessed. In Brown's *Clotel*, for example, the inability to belong to the United States creates, for the characters who survive at the end of the novel, an occasion to yearn for a more racially inclusive American Revolutionary history. Thus, every narrative examined in this book directs more familiar manifestations of nineteenth-century nostalgia toward political visions that may seem less intuitively nostalgic in the end. These narratives translate the affect of nostalgia into a mode of emplotment: homes are always imagined as lost, but the longing to recover them assumes a variety of politically charged forms, from fantasies about the Confederacy rising again to dreams of bringing a socialist international to Middle America.

Novel Nostalgias establishes a line of cultural continuity between antebellum and postbellum literary culture. A longing to recover the founding moment of the United States surfaced at various moments throughout the early nineteenth century, but during the sectionalist debates of the 1850s, nostalgia emerged as a particularly popular sentiment. After the Civil War, it continued to emerge in popular culture as narratives that animated a variety of other political and literary endeavors. Although the chapters in this book loosely follow a chronological order, they are not invested in providing an account of the genealogical development of nostalgia from an eighteenth-century mental illness into a twentieth-century mawkish sentiment. Instead, each chapter attests to how select narratives seized upon nostalgia's protean and aesthetically disruptive qualities to articulate an antagonistic politics within a variety of discursive contexts. I focus on those texts that richly exploit the conceptual malleability of nineteenth-century nostalgia to establish the possibilities and limitations it generates. For example, in the third chapter, I examine how Hamlin Garland forged a populist political imagination by seizing upon forms of agrarian nostalgia only to then show how populism erected racial barriers that Pauline Hopkins would critique by using the language of homesickness to conceive of a black people apart from the white populists. In some cases, as in the fifth chapter when I address the work of L. Frank Baum and Henry James, these counterintuitive pairings illustrate how nostalgia circulated in both culturally elite and popular literary forms to demonstrate the democratic reach of this affect. This book thus examines how nostalgic narratives shaped the political imaginations of abolition, sectionalism, populism, socialism, anarchism, and cosmopolitanism.

The first chapter situates nostalgia within the sectionalist debates of the 1850s. The popularity of poems such as "The Loved of Other Years," which pined for lost places and times awaiting recovery, testified to the wave of nostalgic feeling that swept across the country after the Mexican-American War. As political factions became more bitterly divided, Northerners and Southerners drew on these nostalgic sentiments to legitimate their competing versions of the nation. In congressional debates, senators and representatives proclaimed they no longer felt at home in their nation. They longed to recover the lost spirit of the Declaration of Independence by inventing competing accounts of the U.S. Revolutionary past that validated their version of nationalism. William Wells Brown and Herman Melville, however, seized upon this nostalgia for the Revolutionary War to take aim at the limitations of both Northern and Southern nationalism. Brown's *Clotel* and Melville's *Israel Potter* (1855) called into question those endeavors to create nationally unifying useable pasts. Brown enlists nostalgic longing in *Clotel* to register not just the legal but the affective exclusion African-Americans felt from the nation of their birth. His novel begins as a kind of antinarrative that upends the consensual logic of historical romances about the U.S. Revolution and the historiographical premises behind the sprawling histories of that era. In the place of these narratives, he imagines a more racially inclusive but politically qualified form of American affiliation through nostalgic longing. Melville, conversely, establishes in *Israel Potter* how the desire to belong to the nation condemns his Revolutionary War–era protagonist to a life of suffering and enslavement. Potter's intense longing to return home from exile in Europe only renders him more susceptible to abuse. The novel closes, however, on a note of subnational nostalgia, suggesting that he may find freedom though a local yearning to recover the Berkshires of his youth rather than remaining faithful to the nationality of his adulthood. While these novels depict the desire for American citizenship in opposing terms—as either emancipation or enslavement—both register nostalgia's political limitations as much as they do its possibilities.

The second chapter argues that nostalgic literary texts carried forward the culture of sectionalism after the Civil War. Most literary histories of this period emphasize the importance of national reconciliation romances that cast soldiers who fought on both sides as brothers in arms. While a large body of writing published in the North romanticized a national reunion, the runaway commercial success of Augusta Evans's Southern nationalist *St. Elmo* (1866) recasts the literature of Reconstruction as a cultural battlefield. The chapter first turns to a repository of pamphlets, newspaper articles, and polemical books that used nostalgia to grapple with the psychological turmoil wrought by the conflict and the policies of Reconstruction. It could be used to describe a range of traumas, from the spiritual homesickness one might feel for a heaven where families could again be reunited to the sense of disorientation many white Southerners felt living under what they saw as an occupation. This sentiment became integral to Southern plantation literature that glorified the antebellum South and motivated the vicious acts of the Ku Klux Klan. In this literary and cultural context, Evans's *St. Elmo* and María Amparo Ruiz de Burton's *Who Would Have Thought It?* (1872) revealed how nostalgia could create a robust and homogenous idea of Southern nationalism after the Civil War. During the war, the South struggled to quell the class divisions among the white population. Repurposing the generic logic of the reconciliation romance, *St. Elmo* imagines how a poor white Southern woman might come to embrace a member of the Southern gentry. After suffering a bout of intense nostalgia for her home while living in New York, the novel's protagonist embraces her longtime Southern suitor, and their reunion signals a consolidation of white Southern identity that simultaneously silences the minor black characters that haunt the text. Although Ruiz de Burton's novel differs from Evans's romance in many respects, *Who Would Have Thought It?* uniquely establishes how sectional cohesiveness emerged out of a resentment directed toward racially inassimilable subjects. Ruiz de Burton's formally idiosyncratic work illustrates how nostalgia could dangerously sow racial discord. Both texts ultimately use tropes of diaspora, exile, and nostalgic longing to depict the United States as a loose confederation of sectional cultures produced by mutual regional intolerances.

The third chapter maintains that the Populist movement nostalgically redrew the regional and sectional affiliations forged during the Civil War and Reconstruction. Parts of the Midwest, West, and South became politically aligned in opposition to the cultural and economic supremacy of the Northeast. The challenge facing what historians have described as the *movement culture* of the late nineteenth century was how to define the content and shape the form of its operative political subject: *the people*. For Populist leaders, a Jeffersonian nostalgia for both the agrarian and artisanal underpinnings of U.S. democracy became a way to imagine a type of political mutualism that united urban laborers with rural farmers. The short fiction of Garland exemplified this effort by fusing together a new amalgam of regions in the service of Populism to bridge the divide between the interests of metropolitan workers and rural farmers. By contrast, Pauline Hopkins's *Contending Forces: Romance of Negro Life North and South* (1900) draws attention to white Populism's color line by demonstrating how many of its Southern adherents terrorized blacks. She nevertheless envisions how nostalgia for lost transatlantic family genealogies might be put in the service of creating a regionally diverse black people. As someone who first wrote musical dramas, Hopkins displayed an awareness of nostalgia's political potential when she made her own rendition of "Home, Sweet Home" the centerpiece of her play about the underground railroad. In *Contending Forces*, nostalgia becomes the vehicle for envisioning a black interlocalism that united disparate communities in the North, the South, and the Atlantic World.

The fourth chapter argues that turn-of-century anarchist and socialist writings employed a *left nostalgia* to construct a radical historiography of past revolutionary events in the United States and around the world. For organizers like Eugene Debs, Daniel De Leon, Emma Goldman, and Lucy Parsons, the U.S. Revolution, slave revolts, labor strikes, and the Haymarket Affair had become estranged from their rightful places in an international leftist history. Longing to recover the lost spirit that animated these events, they used left nostalgia to legitimate their commitment to radical internationalism in the present. The politically committed novels of this era imagined how this historiographical and radical affect could work as a personal sentiment. Left nostalgia assumed a distinctly spatial and transnational character in novels about laborers, as they were often written by or about immigrants whose diasporic homesickness underscored the alienation they felt in the workplace. To illustrate how nostalgia operated in the radical novel of the 1890s and early 1900s, this chapter turns to Sinclair's *The Jungle* and Frank Harris's *The Bomb* (1908). In Sinclair's novel, the nostalgia felt by immigrants for the familiar pasts and places they left behind counteracts the seductiveness of industrial wonder. For the novel's protagonist, Jurgis Rudkus, it motivates him to surrender himself to the cause of socialism. *The Bomb* revisits the events surrounding the Haymarket Affair to imagine how disenchanted immigrants may feel nostalgia not for the homelands they left behind but for the unrealized promise of U.S. democracy. This intense feeling provocatively compels the characters in this novel to commit revolutionary violence against the state.

The final chapter examines how Baum's *The Wonderful Wizard of Oz* and Henry James's "The Jolly Corner" (1908) and *The American Scene* (1905–06; 1907) cast nostalgia and cosmopolitanism as mutually constitutive sentiments rather than as two opposing poles of desire. As the United States' imperial pursuits became more global, newspaper coverage of the Spanish-American War and political science journals expressed anxiety about what would happen to U.S. soldiers stationed abroad for too long. Many writers found comfort in reports of nostalgia spreading through the ranks when they surfaced because they believed these incidents confirmed Anglo-Saxon purity through an attachment to home could be preserved. In *The Wonderful Wizard of Oz*, Baum provides this cosmopolitan nostalgia with a narrative logic whereby Dorothy Gale plays the part of the reluctant imperialist who intervenes in the affairs of Oz only to return home. James, in "The Jolly Corner" and *The American Scene*, imagines how cosmopolitan nostalgia could drive the desire not just to return home but to make a home in the world by giving rise to what he calls the United States' "hotel spirit." Nostalgia, in this context, becomes a marketable commodity now capable of generating consumer consensus as much as it could stimulate political disagreement. Baum and James thus provide us with one way of accounting for the conceptual transformation of nostalgia from a multivalent affect into a consumer feeling attached to objects representing past fashions. While Baum largely embraces cosmopolitan nostalgia, James recoils from it in horror. Both authors nevertheless maintained that twentieth-century Americans must venture abroad to experience an intensified nostalgic longing to return home that made them even more American.

The epilogue surveys nostalgia's reemerging role within twenty-first-century political discussions as well as in popular culture. TV serials such as *Mad Men* have directly reflected upon the aesthetics of nostalgia at a moment when political projects have seized upon its aesthetic power again. Members of two opposing movements—the Tea Party and Occupy Wall Street—looked backwards to outline their visions for a more just future. Within the courts, constitutional originalism has become a powerful legal hermeneutic that derives its legitimacy from the claim that the fundamental meaning behind the Constitution can be recovered. I note, for example, how Justice Antonin Scalia asserts the superiority of his judicial interpretations precisely on these grounds. In these various ways, we find ourselves not as far separated from our nineteenth-century predecessors as we might imagine.

CHAPTER 1

BAD ROMANCES

HOMESICK NATIONALISMS IN THE ANTEBELLUM UNITED STATES

DESPERATELY attempting to prevent Southern secession, James Buchannan called for a National Fast Day during the final weeks of his presidency. In a letter appearing in newspapers and periodicals across the country, he instructed his fellow citizens to mark January 4, 1861, as a day for praying that God "remember us as he did our fathers in the darkest days of the Revolution, and preserve our Constitution and our Union, the work of their hands, for ages yet to come."[1] National days of remembrance, such as this fast day and every annual Fourth of July celebration, were supposed to perpetuate the nation's founding narrative to guard against disunion. These commemorations exhume the Revolutionary past to imagine the continuing progress of the nation, but Buchannan's origin story failed to revive any strong unifying national sentiments.

Days after he announced his planned fast day, the South Carolina Secession Convention convened to declare its independence from the United States. They believed the North had betrayed the wishes of their "ancestors" by establishing "exactly the same sort of Government they had overthrown."[2] Longing for a return to the glories and ideals of the Revolutionary and Early National eras, the conventioneers asserted, "All

---

1. "A National Fast Day: Proclamation of the President," *New York Observer and Chronicle*, December 20, 1860.
2. South Carolina Secession Convention, "The Address of the People of South Carolina," 121.

fraternity of feeling between the North and the South is lost." They would embrace "the grand mission of vindicating and reestablishing" the liberties originally won by the U.S. Revolution.³ Faced with an impending crisis, Southerners and Northerners alike would continue, as Karl Marx insisted the French revolutionaries of 1848 had done, to "anxiously conjure up the spirits of the past to their service."⁴ Borrowing the language of 1776, the citizens of South Carolina clothed their revolution of 1861 in the habiliments of a restoration. It was not just the case that, as John Richard Dennett later reported in the pages of *The Nation*, "the North don't understand the South," but that they understood their shared history in completely incompatible terms.⁵

Yet Buchannan's and Dennett's reflections on sectional acrimony followed a period in literary history that saw the proliferation of historical and fictional writing committed to the creation of a national imagination. Scholars resolve this paradox by insisting the Civil War served as a necessary but tragic fulfilment of a national culture. Despite decades of important revision, F. O. Matthiessen's characterization of the antebellum era as an *American Renaissance* committed to giving "fulfillment to the potentialities freed by the Revolution" still looms large.⁶ Matthiessen's moniker became the truism of Cold War intellectuals who extolled George Bancroft's, Francis Parkman's, and Jared Sparks's conciliatory romantic histories and reveled in the achievements of James Fenimore Cooper's and Nathaniel Hawthorne's distinctively American historical romances. We still generally continue to regard many sentimental novels and historical romances as able—though ideologically suspect—generators of antebellum nationalism. Approaching the historical romance from a variety of critical angles, readers often accept Georg Lukács's enduring account of the genre as one capable of sustaining an "idea of totality" and eliciting social cohesion.⁷ Romances also spun national fantasies through sympathetic identification among readers, authors, and characters. Whether dramatizing struggles among family members or reciting celebratory tales of interracial fraternity on the frontier, sentimentally inflected romances united "disparate political, national, class, and even racial positions."⁸ These historical and literary works labored to create

---

3. Ibid., 126.
4. Marx, *The Eighteenth Brumaire of Louis Bonaparte*, 15.
5. Dennett, "The South as It Is," 431.
6. Matthiessen, *American Renaissance*, xv.
7. Lukács, *The Historical Novel*, 91.
8. Samuels, *Romances of the Republic*, 20.

a tradition that would establish social cohesiveness and legitimate the institutions of the federal government. But then, why did they fail to help pacify the sectional acrimony of the 1850s?

It of course would be reductive to fault these literary works for having lacked the requisite agency to prevent the outbreak of the Civil War on their own, but the apparent disconnect between the rise of literary nationalism and the intensification of political sectionalism in the final decade before the secession is one worth pondering. One compelling answer offered by some studies of the historical romance is that the genre remained too protean and too heterogeneous to work toward a nationalist telos. By this account, these texts could be read, as Lloyd Pratt eloquently puts it, "as a literature of the socially impossible" composed of multiple and oftentimes irreconcilable temporalities.[9] Meredith McGill and Lauren Berlant similarly detect, when discussing Hawthorne's work in particular, "narrative ruptures" that underscore his romances' oscillating complicity with and repudiation of nationalism.[10] His fiction outlined a space for a national fantasy, but it also could "break apart the hegemony of dominant culture over politics, consciousness, and bodies."[11] I want to move a step beyond these incisive readings by contextualizing the genre more squarely within the sectionalist tumult of the 1850s by arguing that the same literary marketplace that nourished romances of the republic made another, more contentious affect available to antebellum Americans: nostalgia.

Americans became reacquainted with this affect in the wake of the U.S. invasion of Mexico in 1848 when newspapers reported that scores of soldiers had succumbed to this disease. Assuming the status of a cultural keyword during this volatile time, nostalgia represented a broader sensation of spatial and temporal estrangement that many in the United States felt from the nation. I am especially interested in how two particular historical romances used nostalgia to expose the obstacles to nationalism and the political oversights of sectionalist politics. I focus especially on William Wells Brown's *Clotel; or, The President's Daughter: A Narrative of Slave Life in the United States* (1853) and Herman Melville's *Israel Potter: His Fifty Years of Exile* (1855) because they both clearly intervene within the nostalgic rhetoric of the sectionalist debates to outline the possibilities and limitations of this affect. Both novels abandon the consensus-driven conventions of the historical romance for a nostalgic

---

9. Pratt, *Archives of American Time*, 68.
10. McGill, *American Literature and the Culture of Reprinting*, 220.
11. Berlant, *The Anatomy of National Fantasy*, 188.

narrative logic that transforms the past into a politically contested terrain.

Clotel and *Israel Potter* revolve around subjects that psychological diagnostic manuals deemed especially susceptible to nostalgia—slaves and sailors—and narratively map forms of homesickness onto a historical nostalgia for the Revolutionary War. They faithfully appropriate the same revolutionary rhetoric used by congressmen on both sides of the sectionalist debate but to different ends. They reveal lines of exclusion and, in the case of Melville's historical fiction, the perils of a nationally inflected nostalgia. Brown's use of nostalgia is far more muted than Melville's, emerging out of the text's dense intertextual web and its sprawling political dialogues. It also arrests the progression of its black characters' nostalgic feelings, especially those of Mary and George, who escape to Europe. That deprivation should not be conflated with political resignation, though. As if to underscore that point, when Brown later revised and dramatically altered *Clotel* into *Clotelle; or, A Tale of the Southern States* (1861) and *Clotelle; or, The Colored Heroine* (1867), he added the crucial chapter "The Return Home," in which Brown's exiled slaves happily "hastened home to take part in the struggle" to take their homeland back.[12] Only when the Civil War broke out was Brown able to narrate his black characters' nostalgia directly, casting the more formally idiosyncratic *Clotel* as a novel every bit as estranged from its genre as its characters are from their Southern homes. Indeed, both Brown's and Melville's novels revolt against the reconciliatory promises of many historical romances and even reflect on the dangers of nostalgia, but they still testify to nostalgia's capacity to generate forms of communal and political affiliation from positions of social disaffection.

In the sections that follow, I establish how the reemergence of nostalgia in the late 1840s enabled antebellum writers and political figures to construct conflicting definitions of the nation by casting their projects not as revolutions but as restorations of an imagined past. Sectionalist writers and politicians manipulated this regnant feeling to contend the nation had become estranged from their versions of its founding principles. I then argue that *Clotel* and *Israel Potter* move beyond these sectional rivalries to redress wrongs in the U.S. political system: the denial of equality to slaves in *Clotel* and the exploitation of the poor in *Israel Potter*. They unmask the ways citizenship and romances about the nation's formation deny rather than establish equality. *Clotel* imagines how blacks

---

12. William Wells Brown, *Clotelle*, 316.

can asseverate their American nationality through an understated nostalgic longing. *Israel Potter* equates American citizenship with enslavement by demonstrating how his protagonist's longing to return to the United States consigns him to a life of misery.

"THE LOVED OF OTHER YEARS": NOSTALGIC NATIONALISMS IN THE 1850s

Why in 1861 did cataclysm, not triumph, answer these repeated calls for a unified national history, literature, and cultural tradition? A representative clue from the archive addresses this question. In 1851, a seemingly inconsequential lyric by Edward J. Porter, "The Loved of Other Years," appeared in the pages of *Graham's Magazine*. Composed of three octets, Porter's poem begins by conventionally alluding to the transition from spring to "when summer-flowers are weaving."[13] Instead of embracing this seasonal progress, however, it describes how "memory's spirit, stealing" removes the speaker from the present into a state of analeptic reverie about "the loved of other years."[14] Memory assumes agency in the first stanza of the poem and throws the speaker into a state of suspended animation. No longer able to contemplate futurity, the speaker becomes estranged from the present and can only longingly "recall life's fondest dreams."[15] Circumscribed by memory, the oneiric possibilities of the imagination can be commemorated but not summoned. The poem's guiding motifs—the collapse of the imagination into memory, the speaker's loss of volition, and the prevailing evocation of spatial and temporal estrangement—bear the hallmarks of what Porter's readers unmistakably would have recognized as nostalgia. Soon after appearing in newspapers and periodicals in every region of the country, "The Loved of Other Years" was set to music by J. C. Bekel for a subsequent issue of *Graham's* and again later by Hermann L. Schreiner. Schreiner's score became the more widely circulated version, and he continued to capitalize on the cultural ascension of nostalgia as one of the most prominent composers of Confederate nationalist music. Schreiner revised the "Battle Hymn of the Republic" to accommodate a new set of pro-Confederacy lyrics, and he composed "Take Me Home" (1865), a ballad that opened with "Take me Home to the place where I first saw the light, To the Sweet Sunny South

---

13. Porter, "The Loved of Other Years," line 1.
14. Ibid., lines 5–8.
15. Ibid., line 20.

take me home."[16] Antebellum writers may have frequently appealed to the power of sympathy in their national romances, but Porter's poem represents a growing body of 1850s writing that explored the potency of "homesickness," which elicited a sense of longing and "sorrows that human sympathy has never reached."[17]

The success of "The Loved of Other Years" and Schreiner's songs on Southern homesickness demonstrate that nostalgia had emerged out of the obscurity of psychological nosology. As a pathological term, *nostalgia* resurfaced in the United States during the Mexican-American War, when army doctors diagnosed soldiers with the disease.[18] *The Boston Medical and Surgical Journal* cited a number of physicians who had found "cases of it" during the "late campaign in Mexico."[19] While a wide range of individuals could fall victim to nostalgia, physicians generally agreed that, aside from soldiers, two groups of people proved especially vulnerable to the illness: slaves and sailors, the very two kinds of subjects that Brown and Melville selected as their protagonists in *Clotel* and *Israel Potter*. Nearly every study of nostalgia since the seventeenth century included case histories of sailors who fell ill and sometimes eventually died of homesickness. Reports about slaves' vulnerability to the disease also circulated in the nineteenth century. James Montgomery retrospectively depicted the threat nostalgia posed to the Atlantic slave trade in his poem "The Voyage of the Blind." Distilling the subject of his verse in a prefatory note, Montgomery explains how 160 slaves went blind and became "affected with *nostalgia*," prompting them to throw "themselves into the sea locked in each other's arms."[20] Nostalgia and likely scurvy infected the crowded hold with unusual rapidity, implying that transplanted Africans must be especially vulnerable to the disease.

The United States outlawed the importation of slaves in 1808, but fears about African homesickness remained part of the popular imagination. Marmaduke Blake Sampson, in a published letter to Daniel Webster,

---

16. Schreiner, "Take Me Home," line 1.
17. Madam Tell, "Heart Loneliness," 262. For other examples of poems that traded in nostalgic tropes, see A. M. P., "Stanzas: Progress," and William Ross Wallace, "The Mounds of America."
18. Entries on homesickness, nostalgia, and *maladie du pays* remained a staple of many mid-nineteenth-century psychological handbooks, rehearsing the eighteenth- and early-nineteenth-century understanding of nostalgia. See Bucknill and Tuke, *A Manual of Psychological Medicine*, 160–63; Guislain, "Traité sur L'Alienation Mentale, &c."; and Rush, *Medical Inquiries*, 113–15.
19. "Nostalgia, or Home Sickness," 9.
20. Montgomery, "The Voyage of the Blind," 261.

noted that the "attachment to home or country" presented "itself with singular force in the character of the negro."[21] Sampson and others conceded that the "emotion itself is common to human nature" but insisted that blacks fell victim to the disease more readily because they possessed less advanced mental faculties.[22] Concurring with Sampson, those who wrote about life in the South observed that slaves who displayed an "inability to labor" must assuredly suffer from an especially virulent variation of nostalgia called "negro-consumption."[23] Although proponents of slavery often voiced concerns about the negative impacts "negro-consumption" could have on productivity, abolitionists cited similar cases to bolster their moral argument. Writing about the American slave states, the Edinburgh medical professor Jonah Horner explained that the *"vehement desire for return to home and country"* is most often "seen amongst those of the wronged race of Africa, who have been torn from home with all its charms of the silver-toned names of father, mother, sister, brother, wife, and children; torn from all these by the civilized white man!"[24] Abolitionist sentiments like Horner's relied on the assumption that a slave's home would always be somewhere in Africa, even if he or she was born in North America or in the Caribbean. These writings set the stage for Brown and other African-American writers to conversely enlist the language of nostalgia to lay claim to a more racially inclusive United States.

Nostalgia's career as a debased and pedestrian affect—in stark contrast to its more dignified cousins, melancholy and ennui—may have very well begun with these writings, which aligned the feeling with the simplemindedness of women, children, mendicants, and slaves. European writers, for this reason, would sometimes bluntly cast it as a disease of the "lower classes of society."[25] While nostalgia was also more closely associated with certain groups of people in the United States, it eventually attained the status of a democratic affect that the entire populace could widely experience. In the 1850s, a pervading fascination with the homesick's loved of other years became entwined with the debates over sectionalism and the legacy of the U.S. Revolution. During these years, writing that integrally shaped a multiplicity of American nationalisms was saturated with nostalgia.[26]

---

21. Sampson, *Slavery in the United States*, 68.
22. Ibid., 70.
23. Olmsted, *A Journey in the Seaboard Slave States*, 193.
24. Horner, *On Health*, 135.
25. Sampson, *Slavery*, 69.
26. Benedict Anderson's study of nationalism has been a hallmark of literary studies

Nostalgia, as an antipode to familial feeling, provided an affective language for sectionalists and political dissenters to draw upon. The political writings of the antebellum era bear evidence of the obsession over the relation between the various interpretations of America's Revolutionary legacy and the different nationalisms vying for cultural dominance. Presciently in 1838, Abraham Lincoln articulated what he regarded as a fundamental connection between the nation's past and the future "perpetuation of . . . political institutions" in one of his earliest political speeches, the "Address to the Young Men's Lyceum of Springfield, Illinois."[27] He feared that as the "state of feeling" fostered by the revolutionary "*passions* of the people" faded "upon the memory of the world," it would become progressively more difficult for each generation succeeding that of the founders to hold the nation together.[28] Rather than imploring his auditors to preserve the past, he insists that the memory of the Revolutionary Era will inevitably fade away. He encourages his listeners in terms reminiscent of Emerson to replace the crumbling "pillars of the temple of liberty" with their own new ones.[29] He mourns the loss of the once "living history" of the Revolution in nostalgic terms but attempts to cure himself and his compatriots of this longing by looking forward to the future with "cold, calculating, unimpassioned reason."[30] Lincoln remained committed to replacing the past with a democratic vision of the present in 1838, but by the 1850s Northern and Southern politicians dwelled upon and constructed grand narratives of the past to legitimate their competing constitutional claims. This debate became

---

for the last thirty years, but his theoretical formulation of the national imagination as one characterized by Walter Benjamin's idea of "'homogeneous, empty time' . . . marked not by prefiguring and fulfilment, but by temporal coincidence" cannot fully describe the way U.S. nationalism functioned in the antebellum era. Anderson, *Imagined Communities*, 24–25. As the historian Peter S. Onuf explains, "sectionalism may seem like . . . an imaginative pathway toward idealized local communities," but "the thrust of sectionalist alliance-building was integrative and nationalizing." Onuf, "Federalism, Republicanism, and the Origins of American Sectionalism," 36. A spatial battle over the slave status of newly acquired territories raged between sectional factions and supplanted old party loyalties in favor of sectional ones, and a temporal debate unfolded over the legacy of the American Revolution and the way the nation's past might be remembered. In her sweeping examination of antebellum print history, Trish Loughran also establishes how improvements in infrastructure and greater national print circulation actually stoked rather than smoldered sectional tensions. See Loughran, *The Republic in Print*, 1–29.

27. Lincoln, "Address to the Young Men's Lyceum of Springfield, Illinois," 28.
28. Ibid., 35.
29. Ibid., 36.
30. Ibid.

further magnified through the lens of the 1848 revolutions that erupted across Europe.

In the late 1840s and early 1850s, *The Congressional Globe* was peppered with alternating orations on the future of slavery and the position the United States should adopt toward the 1848 revolts; frequently, the two discussions bled into one another. On one such occasion on February 20, 1850, Representative Alex W. Buel of Michigan apologized for interrupting the debate over "the *dissolution of the Union*" in order to call upon the Congress to "recognize the independence of Hungary" from Austria.[31] Buel stressed that the nation's position on the Hungarian revolution "concerns the principles and policy of our government in its earliest foundations," recalling the "gloomy winter of 1776 and '77."[32] Appealing to the United States' Revolutionary tradition by looking upon it as the Hungarians might—as an inspiration that could underwrite "a new period in the history of the world," he believed an expression of "American sympathy" in the form of national "recognition" could awake "the patriot with new zeal" in Hungary and at home.[33] Lewis Cass expressed a similar sentiment a month earlier in the Senate when he implored his colleagues to "add to the value of the lesson of 1776, already so important to the world" by suspending diplomatic relations with Austria.[34] Senator John C. Calhoun of South Carolina, though not caring for France's widespread emancipation of slaves, praised the revolution in France as a "wonderful event," acknowledging the rebellion's connection to the mythology of the American Revolutionary War.[35]

The 1848 revolutions illuminated the historical terms Northern and Southern nationalists drew upon. The Free Soil Party fashioned itself as an American accomplice to those "revolutions" that "tore across Europe in 1848," and Northern nationalists would later welcome the Hungarian revolutionary leader Lajos Kossuth to America's shores as an Eastern European George Washington.[36] Although pro-slavery Southerners bristled at Kossuth's condemnation of slavery in the United States, they too initially celebrated his visit, and "the founders of the Confederacy" came

---

31. Buel, "Hungarian Independence," 143.
32. Ibid., 147.
33. Ibid.
34. Cass, "Diplomatic Relations with Austria," 55.
35. Quoted in Larry Reynolds, *European Revolutions and the American Literary Renaissance*, 16. For more on the importance of 1848 in the U.S. imagination, see Lott, *Love and Theft*, 169–210.
36. Wilentz, *The Rise of American Democracy*, 610.

to see "themselves as participating in a widespread European movement" by fighting for "the self-determination of a people."[37] Partisans from both sections, such as Senator Jeremiah Clemens of Alabama, recalled that "side by side the North and the South struggled through the Revolution," but only one version of that conflict and its ongoing national legacy could prevail in the coming decade.[38]

The compulsion to repeat the story of the U.S. Revolution displayed by these political figures surfaced within sentimental fictions that attended to the traumas and unfulfilled promises of the U.S. Revolution. Julia Stern has shown how Susanna Rowson's *Charlotte Temple* (1791/4) forged a sympathetic bond among her melancholic readers to imagine a "more cohesive and more inclusive" democratic polity.[39] By creating a space where rich and poor as well as men and women could come together to mourn the death of the novel's eponymous heroine, Rowson sought but ultimately failed to complete "the unfinished business of post-Revolutionary American society."[40] Stern rightly reminds us that sentimental novels, whatever their aims, often unleashed a grief that could not be contained; they produced an "affective leakage" that "suggests the extraordinary difficulty underlying imaginative realization of this egalitarian impulse."[41]

Those succeeding Rowson in the 1850s would fail to stem the flood of tears and repair the fissures within the American society they represented. Harriet Beecher Stowe's most celebrated novel, *Uncle Tom's Cabin*, may have held fast to the promise of the healing power of feeling, but *Dred: A Tale of the Dismal Swamp* (1856) could not keep the faith. While commentators register the way *Uncle Tom's Cabin* imagines a republican community organized around the mourning of the death of the angelic Little Eva, *Dred* unceremoniously dispenses with its two central characters, Nina Gordon and Dred. Nina, a plantation owner committed to the reform of the slave system, envelops her slaves within her sphere of sympathy. When she dies of cholera, however, her lover Edward Clayton and her slaves mourn her death, but Stowe devotes a paltry sum of pages to the mourning of a character whose exploits had occupied the better portion of a sizable novel. In place of a community of mourners composed of the poor and privileged, Stowe forces us to confront the

---

37. Ayers, *What Caused the Civil War?*, 114.
38. Clemens, "Resolutions Regarding Slavery," 56.
39. Stern, *The Plight of Feeling*, 37.
40. Ibid., 42.
41. Ibid., 68.

fate of Nina's enslaved half-brother, Harry, who will soon become the property of her tyrannical brother. Harry possessed a contract that promised him his freedom after Nina's death, but we learn it lacks validity; he holds a document that is *"pro nullis, pro mortuis;* which means . . . that he's held as nothing—as dead, inert substance."[42] Harry's contract is a dead letter; he does not live before the law. Stowe no longer wants us to mourn the death of an innocent woman of feeling but instead acknowledges that no amount of tears can repair the familial and political ties broken by the law. And much like the historical romances and histories of its day, *Dred* incessantly rehearses the legacy of the U.S. Revolution, but this rehearsal cannot bring back this loved tradition of other years.

These sectional debates and the surge of revolutionary romances and sentimental novels provided the backdrop for Buchannan's fast day announcement and the secession documents that cast their actions as following in the "footsteps" of the Founding Fathers who "separated from the Crown of England."[43] Both sections felt estranged from their nation and their past, and they longed to return to the rising glory of the Revolutionary epoch. It is this discussion that Brown and Melville entered and challenged by using nostalgia to expose the political failures of the Revolutionary tradition and U.S. citizenship.

CLOTEL'S "HISTORY OF AFFECTIONS"

"Death Is Freedom," the twenty-fifth chapter of *Clotel*, bears all the hallmarks of a conventional sentimental dénouement. The chapter opens with Clotel, Thomas Jefferson's unacknowledged African-American daughter, incarcerated in a slave prison located at a symbolic point "midway between the capitol at Washington and the president's house."[44] She soon escapes but only manages to reach the Long Bridge, which crosses the Potomac connecting D.C. to Arlington, before her captors surround her. Seeing no other alternative, she takes a suicidal plunge into the river. With a tone of unquestionable finality, Brown proclaims: "Thus died Clotel, the daughter of Thomas Jefferson" (207). The remaining paragraphs reiterate the hyperbolic symbolism of her tragic demise and culminate with a didactic poem memorializing her death.

---

42. Stowe, *Dred*, 385.
43. Mississippi Secession Convention, "A Declaration of the Immediate Causes Which Induce and Justify the Secession of the State of Mississippi from the Federal Union," 129.
44. Brown, *Clotel*, 204. Hereafter cited parenthetically as *Clotel*.

But while Clotel's story ends in this chapter, the novel *Clotel* does not. Defying the expectations of the sentimental novel and the historical romance, Brown devotes several chapters to recounting the fate of her daughter, Mary. In these final pages, he introduces an entirely new character, George Green, who has both won Mary's heart and participated in a slave revolt. Barely mentioning the novel's eponymous character again, Brown narrates George's trial, his escape from prison, and his eventual reunion with Mary in Europe. Having lucidly critiqued the institution of slavery by underscoring the injustice of Clotel's death, why would Brown forego the immensely popular generic conventions of the sentimental novel by seeing this tangential subplot to its conclusion?

Formal idiosyncrasies, like its bifurcated ending, have repeatedly vexed readers of *Clotel*. Across multiple storylines, Brown weaves an intricate intertextual web of lyrics, ballads, political treatises, legal decisions, newspaper reports, and other works of fiction. Noting its assemblage of allusions, Ivy Wilson rightly characterizes "*Clotel* as an example of bricolage."[45] Written when bestsellers such as *Uncle Tom's Cabin* had whetted the literary marketplace's appetite for slave narratives, *Clotel* flopped commercially in no small part because reviewers decried its peculiar form and historical anachronisms.[46] Until very recently, critics continued to deride Brown's novel for its formal and discursive aberrations. Early African-Americanist commentators regarded *Clotel* "as almost an embarrassment" for its structural inconsistencies, reproduction of black stereotypes, and failure to champion the Black Nationalism of Frederick Douglass and Martin Delaney.[47] These attitudes have largely shifted, with proponents of the book celebrating the novel for deploying subtle textual forms of black resistance or for meditating on the imperfections of U.S. legal discourse.[48]

I push these discussions in a different direction by insisting that *Clotel* recalibrates the affective mechanisms that produce feelings of national

---

45. Ivy Wilson, *Specters of Democracy*, 38.

46. The contemporary response to *Clotel* has been well documented in Farrison, *William Wells Brown*, 228–31. *Clotel*'s commercial failure would appear to have little to do with Brown's reputation as an author. As Augusta Rohrbach notes, his more conventional *Narrative of William W. Brown, A Fugitive Slave* (1847) "sold 8000 copies," suggesting that he "was enormously successful as an author." Rohrbach, *Truth Stranger Than Fiction*, 33.

47. Reid-Pharr, *Conjugal Union*, 38.

48. Prominent examples of this scholarship include duCille, *The Coupling Convention*, 17–29; Ernest, *Liberation Historiography*, 331–43; Fabi, *Passing and the Rise of the African-American Novel*, 7–28; Jennifer James, "Civil War Wounds"; and Schweninger, "*Clotel* and the Historicity of the Anecdote."

affiliation in light of how unsettled the content and form of national memory remained in the 1850s. I argue that Brown's novel introduces a competing American national narrative that challenges who may or may not write national histories while drawing attention to citizenship's logic of political denial. Nostalgia serves this end in two ways. Brown engages the sectionalist nostalgia circulating in 1850s political discourse to demonstrate how pro-slavery appropriations of the Revolution run amok. But he also registers the possibility of a black nostalgia—one that wrests the Revolution away from sectionalist discourse to return it to its democratic and republican context. Instead of dispensing with national literary and historical tradition, Brown nostalgically reinvents it. For him, then, tradition constantly changes, remaining subject to constant alteration and contestation.[49] *Clotel* nostalgically conjures up a new vision of the nation and its history by envisaging it as a recoverable place or past. By intervening within the traditions of U.S. history and the antebellum romance, *Clotel* brings about a formal revolution by breaking with the historical romance's and the sentimental novel's conventional "rules for fabrication and criteria of evaluation" and their mechanisms of social cohesion.[50]

Brown's aesthetic revolution works toward three aims: first, it unearths the indispensable contribution blacks made to a U.S. Revolutionary tradition that excludes them; second, it establishes how both the law and sympathy bar African-Americans from attaining citizenship; and thirdly, it foregrounds the spatial expression of nostalgia as a democratic affect capable of forging national affiliation from a place of estrangement. To be sure, the novel does not reproduce the affect of nostalgia in exactly the way broader sectionalist discourse did. Instead, it constructs a nostalgic narrative—one where the loss of a nation is registered and where a temporal longing occurs for the recovery of a truly revolutionary tradition.

Clotel also draws attention to how the spatial estrangement its African-American exiled characters experience cannot completely give rise to homesickness in the present because legal barriers to citizenship imperil their return, leaving them in a state of diaspora for an uncertain duration. It thus inserts "democratic disorder" within the Revolu-

---

49. Brown's conceptualization is consistent with what Paul Gilroy sees as the "nontraditional tradition" of the Black Atlantic that draws upon the "narratives of loss, exile, and journeying which . . . serve a mnemonic function" in order to create a "common history and its social memory." Gilroy, *Black Atlantic*, 198.

50. Rancière, *Politics*, xlv.

tionary tradition and the historical romance that calls attention to the exclusion of African-Americans from both citizenship and a national memory as a people who should not write their own competing history of the whole nation.[51] These qualities differentiate Brown's project from the one pursued by William C. Nell in *The Colored Patriots of the American Revolution* (1855). Nell's controversial imperative—that the participation of blacks in the Revolution be recognized as a part of U.S. history—means they can only claim a portion, not the whole, of the revolutionary tradition. Brown rejects Nell's approach because it accepts a color line that Bancroft and his contemporaries could comfortably gaze across to appreciate the heroics of a group of separate and unequal soldiers; he conversely critiques the exclusionary logic of the Revolution.[52] By chronicling the fate of Jefferson's mulatto slave daughter and her children, *Clotel* brings a new narrative of America's Founding Fathers into focus. Brown brilliantly exploits nostalgia's conceptual malleability to show how the slave's desire to be at home in the South can animate a drive to discover a home for African-Americans in U.S. history. He shifts modalities again to reveal that, without this historical recognition, exiled fugitive slaves will never be able to indulge in the fantasies of homecoming realizable by white secessionists.

Brown stresses that the presence of blacks within the American Revolutionary tradition cannot be integrated into a social totality. Like many antebellum historical romances, *Clotel* reflects on the deeds and writings of world-historical figures, such as Thomas Paine, Jefferson, and Andrew Jackson, and foregrounds the actions of a minor set of characters that embody these political and historical positions. It explores shifting class and racial antagonisms, displaying what Lukács considers historical fiction's ideological aim of "portraying the totality of national life in its complex interaction between 'above' and 'below.'"[53] Like the fiction of Walter Scott, *Clotel* appeared at a moment of historical crisis that its most astute readers variously associated with the inflaming of sectional passions, the historiographic failings of romantic historians, and the epistemological limitations of natural law philosophy. Past crises and a shared revolutionary tradition often surface in historical romances to "defend progress" as "a process full of contradictions . . . between

---

51. Rancière, *Dissensus*, 158.

52. As Ernest notes, Nell's work may have inspired Bancroft to "mention" the role black soldiers played in the Revolution in his ten-volume *History of the United States from the Discovery of the American Continent*. Ernest, *Liberation*, 132.

53. Lukács, *Historical Novel*, 49.

conflicting historical forces, the antagonisms of classes and nations."[54] Philip Gould, in his reading of the U.S. historical romance, observes that this process attempts to reconcile the "dual imperatives of republican and liberal historicism" where the former anticipated cycles of decline and the latter embraced an unwavering "faith in progress and national exceptionalism."[55]

Brown's novel appeared on the coattails of a string of popular historical romances that immortalized the Revolutionary and Mexican-American Wars. George Lippard—the author of *Quaker City*—wrote *Legends of Mexico* (1847), which celebrated the conflict in nationalistic terms as "the crusade of the nineteenth century" and as an extension of America's republican project.[56] Cooper and William Gilmore Simms wrote several romances between them about the Revolutionary War and the novels *Jack Tier* (1848) and *Areytos* (1846), respectively, to place the Mexican-American War within a nationalizing framework.[57] Many of these romances negotiated sectional tensions by making the political writings of the Founding Fathers "clear and accessible" in order to invite their readers to find themselves "at home" in their time and nation.[58]

Propagandistic literary works inundated the literary marketplace in the wake of *Uncle Tom's Cabin*, but these books adhered to a formula found in most romances and sentimental writing. They did not upset nor call into question these genres' capacity for generating social cohesion. Even anti–*Uncle Tom's Cabin* novels drew upon sentimental and romantic forms to imagine reconciliation between sections in Southern terms. Caroline Lee Hentz's enormously popular *The Planter's Northern Bride* (1854), for example, describes how Eulalia, the daughter of a New England abolitionist, travels south only to discover that her father's views of slavery are grossly ill-informed. Reconciliation between the sections manifests itself as a marriage between her and a Southern plantation owner. Hentz's novel, like so many of the responses to *Uncle Tom's Cabin*, appealed to the hopes "that there are a host of noble, liberal minds, of warm, generous, candid hearts, at the North" that will come to embrace the "Southern character."[59] These literary works remained

---

54. Ibid., 53.
55. Gould, *Covenant and Republic*, 55.
56. Lippard, *Legends of Mexico*, 11.
57. For a more extensive account of the cultural and aesthetic significance of these popular romances, see Streeby, *American Sensations*.
58. Lukács, *Historical*, 53.
59. Hentz, *The Planter's Northern Bride*, iv.

squarely within the generic family of the historical romance, striving to produce social cohesiveness in terms amenable to Southern sensibilities. Brown, however, mobilizes the language of nostalgia to unsettle the democratic teleology of the U.S. historical romance. Although they all have a genealogical right to inherit the tradition of the Revolution, Jefferson's daughter and his grandchildren can never feel at home within it. Unable to integrate or be integrated by this tradition, Clotel and her children haunt American liberal and republican historical discourses as political remainders evidencing that the U.S. Revolution cannot make good on its democratic claims.

One of the clearest moments in the text when Brown maps spatial homesickness onto a temporal nostalgia for Revolutionary principles occurs in the chapter "Retaliation." In this short chapter, Horatio Green's wife humiliates her husband by forcing Mary, one of Clotel's daughters, to work as a servant in their kitchen. Mary cannot feel at home in her father's house because neither he nor Dinah, the black cook, will accept her. She never directly expresses her homesickness, but the chapter is crucially introduced by an epigraph, consisting of a series of lines from a popular ballad by Charles Jeffreys, "Phoebe Morel; or The Slave's Dream" or "The Georgian Slave": "I had a dream, a happy dream; / I thought that I was free: / That in my own bright land again / A home there was for me" (*Clotel*, 156). The use of Jeffreys' ballad is enormously significant. The ballad's composer, Stephen Glover, dedicated it in 1852 to Stowe and explained in the preface that "Phoebe Morel was the daughter of a wealthy planter in Georgia who had imprudently contracted marriage with a beautiful creol, a slave on the estate of his father."[60] The poem describes how Morel dreams longingly of returning to her "own bright land again," where "a home there was for me."[61] The excerpt might initially lead Brown's readers to believe Phoebe yearns for Africa, but she clearly desires to return to her "Georgian cot" within "the vaunted home of liberty."[62] Brown uses this ballad to introduce the possibility of being nostalgic for a space that one currently inhabits—the Southern states—and for a past that might have been. This longing becomes a way for slaves to feel as though they are a part of a nation that denies them citizenship. Nostalgia emerges, for the slaves it affects, as the democratic antithesis of the republic of sympathy. Phoebe's and Mary's emotional plights are almost perfectly analogous, but the fact that Brown never

---

60. Glover, "The Georgian Slave," 3.
61. Quoted in Glover, "Georgian," lines 3–4.
62. Ibid., lines 10–11.

explicitly registers her homesickness underscores her alienation from her father's home all the more.

Brown further reminds his readers, "This child was not only white, but she was the granddaughter of Thomas Jefferson" (156). Following this observation, he inserts an extended excerpt from Jefferson's *Notes on the State of Virginia* that brings the plot of the novel to a momentary stop. The quotation's length is visually arresting, formally reproducing Mary's own estranged place within her father's home. Mary's experience anecdotally embodies what Jefferson observes of the peculiar institution in toto: it allows "one half the citizens thus to trample on the rights of the other, transforms those into despots and these into enemies, destroys the morals of the one part, and the *amor patriae* of the other!" (157). Brown uses Jefferson to reflect on the legal basis of citizenship. Jefferson's *Notes* does not draw a distinction between people of European and African ancestry. Citizenship, for him, is a natural right possessed by both groups of people that positive law can only violate. This claim does not rest upon reason, but on a passion or the *amor patriae* that all natural-born citizens ought to feel for their country. Within her own home—a nation in miniature—Mary displays this feeling, but it manifests itself as homesickness. Subjected to "unfeeling and fiendish designs," she can love her home only from a position of estrangement (156). Brown powerfully counteracts pro-slavery and American Colonization Society proponents alike by suggesting that even Jefferson felt that anyone born in North America would identify his or her place of birth as home regardless of ancestry.

While Brown treats Jefferson reverentially and ironically, he principally evokes his writings as a justification for reanimating the logic of the U.S. Revolution. Using language similar to the rhetoric of the Declaration of Independence, Jefferson describes slave owning as a form of "unremitting despotism" in *Notes* (*Clotel*, 157). Commandeering Jefferson's own words to cast slavery as a form of arbitrary power, he acknowledges the Founders' debt to Lockean political philosophy, foregrounding that within this tradition slave-owning "is a power, which neither nature gives . . . nor compact can convey; for man not having such an arbitrary power over his own life, cannot give another man such a power over it."[63] Locke's *Second Treatise*, which contributed to the philosophical foundation of the U.S. Revolution, is repurposed in *Clotel* to justify revolting against this same tradition. Jefferson recognizes that the destruction of African-American patriotic love poses a direct threat

---

63. Locke, *Two Treatises of Government*, 177.

to the stability of the union. He could not be more candid: he concedes that blacks, as Americans deprived of their natural rights, possess a *casus belli*. Brown, however, does not conclude this chapter by calling his countryman to arms. He mockingly laments: "Sad to say, Jefferson is not the only American statesman who has spoken high-sounding words in favour of freedom, and then left his own children to die slaves" (158). This platitude sounds so out of tune with the preceding excerpts that it raises a question about why Brown would conclude this chapter in a falsely understated fashion.

Important readings by Deak Nabers and Ivy Wilson offer two possible answers. Their accounts of *Clotel* fundamentally differ, but both frame their analysis of chapters such as "Retaliation" around legal and philosophical discussions pertaining to sovereignty. For Nabers, Brown brilliantly understands that since "freedom becomes an endowment of the state rather than of the Creator," only legal reforms—a constitutional amendment, not natural law's guarantee of inalienable rights—can grant African-Americans the privileges of citizenship.[64] Wilson too insists that Brown appeals to Jefferson's writings to illustrate how slavery "corrupts and transforms the idea of sovereignty . . . into an excessive dominion over others."[65] Both of these salient readings conclude that *Clotel* calls for reform rather than for revolution. Yet at the end of "Retaliation," an aesthetic revolution has already occurred. Genres may be fundamentally provisional and composed of "a broad spectrum of affinities," as Wai Chee Dimock argues, but they still must exhibit a "family resemblance."[66] In *Clotel*, family and genre alike undergo a process of defamiliarization. Genres, at their core, are structured around a subject proper to their genus, so that instances of impropriety threaten what Rancière describes as these genres' distributions of the sensible, or the way they produce a republican hierarchy of subjects through a process of exclusion.

As the granddaughter of a revered political figure, Mary embodies one of the defining features of the American historical romance. As a slave and the child of miscegenation, however, she bears an axiomatic relationship to the home and the genre she inhabits. This paradoxical dynamic pervades Brown's discussion of Jefferson. He extols the former president's political theory but decries his character and political practices. Brown violates the established conventions of what George Dekker identifies as the *Waverly* and stadialist models of the histori-

---

64. Nabers, "The Problem of Revolution in the Age of Slavery," 87.
65. Ivy Wilson, *Specters*, 41.
66. Dimock, *Through Other Continents*, 74.

cal romance. If the former resolves the cultural conflicts wrought by revolution through a synthesis of antagonistic ideologies, Jefferson then represents not one but both sets of "opposed cultural values"; he championed the rights of blacks, but he also deprived them of these rights as an owner of slaves.[67] The stadialist model of historical progression breaks down too, as Jefferson's words elevate the time of the U.S. Revolution over the present as a moment where the inalienable rights of all Americans could have been secured. Brown romances a counterfactual past that fulfilled the promise of Jeffersonian republicanism rather than establishing how the present moment progressed to a happier and more advanced state.

Brown also wrestles with the legacy of Jacksonian democracy—a legacy that overlaps chronologically with the historical period of *Clotel*. Juxtaposed against "Retaliation," the chapter preceding it, "The Liberator," adopts the legend of William Lloyd Garrison's famous antislavery periodical, which railed against the aims of the American Colonization Society. This chapter describes the dilemma facing Georgiana Peck Carlton, the daughter of a deceased plantation owner who wishes to liberate her slaves. One of these slaves happens to be Currer, Thomas Jefferson's mistress and Clotel's mother. Georgiana's husband, a Northerner, suggests sending them to Africa, parroting the guiding tenet of the American Colonization Society and the central argument of *Uncle Tom's Cabin*: the belief that emancipated slaves ought to be deported to their own nation-state in Africa. Georgiana repudiates him: "What right have we, more than the negro, to the soil here, or to style ourselves native Americans?" (160). Answering her own question, she argues: "It is as much their home as ours, and I have sometimes thought it was more theirs. The negro has cleared up the lands, built towns, and enriched the soil with his blood and tears; and in return, he is to be sent to a country of which he knows nothing" (160). Georgiana then recollects the American Revolutionary tradition by inscribing another founding father, "a negro, by the name of Attucks, was the first that fell in Boston at the commencement of the revolutionary war," into her rebuke (160–61). Underscoring the role of black soldiers in the U.S. Revolution, Brown maintains that they have an equal claim to the place and therefore the history of the nation.

Brown's nostalgic historiography exposes the Constitution's commitment to the perpetuation of an oligarchy—not a democracy—dependent on the inclusion of slave labor and on the exclusion of blacks from the

---

67. Dekker, *The American Historical Romance*, 47.

administration of the state. He uses the past to overturn the consensual logic of republican representation found in other historical romances. Cooper's novels, for example, integrate and archive insurgent histories into a larger stadialist narrative. Loyalists and rebels belong to a common family in *The Spy*, and Native American cultures become relics of a bygone era emptied of their political force in the Leatherstocking tales. Brown introduces an alternative timeline—one that cycles back to a revolutionary moment that could have produced a democracy. He violates what is "proper to a particular genre," the historical romance, in order to make his readers sensible of the nation's democratic fallacy.[68] Brown's evisceration of the historical romance's social cohesiveness reaches a crescendo with the presentation of two mutually constitutive yet dissonant histories of the United States' pre-national past. He acknowledges the liberation mythology of the *Mayflower* but also draws attention to the coterminous existence of another founding narrative embodied by the "low rakish ship" that landed in Jamestown "freighted with the elements of unmixed evil"—the "rattling chains" of slavery (*Clotel*, 180). These two rival histories cannot be synthesized into a single, coherent narrative that presaged the U.S. Revolution. By highlighting their antagonistic irreconcilability, Brown takes direct aim at the sectionalist nostalgia promoted by the advocates of Southern rebellion.

This negative dialectic becomes the most pronounced in the chapter entitled "The Escape" when George stands trial for his revolutionary activities. Beginning with several charged allusions to the revolutionary movements in Europe that used the U.S. Revolutionary War as a legitimating historical precedent, Brown wonders why white slave owners could consider "going to Greece to fight for Grecian liberty" while simultaneously depriving their slaves of freedom (211). When called upon to defend himself, George brazenly synthesizes the nation's two pre-national histories:

> I will tell you why I joined the revolted negroes. I have heard my master read in the Declaration of Independence "that all men are created free and equal" . . . . The grievances of which your fathers complained, and which caused the Revolutionary War, were trifling in comparison with the wrongs and sufferings of those who were engaged in the late revolt. Your fathers were never slaves, ours are; . . . . You say your fathers fought for freedom—so did we. You tell me that I am to be put to death for

---

68. Rancière, *Mute Speech*, 46.

violating the laws of the land. Did not the American revolutionists violate the laws when they struck for liberty? They were revolters, but their success made them patriots—we were revolters, and our failure makes us rebels. (212)

Here George mimics the rhetorical maneuvers of Lajos Kossuth and other 1848 European revolutionaries by using the American War for Independence as a justification for revolt. But for George, as well for Brown, this temporal nostalgia—the romancing of the U.S. Revolution—equally becomes a moment of spatial estrangement. Slavery sabotages the imaginative origin of the Revolution. George's justification for revolting and the law that will condemn him to death derive their legitimacy from a shared revolutionary history.

This irony is not lost upon George, who professes to his judge: "You boast that this is the 'Land of the Free'; but a traditional freedom will not save you.... Worse for you that you have such an inheritance, if you spend it foolishly and are unable to appreciate its worth" (212–13). By describing the Revolutionary tradition as an "inheritance" squandered by its supposed beneficiaries, he suggests that the traditional freedom his persecutors extol has become bankrupt. He assumes responsibility for remembering the past for his auditors to project it onto the present. His account prevails, but he ultimately fails to exonerate himself. The two founding timelines introduced by Brown remain, for the moment, in tension with one another; the promised inheritance of the Revolution still appears lost. Brown cannot necessarily recover it, but he exposes the hypocrisy of secessionist nostalgia through intertextuality. When he laments, "O land of Washington, how often would I have gathered thy children together, as a hen doth gather her brood under her wings, and ye would not; behold your house is left unto you desolate," George cites almost verbatim chapter 23 of the Gospel of Matthew (213). In this chapter, Jesus chides the Pharisees for deriving their legitimacy from Moses, a liberator of the oppressed, while hypocritically subjecting their people to undue hardship and demanding deference to their authority. Substituting Washington for Jerusalem, George suggests that anyone who truly embraces the ideals of the Revolution will find the nation to have become a "desolate" home; Washington represents its ideals in *Clotel* no more than Jerusalem does in Matthew. "Nearly every one present was melted to tears" in response to George's declaration because he exposed the political bankruptcy of the Revolutionary nostalgia of his white counterparts (213).

Let us now return to the novel's two endings, which allow Brown to imagine the possibility of a form of national affiliation neither based on citizenship nor born out of sympathetic identification. Brown makes abundantly clear when describing Clotel's suicide, "she was a slave, and therefore out of the pale of their [the American people's] sympathy" (207). If *Clotel* had remained faithful to the generic conventions of the sentimental novel or the historical romance, it would have terminated along with the cessation of Clotel's own life. The prose of this chapter gives way to verse drawn from another source. The poem, "The Leap from the Long Bridge," parallels Clotel's own leap by describing the suicide of another tragic mulatto figure who also leapt to her grave. Both corpses find their way floating down the Potomac, so that the dead slave eventually comes to pass by "Washington's grave" (209). Clotel's corpse becomes one with Washington and participates in the history of the U.S. republic in a way that in life she never could; death becomes essentially the only form of democracy imaginable. Her death does not successfully contain the threat that she, as the product of miscegenation, poses to U.S. national identity.[69] The novel escapes the generic limitations and nationalizing aims of the sentimental historical romance by returning to Mary's unfinished narrative.

In "The Escape" Brown reveals how nostalgia can render one affectively aware of being politically wronged while simultaneously fostering its mode of national affiliation divorced from citizenship. George and Mary become romantically involved while both serving in the same house. After being jailed for participating in a slave revolt, George escapes when Mary voluntarily chooses to masquerade as him. The plan ultimately succeeds, and they part ways. George—as Brown did—finds himself exiled in Britain. Rather than remaining forever separated or reuniting in the United States, they eventually rediscover each other abroad. They meet unexpectedly and unwittingly in a graveyard located in France. Reading a copy of William Roscoe's *Leo X*, a book Brown claims himself to have read in his *Narrative*, George encounters a veiled lady who screams and faints after laying eyes on him. After this mysterious encounter, he returns to his hotel only to find that he had forgotten his book. It is the material book itself—a kind of *mise-en-abyme* for *Clotel*—that leads George to discover that Mary is the woman behind the veil. The fulfillment of this marriage plot ends, however, in a moment of displaced

---

69. See Armstrong, "Why Daughters Die," and Tawil, *The Making of Racial Sentiment*, 92–128.

nostalgic yearning. The chapter becomes enmeshed in an intertextual moment when Mary's life is universalized in the words of Washington Irving, who notes, "A woman's whole life is a history of affections" where "she sends forth her sympathies on adventure; she embarks her whole soul in the traffic of affection; and, if shipwrecked, her case is hopeless, for it is a bankruptcy of the heart" (*Clotel*, 225). These lines by Irving, which appear in "The Broken Heart," are linked to another literary work by the poet Thomas Moore: "She Is Far From the Land."

The intertextual chain formed by these works repeats the circuitous nostalgic logic of Brown's earlier chapters. Nostalgia is expressed, but indirectly through a series of allusions, so that the homesickness Mary and George undoubtedly feel is formally exiled from the central narrative as much as they remain exiled from their American homes. Both Irving's essay and Moore's poem refer to the fate of the Irish revolutionary Robert Emmet and his lover, Sarah Curran. Evoking the memory of Emmet places Mary's and George's fate within the broader transatlantic revolutionary discourse of the 1840s and 1850s as well as the U.S. and French Revolutions. Emmet participated in both the 1798 and 1803 uprisings, doomed insurgencies born out of French Revolutionary political thinking. In their reflections on his death, Irving and Moore emphasize Curran's fate over Emmet's execution. They portray her as yearning to reunite with her deceased lover after leaving Ireland with her husband in an effort to overcome her melancholic state. In Moore's poem, her mourning becomes amplified by her nostalgia for her home. "Her heart in his grave is lying," Moore writes, but "she sings the wild songs of her dear native plains."[70] Moore interweaves her longing to return to Ireland with her desire to see Emmet; she represents the exile all Irish nationalists feel from a land that remains subject to British rule.

Brown invites us to associate Mary's emotional position with Susan Curran's, even though her revolutionary suitor lives. They both, however, share an untenable nostalgia for a homeland that would meet their political expectations. Returning to the United States will not be possible for Mary or George until they can achieve the legal protections of citizenship. The promise of the U.S. Revolution thus remains as dead as Robert Emmet until it can be reanimated by a future generation. Including this loaded allusion surely invites us to project a sense of homesickness onto Mary and George, but their nostalgia is qualified and halted, teetering on the edge of melancholic resignation. In all three of these

---

70. Quoted in Irving, "The Broken Heart," lines 4–5.

texts—*Clotel*, "The Broken Heart," and Moore's poem—the foundation for a new form of social affiliation emerges within a diasporic and nostalgic context. Mary's and George's pilgrim's regress back to Old Europe and the impossibility of returning home are precisely the conditions that allow them to claim "their native land without becoming slaves" (225).

The understated, racially inclusive nationalist nostalgia in *Clotel* is supplanted by what Gillian Johns describes as "the ideological promise of a post-emancipation future for Americans . . . who live through an internal experience of slavery" in the novel *Clotelle* nearly a decade later.[71] Johns and other critics rightly encourage us to read the various *Clotelles* as separate novels rather than as revisions of *Clotel*, but these more conventional narratives still preserve many of the elements of Brown's first novel. Most relevant to my reading of *Clotel*, though, is the way these romances, one of which was issued as part of James Redpath's *Books for Campfires* series and circulated among Union troops on the frontlines, realize the understated nostalgic hopes of *Clotel*. In the 1861 *Clotelle*, Redpath insists Brown wrote the story to harden the resolve of Union soldiers fighting against the evils of slavery. And in the 1867 *Clotelle*, Brown's main characters, now named Jerome and Clotelle instead of George and Mary, return to the United States to assist with the war effort. Jerome perishes in battle, but the novel ends triumphantly with Clotelle reuniting not with her lost lover but with her Mississippi home. "In the summer of 1866," Brown writes, "the Poplar Farm, on which she had once lived as a slave . . . was purchased by Clotelle, upon which she established a Freedmen's School."[72] With the object of her nostalgic desire reclaimed, we get a glimpse of a racially integrated future that still lay beyond the shores of *Clotel*'s diasporic imagination.[73] And in the years after the Civil War, Brown expressed his attachment to the South and his desire to recover the place of blacks within it in his post-Reconstruction book *My Southern Home* (1880), which includes a wide array of vignettes about Southern life and the bonds African-Americans forged with this region that they called home, even in bondage.

---

71. Johns, "'Moral Authority,' History, and the Case of Canonization," 234.
72. *Clotelle*, 327.
73. In a different but complementary reading, Martha Schoolman brilliantly establishes how Brown developed a critical cosmopolitanism in his travel writing that advances "a hopeful message for the future of all enslaved persons" and invites "his international readership to ponder history on a broader scale." Schoolman, *Abolitionist Geographies*, 115.

SIRENS OF NATIONALITY IN *ISRAEL POTTER*

At the moment in his autobiographical slave narrative that Brown adopts the surname of the Quaker who liberated him, he ruptures the temporal continuity of his story to comment upon the scene of writing. Revealing that he composed his narrative "in sight of Bunker Hill Monument," Brown reflects on the irony of his position: that he, an American, had to flee from a "Democratic, Republican, Christian government" to monarchial England to "receive protection" from enslavement.[74] Since its construction, the Bunker Hill Monument functioned as a master trope for the legacy of the American Revolution. Brown seized upon it the same way he did the legacy of Jefferson in *Clotel*. Melville similarly bookends *Israel Potter*, a historical romance about an American Revolutionary War veteran, with this same monument. Yet while both of the protagonists of their novels become Americans only in exile, Brown and Melville call upon this emblem of the Revolution and enlist the discourse of nostalgia to achieve different ends.

That monuments to the Revolution and the Founding Fathers figure prominently in antebellum literary culture has not escaped the notice of other readers. Russ Castronovo writes extensively about what he refers to as the "monumental culture" of the period, placing it within the context of other forms of antebellum "filiopietism."[75] The monument contributed to the ascension of dominant antebellum nationalism, leaving writers like Melville or Hawthorne to ambivalently imbue these monumental symbols with nationalizing power while simultaneously exposing "the political pitfalls of figuring history within nationalist discourse."[76] I extend these readings by exploring how Melville exposes the undemocratic character of U.S. citizenship and nationality to propose an alternate, non-national form of communal affiliation.

Melville addresses the problem of national citizenship in many of his novels, but he never does so as directly and caustically as he does in *Israel Potter*. These other novels also often draw on the sentiment of wanderlust more so than on the countervailing desire to return home (though even in novels such as *Typee* or *Moby Dick*, the protagonists often find themselves wishing to return home after the events of the narrative unfold). *Israel Potter* satirically rewrites the legacy of the Revolution and the Founding Fathers. The earlier Melville of *White*

---

74. William Wells Brown, *Narrative of William W. Brown, A Fugitive Slave*, 58.
75. Castronovo, *Fathering the Nation*, 106.
76. Ibid., 141.

Jacket (1850) rejects the past to forge a new sense of American identity, but the Melville of *Israel Potter* joins his contemporaries by working through rather than abandoning the past. Like Brown, Melville revolutionizes the tradition of the Revolution and eschews the generic conventions of the historical romance. Chronicling the adventures of a Revolutionary War soldier that largely unfold in Europe instead of North America, Melville sets his novel apart from paragons of the form such as *The Spy* or the embellished historical biographies penned by Mason Weems. *Israel Potter* differs from its picaresque forbearers, such as Royall Tyler's *The Algerine Captive* (1797), by rejecting federal citizenship and its call for a national "union among ourselves."[77] Melville's novel, which deploys many of the conventions of the Anglo-American captivity narrative and the African-American slavery narrative, depicts any form of American nationality as a type of enslavement. Paradoxically, it is Israel Potter's very longing to be at home in the nation that prevents him from returning to his native land.

Critics have not radically veered away from Michael Paul Rogin's touchstone reading of *Israel Potter* as a novel that "mocked the cult of the fathers" by exposing the flaws and unfulfilled promises of their revolution.[78] Though a good deal of mockery at the Founding Fathers' expense occurs in its pages, the novel is not solely an exercise in patricidal character assassination. Melville reminds his readers, in an era of newfound revolutions and an impending civil conflict, of the political character of the U.S. Revolution. When comparing the French and U.S. Revolutions, Arendt purposefully turns to Melville as a figure that "knew better how to talk to the theoretical proposition of the men of the French Revolution" to cement her distinction between the philosophical underpinnings of that insurrection from the one that took place in North America.[79] Not unlike Arendt, Melville uses *Israel Potter* to explore the idea of "revolution" on the eve of an unprecedented national crisis. Excavating the meaning of this concept, Melville establishes the relationship between revolution and the foundations of American identity and citizenship. In *Israel Potter*, what appears as a classic case of the psychoaffective disorder nostalgia becomes the vehicle for an exploration of several pressing cultural and political questions. This novel links the success of the American Revolution to the problem of the subject that Arendt referred to as the *homo*, or the "rightless person"

---

77. Tyler, *The Algerine Captive*, 226.
78. Rogin, *Subversive Genealogy*, 224.
79. Arendt, *On Revolution*, 75.

who inhabits but is not entitled to citizenship within the classical conception of the *polis*.[80] *Israel Potter* reminds its readers that the American Revolution succeeded precisely because it denied certain groups political and economic privileges rather than inaugurating an economically and politically egalitarian state. Melville's historical romance does not just produce a misanthropic portrait of the self-proclaimed land of the free; it also gestures toward an entirely different form of sociality tied to a specific locality: the Massachusetts Berkshires. *Israel Potter* fashions its own understanding of nostalgia that would become an important aesthetic force in the postbellum United States.

Since *Israel Potter* first appeared as a serial in *Putnam's Monthly* in 1854, which dubbed the series "A Fourth of July Story," readers have debated Israel Potter's nationality.[81] Despite the nearly uniform focus on Potter's national characteristics, two distinct and wholly incompatible ways of assessing the national identity of the novel's namesake exist. Reviewers from Melville's own time onward have held up Israel Potter as both the American *par excellence* and as hardly American at all.[82] Despite the apparent irreconcilability of these interpretations, they can be fully compatible with a certain way of conceptualizing "Americanness" in the 1850s. Although Young America vanguards John L. O'Sullivan and Evert Augustus Duyckinck had sought for over a decade to establish a recognizably American literature by the time *Israel Potter* began to appear in print, Edward L. Widmer questions the claim that "in the 1850s" Young American "cultural nationalism had never been stronger."[83] In an article that appeared in the October 1854 issue of *Putnam's*, which included the fourth installment of *Israel Potter*, an

---

80. Ibid., 36. Giorgio Agamben revitalized the discussion over the status of the rightless person, or what he refers to as the *homo sacer*. I use Arendt in this case because her work, which Agamben also draws upon, addresses my interests more directly by examining the case of the American Revolution in particular. But for more on Agamben's thought on this concept, see Agamben, *Homo Sacer*, and Agamben, *State of Exception*. Additionally, Rancière singles out Agamben more so than Arendt for assigning those who suffer "the wrong" (i.e., deprivation of rights) an infinite "ontological destiny" or status that forecloses any possibility of revolt. Rancière, "Who Is the Subject of the Rights of Man?," 308. Rancière insists that the ethical turn galvanized in part by the work of Agamben and Alain Badiou is really a turn away from politics, as the latter does more than work within or resist the order of things; politics is precisely that which seeks to overturn this order.

81. Melville, "Israel Potter," 66.

82. For examples of the reviews written by Melville's contemporaries, see Higgins and Parker, *Herman Melville*. Paul Giles regards *Israel Potter* as a novel in which "national identities become 'snarled.'" Giles, *Virtual Americas*, 70.

83. Widmer, *Young America*, 202.

anonymous writer confidently declared that "America has no national novel, for the very good reason that there is no such thing as American Society."[84] Even Melville's own hallmark piece of Young American literary criticism, "Hawthorne and His Mosses," remains enclosed within a frame of non-national identity. Its byline reads "By a Virginian Spending July in Vermont," and the opening paragraphs indulge in florid local-color descriptions of the New England countryside.[85] Such a framework coupled with comments that stress Hawthorne's "New-England roots" moor him just as much—if not more—to a local rather than to a national literary space.[86]

Israel Potter's national identity remains tenuous. In the opening chapters, Melville squarely inserts Potter into the narrative of an archetypal American Revolutionary *bildungsroman*. Loosely following the historical romance's stadialist model of progress, Melville establishes that Potter began his adult life by first rebelling against "the tyranny of his father" to become a successful hunter and profitable fur trader before embarking upon a whaling expedition (8).[87] Making the allegory obvious for even the most obtuse of readers, he explicitly characterizes his protagonist's progressive narrative as illustrative of Potter's "fearless self-reliance and independence which conducted our forefathers to national freedom" (9). These statements recall the paradigmatic definitions of American identity found in Emerson's essays or even earlier in Crèvecoeur's *Letters from an American Farmer* (1782). That Americans often seem recognizable by their behavior is an observation Melville seizes upon. When a pair of American sympathizers in Britain identify Potter as "a Yankee of the true blue stamp," they do so by taking stock of his conduct (34).[88]

---

84. "Novels," 394.
85. Melville, "Hawthorne and His Mosses," 93.
86. Ibid., 100.
87. Melville, *Israel Potter*, 8. Hereafter cited parenthetically as *Potter*. George Dekker identifies stadialism as one of the key philosophical discourses that contributed to the development of the American historical romance. This historical outlook mapped the progression of humankind onto a series of stages, ranging from the "'savage' stage based on hunting and fishing" to an "over-civilized" stage built on "commerce and manufacturing." Dekker, *American*, 75. As Dekker rightly notes, stadialism figured prominently in the work of Adam Smith as well as in Cooper's Leatherstocking tales. In *Israel Potter*, Melville has his protagonist proceed through a series of stages, from one of hunting to one where he participates in the world of commerce as a sailor. Potter's fate, however, suggests that this movement is not a progressive one.
88. Rooting American or "Yankee" identity in New England, Melville gestures to the New England literary tradition that produced a "prolific" amount of "fictive works on historical themes" to imagine this region's history as the history of the nation. Buell, *New*

Melville eventually jettisons these earlier characterizations to critique the nationalist narrative that encloses Potter. While some readers see Potter's ever-vigilant minding of "the main chance" as quintessentially American, his continuous escapes force him to perform a series of masquerades that destabilize the narrative and whatever underlying national identity Potter might have possessed (*Potter*, 16). The challenge of pinning Potter down is best expressed metaphorically by the most outrageous of the various disguises he adopts: the scarecrow, which embodies his own ontological ambiguity. Breaking out of another place of confinement (this time a secret enclosure within the residence of the recently deceased Squire Woodcock), he stumbles across what he first believes to be a "mysterious stranger" (77). As he "drew still nearer," he finds himself staring into "the face" of a scarecrow "lost in a sort of ghastly blank" (77). He quickly realizes that he should don its clothes in order to cross the English countryside undetected as an impoverished "wretch" (78). Like the scarecrow, he later finds himself "gazing blankly about," implying that his American identity is no more substantive than that of a straw man (167).

Potter nevertheless repeatedly insists upon his own American identity, even if the content of his nationality remains obliquely blank. So, then, what makes him an American in spite of his ontological vacuity? Although the novel "reflects the muddled and arbitrary status of national identity," the fact that Potter "remains nostalgic for his homeland" should not be regarded as a curious but insignificant detail.[89] The importance of nostalgia to the text cannot be overstated, since it is Potter's nostalgia that keeps him committed to his American identity and propels the narrative forward. Like George and Mary in *Clotel*, Potter can imagine his place within the nation only in a state of exile. Unlike Brown's novel, however, Melville portrays nationality as a form of entrapment, not of emancipatory possibility. By portraying U.S. nationality in these terms, Melville uses the language of national longing to comment upon the character and consequences of the U.S. Revolution. Potter's identity may at first seem empty, but like the shallow "recesses" in the boots he uses to smuggle documents into Paris, this emptiness is "full of meaning" (40).

Potter repeatedly succumbs to fits of delusional reverie characteristic of nostalgia. Shortly before assuming the appearance of a scarecrow, he

---

England Literary Culture, 196. By the end of the novel, however, Melville undermines this association by having his protagonist abandon the national in favor of his regional identity.

89. Giles, *Virtual*, 71.

comes "to a hilly land in meadow" where "the whole scene magically reproduced . . . the aspect of Bunker Hill, Charles River, and Boston town" (76). And during Potter's forty-five years in London, "sometimes . . . thoughts of home would—either by gradually working and working upon him, or else by an impetuous rush of recollection—overpower him for a time to a sort of hallucination" (163–64). Once overcome by these moments of reverie, he would soon find himself "bewitched by the mirage of vapors" (165). These delusions fit the description of one of the hallmark symptoms of nostalgia outlined by the antebellum medical establishment. For the nostalgic, as described in one of the authoritative diagnostic manuals of the nineteenth century, "the prospect of their native home presented itself to their mind's eye, like the *fata morgana* to travelers in the desert, depicted in the most extravagant and delusive hues which a morbid fancy could suggest."[90] That Potter appears to suffer from a particularly virulent form of nostalgia explains why, after decades of exile, he insists on compulsively "declaring himself an American" (36).

His nostalgic impulse to return home to the land of liberty has grave consequences: it condemns him to a life of almost ceaseless impressment. As Melville explains after Potter speaks with the king in his garden, "had it not been for the peculiar disinterested fidelity of our adventurer's patriotism, he would have sported the red coat" and "advanced in time to no mean rank in the army of Britain" (32). Instead of thriving in the British army, his mental state renders him vulnerable to manipulation. In the intervening pages, a who's-who list of American Founding Fathers, including Franklin, promise to help Potter find a "ship for America" only after they ensnare his aid in the Revolutionary cause (43). Because Potter has no hope of finding passage back to America on his own, he must depend on Franklin for assistance. This dependency condemns him to a state of servitude, and while in Paris, Franklin consequently informs him, "You must absolutely remain in your room, just as if you were my prisoner, until you quit Paris for Calais" (43). Unlike *Clotel*, which draws upon the language of nostalgia to call attention to the limits of citizenship, Melville puts the shortcomings of nostalgia on display. A slave to his desire to be at home within the nation, Potter finds himself in the position of a "subaltern" under the command of John Paul Jones (94).

If Potter's national nostalgia imprisons rather than liberates him, what does the novel say about the Revolution and its legacy? Many critics read *Israel Potter* as a novel that exposes the failure of the American Revolu-

---

90. Bucknill and Tuke, *Manual*, 161.

tion by portraying a working-class patriot condemned to a life of exiled misery and whose heroics "faded out of print," disappearing from the nation's collective memory (169).[91] Such a reading would liken Melville's understanding of nostalgia with its use in *Clotel*, which recasts the past to make political claims about the present. But rather than trying to reclaim the Revolution for radical political ends, *Israel Potter* reminds readers of its real aims. Melville underscores that the founders imagined their idea of revolution as more of a return to the republicanism of ancient Greece and Rome.

Arendt portrays the Revolution as an event as a "revolving back" to a time when men "had been in the possession of rights and liberties of which tyranny and conquest had dispossessed them."[92] She also casts the American Revolution as a restoration, because it established a free constitutional republic as opposed to an economically egalitarian society. Economic equality, Arendt explains, became a part of revolutionary rhetoric only during the French Revolution, which expressed pity for the people who lived lives of scarcity. Whereas the Founding Fathers sought to "liberate men from the oppression of their fellow men," the French revolutionaries wished "to liberate the life process of society from the fetters of scarcity so that it could swell into a stream of abundance."[93] As Gordon Wood stresses, the American "revolutionaries had not intended to level their society" as "they knew that any society . . . would still have to have 'some Distinctions and Gradations of Rank arising from education and other accidental Circumstances.'"[94] Potter's descent into poverty does not signal the Revolution's failure, but it emphasizes an important difference between the aims of the American Revolution and the rationale of the 1848 insurrections. While various members of Congress eagerly imagined Kossuth as a Washington reborn, Melville implicitly regards this analogy as an inherently false one. Reflecting upon the success of Jones's and Franklin's endeavors much like Arendt later does, Melville reminds his readers that for these men, as metonyms for the Founding Fathers, "compassion" for the misery of the people "played

---

91. See Reising, *Loose Ends*, 117–85.
92. *Revolution*, 35.
93. Ibid., 54.
94. Wood, *The Radicalism of the American Revolution*, 233. Many historians would reject Wood's characterization. Joyce Appleby, for example, contests the view that there was really never "a possibility of a fully participatory democracy in the United States." Appleby, *Liberalism and Republicanism in the Historical Imagination*, 220.

no role in the motivation of the actors" of the American Revolution.[95] Franklin may display "condescending affability" toward Potter, but he does not pity his imprisoned patriot's state of impoverishment (*Potter*, 52). Franklin nevertheless enlists his service, revealing that without this distinction in rank, the latter may have never played the role necessary for him to perform.

Israel Potter does not trumpet the superior virtues of the U.S. Revolution. Potter's nostalgia for the American Revolution can never grant him the "abundance," or the material and political freedom, that the novel implicitly suggests he justly deserves. He appears trapped within a captivity narrative that ironically contains the story of his supposed liberation from tyranny. This story relentlessly pursues him during his time England until he becomes subsumed into the crowds of London. His momentary refuge as "the king's gardener at Kew," for example, becomes compromised "when the old story of his being a rebel, or a runaway prisoner, or a Yankee! or a spy, began to be revived with an added malignity" (*Potter*, 32). At every possible turn, Potter runs away from his own story, suggesting the story itself has him held captive. This captivity narrative mimics the Whiggish captivity narratives of the Revolutionary era by inverting the "incessant dialectic between corruption and virtue."[96] Potter, like the heroes of the rebellion, revolts against his father and puts his duty to country ahead of his private interests. But instead of setting him free, the romantic plot of this story entraps him and his public virtue goes unrewarded. *Israel Potter* indicts the practice of drawing upon the iconography and mythology of the American rebellion. It establishes that the Revolution cannot be allegorically applied to contemporary debates surrounding abolition, popular sovereignty, or the U.S. position on the mid-century European revolutions. While for Brown nationalist nostalgia can be revolutionary when it uses the past to legitimate what was for him a battle to expand the definition of American identity in the present, Melville insists the same narrative forecloses this possibility because it seeks to restore an order of society founded on a necessary inequality.

After living in London for forty-five years, Potter's story ceases to pursue him. Thanks to the efforts of his English son Benjamin, he finally manages to return home. Arriving in Boston on the Fourth of July, Potter "narrowly escaped being run over by a patriotic triumphal car in the

---

95. Arendt, *Revolution*, 61.
96. Burnham, *Captivity and Sentiment*, 69.

procession" for the commemoration of the Battle of Bunker Hill (167). His homecoming on this national day of remembrance nearly kills him, confirming that monumental nationalism can only terminate his life and cannot satisfy his longing. Potter can represent American nationality, but he cannot be represented within the United States. Having returned to the United States, his national nostalgia evaporates. Somewhat aimlessly, he proceeds to leave Boston, which serves as a synecdochal metropole for the nation, toward his childhood home in the Berkshires. Upon approaching the spot where his "father's homestead" once stood, he discovers that "it had been burnt down long ago" (168). He stumbles upon an unfamiliar "walnut grove" but soon remembers "that his father had sometimes talked of planting such a grove" (168). At this moment in the novel, the nation becomes completely displaced by Potter's regional ties to the Berkshires. This region does not occupy the empty time of the nation, and the local inhabitants view his unexpected appearance in a kind of messianic light, seeing it "less a return than a resurrection" (168). Potter learns that his father had "gone West" some time ago (169). His childhood home in the Berkshires is neither a space of filiopietism nor a scene of patricide; it is a place of fatherly absence. He still slips back into a nostalgic reverie, recalling when his "father would sit" along with the rest of his family "on the very same spot" that Potter does now (169). This form of nostalgia is not composed of a longing to return to a national homeland but instead consists of a mourning of the loss of an irrecoverable locality.

Melville proposes but does not fully define a viable alternative to national nostalgia. Within this place of national absence, Potter may indeed disappear "out of [the national] memory," but only in the Berkshires do "the ends meet," securing the very restorative ending that Potter longed to achieve (169). The implication here is that an innocuous regional imagination might function as an alternative to vitriolic sectionalism and its battles over the content and form of the nation's memory—a form of memory that will never recognize or remember the class of Israel Potters. Melville focuses less on Potter's fading out of print than upon the moment in which he comes to embrace a different form of communal affiliation and memory.[97] Nostalgia, as *Clotel* and *Israel Potter*

---

97. Castronovo concludes that *Israel Potter* also produces a local knowledge in the Foucauldian sense of that term, but he locates the site of this knowledge not in the Berkshires but in the London crowds that Potter loses himself within. He reads Potter's incorporation into this "critical mass" as a moment when it becomes possible to "effectively challenge the hegemonic structure of American nationalist discourse." Castronovo, *Fa-*

demonstrate, became a way for writers to revisit the past aesthetically and its relation to the political and cultural crises of the 1850s. Throughout the second half of the nineteenth century, writers would continue to revisit and redefine the affect and aesthetics of nostalgia that initially took shape before the Civil War.

---

thering, 154. My reading of nostalgia casts Melville's regional imagination as an alternate, not necessarily an oppositional, way of imagining a community and a collective memory in the 1850s.

CHAPTER 2

CONFEDERATE NARRATIVES AND THE PROBLEM OF RECONSTRUCTION

*T*WO YEARS into the Civil War, *The Atlantic Monthly* published the short story "The Man without a Country" by Edward Everett Hale. Engineered to embolden Union sentiment, it followed the fate of the American exile Philip Nolan. A quintessential frontier man, Nolan unwittingly became involved in the Burr Conspiracy. For many Americans, this insurrectionary event exemplified the peril of committing treason against the U.S. government. In the early nineteenth century, Jefferson suspected Aaron Burr had organized a small group of farmers to found a new nation in the center of North America, encompassing parts of Texas and Mexico. After this alleged plot became exposed, Burr was publicly disgraced but legally acquitted.[1] Nolan receives a far worse verdict in Hale's story. Court-martialed and disillusioned, he declares before the court, "D—n the United States! I wish I may never hear of the United States again!"[2] Incensed by this eruption, the judge hands down a peculiar sentence: he will spend the rest of his life on a series of naval vessels where he will "never hear the name of the United

---

1. Burr repeatedly surfaces in antebellum writing as a shorthand for illegitimate or anti-federal rebellion. Michael Drexler and Ed White provocatively examine how representations of "Burr's rise and fall" functioned as "a coded response to the consolidation of slavery" in the United States. Drexler and White, *The Traumatic Colonel*, 10. That Burr emerges in Hale's story as a figure responsible for Philip Nolan's exile from his country and the nation's history is consistent with their analysis of Burr as a traumatic entity.

2. Hale, "The Man without a Country," 667. Hereafter cited parenthetically.

States again" (667). The remainder of the narrative describes how each successive crew deprives him of any connection to his former country, excising maps of the nation from atlases and removing articles on the United States from newspapers. Rather than tearing him emotionally away from his homeland, these acts throw him into a state of nostalgia. Over time his homesick patriotism becomes so intense that he takes up arms to defend his countrymen during a sea battle. Nolan's actions earn him the respect of the current captain, who requests but ultimately fails to secure a pardon for him.

The most significant moment in the text occurs when his vessel liberates a group of slaves. They speak Portuguese, a language that only Nolan knows. He must translate their request: "Take us home, take us to our own country, take us to our own house" (674). After relaying their petition, he breaks down completely, and everyone around him expresses an "almost equal agony of sympathy" (675). Few had empathized with him until this point; his display of homesickness efficaciously transmits his affective condition to others, compensating for their initial lack of sympathy. At the end of his life, Nolan learns about his estranged nation, marveling at the news of its expansion and extension of federal power and infrastructure. His nostalgia made it possible for him to love "his country as no other man has loved her" (679). Hale clearly intended Nolan to serve as an object lesson in redeemed patriotism, noting in the final lines of the story that the "infernal rebellion" of the South would have seemed incomprehensible to him (679). It certainly captured the Union imagination, as Northerners found themselves moved by the figure of Philip Nolan.[3] But by capitalizing on the fascination with nostalgia in both the United States and the Confederate States of America, his story did not necessarily work in the service of reunion. The same logic of estrangement that repatriated Nolan forged Confederate bonds too.

This chapter argues that the termination of the Civil War did not bring an end to this discord of nostalgic feeling, giving rise to widespread longing for fallen soldiers and lost homes. Southern writers redirected these broader discussions of nostalgia to preserve their cultural independence in the face of Reconstruction. The growth of a literature of Southern nostalgia helps explain why the policies of the Lincoln, Johnson, and Grant administrations struggled to assimilate the South culturally. Writers registered, bolstered, and combated sensations of

---

3. For a study of the reception of "The Man without a Country," which acknowledges the role of nostalgia in the story in a manner that anticipates my own reading, see Hyde, "Outcast Patriotism."

affective dislocation that included the freedmen's longing for national inclusion, the North's hopes for a nation made whole, and Southern desires for cultural preservation. The first section of this chapter attends to an archive of newspaper and magazine articles, poems, medical studies, treatises, and military reports that document nostalgia's use as an emotion expressing the disorientation so many felt in the United States after the war. I then devote sustained attention to Augusta Jane Evans's *St. Elmo* (1866) and María Amparo Ruiz de Burton's *Who Would Have Thought It?* (1872), because they representatively demonstrate how nostalgia generated antipathetic forms of communal and sectional affiliation. Building on the success of *Marcaria* (1863), *St. Elmo* addressed the challenge of white reconciliation in the South: many nonslaveholders had opposed the rebellion and had continued to express anti-Confederate sentiments throughout the conflict.[4] Defeat took a severe toll on the livelihood of these working-class Southerners who, sometimes against their will, disproportionately gave their lives to defend the Confederacy.[5] Evans superintended this resentment by imagining a new form of postwar Confederate nationalism. A commercial success, *St. Elmo* was not a novel of protest but one saturated with the ideology of prostration. Set in a South doomed by military downfall, it enacts a cultural reconciliation among white Southerners of varying social classes, substituting Confederate bellicosity with a Dixieland nostalgia founded on resentment toward Northern cultural institutions and a silently subservient black population.[6] *Who Would Have Thought It?*, written later during the Reconstruction Era, clarifies the relationship between sectional nostalgia and the place of the West. It establishes how both postwar Northern and Southern social cohesion emerged out of antipathy directed not just toward freed blacks, but also toward inassimilable subjects closely associated with the West, such as the novel's young Mexicana protagonist. Revealing the limits

---

4. For an account of how Evans deliberately sought out Northern and Southern readers for *Marcaria*, see Homestead, *American Women Authors and Literary Property*, 197–226.

5. For a detailed historical examination of the Southern dissenters, see David Williams, *Bitterly Divided*, 2–3 and 53–107.

6. William Perry Fidler claims *St. Elmo* was the third-best-selling novel in the nineteenth century behind *Uncle Tom's Cabin* and *Ben-Hur*. He admits, however, that "the absence of reliable records and indexes of sales before the year 1895" makes it difficult to be absolutely certain of *St. Elmo's* sales ranking. Fidler, *Augusta Evans Wilson*, 129. The novel continued to be widely sold well into the early twentieth century, though. Frank Luther Mott also lists *St. Elmo* among his list of all-time best sellers. See Mott, *Golden Multitudes*, 309.

of nostalgia's power, Ruiz de Burton employs topi of exile to show how the nostalgia fomented by the war will remain an incurable feature of U.S. cultural and political life. By representing the fluctuating regional alliances of the 1870s and complicating the North's relationship to ethnic difference, her romance rounds out my account of nostalgia in the Reconstruction Era in ways that another Southern Confederate or Northern republican reconciliation work of fiction simply could not.

Even though both historians and literary critics acknowledge the cultural tensions that strained the nation during the era, when they turn to the literature of Reconstruction, they usually focus on those works committed to national reconciliation.[7] Repudiating the long-standing myth of the Civil War as an "unwritten war," Alice Fahs chronicles the important differences between Northern and Southern Civil War writing, but she concludes that after the war, popular literature gave rise to "diversified nationalism" congenial to Northern hegemony.[8] Other commentators note how "the punitive desire to impose a new order on the South lasted probably about seven or eight years, until 1873" and conclude that Northerners and Southerners largely accepted their cultural differences.[9] These studies thus see the literature of the Reconstruction period as paving the way for the work of late-nineteenth-century writers that David Blight asserts "embraced the romance of the Lost Cause" to forge reunion narratives that celebrated "the mutuality of the soldiers' faith" on both sides of the conflict.[10] Reading proto-realist novels like John William De Forest's *Miss Ravenel's Conversion from Secession to*

---

7. For example, see Arac, *The Emergence of American Literary Narrative*; Bramen, *The Uses of Variety*; Brodhead, *Cultures of Letters*; Glazener, *Reading*; Lutz, *Cosmopolitan Vistas*; Samuels, *Facing America*; Warren, *Black and White Strangers*; and Young, *Disarming the Nation*. Also see Edmund Wilson's intrepid study of the literature of the Civil War: *Patriotic Gore*.

8. Fahs, *The Imagined Civil War*, 1, 16. Focusing on Northern women writers, Lyde Cullen Sizer persuasively documents the various strategies these authors used to critique republican institutions that denied them equal rights. But even though they "had diverging positions on the reigning ideologies supporting the Union war effort," they affirmed "the war's necessity and purpose." Sizer, *The Political Work of Northern Women Writers and the Civil War*, 13.

9. Martin Griffin, *Ashes of the Mind*, 5. Displacing the ideology of sectionalism, Southern regional writing "created an alternative world of stability, loyalty, and community in which racial problems and tensions disappeared behind a rose-tinted fiction of plantation slavery." Griffin, *Ashes*, 5–6.

10. Blight, *Race and Reunion*, 211. It should be noted he acknowledges the presence of late-nineteenth-century dissenters who, as in the case of W. E. B. DuBois, issued a "direct challenge to the history of the war and Reconstruction as it stood at the turn of century." Blight, *Race*, 253.

Loyalty (1867) or Oliver Optic's many popular children's books, critics insist that through homosocial battle scenes or heteronormative marriage plots North and South reunited as one.[11] But when placed alongside romances such as those written by Evans and Ruiz de Burton, these narratives no longer appear to express dominant cultural attitudes. They belong to a larger web of antagonisms, striving to narrate a regenerated nation in their own sectional terms. Rather than relying on a shared tradition, the Union and the Confederacy preserved their legacies through competing nostalgias.

The cultural significance of postwar novels of cultural disunion, as represented by *St. Elmo* and *Who Would Have Thought It?*, rested upon their particular formal qualities. Recent theories of genre and community provide a starting point for explicating how these texts operate aesthetically. Dimock models her understanding of genre around notions of kinship. Heeding poststructural critiques of generic classification as "border policing," she maintains that genres denote networks of affiliation.[12] They encompass a "broad spectrum of affinities" produced by a convergence "of contextually induced parallels."[13] But while genres do not obey rigid laws, I maintain, they create a shared perception of the world in the aggregate.[14] When a literary work that bears a "family resemblance" to an established genre begins conceiving a different sensible world, its departure must be deemed aesthetically significant.[15] The text becomes estranged from its family even if it cannot be said to have broken a set of formal laws. Rancière regards any text engaging in this kind of derivation as practicing the "'orphan' system of writing," which dislodges the genre to which it belongs.[16] These textual orphans break a law, but their transgression is a communal, not a strictly generic one. They render an absence previously unperceived by the genre to envision new communities of affiliation. For Rancière, these orphans are inherently democratic,

---

11. Randall Fuller, for example, establishes how prominent literary figures from Ralph Waldo Emerson to Louisa May Alcott enflamed Union passions during the war, but this bellicose body of letters became eclipsed by the "countless postwar narratives" that "obscured the political and social contexts of the conflict in order to emplot the theme of reunion and reconciliation that often united southern and northern lovers through marriage." Fuller, *From Battlefields Rising*, 221.

12. Dimock, *Through*, 73.

13. Ibid., 74.

14. In a similar vein, James Lilley urges us to approach genre as that which "names a collective idea, not a singular essence or totalizing concept." Lilley, *Common Things*, 21.

15. Ibid.

16. Rancière, *The Flesh of Words*, 104.

projecting the semantic power of the "people, equality, liberty, etc."[17] *St. Elmo* and *Who Would Have Thought It?* are orphans like their protagonists, but their formal estrangement does not revolve around the radical promise of the *demos*. They reconfigure hierarchies of power in the wake of Reconstruction, but in ways that create new communities that still obfuscate political subjugation. The communities featured in Southern romances and outlined by Ruiz de Burton's first novel are defined through negation rather than through a common set of political properties.

Roberto Esposito powerfully introduces a vocabulary for describing how negative communities are "united by an 'obligation,' in the sense that we say 'I owe *you* something.'"[18] Individuals surrender themselves out of the need to repel a shared threat or that which is not proper to the community. Only after they are brought into relation around "the memory of common danger" do they construct an origin story that enumerates a shared set of fictional properties.[19] This "dialectic of lost and found, of alienation and reappropriation" that defines all philosophies of community for Esposito, I argue, is affectively expressed through nostalgia.[20] In the decades immediately succeeding the Civil War, authors refined abstract feelings of nostalgia into Southern and Northern fantasies of reunion predicated on overlapping fears of scallywags, carpetbaggers, freed slaves, and non-European immigrants. The orphan as a trope for generic discord, political dissent, and a terrifying subject accordingly emerges in this chapter as a potent metonym for a moment in literary and cultural history overwhelmed by a surge in orphaned children. Steeped in nostalgia, these orphaned texts profoundly shaped the literary, cultural, and political landscape of the late nineteenth and early twentieth centuries.

LOCATING POLITICS IN THE ERA OF RECONSTRUCTION

The Mexican-American War brought nostalgia out of obscurity in North America, but it became a household word during the Civil War as reports of its prevalence among soldiers of both sections circulated.[21] Through this language of longing, writers expressed their desire for national unifi-

---

17. Ibid.
18. Esposito, *Communitas*, 6.
19. Ibid., 11.
20. Ibid., 16.
21. See David Anderson, "Dying of Nostalgia."

cation and imagined forms of sectional preservation. Essays, poems, and fictional prose steeped in it became a hallmark of debates over the viability of Reconstruction. As the failure of the Radical Republicans' efforts to remake the South in the image of the North became clear in the late 1870s, Confederate sympathizers appealed to nostalgic feelings to mollify divisions among poor and aristocratic white Southerners. The South, as a distinct and contested cultural identity, blossomed out of a longing to reclaim a more monolithic image of the Confederacy and antebellum plantation life. These Lost Cause images contrasted sharply with the economic and cultural divisiveness that plagued the short-lived nation during its rebellion.[22]

While nostalgia's etiology changed very little during these decades, the idea of homesickness became a way to process the psychological toll of the war's aftermath for citizens of both sections.[23] Newspapers contained vignettes about returning soldiers whose "blessed memories" of home "steadied [their] brain," only to struggle when readjusting to home life again.[24] As homesickness became a part of U.S. culture after the war, the pathological designation of nostalgia—though still mentioned—waned. Everyone experienced a moment when, as one author confessed, "Homesickness hath my heart possessed."[25] It became such a widely embraced feeling that some even suggested that never experiencing this emotion could be misanthropic. Thomas Cogswell Upham, a prominent Bowdoin professor of moral and mental philosophy, postulated that moderate nostalgia preserved "the natural tie of brotherhood, which binds man to his fellow-man."[26] As a writer for the Missouri-based *The Union Literary Magazine* claimed, "Even the savage, dead as is his heart to sympathy for the white man, cherishes an almost idolatrous reverence for his hunting grounds and the graves of his forefathers . . . [T]he sentiment is universally received, that 'There is no place like home.'"[27] Following this logic, those celebrating the Emancipation Proclamation cast it as a homecoming. *The Elevator* recited the story of Chester, a slave who finally could return to Florida, where he "felt at home in no other, and when

---

22. See Blight, *Race*, 99–139, and David Williams, *Bitterly*, 9–107.
23. For extensive accounts of the disease during the Civil War, see Dean, *Shook over Hell*, 135–60, and Matt, *Homesickness*, 75–101.
24. "Coming Home," *Salem Register* (Salem, MA), July 19, 1866.
25. "Over the Sea," *Pomeroy's Democrat* (New York, NY), October 17, 1874.
26. Upham, *Abridgement of Mental Philosophy*, 458.
27. Staples, "Mother, Home and Heaven," 6.

away, long to sing 'Home, sweet home.'"[28] These stories set the stage for African-American writers, such as Charles Chesnutt, Frances Harper, and Pauline Hopkins, who would recast Southern identity in their own terms.

During the early years of Reconstruction, most of the North optimistically believed the nation could be forged anew and embraced by the Radical Republicans' postbellum plans. They were aware that "the sword, though it practically settles many great political questions, does not immediately change convictions."[29] Northern essayists expressed anxiety over how many esteemed former Confederates vowed to pursue a cultural counter-revolution. The Confederate founding father Howell Cobb of Georgia confirmed these fears when he declaimed, "In war, we drew the sword, and bade them (loyal men) defiance; in peace, we gather up the manhood of the South, hurl into their teeth the same defiance."[30] To stem this "state of chronic rebellion," prominent organs of the federal cause aspired to transform the culture of the former Confederacy.[31] Northern periodicals would foster a "spirit of healing" in the South by combating the "sectional and one-sided . . . tone" of the now-defunct Southern magazines.[32] They saw the South's nostalgia for its past as many saw all forms of nostalgia, as "an abnormal condition, in a kind of diseased state."[33] To rid Southerners of their fidelity to the Confederacy, *Putnam's Magazine* proposed the following cultural synthesis: the "Northerner will carry South his thrift, his caution, his restless activity," while "the Southerner will temper these with his reckless liberality, his careless confidence, his fiery energy, and his old-time conservatism."[34] This kind of unbalanced amalgamation was the aim of those who committed themselves to the Republican blueprint for the South.

Those who relocated to the South saw this region much like they saw the West: it was an opportunity to improve their own economic lot. These individual motivations assumed a distinctly regional character draped in nostalgic hues. A Vermont native appealed to the exceptionalism of New England when he outlined his vision of a New South. Noting that "New England has taken possession" of the West, he declares that "her next work will be to New Englandize the South" in order to

---

28. "The Exile's Return," *The Elevator* (San Francisco), September 17, 1869.
29. "Southern Reconstruction," *Methodist Quarterly Review*, 379.
30. "Chronic Rebellion," *Advocate of Peace*, 120.
31. Ibid., 121.
32. "Southern Reconstruction," *Lippincott's Magazine*, 226.
33. "Southern Reconstruction," *Methodist Quarterly Review*, 381.
34. "The New South," *Putnam's Magazine*, 459.

extend its influence farther "from Plymouth Rock."[35] In his travel writing about Dixie, Sidney Andrews stressed that importing "Northern civilization, no less than the Northern idea of right and wrong, justice and injustice" to the former Confederacy "is the work ready for the hand of every New England man and woman."[36] Even under the auspices of national reunification, these comments exemplify the regional tensions and rivalries present during the Reconstruction decades. These views, uttered by Northerners, confirmed those held by Southerners before the war who insisted, "States have become the great factors by which nearly all of our results are accomplished," so that "if an American be asked abroad of what country are you, his first impulse is to answer, I am a New Yorker, a Virginian, a Massachusetts man, or a Carolinian, as the fact may be."[37] These localities spurred rivalries over other sectional affiliations during the postwar era. Northerners maintained that a strong connection existed between the "North and West," which conjoined "under homogeneous influences."[38] Yet Southerners, in defiance of the North, claimed their own affinities with the Midwest and the West, as regions that challenged the nationalizing aims of the Northern press and its elitist culture.

While the Radical Republicans struggled to reunite the nation, those who lived through their policies longed to restore Southern culture or to remake the South in the image of their own state. The most vicious manifestation of Southern resentment assumed the form of the Ku Klux Klan. Eric Foner provides a comprehensive list of the Klansmen's transgressions, from the murder of black members of the 1867–68 constitutional conventions to the whippings of white sympathizers.[39] Aligned closely with the economic interests of the planters, this notorious group attracted new members through its nostalgic vision of the antebellum South. Klan members wanted to take their country back from the federal government by restoring the racial hierarchy that the Reconstruction amendments and Civil Rights Acts dismantled. *Every Saturday*, the Boston-based magazine edited by Thomas Bailey Aldrich, surmised that "nothing could have prevented" the rise of the Klan "except the preservation of the exact condition of the South before the war."[40] Like many Northern periodicals,

---

35. Hough, *Our Country's Mission, or the Present Suffering of the Nation Justified by Future Glory*, 15.
36. Andrews, *The South Since the War*, 4.
37. Trescot, "Oration Delivered Before the South Carolina Historical Society," 289.
38. "Southern Reconstruction," *Lippincott's Magazine*, 223.
39. See Foner, *Reconstruction*, 425–44.
40. "What to Do," 362.

it urged Congress to adopt a less aggressive program of reconstruction, but Washington lawmakers did not waver. The Republicans passed the Ku Klux Klan Act of 1871, which brought a swift end to this organization's brutal campaign until enforcement of the law subsided under the direction of the Hayes administration.[41] Just decades later, Thomas Dixon vilified the repression of the Klan in a trilogy of novels romanticizing its exploits that came to embody a virulent strain of racist nostalgia in the twentieth century.[42]

The Ku Klux Klan was not alone in drawing upon the affective power of nostalgia to express or indict the interests and regional affiliations of Southern planters, poor whites, freedman, scallywags, and carpetbaggers. Democratic politicians rallied to curtail federal power over the governance of the former Confederate states by appealing to the section's glorious past. Even before the end of the war, Northern Democrats expressed concerns over the perceived radicalism of the Republican Party when it came to the treatment of former slaves. Ohio Representative Samuel Cox chided them for calling upon everyone "to forget the past—not to inquire how these poor people have become free, whether by law or usurpation."[43] Fearing the spread of miscegenation, he underscored that the road to a proper reunion and cessation of unrest could be achieved only by recapturing the South's now-estranged Anglo-Saxon and aristocratic past. "The question shall be," Cox declared, will the South be overseen by "the old order with Democracy to administer it, or continued revolution with destructives to guide it; the old Union with as much of local sovereignty as may be saved from the abrasion of war, or a new abolition and military unity of territory."[44] In a separate pamphlet, he decried the "the oath required both of loyal and disloyal

---

41. See Foner, *Reconstruction*, 456–59, and Martinez, *Carpetbaggers, Cavalry, and the Ku Klux Klan*, 68–79.

42. In these novels, Republican politicians, carpetbaggers, and scallywags emerge as the greatest villains. In *The Clansman*, for example, he paints a nostalgic portrait of Lincoln as a kindly conciliator with Southern roots. His assassination thrusts House Speaker Austin Stoneman and the Radical Republicans into power, who embark upon what Dixon describes as a "reign of terror." Dixon, *The Clansman*, 187. Instead of reunion, these Radical Republicans solidify Southern pride and give rise to the heroic Ku Klux Klan, who long to recover what they deem the ancient Anglo-Saxon principles of freedom extending from "the Magna Charta rights of every man who speaks the English tongue." Dixon, *Clansman*, 230. Dixon played a principal role in the creation of a Confederate nostalgia industry that thrived at various moments throughout the twentieth century. Tara McPherson provides a rich account of this brand of nostalgia in *Reconstructing Dixie*.

43. Cox, "The Nation's Hope in the Democracy," 3.

44. Cox, "Miscegenation or Amalgamation," 11.

men in the South" as an "oath to aid anarchy, and out of anarchy create a 'new nation.'"[45] Just as supporters of the Reconstruction Acts framed them as a return to an earlier U.S. Revolutionary ideal, so too did the Acts' detractors frame their opposition around the idea of preserving the nation's founding principles. For many Democrats, Reconstruction was a revolutionary program; it revived the spirit of the French, not the American, Revolution by imposing a reign of terror on a conquered and now-prostrate South.[46]

For Americans of both sections, as people longed to restore the home life they knew before the war, the question of what the home looked like and how regional identity would be defined was a hotly debated one. These regional attachments organized around feelings of nostalgia provided a rationale for what became seen as the failure of Reconstruction in the eyes of both Democrats and Republicans. African-Americans played the principal role of scapegoat, but those who penned screeds against them and other Republicans also couched their views in regional and nostalgic terms. Nostalgia worked in two directions in many Southerners' minds: they cast their antagonists as homesick Unionists and themselves as committed to reviving the Lost Cause. To establish that carpetbaggers could not assimilate to Southern society, they argued these Northerners remained too emotionally attached to their old homes. The *New Orleans Times* noted approvingly that Mississippi witnessed a "Northern flight" when "a species of nostalgia" afflicted Republican emigrants "in the form of an epidemic."[47] Northern publications subscribed to this view when doubt in the efficacy of Reconstruction arose. Among those who returned from the South, the

---

45. Cox, "The Nation's Hope in the Democracy," 3.
46. Although historians rightly have dismissed the ideology of the prostrate South, the effects of this cultural fiction were profoundly devastating. In the 1870s, as Reconstruction seemed doomed, racism became a socially acceptable way of expressing disappointment in the North as well in the South. In addition to James Shepherd Pike's *The Prostrate State: South Carolina under Negro Government* (1874), articles appearing in many Northern periodicals and Charles Nordhoff's *The Cotton States* endorsed the view that white—especially patrician—Southerners had "paid a heavy penalty for their mistake, for most of them were wealthy, and are now poor." Nordhoff, *The Cotton States in the Spring and Summer of 1875*, 11. They likened the political power held by carpetbaggers and black Republicans to the socialism of the Paris Commune of 1871. Thus, regional identity played a key factor in shaping the conversation over cultural reconstruction, and literary regionalism sometimes responded to anxieties about black social equality and the cultural revolution it could bring to the South. See Baker, *What Reconstruction Meant*, 14–20, and Foner, *Reconstruction*, 525–37.
47. "Our Standard Bearers," *New Orleans Times*, August 9, 1868.

Duluth Minnesotan reported, "the chief reason of discontent . . . is— homesickness. They miss the excellent schools, the churches and social elements of the North."[48] The person who relocated South would soon find that he "must necessarily be long time a stranger."[49] Reconstruction's pitfalls could be explained not by policy alone but by its inability to trump the power of local affections. The epithet *carpetbagger* underscored the paramount importance of locality by permanently assigning all Northern migrants the status of strangers. As Lewis Taylor of *The Independent* conceded, the important question of whether the United States is "a *league of states*" or "a nation" had not yet been "settled, as it ought to be."[50]

The presence of these strangers intensified the nostalgia many Southerners felt for the antebellum era, consolidating a shared identity that did not exist previously among the planters and poor white Southerners. In his intellectual history of the Confederacy, Michael Bernath describes how the South created its own national culture during the Civil War through an unprecedented expansion of literary and cultural materials tailored to a Southern audience. As the war reached its twilight, he maintains, Southern presses collapsed and Confederate intellectual nationalism floundered. After Lee's surrender, these cultural nationalists no longer "looked hopefully to the future," but they instead "looked regretfully back to the past."[51] The sense of occupation that many white Southerners shared during the Reconstruction nonetheless eroded the divisions that had once existed among them, and this shared feeling of besiegement gave rise to a reconstructed Southern literary culture.

Even though the war eventually decimated the Southern publishing industry, many new and widely circulated periodicals, such as *The Land We Love*, *The South-Land*, and *The Southern Review* in the South and *The Old Guard* in the North, arose out of the war's ashes to champion Southern culture. They combated the perception that the South "had neither literature nor science" to draw upon and so could be easily "denationalized."[52] These periodicals offered an ensemble of political essays, historical sketches, philosophical meditations, regional poems, and local-color stories that sounded chords of Southern nostalgia in

---

48. "The Reverse Side of Virginia," *Duluth Minnesotian*, November 11, 1871.
49. Ibid.
50. Taylor, "The 'Carpet-Baggers' and 'State Rights,'" 1.
51. Bernath, *Confederate Minds*, 297. For another important account of Confederate nationalism, see Faust, *The Creation of Confederate Nationalism*.
52. "The Old and the New South," *The International Review*, 215.

various registers. In some cases, this longing expressed itself indirectly by casting the South as a section that once embodied the ideals of classical republicanism. To repel what they deemed the federal government's usurpation of power, these sympathizers called for resurrecting the Roman Republican "spirit of liberty" that never "hesitate[d] to resist and punish both the consuls and the Senate" when they exceeded the powers delegated to them.[53] Often these publications printed ballads commemorating their lost nation. A poem dedicated to a fallen war general laments, "The land we love—a queen of lands / No prouder one the world has known, / Though now uncrowned, upon her throne / She sits with fetters on her hands."[54] It concludes with the hope that the South will someday rise again.

Nurtured by these publications and readers, the literatures of the Lost Cause and national reunion that began to flourish during Reconstruction were a regional enterprise in more ways than one. Against this cultural backdrop, reconciliation novels flooded the literary marketplace. Northern romancers waged their cultural war on this front. *Miss Ravenel's Conversion from Secession to Loyalty* exemplified the genre. De Forest's novel, which covers the span of the Civil War and the early years of Reconstruction, centers on the romantic fate of Lillie Ravenel, an exile from New Orleans residing in the fictional Northern town of New Boston. Her father sought refuge in the North because he remained loyal to the Union and could not be tolerated in his native South. De Forest describes Lillie as "strictly local, narrowly geographical in her feelings and opinions" and states that "no flower could be red, white and blue in Louisiana."[55] At odds with the views of her father, Lillie's exile awakens her "homesick sensibilities" and strengthens her commitment to the rebel cause from afar (45). She then enters into a love triangle that includes the Unionist lawyer turned soldier Edward Colburne and the Colonel Carter. Though a Union officer, Carter betrays sympathy for the rebel cause. He also belongs to a Virginian family that "boasted a purer strain of old colonial blue blood" (22). He develops a deep attraction toward her and "her homesick eyes" (81). Southern homesickness or nostalgia brings them together to preserve the Southern aristocracy regardless of the conflict's outcome. Carter proves unfaithful to Lillie and eventually perishes in battle. She finally marries the right man, Colburne, who exhibits an

---

53. "The Limits of Obedience to Acts of Government," *The Old Guard*, 727–28.
54. "The Land We Love," *The Land We Love*, lines 1–4.
55. De Forest, *Miss Ravenel's Conversion from Secession to Loyalty*, 11. Hereafter cited parenthetically.

unwavering love of the Union and embodies the intellectual vitality of the North. Her embrace of him cures her of nostalgia, prompting her to declare she "never" wishes to return to New Orleans but instead wishes to remain "always at the North!" (464).

Many other Northern novels emulated the generic features of De Forest's novel. Nearly all of them contain a marriage plot where a woman or man possessing strong Southern sympathies surrenders herself or himself to a suitor who practices Northern values. In other cases, these Northern romances grappled with the racial legacy of the war by introducing orphaned characters of dubious ethnicity. After relocating to the North, these characters, like Flora Delano of Lydia Maria Child's *A Romance of the Republic* (1867), feel "oppressed with homesickness" as they try to acclimate to their new surroundings.[56] The Northern households who take in these children successfully manage ethnic differences, Child opined, testifying to the assimilative power of the North. *A Romance of the Republic* is set largely in the antebellum era, but it projects an image of the North and the national culture it promotes as one conducive to racial inclusion and where convoluted and secret family trees get exposed and incorporated. Collectively, these Northern narratives cast nostalgia as a dangerous Southern sentiment. Homesickness obstructs reunion, but the virtues of national patriotism and republican unity prevail in these novels.

Writing retrospectively of Reconstruction's failure, Albion W. Tourgée depicted the foundation of reunion giving way to the weight of Southern nostalgia. In *A Fool's Errand* (1879), he reflected on the power of "the dead leader" who "has always more followers than his living peer," capable of summoning followers to "the burning cross."[57] He witnessed with dismay how Southern Unionists "who were true to the Union of their faith" throughout the war eventually turned against the North in the face of Reconstruction. The war in concert with the Radical Republican policies of the 1860s and early 1870s transformed Southern whites into a people without a country. The Northern protagonist, an erstwhile emigrant to the New South, begins his journey by eschewing the "sweets of the return home" but dies in the South not as a Southerner but as a fool-hearted alien.[58] It was within this affective atmosphere of postwar nostalgia that Augusta Evans wrote the most popular Reconstruction romance in the service of preserving Southern culture in the wake of its martial downfall.

---

56. Child, *A Romance of the Republic*, 145.
57. Tourgée, *A Fool's Errand*, 141.
58. Ibid., 19.

ST. ELMO'S CONFEDERATE RECONSTRUCTION

Throughout a better portion of the nearly six-hundred-page *St. Elmo*, the novel's protagonist, the orphaned Edna Earl, rebukes every major institution of the patriarchal and aristocratic South. Her dislike of this brand of Southern culture begins in the opening pages when, as a child, she witnesses a duel. This event traumatizes her to so great a degree that she sees it and the "Honorable Satisfaction" that it bestows as "a monster which custom had adopted and petted."[59] Her rejection of this Southern institution inspires her to become a writer and governess in New York, where she achieves literary renown. While pursuing her career, she rejects several male suitors, chief among them the Byronic Southern plantation owner St. Elmo, who has a "low estimate of female intellect" (259). St. Elmo plays the part of the consummate rake, taking pleasure in dueling, ruining women, and blaspheming the Bible. Although Edna finds herself inexplicably drawn to his "wicked magnetism," she resists him for most of the book, until he becomes a minister (226). After he finds the faith, Edna enthusiastically marries him. Once their union seems imminent, he gleefully proclaims to Edna's delight: "To-day I snap the fetters of your literary bondage. There shall be no more books written!" (562). Contemporary commentators invested in rehabilitating Evans as a successful woman writer could not imagine a resolution more disappointing than this one; the novel's strong female protagonist relinquishes her authorial agency to become a stereotypical Southern gentleman's belle.

Its conclusion may appear incongruous with Evans's successful literary career, but details of her biography suggest otherwise. As the South's answer to Stowe, she insisted motherhood and authorship were incompatible and railed against the idea of universal suffrage.[60] Drew Gilpin Faust accordingly asserts that "Augusta Jane Evans regarded herself as anything but a feminist."[61] Despite these biographical details and *St. Elmo*'s resolution, some commentators still see antipatriarchal elements in the novel.[62] Irrespective of how they regard Evans's status as a found-

---

59. Evans, *St. Elmo*, 20. Hereafter cited parenthetically.
60. See Sofer, *Making the "America of Art,"* 103.
61. Faust, *Mothers of Invention*, 177. For a similar reading, see Russell, "A Southern Patriot's Sacrifice," 55.
62. Notable readings that cast Evans in these terms include those by the following: Brusky, "Beyond the Ending of Maternal Absence *in A New-England Tale, The Wide, Wide, World*, and *St. Elmo*"; Susan Harris, *Nineteenth-Century American Women's Novels*; and Bradley Johnson, "Dueling Sentiments."

ing mother of an American women's literary tradition, all readers of *St. Elmo* must grapple with the narrative problem Edna's reunion with St. Elmo creates. Melissa Homestead addresses this question by contextualizing Evans's place in postbellum print culture and relation to the vexed status of Confederate copyright law. As a passionate advocate for these legal protections, Evans had to come to terms with the Northern literary market's power after the war. *St. Elmo* and its ending, for Homestead, "strategically staged" Evans's "own authorial dispossession and reassimilation into the American literary market."[63] I share Homestead's view that the Confederacy "concretely differentiated . . . its literary culture from the North's," but I see Edna's fate as indicative of Evans's attempt to preserve Southern cultural independence by challenging the ascendency of the Northern Reconstruction romance.[64]

The novel recites a different reunion story that renders a vision of a unified Dixieland imaginable in the wake of the Confederacy's downfall by marshalling the logic of marriage plots in antebellum and postbellum Northern romances and sentimental novels. But rather than renewing the country through the construction of new "fictions of nationhood," *St. Elmo* completes a different reunion at the expense of national reconciliation: a marriage between white Southerners of conflicting socioeconomic backgrounds in opposition to the North's cultural chauvinism.[65] In Evans's Reconstruction novel, tropes of submission channel the ideology of the prostrate South and embolden Southern cultural resistance. In the spirit of other Southern apologists, she reproduces the ideology of prostration by placing her protagonist in a position equivalent to *Clotel*'s nostalgic slave or *Israel Potter*'s homesick sailor. Regardless of how reactionary Evans may now appear, *St. Elmo*—not *Miss Ravenel's Conversion from Secession to Loyalty*—sold out within two weeks of its initial release and put a strain on its publisher's printing presses for the better part of the year.[66] Edna's conversion from loyalty to secession envisages a culturally independent prewar South impervious to the Reconstruction policies of the Radical Republicans.

Like many sentimental heroines, Edna is an orphan, but this has less importance than the particularities surrounding the young girl's regional and economic background. Soon after she endures the trauma of witnessing her first duel, the novel reveals that she lives with her grandfather,

---

63. Homestead, *American*, 196.
64. Ibid., 195–96.
65. Young, *Disarming*, 17.
66. See Fidler, *Augusta Evans Wilson*, 129.

a blacksmith by trade. That she clearly comes from the laboring and not the plantation class of Southerners conforms to the logic of Evans's Confederate romance. Her grandfather's blacksmith shop stood a mile from the "straggling village of Chattanooga" and "like the majority of blacksmith's shops at country cross-roads, it was a low, narrow shed, filled with dust and rubbish" (24). Just pages later, Evans informs us that Edna's grandfather has a "debt" to "pay off" before he can help secure her the education she needs to become a schoolteacher (29). These details underscore Edna's position within the South's class hierarchy and gesture to the historical reluctance of the Southern yeomen to enter the Civil War. Setting the early chapters in Chattanooga assumes significance given that "disloyalty" to the Confederate cause "was rife" in east Tennessee and the mountainous regions around Chattanooga especially.[67] The yeomen in these areas felt that secession would largely benefit only the planters. Evans thus provides us with a protagonist who inhabits a social and physical space lying on the border between North and South.

Edna's defining struggle is deciding whether to abandon her past and the South or to embrace her Southern heritage nostalgically. The unexpected and sudden death of her grandfather sets this dilemma into motion. Upon learning of his death, she feels "an abiding sense of irreparable loss" (35). This loss unmoors her from her particular region and forces her to think about how she might support herself without her grandfather. While mourning his death, she wanders around "the steps of the dreary homestead" (37). Describing Edna's now-deserted home as a "country graveyard," Evans alludes to Thomas Gray's "Elegy in a Church Graveyard"—a poem closely associated with the emergence of nostalgia in late-eighteenth-century Britain (37).[68] Instead of experiencing a longing for her home and her past, Edna finds her surroundings impoverished and so "spectre-thronged" that she can find no "allusion to the future" (38). The intertextual quality of these paragraphs diegetically embodies her perception of her old home by inundating the reader with a relentless list of allusions to poets, such as Charles Lamb and Oliver Goldsmith, who dwell upon the past. After completing her survey of the desolate homestead, she declares to a local miller, "I don't love this place now" (39). She decides to abandon her dreams of attending school and resolves to look for factory work in Georgia. She declares to a neighbor

---

67. Foner, *Reconstruction*, 13.
68. For an account of nostalgia in Gray's work, see Löwy and Sayre, *Romanticism Against the Tide of Modernity*, 52–53.

that "I have no home and nobody to love me, how then can I ever be homesick?" (41).

Her journey to Georgia represents an attempt to break her ties with the past and the Old South, but a catastrophic train crash prevents her from realizing this aim. The collision, however, inadvertently introduces her to Mrs. Murray, the widow of a wealthy Southern patriarch and planter, who immediately assumes care of her. By inserting Edna into Mrs. Murray's domestic space, the novel poses to its readers a crucial question: can a yeoman's granddaughter reconcile her differences with a family of planters? By answering this question in the affirmative, Evans preserves a sectional imagination after the Civil War. She imagines how white Southerners of various class and regional backgrounds can cohere into a single community culturally independent from the North. If seduction and sympathy work as registers of "familial feeling" to create "model[s] for sociopolitical union," then moments of sympathy and seduction in *St. Elmo* decipher Edna's cultural position within a nation that remains very much divided.[69] Evans reformulates the genres of the domestic novel and the seduction romance in order to imagine a way of integrating Edna—a white working-class orphan—into the home of a wealthy patrician family.

From the moment that she enters her home, Mrs. Murray regards her as an object of pity as opposed to an object of sympathy. She insists on becoming Edna's benefactress but explains, "Understand me, I do not adopt you; nor shall I consider you exactly as one of my family" (54). By not *exactly* admitting her into the family, Mrs. Murray underscores Edna's inferior class position. The servants repeatedly remind her that she is "a stranger in this house" (60). By residing in a home that she cannot call home, Edna's situation foregrounds the stark class divisions within the South as obstacles to creating a unified Southern cultural consciousness. Ironically, Edna's position in the home is remarkably similar to that of a slave or black servant. This formal maneuver musters the ideology of the prostrate South to suggest that whites from the lower orders possess a social standing comparable to slaves in the former Confederacy. Evans barely mentions the new conditions of blacks in the South, and these figures appear only intermittently as servants who silently maintain the Murray household and the plot of the book. Their conspicuous absence supports the narrative logic of a novel committed to unifying the South around a shared whitewashed culture. But being white, Edna

---

69. Barnes, *States of Sympathy*, 3.

can surmount the barriers to domestic acceptance, while the presence of freed slaves remains unrecognized.

Edna is courted by several suitors who illuminate her class position and what she must do to overcome it to become accepted into this Southern aristocratic world. The first of these suitors, Gordon Leigh, a wealthy Southern planter who studies Hebrew and Greek with her, occupies a social station higher than her own. When other women observe his interest in Edna, they assert she has no right to marry such a man, as she comes from "unknown parentage and doubtless low origin" (120). Her lower station empowers her in the face of Leigh's amorous onslaught. When he finally proposes marriage, she insists she has no desire to wed him and wishes to "earn a home" rather than "marry for one" (187). Rather than undermining patriarchal authority, Edna's rejection of Leigh elevates her into a position where she becomes further incorporated into a patriarchal structure. Mrs. Murray's son, the tempestuous St. Elmo, makes his romantic interest in her known. Regularly surveying his many plantations when not abroad, he embodies the very Southern culture Evans devoted her own literary career to preserving. Unable to forgive St. Elmo for his participation in a duel, Edna moves to New York, where she can devote her energies to her literary career. Her relocation is equally framed as a desire to shed her Southern identity, signaling her embrace of the North's cultural capital as the center of a new nationalized American society. Read as a conflict between two competing geographical allegiances, the novel diverges from its Northern literary counterparts. In a typical Northern sentimental romance, St. Elmo would play the part of the rakish seducer and New York would serve as the place where Edna might find a suitable Northern husband. Just such a husband presents himself in New York in the form of her publisher, Mr. Manning, who eventually proposes to her. Following the conventions of the genre, Edna should marry him and bear his children to fulfill the fantasy of national reconciliation. But Evans alters the generic formula by depicting New York and its promises of literary fame and fortune, not St. Elmo, as the real rake of her romance. Another Southern gentleman even suggests as much when he suspects that "there is a spring of selfishness underlying" Edna's desire to become an authoress and move north (293).

Once Edna arrives in New York, Evans introduces a subplot that resembles Fanny Fern's best-selling and highly influential antebellum novel *Ruth Hall* (1854), only to dismantle it. After the death of her husband, Ruth struggles to establish herself as a writer in New York. Like Edna, she forgoes the comfortable familiarity of a rural life for the pecuniary rewards of the city. Both characters also strive to find editors who will support their work. Edna's editor reminds her how much he deplores women's writing and bemoans the state of the "republic of letters" (372). He assures her that she "will not find life in New York as agreeable as it was under his [St. Elmo's] roof" in the South (372–73). But like Ruth Hall, Edna eventually achieves "celebrity" as an author (467). Her popularity swells to such a size that "letters came from all regions of the country" addressed to her, "asking for advice and assistance in little trials of which the world knew nothing" (465). An almost exact series of scenes appear in Fern's novel when Ruth peruses "a bundle of letters" from around the nation that beg her for advice or share stories about how they found her work comforting.[70] Fern's novel affirms New York as the nation's cultural capital, capable of unifying the nation through its dissemination of literature. Ruth eventually leaves the city, but she does not repudiate it and maintains her writing career. Evans also establishes that by moving to New York, Edna won a national audience that the South could never afford her. She eventually develops an affection for Mr. Manning, bringing the novel closer to imagining a national reconciliation between North and South. If it reached this anticipated conclusion, it would place New York at the cultural center of a reconstructed nation. But unlike her literary relative, Ruth Hall, Edna does not fare very well in the city, as it takes an incalculable toll on her health. She becomes increasingly paler and suffers regularly from fainting "attacks" (495). Eventually, news of her deteriorating health reaches Mrs. Murray, and she travels north to visit her beneficiary. Upon meeting, Mrs. Murray informs Edna that she will now receive her as a social equal and as a daughter. Realizing that the budding writer has become gravely ill, she inquires, "My child, why did you not come home long ago?" (469). Having become fully accepted into the Murray plantation household, Edna decides to "go home" at last (478). New York, in Evans's estimation, cannot denationalize the South, as so many Republicans had hoped.

Her acceptance into the Southern pale of sympathy cannot immediately mend the wounds between her and St. Elmo. He remains ready to embrace her at a moment's notice, but she refuses to forgive him for his transgressions. Their reconciliation becomes imminent at the moment her nostalgia for the South unleashes her repressed longing to be with him. When she returns, she consistently dwells on the past—something that she avoided throughout most of the novel. Upon laying eyes on St.

---

70. Fern, *Ruth Hall*, 180.

Elmo's treasured possessions, however, "her lip began to quiver as every article of furniture babbled of the By-Gone—of the happy evenings spent here" (492). Among St. Elmo's writings, she discovers a copy of Henry Soame's poem "Pleasures of Memory," which sends Edna into another reverie and triggers one of her fainting spells. These fainting episodes, along with her delusions and progressive weight loss, are the hallmark symptoms of nostalgia. This fact is in no way lost upon Edna, who after once again stressing that she will not allow herself to forgive St. Elmo, launches into the following speech:

> There are many reasons why I ought not to come here again; and, moreover, my work calls me hence, to a distant field. My physical strength seems to be ebbing fast, and my vines are not all purple with mellow fruit. . . . Not until my fingers clasp white flowers under a pall, shall it be said of me, "Yet a little sleep, a little slumber, a little folding of the hands to sleep." *In coelo quies!* The German idea of death is to me peculiarly comforting and touching, "Heimgang"—*going home*. Ah, sir! humanity ought to be homesick; and in thinking of that mansion beyond the star-paved pathway of the sky, whither Jesus has gone to prepare our places, we children of earth should, like the Swiss, never lose our homesickness. Our bodies are of the dust—dusty, and bend dustward; but our souls floated down from the sardonyx walls of the Everlasting City, and brought with them a yearning *maladie du pays*, which should help them to struggle back. . . . Thank God! going home for ever! (499–500)

This revelatory moment uses an eschatological nostalgia for heaven to underscore the force of Edna's earthly homesickness for the South.[71] As with many who became stricken with it, Edna realizes her time away from St. Elmo and her Southern home is gradually killing her. For the first time in the novel, she is capable of being homesick, a sentiment she believed as a young child she would never experience. She imagines her home as heaven, but this longing for a life after death allegorizes the Southern desire for a cultural life after martial defeat. Rehearsing the

---

71. For the aggrieved mourning the dead or for soldiers struggling to readjust to home life, nostalgia best described the affect that permeated their families and communities. It surfaced in fiction by spiritualists, such as Elizabeth Stuart Phelps's best-selling *The Gates Ajar* (1868), a novel about an orphan who feels estranged in her own home upon learning of her brother's death during the Civil War, until she begins to commune with his dead spirit. This spiritualism, inspired by Swendenborgianism, reflects the longing to be in heaven: the one place where families could be reunited with each other and God.

genealogy of nostalgia, Evans limns this affect's capacity for supplementation: where the familial sympathy of the Murrays faltered, the bond of homesickness succeeds in making it possible for Edna to claim her Southern heritage. This episode prefigures not death but her marriage to St. Elmo and an imaginary reconstruction of Confederate culture.

If genres operate not only as systems of classification, as Dimock contends, but also as "families subject to change" that encompass "a broad spectrum of affinities," then *St. Elmo* is a mutation of the reconciliation romance.[72] Its dislocation from its generic relatives is registered affectively through nostalgia. *St. Elmo* cannot belong to the Northern literary tradition as reflected though Edna's personal experience of homesickness. Paradoxically, Evans's novel is a formally exogamous permutation of the genre designed to sustain a culturally endogamous fantasy. It recognizes how working-class women in Southern society can nurture Confederate culture after the war. Evans accords Edna this role by having her reject Mr. Manning's hand in marriage and write domestic treatises instead of studies of ancient Greek and Roman civilization. She now fully rejects the "progress" of the North (523). Her changing attitudes find their corollary in St. Elmo, who renounced his violent past and embraced the ministry. His change in behavior makes it possible for Edna to become his wife and heralds a shift in the nature of sectionalism after the Civil War; in place of outright violent revolt, she imagines a culturally independent South—one that rejects both the political policies and the cultural superiority of the North. Their nostalgia for the South brings them together in marriage, uniting a granddaughter of a yeoman with the son of a planter.

This endogamous ending comes at the cost of leaving the recently emancipated slaves of the South unrecognized. They remain an unseen centripetal force around which the South orbits; behind Evans's sectional romance lies a fear of what the South might become if the Radical Republicans succeeded. The fleeting references to the Murray household's antebellum slaves as black servants, such as the "staid-looking elderly negro woman" who "sewed silently," reassure readers that Evans envisions a postbellum South where one part of the labor force will never participate in its polis (51). The nostalgia endemic to the ideology of the prostrate South mutes these subjects and propels the plot of *St. Elmo*. To wish for a South that never existed and to consummate an improbable marriage is to imagine a community out of a shared sense of dispossession

---

72. Dimock, *Through*, 74.

organized around the fear of a common enemy: their revulsion toward, in the words of one Southern Democrat, the "nigger, carpet-bag, and scalawag."[73] This political community is not formed out of a common set of properties or a sense of shared ownership but instead evolves out of "managing the only social bond possible, namely, enmity."[74] Edna's and St. Elmo's marriage is a union predicated on a divorce from the Northern culture and resentment toward Radical Republican politics. The failure of Reconstruction presaged by Evans was not yet apparent when *St. Elmo* first appeared in print, but the demise of these policies became a foregone conclusion by the time Ruiz de Burton sat down to write *Who Would Have Thought It?* Her novel rounds out our understanding of the literary and political climate of these decades by capturing the twilight of the Reconstruction Era as one fraught with social instability.

REJECTING THE REPUBLIC IN *WHO WOULD HAVE THOUGHT IT?*

When Dr. John Norval returns to New England from a geological expedition in the West with a Mexicana child in *Who Would Have Thought It?*, his family becomes plagued by internal division. He rescued the young Lola Medina from a band of Apaches who had held both her and her mother captive. Lola's mother, who perished before being able to escape, entrusted her daughter and a cache of plundered riches to the doctor. But rather than welcoming Lola with open arms, the doctor's wife, Jenny Norval, finds the young girl's racial composition repulsive. Determining Lola's place in the home is one of the guiding dilemmas of the novel, as characters struggle to situate her both within the household and within normative racial categories. Matters are complicated by the black dye the Apaches applied to Lola's skin, so that she becomes progressively whiter as it wears off during the course of the narrative. She longs to have "her own home" but always verges on being "homeless."[75] Jenny Norval's inability to assign Lola a clear position within her domicile thwarts what Lori Merish describes as "the persistent effectiveness of sentimental texts in enacting forms of subjection and identification within liberal polit-

---

73. Carey, *The Democratic Speaker's Hand-Book*, 373.
74. Esposito, *Communitas*, 27.
75. Ruiz de Burton, *Who Would Have Thought It?*, 180. Hereafter cited parenthetically as *Who*.

ical culture."[76] As with many Reconstruction novels not written from a Northern perspective, *Who Would Have Thought It?* uses nostalgia to express affectively the limits of sympathy.

Written at Reconstruction's nadir, the novel casts the West as an object of sectional rivalry with culturally unsettling immigrant and American Indian populations. *Who Would Have Thought It?* explores multispatial and multiethnic phenomena by mobilizing several genres, including the captivity narrative, the picaresque, and the historical romance. The novel's amalgamation of forms has confounded previous readers, making the book as difficult to classify generically as much as it is to place Lola within the Norval Republican household. Encumbered with countless literary references and character names that fuse classical first names with Dickensian surnames, like "Marcus Tullius Cicero Cackle" and "Sophocles Head," the novel's dense intertextuality obfuscates the plot. The disorderly structure of *Who Would Have Thought It?* demonstrates that a novel's heteroglossia may not necessarily exhibit the "centralizing tendencies of a new literary language" but instead may produce a cacophony language "outside the centralizing and unifying influence of the artistic and ideological norm established by the dominant literary language."[77] Like its protagonist Lola, Ruiz de Burton's novel is something of an orphan, belonging to no one particular genre or national literary tradition.[78]

---

76. Merish, *Sentimental Materialism*, 23.

77. Bakhtin, *The Dialogic Imagination*, 67. Unlike Evans's *St. Elmo*, Ruiz de Burton's first novel failed commercially and went out of print in the nineteenth century. Its generic idiosyncrasies and subject matter, however, shed light on the varied reaction against Reconstruction and the Northern literary culture that worked in tandem with this policy.

78. The novel's position within U.S. literary history and Chicano/a studies has been hotly contested. Ruiz de Burton's entire body of writing remained largely unread for over a century until Rosaura Sánchez and Beatrice Pita began producing newly annotated editions of her novels in the early 1990s under the auspices of the Recovering the U.S. Hispanic Literary Heritage Project. They consequently maintained that the novel's "subversive" character as a "critique of the empire" of the United States "from within" merits our attention as a literary forebear to the Chicano/a tradition. *Who*, lviii. Others embraced *Who Would Have Thought It?* as a novel that "turn[s] the tables on all the 'Yankees' who wrote about the West" by critiquing New England culture. Jacobs, "Mixed Bloods, Mestizas, and Pintos: Race, Gender, and Claims to Whiteness in Helen Hunt Jackson's *Ramona* and Maria Amparo Ruiz de Burton's *Who Would Have Thought It?*," 213. These kind of claims invited criticism from commentators who viewed Ruiz de Burton's relationship to Chicano/a literary studies as mired by her privileging of whiteness to construct "racist and classist narratives of white Hispanic superiority." María Carla Sánchez, "Whiteness Invisible," 66. No commentator, however, has cast her work as fully complicit with Anglo-American hegemony, even if some have insisted upon portraying her as unimpeach-

Two important readings of the novel single out its two opposing geographical trajectories. Carrie Tirado Bramen examines the regional character of Ruiz de Burton's work by insisting that *The Squatter and the Don* (1885) and, to a lesser degree, *Who Would Have Thought It?* reclaim the "tradition" of "federalism" in order "to integrate the various parts within the union" under the banner of liberal republicanism.[79] By contrast, Gretchen Murphy seizes upon the transnational dimension of Ruiz de Burton's work by arguing that she "criticizes mythic American independence and virtue" while "valorizing instead the manners of civilized cosmopolitanism."[80] While Bramen's and Murphy's views of Ruiz de Burton differ in some respects, both compellingly contend that in spite of its racist and classist pretensions, her work possessed a clear *telos*: to critique U.S. imperial ambitions by privileging either the regional or the transnational. This chapter also considers Ruiz de Burton's cultural relevance to Reconstruction-Era debates over national reunification, citizenship, and race, but it devotes particular attention to the aesthetic qualities of her work and their relationship to sectionalism's resilience.

If *St. Elmo* illustrates nostalgia's power to revitalize sectional culture, then *Who Would Have Thought It?* underscores the dangers inherent in this power. Ruiz de Burton prefers thought over feeling as a way of bringing individuals together. Nostalgia emerges in the novel initially as an ambivalent form capable of dismantling established literary genres to reveal the political and economic iniquities they conceal. As the novel progresses, however, the characters' various nostalgias render them incapable of forging communal bonds with one another. In place of either sympathetic belonging or nostalgic longing, Ruiz de Burton's central protagonists accept exiled resignation as their only alternative to a nation that they "no longer loved" (286). All of the novel's most laudable characters—Lola Medina, Julian Norval, Isaac Sprig, and Dr. John Norval—enter into states of exile in which homecoming ceases to be possible.

---

ably counterhegemonic. Those who read Ruiz de Burton's work as participating in the Chicano/a resistance tradition include Bost, "West Meets East"; Beth Fisher, "The Captive Mexicana and the Desiring Bourgeois Woman"; de la Luz Montes, "María Amparo Ruiz de Burton Negotiates American Literary Politics and Culture"; Pita, "Engendering Critique"; Rosaura Sánchez, "Dismantling the Colossus"; Sánchez and Pita, "María Amparo Ruiz de Burton and the Power of Her Pen"; and Saldívar, "Nuestra América's Borders." Those who cast her work in more ambivalent terms include González, *The Troubled Union;* Luis-Brown, *Waves of Decolonization;* Rivera, *The Emergence of Mexican America;* and Rodríguez, "Textual and Land Reclamations."

79. Bramen, *Uses*, 136.
80. Murphy, *Hemispheric Imaginings*, 103.

These tropes of nostalgia and exile cast the forging of national culture in the wake of the Civil War as an untenable goal.

This novel exhibits one of the defining formal traits of the historical romance: "*sedimentation,*" or the narrative quality of incorporating a multiplicity of layered discourses and genres.[81] According to Jameson, "*generic discontinuities*" inevitably arise within any densely sedimented genre like the historical romance.[82] Typically, these discontinuities work in concert with one another, even if they achieve only a kind of negative reconstruction. But what about when these diffuse elements fail to cohere, destabilizing the romance's harmonic heteroglossia? Rancière refers to this narrative discordance as "the 'orphan' system of writing," which unravels formal hierarchies and disturbs social cohesion.[83] This writing supplants the regime of representation, or the realm of rule-bound genres, with the regime of the aesthetic. *Who Would Have Thought It?* follows this course, leaving the form of the novel in shambles to render various social inequities "perceptible."[84]

Ruiz de Burton exposes the captivity narrative's inability to integrate ethnic diversity on the frontier. Its formal shortcomings emerge out of the divergent legacies of the Anglophone and Hispanophone versions of the genre. While exhibiting several similarities, these narratives manage racial hybridity differently, as miscegenation in the Anglophone literature and *mestizaje* in the Hispanophone tradition. Scholarship on the Anglo-American captivity narrative assigns it one of two principal cultural functions. They may challenge "the fixity of race and gender" by imbuing their female protagonists with at least a modicum of agency and by enabling them to transgress once impermeable racial boundaries.[85] But many readers conversely view the genre less as one that transgresses various identities than as one that constitutes them. Proponents of this interpretation argue that the Anglo-American captivity narrative preserved English identity in British North America by always ensuring that the "blood" of the captive "remained pure" by either returning her "undefiled to her family" or by having her die in captivity after becoming

---

81. Jameson, *The Political Unconsciousness*, 140.
82. Ibid., 144.
83. Rancière, *The Flesh of Words*, 104.
84. Rancière, *Disagreement*, 57.
85. Castiglia, *Bound and Determined*, 9. Also see Burnham, *Captivity*; Ellison, *Cato's Tears and the Making of Anglo-American Emotion*, 148–70; and Tinnemeyer, *Identity Politics of the Captivity Narrative after 1848*.

corrupted.[86] While providing antithetical interpretations of the Anglo-American captivity narrative, these two accounts contend that the genre produced subjects and communities either through transgression or by reproducing English identity in a diasporic context. They seize upon the same two key formal features that define the Anglo-American captivity genre: the protagonist is almost always white, and her captivity throws her racial and cultural purity into jeopardy. But what happens when the conventions of the genre are not honored? *Who Would Have Thought It?* fails to do what Jameson insists every novel must do: "reunite or harmonize heterogeneous narrative paradigms" that appear within its pages.[87] Behind Jameson's claim, one can hear the unlikely echoes of Matthew Arnold's idea of harmonious culture, but Ruiz de Burton's anarchical use of the captivity narrative is discernibly out of tune with its narrative traditions and with the project of cultural and political reconciliation.

Who Would Have Thought It? produces disharmonious heterogeneity by forcing the Anglo-American version of this genre to contend with its formal relative, the Hispanophone captivity narrative. Ruiz de Burton attends to how the nineteenth-century Hispanophone "ideal of *mestizaje*" is "pejoratively rendered in English as miscegenation."[88] Before the nineteenth century, both Hispanophone and Lusophone colonists feared that "mestizo captives, born or raised among the Indians, love their vices, customs, and freedom so much that they are harmful."[89] They often dealt with these figures differently by imagining new ethnic possibilities to achieve a different set of literary and cultural ends. Instead, these narratives, as Lisa Voigt asserts, "contributed to the sharing of knowledge—whether through coercion or cooperation—across national, religious, and linguistic boundaries."[90] Articles routinely appeared in U.S. periodicals on Mexico and the West, establishing that people in both the North and the South took a keen interest in this part of the continent.[91]

---

86. Tennenhouse, *The Importance of Feeling English*, 57. For like-minded approaches, see Gardner, *Master Plots*, 30–51; Gould, *Barbaric Traffic*, 98–109; and Tawil, *Making*, 92–128.
87. Jameson, *The Political Unconsciousness*, 144.
88. Sommer, *Foundational Fictions*, 78.
89. In Jerónimo de Quiroga, *Memorias de los sucesos de la guerra de Chile* (ca. 1690) (quoted in and translated by Voigt, *Writing Captivity in the Early Modern Atlantic*, 12).
90. Voigt, *Writing*, 25.
91. One characteristic account of Mexico appeared in *Frank Leslie's New Monthly*, which detailed the state of Mexican culture before and after the Mexican-American War. The reporter "dressed in Mexican style" at one point to gather information about various ranchos and Indians he encountered. "Reminiscences of Mexico," 405. He also gleaned information from prisoners held captive in the country. Interest in Mexico stemmed in

Dr. Norval regards Lola's captivity as an opportunity to gather information, yet the knowledge he and the rest of his family hope to glean from her circumstances proves elusive. Ruiz de Burton does not synthesize these two iterations of the captivity narrative, and their formal discord contributes to her narrative's larger exploration of disunion.

Dr. Norval recounts the story of Lola's captivity shortly after returning home from his expedition. Having brought with him what everyone initially believes to be either a young black or Native-American child, the doctor recites the details of Lola's captivity and her eventual redemption. She does not provide firsthand testimony, permitting Dr. Norval to relay her tale within the masculine frame that typically surrounds the female captivity narrative. His framework rests upon a fetishization of her Mexicana heritage. He is part geologist, part explorer, and part ethnographer, making him wholly a collector of exotica. For this reason, when he introduces Lola to his family, his wife mockingly concludes that his collections must have "exhausted the mineral kingdom," so he "is about to begin with the animal" by claiming Lola as his "first specimen." (16). He dismisses her xenophobic comment out of hand, but it does not miss the mark. Lola is an anthropological curiosity for him, and he regards her as an acquisition, even if he cannot quite assign her a proper genus. Her classification proves difficult partly because he knows, despite appearances, that her "blood is pure Spanish blood" (28). Lola can trace her lineage back to Spain, complicating Ruiz de Burton's use of the genre in three interconnected ways: first, her Spanish bloodline raises the question of whether the tradition of the Anglo-American captivity narrative is relevant to her cultural circumstances; second, her Spanish identity and ties to Mexico elicit confusion by making her racially indiscernible to those around her; and third, her convoluted ethnic identity excites feelings of both nostalgic desire and xenophobic revulsion in the hearts of those around her.

The novel holds in abeyance the question of whether the rules of the Anglo-American captivity narrative apply to Lola. It initially reproduces

---

no small part from the publication of William Prescott's *History of the Conquest of Mexico* (1843). The entire multivolume study and excerpts from it were reprinted widely throughout the second half of the nineteenth century. In his critical reappraisal of the United States' territorial expansion in the nineteenth century, Andy Doolen attends to "the major effects" U.S.-Mexico relations and more broadly "Latin American independence" had upon the growth and character of the United States' empire and its "process of territorialization." Doolen, *Territories of Empire*, 91. Doolen's literary analysis and wide-ranging archive, to my mind, reveals that *Who Would Have Thought It?* taps into a cultural and political discourse of paramount importance.

the genre's convention faithfully. That Lola's purity is insisted upon by Dr. Norval recalls Mary Rowlandson's captivity narrative, which underscores the "*English*" purity of its "Gentlewoman" protagonist.[92] Ruiz de Burton emphasizes Lola's chastity and virtue, two other crucial attributes she shares with the archetypal Anglo-American female captive. Despite these typical generic overtures, her captivity narrative deviates from the norm by acknowledging Lola's cultural corruption. Although she is of "pure Spanish descent," she "was born five months after her capture" and raised in captivity among a tribe of Apaches (28). Dr. Norval reveals that an Apache chief had taken her mother, Doña Theresa Medina, as his wife. Aware of the threat cultural miscegenation poses to her daughter, Lola's mother beseeches Dr. Norval to "take her child away from among savages and bring her up as a Christian" (35). Having spent her formative childhood years among the Apaches, Lola does not possess the same degree of perceived cultural purity that many Anglo-American captive women did.

Doña Theresa Medina's and her daughter's story, nevertheless, is not entirely without literary precedent. Doris Sommer has shown how Latin American foundational stories, from captivity narratives to romances, used the model mestiza to create nationally integrative fictions. These romances of racial amalgamation whiten the indigenous population, providing "elite control" with "another fictional grounding: falling in love and getting married to the object of control."[93] Read in this context, Dr. Norval's actions modify this hegemonic gesture through an attempted act of adoption rather than matrimony. There are more idiosyncratic Anglo-American captivity narratives that embrace forms of cultural or racial hybridity. Mary Jemison's narrative, for example, resembles the story of Lola's mother, as she too goes native and manages to "reproduce an English household" for her children in this environment.[94] Lola's story, however, does not realize either of these ends. She cannot be mastered in the Norval household, and her mother, unlike Jemison, cannot replicate a Spanish household in captivity. Dr. Norval observes that while her "bedclothes . . . were as white as snow, and everything about her was clean and tidy," her surroundings "were cheerless enough to kill any civilized woman" (36). She failed to preserve the cultural integrity of her daughter, lamenting that Lola had yet to be baptized or taught the ways

---

92. Rowlandson, *A True History of the Captivity and Restoration of Mrs. Mary Rowlandson*, 28.
93. Sommer, *Foundational*, 288.
94. Armstrong, "Why," 11.

of the Catholic Church. Here the narrative overturns the conventional cultural logics of both the Hispanophone and Anglo-American captivity narratives. The captivity narrative fails to incorporate or render Lola's and her mother's racial and cultural status legible.

Her dubious Spanish ancestry further muddles the normative racial parameters of the captivity narrative genre. As the circumstances of her captivity suggest, Lola can assert only a genealogical and not a cultural connection to her Spanish identity. And since the Apache had regularly dyed her skin black, one of the two Norval daughters proclaims Lola "a nigger girl" but revises her initial assessment moments later when she recognizes that her "hand is as white as mine—and a prettier white" (16–17). Her dyed skin, which eventually fades to white, dispenses with essentialist notions of whiteness to undermine uncannily "the boundaries of 'foreign' and 'domestic,'" as her changing complexion and uncertain white European status make her both familiar and strange at the same time.[95] Blurring the line between alien and citizen, the narrative allegorizes the shifting status of Mexicans in the United States in the wake of the Treaty of Guadalupe Hidalgo, the Gadsden Purchase, and the Civil War.

While Mexicans living within the various annexed territories initially had legal assurances that they would receive the full benefits of American citizenship from the federal government, historian Manuel G. Gonzales notes that the material success of those working in the gold mines inspired Anglo-American envy that would "encourage the portrayal of Mexicanos as a foreign and unfriendly element."[96] Yet articles appearing in Western periodicals, such as *The Overland Monthly*, also published sketches expressing great interest in "the high noon of the Mexican Empire" or "the newborn nation of the West."[97] Highlighting the nation's disparities in wealth and social ills, *The Overland* indulged in the "romance in the mysterious past of that distant land" and averred that "enough of hope for its future" existed for "regeneration" to occur.[98] *The Land We Love* also issued a piece that portrayed Montezuma in sympathetic terms as someone who fought the overbearing "arms of the Senate" and the Spanish Empire.[99] It implicitly considered whether a prostrate people could recover from an oppressive defeat. Described in this manner,

---

95. Tinnemeyer, *Identity*, xvi.
96. Gonzales, *Mexicanos*, 84.
97. "High Noon of the Empire," 21.
98. Ibid., 28.
99. "A Fragment from Mexican History," 427.

Mexico figured as an analog to the recently reunited United States: Mexico's fate and the fate of the West might be portended by Mexico's success or failure. Lola's racial indeterminacy and the place of Mexicans in the United States work not just as a locus for the uncanniness of ethnic mimicry; she functions as a palimpsest overwritten with layers of unfulfilled national desire.[100] Lola is an object of transference more than a subject of resemblance. Ruiz de Burton pins the hopes and anxieties surrounding the future of federalism and its ethnically integrative promise.

The generic instability accompanying Lola's uncertain cultural status incites a series of incongruous receptions of her that oscillate from revulsion to desire. The black paint covering her underlying whiteness involuntarily forces her into a cultural position commensurate with Eric Lott's account of blackface minstrelsy. Lott demonstrates that blackface's appropriation of black identity and "cultural practices" yields a "mixed erotic economy of celebration and exploitation" or "love and theft."[101] "Nostalgic longing" for the South and its plantation life as "a kind of timeless lost home" drove this practice of appropriation.[102] Rather than bringing disparate groups of people together, "minstrel nostalgia" excited a longing for slavery that ignited racial and sectional tensions.[103] Ruiz de Burton mobilizes the same forces at work in antebellum blackface practices in *Who Would Have Thought It?*, showing her postbellum readers that the United States remains a nation divided by competing regional nostalgias and conceptions of race. These nostalgias have little to do with recovering an idyllic pre-emancipation South, but they enumerate the many cultural obstacles to Reconstruction in the postbellum period.

Lola's presence in the Norval household entices the imaginations of the people around her soon after the doctor assures them—and Mrs. Norval especially—that "her history is already more romantic than that of half of the heroines of your trashy novels" (17). The romance surrounding her lineage stems from her status as a Mexican, conjuring up fantasies of possible connections to the Aztecs. Even though many find Lola's potential Mexican heritage revolting, they fetishize her imaginary Aztec genealogy and display a nostalgia for these native and noble American empires.[104] These desires appear all the more transparent

---

100. See Bhabha, *The Location of Culture*, 92.
101. Lott, *Love*, 6.
102. Ibid., 190.
103. Ibid., 191.
104. By doing so, they subscribe to what Eric Wertheimer identifies as a "vital tradition" in the United States of locating "exemplars in the New World" that could serve as legitimating precedents for U.S. empire building. Wertheimer, *Imagined Empires*, 3.

when associated with Lola's stash of gold and precious gems. Exemplifying the fantasy of imperialism, she amassed her fortune in captivity because "Indians brought her emeralds and rubies, seeing that she liked pretty pebbles" (29). These precious jewels, along with her stockpile of California gold, tempt others to seize her inheritance both materially and culturally. Lola metonymically fuses together two sides of U.S. imperialism in Central America: the reverence for the traditions of the Aztecs and a romanticized appreciation of the victory of the conquistadors. Cupidity and imperial chauvinism find their perfect incarnation in the figure of the wayward Reverend Hackwell, a lascivious rake who first seduces Mrs. Norval in her husband's absence but then begs Lola "to marry him," insisting that "he had loved her always, even when others thought her an Indian" (147). His greed for her fortune and lust for her beauty become completely entangled, as he obsessively but unsuccessfully pursues her. Her association with the Aztecs and the Spanish Empire also wins her the love of several morally laudable characters, including Dr. Norval, Isaac Sprig, and her eventual husband, Julian Norval, who departs for Mexico with her at the close of the novel.

Lola's ability to set into motion a dialectic of desire and hatred or love and theft unravels the communal harmony of the Anglo-American Norval family and those who associate with them. The interplay between these two antipodal emotions proves unwieldy for another genre mobilized in this romance: the domestic novel. Those who study this form either maintain it unites "subjects in opposition to its figures of the patriarch/slaveholder" or argue it facilitates colonial expansion by assimilating any foreign threats.[105] Whether lauded for its political power or derided for its complicity with imperialism, the domestic romance is structured to incorporate difference for better or for worse.[106] Ruiz de Burton, however, overturns the sentimental power of the home to challenge the Republican matriarchy of the North. Jenny Norval cannot reconcile Lola's skin color with her wealth and pure Spanish stock. She regards Lola's racial mutability as a contagion, adamantly believing that her spots suggest she contracted "some disease" while in captivity (78). Lola goes viral and circulates, akin to the Hispanophone captivity narratives that gave rise to similar mestiza figures, beyond the confines of the Norval household and the captivity narrative genre. Once in circu-

---

105. Romero, *Home Fronts*, 86. Also see Kaplan's account of "manifest domesticity" in Kaplan, *The Anarchy of Empire in the Making of U.S. Culture*, 23–50.

106. For deft examples of this scholarship, see Gillian Brown, *Domestic Individualism*; Hartman, *Scenes of Subjection*; Tompkins, *Sensational Designs*; and Wexler, *Tender Violence*.

lation, she tears apart the Norval household. Julian, Jenny Norval's son, quickly recognizes her as his social equal, and he develops an intense attraction toward her that blossoms into a desire to "marry her" (180). Their transparent affection prompts Julian's mother to send him off to the frontlines of the Civil War and Lola off to a convent. Despite her best efforts, she cannot keep them separated, nor can she manage the danger Lola poses to her Northern household.

Jenny's tyrannical behavior and Lola and Julian's marriage plot lay the foundation for Ruiz de Burton's Confederate apologia. *Who Would Have Thought It?* is a new kind of anti–*Uncle Tom's Cabin*. It does not romanticize plantation life, as the antebellum anti–*Uncle Tom* novels did, but it indicts the institutions of Republican motherhood and the Republican Party. Northern reconciliation romances honor Stowe's model by establishing how orderly homes produce an orderly society. *Who Would Have Thought It?* instead incites disorder on both fronts. Norval's motherly failings parallel the romance's portrayal of the severe shortcomings of the federal government. When Julian and Major Hackwell are wounded in battle, for example, Mrs. Norval behaves despotically by transforming her family into "all her slaves," ordering them to flock to either Julian's or Hackwell's bedsides (138). Her conduct corresponds to the Union's suspension of *habeas corpus* and other fundamental rights accorded by the Constitution. Ruiz de Burton scarifies Lincoln for exercising his wartime powers, as many Southern apologists did, throughout the novel. Far from abolishing slavery, Norval and, by extension, the federal government expand the peculiar institution's reach by enslaving household members and citizens without rights.

Jenny Norval's private behavior presages a long list of public federal transgressions experienced by many of the novel's other characters. After delivering an allegedly treasonous speech, Julian finds himself trapped within an unjust and broken U.S. legal system. He struggles to navigate the bureaucracy of the federal justice system while attempting to get his charges expunged. While set during the war, the Reconstruction-Era implications of Julian's legal misadventures could not be more clear: an expansion of federal power will only breed greater injustice and corruption. He initially has faith in the president's ability to redress his charges, but Ruiz de Burton's Lincoln is not a folksy and conciliatory figure. He is portrayed instead as an overprivileged tyrant with a gold cane who has little patience for hearing the grievances of the people who come to see him. Unable to secure the pardon he wishes from the president, Julian asserts that the nation is not "a country of equals" (209). He laments, "Have we free-born Americans turned into slavish courtiers, and are we to dance attendance at the antechamber of a despot?" (212). Ruiz de Burton channels the ideology of the prostrate South by inviting readers to identify with Julian's position. When the authorities throw him into prison, he continues to reflect upon the failures of federalism. He nostalgically recalls the founders but believes the nation squandered their "inheritance of liberty" (244). He witnesses the poor prison conditions that blatantly homesick Confederate soldiers must endure. These observations compel him to sympathize with the South fully, which he concludes has suffered long enough. He ceases possessing any patriotic sentiments and declares, "I did not bargain to surrender my freedom to give it to Sambo" (241).

Following Julian Norval's fate, Ruiz de Burton musters and then globalizes the ideology of the prostrate South found in Evans's and other Southern romances published after the Civil War. Unable to tolerate ethnic difference or political dissent, the federal government sends its most sympathetic characters packing. Lola reunites with her Spanish relatives in Mexico after learning of their whereabouts from Mrs. Norval's estranged brother, Isaac Sprig. Sprig, who also fought in the war, sought out Lola's Mexican relatives after he too had become disenchanted with his country. Mexico provides both Lola and Sprig with a refuge from federal tyranny, but her father and grandfather are powerful gentlemen who fear the defeat of the South will embolden the United States. They regard the United States as a despotic imperial power that *"will eventually destroy us*—the Mexicans" (198). Here Ruiz de Burton uses Lola's father to indulge in a nostalgia for an aristocratic class bred for enlightened governing. This aristocratic nostalgia gives rise to an image of the global South that encircles the former Confederate states, Mexico, and implicitly, California. As both José Arnada Jr. and John Morán González argue, their "union becomes possible as the dark dye applied to Lola's white skin by the Indian wears off," but their union marries Mexican colonialism to a Confederate, not U.S., colonialism.[107] That Julian and Lola finally realize their romance in Mexico indicates that Ruiz de Burton imagines a regional and national realignment among these regions—a global confederacy separated from a depraved federation of Northern states.

Ruiz de Burton establishes that the captivity narrative, the domestic novel, and the romance that encapsulates them cannot perform their

---

107. González, *Troubled Union*, 92. Also see Aranda, "Contradictory Impulses."

nationalizing cultural work during or after the Civil War. Unlike Evans, Ruiz de Burton sees the various regional and ethnic nostalgias so pervasive during this period as obstacles to rather than mechanisms for creating communal affiliation. None of the heroes and heroines in *Who Would Have Thought It?* belong anywhere. Ruiz de Burton and many of her characters embrace their exile or the state of being at home nowhere in the world. When the doctor is accused of harboring Southern sympathies simply because he attempted to negotiate a political compromise before the war broke out, he commits to "voluntarily exiling himself from his country" (84). Even though Dr. Norval's return home is much anticipated, it is never realized. Once Sprig escapes from his prison in the South, he also becomes so "sick of his country and countrymen" that "he longed to get away" to Mexico (192). Social bonds, insofar as they persist in the novel, orbit around figures of antipathy: Lola unites Mrs. Norval and Hackwell against her, and the North's injustices bring together the exiled characters, and by their association, a geographical union among the South, the West, and Mexico takes shape. They are all women and men without a country. This divisive feature of nostalgia served as the basis for Howells's outright repudiation of it and the historical romance more broadly in the 1880s, and it set the stage for mapping new regional affiliations and political possibilities in the final decades of the nineteenth century.

CHAPTER 3

LONGING FOR A PEOPLE

HAMLIN GARLAND'S AND
PAULINE HOPKINS'S POPULIST FICTIONS

*W*ALT WHITMAN'S "Democratic Vistas" (1871) presciently identified the political and economic challenges of the final decades of the nineteenth century. "Of all dangers to a nation," he prognosticates, "there can be no greater one than having certain portions of the people set off from the rest by a line drawn—they not privileged as others, but degraded, humiliated, made of no account."[1] Congress may hold hearings to address "the suffrage, tariff and labor questions, and the various business and benevolent needs of America," but Whitman avers their measures will not prevent the rise of national unrest (365). What the nation lacks is a coherent collective subject or a clear and shared apprehension of *the people*. He speculates that the rebirth of American nationality will require material changes, entailing "a more universal ownership of property, general homesteads, general comfort—a vast, intertwining reticulation of wealth" (383). This redistribution of wealth, however, must be matched by the equal dissemination of a democratic literary tradition. He calls for "a programme of culture, drawn out, not for a single class alone . . . but with an eye to practical life, the west, the working-men, the facts of farms and jack-planes and engineers, and of the broad range of the women also of the middle and working strata" (396). He concludes with a sprawling paragraph-long sentence, formally uniting a multiplicity of ideas and points of view under the banner of the United States' "literature,

---

1. Whitman, "Democratic Vistas," 382. Hereafter cited parenthetically.

esthetics, &c." upon which "the democratic, the popular," and "all the superstructures of the future are to permanently rest" (425–26).

A decade after "Democratic Vistas" first appeared in print, writers, politicians, and grassroots organizers vigorously contested the form and content of the common people. Battered by the Panic of 1873, rampant land speculation, and predatory lending practices, farmers started organizing. These groups grew and eventually collaborated to found a new political party that invented its own conception of *the people*. Even as they anticipated a better future, what brought these groups together was the desire to resuscitate a lost past or home. Creating a better democracy meant looking backward. They knew, as much as Whitman did, that the present and the future are "but the legitimate birth of the past" (362). To remain politically viable, they had to craft "a new history, a history of democracy" (423). Many of these organizers and writers celebrated the democratic impulse behind Whitman's poetry and prose, but he wanted to cure the country of factionalism though the creation of a shared literary tradition.[2] The Populists, on the other hand, introduced a series of contentious alternative lost cultural and political histories awaiting recovery.[3] As earlier agrarian revolutionaries had done before them, their nostalgia for Jeffersonian agrarianism and Jacksonian egalitarianism worked affectively to bring together rural and urban laborers alike.[4] It was not a question of embracing an antimodern retreat backward or a progressive march forward, as many studies of Populism maintain; it was a question of what kind of nostalgic vision would underwrite the future of the people.

Insisting upon the aesthetic and affective importance of nostalgia to Populism, this chapter shifts attention away from American literary realism and toward regional and romantic writing often placed on the periphery of late-nineteenth-century U.S. literary history. This body of writing, I argue, assisted or competed with Populist efforts to create its own conceptions of the people. While figures such as Sarah Orne Jewett and Mary Wilkins Freeman carved out places in their writing for women in old New England society, Populist writers entertained new political possibilities in their utopian and regional literature. To establish its potential and limitations, this chapter surveys nostalgic Populist political discourse

---

2. See David Reynolds, *Walt Whitman's America*, 448–589.

3. Throughout this chapter I use "Populism" and "Populist" to refer specifically to either The People's Party movement or the Black Populist movement.

4. For an especially compelling survey of agrarian political thought and literary culture in the 1790s, see Ed White, *The Backcountry and the City*.

before turning to a careful examination of writings by Hamlin Garland and Pauline Hopkins. While I remark upon the utopian novels of Ignatius Donnelly and Edward Bellamy at various moments in this chapter, it may seem strange not to devote sustained attention to either author given their importance to the Populist movement. But as critical a role as both Donnelly's *Caesar's Column* (1891) and Bellamy's *Looking Backward* (1889) played, neither book registers the narrative power of nostalgia, nor do they principally concern themselves with how this affect could constitute a people. This chapter thus gravitates toward authors who can shed light on the nostalgic narrative logic that animated an array of divergent populisms. Garland receives sustained attention because I see his *veritist* aesthetics as intimately bound to his use of nostalgia and its creation of a Populist political subject. As a counterpoint, I turn to Hopkins as a writer who attended to the racial limitations of white Populism's "people." My examination of *Contending Forces: Romance of Negro Life North and South* (1900), then, is in keeping with recent histories of Populism attesting to how blacks both participated in and were excluded from this important late-nineteenth-century political movement. And Hopkins crucially uses a diasporic nostalgia of her own to construct her idea of a politically committed black "people," making her literary work central to intellectual concerns of *Novel Nostalgias*.

Garland developed an aesthetic theory and wrote short fiction that oppugned the integrative aims of American literary realism. His work transforms what Ernesto Laclau and Rancière would theoretically deem the necessary "'vagueness' of populist discourses" into an emotionally and imaginatively potent political subject situated within its own historical narrative.[5] Garland uses nostalgia, an emotion now "everybody knows" after the Civil War, to delineate new relations among the nation's regions.[6] The Populist iteration of this affect could cement new allegiances, as in Garland's work, but it also reproduced old and established new categories of differentiation. Many members embraced anti-Semitic financial conspiracy theories, and even though various Black Populist associations emerged in the South, white Populists were reluctant to accept them. Black Populists drew upon their own feelings of nostalgic displacement to expose the limitations of other Populist conceptions of the people. Although she did not belong to any Black Populist organization herself, Hopkins participated actively in late-nineteenth-

---

5. Laclau, *On Populist Reason*, 17.
6. "Nostalgia," *The New York Times*, May 12, 1874.

century African-American politics and registered Populism's limitations: it gravitated toward white nativism, rendering it complicit with the ongoing economic, political, and social oppression of blacks. In her magazine essays and especially in her 1900 historical romance *Contending Forces*, she turned backward to rewrite the past and to fashion her own nostalgic rhetoric of populism. Attending to her body of work broadens the cultural context for assessing the diffuse character of populism at the end of the nineteenth century.

By examining the intersection between Populist and regionalist ideas of the people, I place two bodies of once-maligned historical and literary scholarship into constellation with one another. Studies of Populism and regionalism share a preoccupation with their subjects' temporal orientation: were they analeptic and reactionary or proleptic and progressive phenomena? Early Progressive accounts of the Populists squarely depicted them as forward-driven reformers.[7] Cold War historians conversely castigated them as proto-fascist reactionaries yearning for a return to racial homogeneity.[8] With the rise of the New Left in the 1960s and 1970s, scholars again revised their view of Populism as one that gave rise to a new grassroots *movement culture* that became the boilerplate for later political groups.[9] In recent years, historians moved away from assessing "the Populists by today's measurements of what is progressive or reactionary" to consider how their *"idea of progress"* or "history and tradition" took shape.[10] The literary criticism on regional

---

7. Historians from Frederick Jackson Turner to Solon J. Buck participated in the Progressive cooption of the movement's guiding principles by contending that their "programs which were ridiculed at the time have long since passed beyond the stage of speculation and discussion." Buck, *The Agrarian Crusade*, 198. During these early decades of the twentieth century, what was known as the dialectical struggle between the regenerative West and the economically oppressive East became one of U.S. history's leitmotifs.

8. Hofstadter, exclusively stressing the Populists who embraced anti-Semitism and racism, proposed that "the utopia of the Populists was in the past, not the future." Hofstadter, *The Age of Reform*, 62.

9. Lawrence Goodwyn ambitiously claimed that "out of their cooperative struggle came a new democratic community." Goodwyn, *The Populist Moment*, xxiii. Norman Pollack laid the groundwork for Goodwyn's study by recasting Populism along Marxist lines "as a class movement." Pollack, *The Populist Response to Industrial America*, 11. There are echoes of Pollock in Bruce Laurie's claim that the "radicalism" of the Knights of Labor spread "into the countryside, where it crossed organization lines to help stimulate the agrarian uprising of the 1890s." Laurie, *Artisans into Workers*, 175.

10. Postel, *The Populist Vision*, 10–11. See also McGerr, *A Fierce Discontent*, and McMath, *American Populism*. These inquiries also opened the field to nuanced and archivally rich appraisals of the movement's racial shortcomings as well as an account of "Black Populism as a regional movement with its own integrity." Ali, *In the Lion's Mouth*, 6.

writing parallels the historiography of the Populist movement. This body of literature is usually read in relation to the Northeastern literary establishment rather than alongside the growth of regionally iterative institutions of Populism. Citing Howells's criticism on local-color fiction, generations of scholars maintained that regional fiction, especially stories about quaint parts of New England or the rural South, participated in the broader incorporation of America by preserving these vanishing cultures.[11] Assessments of this writing changed with the advent of feminist and ethnic literary studies. No longer cast as preservers of dying regional differences or as glorified travel writers, these authors now seemed subversive.[12] Far from assenting to the anthropological or realist gaze, writers such as Rose Terry Cooke, Sui Sin Far, Freeman, Jewett, and Zitkala-Ša undermined the imperializing and nationalizing aims of dominant U.S. literary culture. More recently, studies have examined the way regional writing participated in a global literary culture as "cosmopolitan localists."[13]

This chapter casts the final decades of the nineteenth century as ones defined as much by conflict as by consensus. To be sure, the Gilded Age saw an expansion of federal power, the awarding of greater legal protections to corporations, and the consolidation of the publishing industry in New York. But these centralizing forces battled what became a formidable political movement and an explosion in local newspapers and periodicals. This approach rejects the dichotomous logic of the con-

---

11. Howells embraced this short fiction for introducing, through the representation of dialect, characters that "speak true American, with all the varying Tennesseean, Philadelphian, Bostonian, and New York accents." Howells, *Criticism and Fiction*, 137. They cultivated "the appreciation of the common" that he lionized as quintessentially American. Ibid., 139. Howells believed that the local differences they represented did not fuel sectional discord but testified to a vibrant and tolerant pluralistic idea of American nationality. Even skeptical treatments of the genre from the late 1890s conceded that while "life in this country is as yet such a roughly-pieced patchwork of local differences," regional fictions "taken together . . . give to the careful reader a fairly accurate notion of our composite national life." Pancoast, *An Introduction to American Literature*, 311. Influential late-twentieth-century studies of realism's appropriation of regionalism include Bell, *The Problem of American Realism*; Brodhead, *Cultures*; Glazener, *Reading*; and Kaplan, *The Social Construction of American Realism*.

12. Directing this forceful polemic, Judith Fetterley and Marjorie Pryse characterize a number of women's regional writers as "resistant voices" who challenge "the power structures of the political and cultural construction of regions themselves." Fetterley and Pryse, *Writing Out of Place*, 8.

13. Lutz, *Cosmopolitan*, 56. Also see Joseph, *American Literary Regionalism in a Global Age*.

ventional debate surrounding both Populism and local-color writing as one framed by the question of "nostalgic or progressive?"[14] As the next section establishes, nostalgia featured prominently in both Populism and local-color writing, but as an affect that galvanized a political and cultural movement rather than as one that signaled a reactionary retreat.

JEFFERSON'S GHOSTS:
THE PEOPLE UNITED WILL ALWAYS BE DIVIDED

The gradual rolling back of Reconstruction policies, the earlier passage of the Homestead Act, and the financial Panics of 1873 and 1893 created the conditions necessary for the growth of grassroots agrarian and labor organizations. The Grange advocated for fairer railroad rates and rural free delivery for farmers, branches of the Farmers' Alliance campaigned to end the detrimental effects of land speculation and unfair loans in the Midwest and South, and the Knights of Labor advocated for better working hours, pay, and conditions in urban centers throughout the nation. These cooperative associations, many of which embraced the ethos of business, opposed the rise of monopolies as the corporate corruption of capitalism.[15] The growth of these trusts harmed what the Knights' prominent leader Terence Powderly called the nation's *producers,* or "the men and women who dig, delve, and spin."[16] These organizations lobbied elected officials on their members' behalf, but they more importantly nurtured a sense of mutualism among their ranks. Farmers and laborers looked out for one another, offering each other the best possible prices on their goods or making mutual investments. Out of this movement culture emerged one of the nation's most successful third parties, the People's Party. The Midwest, the West, and the South now shared a common enemy: the robber barons and speculators of the Northeast. But as much as the rhetoric of Populism brought a diffuse array of interests into agreement, the Populists' pursuit of racial integration faltered. In many cases, they trafficked in outright racism. Black Populism nevertheless was a force to be reckoned with, but it developed independently and shaped its own agenda.

The organizations that coalesced into the People's Party crafted their own understanding of the *people* as a political subject. Few systematic

---

14. Unger, *Populism,* 1.
15. See Postel, *Populist,* 137–71.
16. Powderly, *Thirty Years of Labor,* 115.

accounts of populist subjectivity exist, and political theorists usually sideline these movements as deviant and irrational at best or as the instruments of elite manipulators at worst. Unfurling the logic behind various populist movements, Laclau argues that "political analysts" harbor "some unformulated political prejudices" that prevent them from apprehending that the power of populism lies in its defiance of "systematicity."[17] Populism's vagueness, Laclau suggests, is "the consequence of social reality itself being, in some situations, vague and undetermined."[18] When approached as an aggregate, these reorganized groups become a people in opposition to a dominant and antagonistic entity. Rancière also celebrates the ambiguousness of *the people* as "a supplement in relation to all logics of counting the population" or a subject without a "statist embodiment."[19] Unlike Laclau, he does not see the people as the realization of new "logics of equivalence and difference"; the people only denotes a subject in the process of formation.[20] Whether deemed a fully realized or an emerging subject, the people's contingency and its open-endedness empower it to name an unrecognizable political entity.

While also abstract and contingent, the People's Party's understanding of populism was an affectively charged form of mutualism. Frank Parsons, a socialist and Boston University professor who wrote about the spirit of the movement for *The Arena,* explained what drove mutualism psychologically: "love—not in the sense of the selfish passion that demands possession and control of the life of another, but love in the sense of sympathy, kindliness, brotherly feeling."[21] Populist love thrived off cooperation, not competition, and nurtured a "social ideal . . . characterized by self-government, not only in political and religious life but in industrial life as well."[22] He captures a widely held sentiment among the Populists that extends the antebellum language of sympathy and nostalgia. This love grows out of a recovery process. The eras that produced the "Magna Chartas and Declarations of Independence" must be recalled.[23] This cooperative spirit culminates with the realization of "a government of the people by all the people and for all the people."[24] For Parsons and other Populist sympathizers, an assemblage of sentiments—

---

17. Laclau, *On Populist Reason*, 10.
18. Ibid., 17.
19. Rancière, *Dissensus*, 85.
20. Laclau, *Populist*, 200.
21. Frank Parsons, "The Philosophy of Mutualism," 784.
22. Ibid., 793.
23. Ibid., 796.
24. Ibid., 794.

a sense of dispossession, a nostalgic desire for reclamation, and mutual love—brings forth the political subject of the people. The Farmers' Alliance sought "to destroy prejudice, local, national, and sectional" as well as "party prejudices" by shaping its own national culture in its agricultural and industrial image.[25] Nelson A. Dunning, an associate editor of the Southern Alliance's *National Economist*, pinned the downfall of democracy since the era of the founders on bankers, arguing their "spirit of avarice . . . threatens the perpetuity of the government itself."[26] Lamenting the erosion of Jeffersonian agrarianism, he wistfully contends that "neither poverty nor crime existed in the same proportion" during the years of the early republic.[27]

Their democratic nostalgia was interwoven with the homesickness exhibited by the destitute in the city and country alike. Homesickness no longer had to be fixed to a particular place or time; it could express a general sense of dispossession. One San Francisco paper reported, "The poor house tenant may feel a sickening longing for the home she has never known, which has never existed for her."[28] Newspapers also printed accounts of people who, because they had recently lost their homes or all their assets, committed suicide after "feeling very homesick" and ashamed of their "dependent condition."[29] Stories about the fate of those who suffered from nostalgia appeared routinely in rural newspapers. Some of them glowingly recollected those men and women who left for the city only to return home to the farm, where there "remains the joy and comfort of the old folks."[30] *The Philadelphia Inquirer* published an anecdote on "Juvenile Nostalgia" about a girl "miles away from home and mamma" who found herself "seasick for home."[31] Southerners also insisted their inhabitants especially struggled with nostalgia. Basil L. Gildersleeve noted, for example, that "notoriously the North Carolinians" possessed an intense "attachment to the

---

25. Dunning, *The Farmers' Alliance History and Agricultural Digest*, 297.
26. Ibid., 3.
27. Ibid., 5.
28. "Homesickness," *Daily Evening Bulletin* (San Francisco), January 8, 1881.
29. "German Shoots Himself," *The Springfield Daily Republican* (Springfield, MA), May 9, 1881. Also see "Leaped to Get Fresh Air," *New York Herald*, October 12, 1889.
30. "Nostalgia," *New Haven Evening Register*, January 14, 1880. While this article appeared in a New Haven newspaper, an uncannily similar account appeared a decade later in "Nostalgia and Homesickness," *Wisconsin Weekly Advocate* (Milwaukee, WI), September 22, 1898.
31. "Juvenile Nostalgia," *The Philadelphia Inquirer*, September 25, 1898. The story was reprinted widely across the country.

soil of their State."³² Even those who had never lived in rural parts of the country, especially out West, found themselves craving this life. In a piece typical of booster literature, one writer insisted gold and silver miners felt "an almost irresistible impulse, a transferred nostalgia, a longing for the clear, bracing mountain air and the liberal ways of the mines."³³ Yet while many of these stories appeared throughout the country, Midwest and Western newspapers often published bleaker accounts of nostalgia. An 1882 article appearing in the Grand Forks *Daily Herald* told of a man who traveled to the city after "having passed all [his] life on a farm" only to become overwhelmed by thoughts of his "old fireside."³⁴ His return home, however, proves uncanny when he realizes that his hometown has fallen into a state of decay. "Alas," he realizes, "a change had come and home was never home again."³⁵ Tales of homesteaders overwhelmed by their relocation to the Midwest or South also circulated.³⁶ Doctors desperately tried untested and outlandish treatments on these men and women because they could never afford to return home.

Whether cherished or reviled, nostalgia figured as a democratic sentiment capable of afflicting all. Deemed "a complaint that outranks all afflictions," one newspaper vignette reminded its readers that "homesickness don't show no favors," as "high er low, er rich er poor, all comes under her jurisdiction."³⁷ The rich, however, could afford to travel home, while everyone else either lost their homes or could not afford to return. As accounts of the fledging Populist movement appeared in these same serials, the once insatiable nostalgia of the financially bereft was overlaid onto narratives of historical recovery. As Phillips Thompson makes clear in his poem "Rouse and Rally," the paths to resurrecting Jefferson and preventing the loss of family farms to the banks were one and the same. Jefferson, he and his cohort believed, would never have permitted "The broad and fertile plains, which stretch / Their leagues of golden grain" to "enrich some greedy, thievish wretch / Who profits by our pain."³⁸

---

32. Gildersleeve, "A Southerner in the Peloponnesian War," 339. See also Julie M. Lippmann, "The Nostalgia of Nancy Knowles," *The Daily Picayune* (New Orleans, LA), July 31, 1898.

33. Albert Williams, "Modern Types of Gold and Silver Miners," 52.

34. "Homesickness," *Daily Herald* (Grand Forks, ND), October 27, 1882.

35. Ibid.

36. See "A Cure for Homesickness," *Jackson Weekly Citizen* (Jackson, MI), July 3, 1888, and Harte, "The Argonauts of '49."

37. "Homesickness," *Grand Forks Daily Herald* (Grand Forks, ND), October 25, 1884.

38. Phillips Thompson, "Rouse and Rally," *Journal of the Knights of Labor* (Chicago),

Sympathetic newspaper accounts of the Populist political conventions noted the important role "the teachings of Jefferson and the warnings of the immortal Lincoln" played in their speeches.[39] Deeming themselves the heirs of the U.S. Revolution and the agrarian revolutionaries who participated in the Shays', Fries', and Whiskey Rebellions, the members of the People's Party scheduled important meetings and delivered key speeches on July 4. Thomas E. Watson, the most influential Southern Populist organizer, used one of his Fourth of July addresses to recite his "Creed of Jefferson."[40] By his account, Jefferson's Declaration of Independence entrusted the nation to the democratic power of the people, in stark contrast to the Federalists, who revered more republican institutions. Watson saw the Senate as "really a House of Lords" that together with the judiciary threatened the "theoretical sovereign of the land—the people" from their inception.[41] He had little use for Alexander Hamilton, whom he denounces as Jefferson's nemesis in his melodramatic history.[42] Jefferson heroically combated many of the Federalists' beloved institutions, according to Watson, including the Treasury Department, the Senate, and the Supreme Court, that from their founding defended the interests of the powerful and wealthy. As the resilience of Jefferson's spirit wavered, Watson feared that federal institutions had grown too powerful and too close to the moneyed aristocracy. To return to Jefferson, Watson maintains, is analogous to a historical homecoming, potentially bringing an end to the people's political exile and introducing the nation to "a new era in the affairs of the Republic" when "happiness" will again "dwell in all her homes."[43]

Populist sympathizers brought their historical lessons home, demanding that these moneyed aristocrats "look at your industrial life . . . and enter the hovels of those whose never ending toil feeds you, clothes you, houses you—and if your soul is as callous as that of a devil in hell, you'll feel no pity and no remorse."[44] For Alliancemen and the Knights alike, the loss of the nation's democratic history materially presented itself as the deterioration or loss of one's home. In *Seven Financial Conspiracies*

June 22, 1893, lines 25–28.
   39. "The People's Party," *The State* (Columbia, SC), June 2, 1891.
   40. Watson, *The Life and Speeches of Thomas E. Watson*, 126.
   41. Ibid., 129.
   42. Hamilton, for the Populists, stood in as a metonym for all that was wrong with U.S. monetary policy. See A. S. Houghton, "On the Idiocy of Isms: The Main Issue is the Money Question," *Journal of the Knights of Labor* (Chicago, IL), December 7, 1893.
   43. Watson, *Life*, 165.
   44. T. E. W., "The Liberty Bell," *People's Party Paper* (Atlanta, GA), October 18, 1895.

(1887), a book widely read in Populists circles, Sarah E. V. Emery equated the betrayal of the nation's Revolutionary history with the decline in home ownership. She saw owning one's home as "the great safeguard of liberty," because "it is impossible for a people long to remain free who do not own their homes."⁴⁵ Day laborers wanted to own their flats and houses in the city, while farmers wished to acquire their farms in the country. For them, property ownership represented the core of Jeffersonian democracy. Literal and historically imagined feelings of dispossession and the attendant nostalgia for a nation that felt like home again intensified as more farmers and laborers became renters, convincing them "no relief can be obtained except by political change."⁴⁶ Those who felt that their past and future had been mortgaged along with their homes became the people of Populism.

Some of the clearest distillations of the Populists' conception of the people can be found in two documents: the "Second Declaration of Independence" and the platform of the People's Party. Reprinted in Populist newspapers, the "Second Declaration of Independence" was authored and adopted by the Confederated Industrial Organizations in St. Louis. They scheduled their convention to coincide with the anniversary of George Washington's birth as a day to commemorate "the illustrious man who led the first great revolution on this continent against oppression."⁴⁷ While socialists and anarchists remembered Washington as a member of the nation's aristocracy, these laborers fondly yearned for the return of a leader who would "restore the government of the republic to the hands of the 'plain people.'"⁴⁸ The Populists believed the common people now suffered from a far greater degree of oppression. As another writer explained, "Modern oppression is satisfied with nothing," as "not even hunger and death will quench its thirst."⁴⁹ The "Second Declaration" thus evokes the language of producerism characteristic of most Populist discourse, pitting them against the millionaires who control the major political parties, the banks, and the trusts. Their grievances defined the people through negation and class antagonism.

---

45. Emery, *Seven Financial Conspiracies Which Have Enslaved the American People*, 8.

46. "General Gloom in Kansas," *The Sun* (Baltimore, MD), July 5, 1891.

47. "Second Declaration of Independence," *People's Party Paper* (Atlanta, GA), April 7, 1892.

48. Ibid. Similar claims can be found throughout other pro-Populist publications. See also "Necessity of Action," *American Nonconformist and Industrial Liberator* (Indianapolis, IN), March 29, 1894.

49. James R. Sovereign, "'The Mantle of Guilt': Place the Blame Where It Belongs." *Journal of the Knights of Labor* (Chicago), January 18, 1894.

For the attendees, "the interests of rural and urban labor are the same," because "their enemies are identical."[50] Yet their understanding of the people remains vague, loosely defined as those producers who cannot earn enough to own property.

The "National People's Party Platform" initially follows a similar line of argumentation, lamenting that the United States is "rapidly degenerating into European conditions" by breeding "the two great political classes—tramps and millionaires."[51] Largely written by Ignatius Donnelly, the platform was adopted by a People's Party delegation that assembled in Omaha on July 4, 1892, the 116th anniversary of the signing of the Declaration of Independence. It reaffirms the people's political agency, predicting "that the union of the labor forces of the United States this day consummated shall be permanent and perpetual."[52] Among their many goals, they call for the nationalization of the railroads, the monetization of silver, a graduated income tax, and a national savings bank. Their platform speaks to the interests of farmers and urban workers, but the exact scope and composition of their imagined constituency remains amorphous. Unlike the "Second Declaration," which borrows the language from the platform verbatim in some sections, the People's Party platform emphasizes the importance of affective bonds. Echoing the rhetoric of the 1848 Seneca Falls Conference's "Declaration of Sentiments," the platform's composers included an "Expression of Sentiments." Each resolution of this section denotes an expression of fellow feeling with a particular issue or aggrieved group. They extend their sympathy to veterans of the Union army in need of better pensions, those who campaign for the eight-hour workday, the victims of the Pinkertons, and the "Knights of Labor and their righteous contest with the tyrannical combine of clothing manufactures of Rochester."[53] Here, as throughout the platform, a *people* emerges out of "a plurality of demands" and the construction of "an internal antagonistic frontier separating the 'people' from power," or an elite minority.[54] But what stabilizes the Populist movement in this document is not a system of signification but mutual feeling. And all of these expressions of sympathy rest upon one affective precondition: a shared nostalgia for Jefferson and the Declaration of Independence.

50. "Second Declaration of Independence," *People's Party Paper* (Atlanta, GA), April 7, 1892.
51. "National People's Party Platform," 91.
52. Ibid., 93.
53. Ibid., 96.
54. Laclau, *Populist*, 74.

No political figure better understood the intertwined modalities of Populist nostalgia than William Jennings Bryan. The polarizing Democratic Presidential candidate who won the endorsement of the People's Party in the 1896 election cleverly integrated his rendition of U.S. history with the quotidian sentiment of homesickness. As he canvassed the country in pursuit of the presidency, he paid a series of visits to Illinois in the vicinity of his childhood home. He recollects these stump speeches in a chapter from his memoir entitled "Homeward Bound." In his hometown of Salem, he declares that "returning to the scenes which surround my first home, the memories of my early days crowd out all thoughts of the subject" of politics.[55] Predictably, his reflections on childhood swiftly segue back to the electoral task at hand. He confides to his old neighbors that "it was in this city that I received my first instructions in democracy."[56] Salem teems with unrealized ideals, and he wishes to recapture the innocence of his and the nation's youth. At another campaign event in southern Illinois, he praises "the greatest Democrat who ever lived, Thomas Jefferson," whose legacy lives on in communities like Jefferson City, where Bryan again "feel[s] at home."[57]

The rhetoric of these Populist documents contributed to an affective atmosphere that writers would imaginatively articulate in more emotionally charged forms. Utopian and dystopian novels capitalized on these sensations of physical and temporal dislocation, but their narrative logics do not rely on nostalgia. In *Looking Backward*, Edward Bellamy's protagonist Julian West slips into a deep sleep and awakes in the year 2000 to a socialist or Nationalist utopia.[58] Although he looks backward to the nineteenth century, he displays no signs of homesickness. Overwhelmed by the wonders of the future, "the memory" of West's "former life was, as it were, in abeyance."[59] His romantic interest, Edith Leete, dispels any lingering thoughts he has of his past life with "the tender human sympathy which thrilled in the soft pressure of her fingers."[60] Their romance embodies the promise of a future Bellamy hoped his readers would embrace; it does not dwell upon the mutualist bonds required to articulate a new political subject or *people*. *Caesar's Column*, Don-

---

55. Bryan, *The First Battle*, 233.
56. Ibid., 234.
57. Ibid., 236.
58. Partly to avoid the stigma already associated with socialism in the United States, Bellamy preferred to describe his utopic political vision as Nationalism.
59. Bellamy, *Looking Backward*, 67.
60. Ibid., 91.

nelly's novel about a dystopic oligarchy set in the future, works through the affective production of fear. While it contains several lengthy digressions on agrarian principles, it largely revolves around the revolutionary Brotherhood of Destruction. Led by Cesar Lomelleni, a Jewish Italian of partial African descent, the Brotherhood embarks upon a violent and fanatical crusade against the state. Their actions culminate with the construction of Cesar's Column, a monument composed of "a pyramid" of the people they killed with "cement over them."[61] Donnelly, in this way, draws only lines of antagonism rather than creating new forms of mutualism. Implicitly, the Populist movement stands apart from both the Jewish-controlled oligarchy of the future and the Jewish radicalism that might oppose it. We must thus turn to Garland's work to witness how literature could incubate the kind of populist imagination essential to the People's Party's aim of uniting urban and rural workers.

HAMLIN GARLAND'S MUTUALIST IMAGINATION

"Among the Corn-Rows," a short story appearing in Garland's *Main-Travelled Roads* (1891), opens with a telling dialogue between homesteader Rob Rodemaker and Seagraves, a local newspaper editor. During their exchange, Rodemaker explains why he left his native Waupac County in Wisconsin to settle farther west in the Dakota Territory: "We fellers workin' out back there got more 'n' more like *hands*, an' less like human beings. Y' know, Waupac is a kind of summer resort, and the people that use' t' come in summers looked down on us cusses in the fields an' shops."[62] Rodemaker complains that as his hometown became more of a tourist destination for urban affluent visitors to indulge their pastoral fantasies, it transformed into a place of agricultural peonage. For the tourists, the farmers became just part of the scenery, reified synecdochally as mere "hands" for the visitors to gaze at like "the cussed European aristocracy" looked upon their peasants (92). Rodemaker alludes to the clashing perceptions of the rural region and the Middle West specifically that framed the debate over the status of regions and regional writing both in the 1890s and in contemporary discussions over the form. His observation raises the question: is regional writing fundamentally a touristic genre that nostalgically converts places into imaginatively "possessible property" for

---

61. Donnelly, *Caesar's Column*, 319.
62. Garland, *Main-Travelled Roads*, 92. Hereafter cited parenthetically as *Main*.

the leisure class, or can it instead serve the economic and cultural interests of the marginalized people that inhabit these spaces?[63]

This question has implications pertaining to Garland's attitudes toward regionalism and Populism. Regional writing and Garland's work in particular became a genre through which turn-of-the-century readers could contemplate the relationship between time and space, history and form, and politics and literature. It is sometimes compared to ethnography for this reason, suggesting that "the process of arriving at the region entails a backward movement" to "nostalgically charged spaces."[64] Regionalism, when read from this perspective, granted its nineteenth- and early-twentieth-century urban readers what Johannes Fabian refers to as an "allochronic" perspective whereby the observer inhabits a time distinct from the object or site of observation.[65] By imaginatively moving from the city to the American countryside, the regional reader moves in space as well as back in time. But while the leisure class may deny rural regions' coevalness by casting them as preindustrial agrarian spaces, Garland continually uses characters like Rodemaker to affirm the Middle West as a region coterminous with the rest of the nation.[66] Responding to the local-color writing that unabashedly trafficked in pastoral and bucolic portrayals of lost rural worlds to pawn them off to urban readers, he presents the rural as a space of "toil" where "the poor and wary predominate" (*Main*, n.pag.).

More so than any other populist writer, including Donnelly and Bellamy, Garland labored to outline his own idea of populist aesthetics. His theory of art, however, does not assume the form of overt commitment. The absence of explicit didacticism in *Main-Travelled Roads* is consistent with the inchoate character of his vision of *the people*. He captures the development of this collective political subject by inserting it within a nostalgic narrative structure. To apprehend how Garland constructs this narrative, Hayden White's classical study of historiography proves instructive. While White's structural dissection of "historiographical style" into "particular . . . modes of emplotment, argument, and ideological implication" exhibits a degree of artificial precision, it elucidates how Garland's populist nostalgia is neither completely reactionary nor

---

63. Brodhead, *Cultures*, 133.
64. Foote, *Regional Fictions*, 59.
65. Fabian, *Time and the Other*, 37.
66. Previous accounts of his work underscore these moments to distinguish him from other late-nineteenth-century regional and local-color writers. See Brodhead, *Cultures*, 139–41.

progressive.[67] In his writing, nostalgia does not work as a mode of ideological implication or a narrative's ethical and political assumptions and prescriptions. It denotes a type of plot structure; to identify the mode of emplotment, in other words, is to determine "the *kind of story* that has been told."[68] What I call the nostalgic mode of emplotment lies between what White describes as the romantic and the satiric modes. The former imagines historical actors can transcend the world, while the latter insists that humanity will always remain "a captive of the world."[69] Garland's nostalgic mode conversely imagines how individuals can collectively and immanently alter their conditions of existence through narratives of spatial and temporal return. The content of this return, or who comes together in a shared homecoming, determines its ideological implication. Nostalgic emplotment could aid in the ideological masking of rural industrialization by temporally detaching these spaces from the urban Northeast. On the other hand, nostalgic Populists decried corporate monopolization and commercial farming based on their rehabilitation of Jeffersonian agrarianism. Rather than sating the consumptive desires of the vacationing leisure class, Garland produces a shared collective memory of the past that could bring together a range of discrete groups such as rural farming associations and urban labor organizations. His use of this affect overcomes aesthetically what the Populists surmounted politically: the division between country and city.[70] He recalls that nostalgia's democratic properties allow everyone to participate in its aesthetics, providing them with a space to examine the political contours of their communal life.[71]

Garland's understanding of nostalgia is a product of his own theory of fiction called *veritism*. His unique aesthetic philosophy alienated many of his readers. Howells, though a supporter of his work, felt his sketches of Midwestern life fell short of perfection. He faulted him for always

---

67. Hayden White, *Metahistory*, 29.
68. Ibid., 7.
69. Ibid., 9.
70. Populism, in other words, unraveled what Raymond Williams described as the "division and opposition of city and country, industry and agriculture" that "developed under [capitalism] to an extraordinary and transforming degree." Williams, *The Country and the City*, 304. For a different but illuminating reading of Garland's aesthetics, see Lutz, *Cosmopolitan*, 65–78.
71. For variations of this argument, which privilege either Garland's politics or his aesthetics over the other, see the following: Bill Brown, "The Popular, the Populist, and the Populace"; Foote, *Regional*, 38–58; Herr, *Critical Regionalism and Cultural Studies*, 90–95; and Henry Nash Smith, *Virgin Land*, 244–49.

producing prose that displayed "a certain harshness and bluntness."[72] Others complained that his work lacked historical and empirical veridicality because it simplified life on the prairie. Both of these criticisms, while seemingly contradictory, stem from Garland's adherence to his own idiosyncratic apprehension of literature that conformed neither to the generic expectations of American literary realism nor to those of naturalism. His rival understanding of veritism stemmed from his study of two widely divergent books: *Progress and Poverty* (1879) by the Spenserian economist Henry George and *Aesthetics* (1879) by Eugène Véron.[73] George's book converted him to the cause of Populism, and he wed this economic outlook to Véron's aesthetic theory, which railed against the kind of realism endorsed by Howells. Véron's definition of aesthetics advanced its original eighteenth-century meaning as the study of "sensations and perceptions."[74] He argues that literature ought to elicit a highly individuated "vivid impression—whether moral, intellectual, or physical" instead of a mere imitation that only aspired to represent the world with empirical accuracy.[75] Synthesizing George's economics with Véron's aesthetics, Garland valued impressionistic and local literature because these works did not subsume the particularities of the region under the universalizing umbrella of the nation. Veritism became a way for him to challenge the economic and literary supremacy of the metropolitan Northeast.[76]

Garland's nostalgically tinged aesthetic and political thought figures centrally in his fiction. Toward the end of one of these stories, "Under the Lion's Paw," the narrator makes a declaration echoed throughout *Main-Travelled Roads:* "There is no despair so deep as the despair of a homeless man or woman" (*Main*, 141). His protagonists find themselves in a state of perpetual homelessness that inevitably produces a corporeal homesickness. His work accordingly begins with passages that recall nostalgia's psychiatric designation but ascribe this illness to the political and economic conditions of the late nineteenth century.

---

72. Howells, introduction to *Main-Travelled Roads*, 4.

73. While he received some formal schooling from a local seminary in Iowa, Garland was largely an autodidact who, because he could not afford a university education, acquired his knowledge of both George's and Véron's work during the course of his self-guided study at the Boston Public Library. For more information on his early intellectual development and literary career, see Pizer, *Hamlin Garland's Early Work and Career*.

74. Véron, *Aesthetics*, 95.

75. Ibid., 108.

76. For a terrific analysis of Garland's critique of Northeastern literary hegemony, see Watts, *An American Colony*, 202–15.

"The Return of the Private" exhibits how he connects the disease of homesickness to Populism. Set in the immediate aftermath of the Civil War, it describes the homecoming of Private Edward Smith to his farmhouse in rural Wisconsin. The story is doubly nostalgic insofar as it portrays the Midwest before the economic upheavals of the late nineteenth century and revolves around a homesick solider: one of the exemplary victims of the illness. He suffers from "a sickness at heart" when he opines on "the joy of homecoming" (114). He succumbs to a fit of involuntary reverie when he returns to his farmhouse, becoming "lost in a dream" as "his wide, hungry eyes devoured the scene" around him (126). Other stories contain similar episodes: Will Hannen in "The Branch Road" and Howard McLane in "Up the Coulee" become "seized" by "a thought" of their old Midwestern homes, expecting them to have remained unchanged (63).[77] These vignettes offer a snapshot of nostalgia operating within the two modalities of time and space. While the protagonists sate their spatial nostalgic desires for home by returning to the Midwest, they continue to yearn for an earlier point in time. True to his notion of veritism, he uses these nostalgic episodes as pretexts for sustaining multiple narrative perspectives and fusing together divergent communities.

Most of *Main-Travelled Roads* operates within a nostalgic narrative structure, but Garland executes it most vividly in "Up the Coulee." It dramatizes the return of Howard McLane, an affluent cosmopolitan actor now living in New York, to his native Wisconsin. Although he blithely expects to reunite with his family and reacquaint himself with the beauties of his boyhood home, Howard finds his brother Grant and their mother downtrodden by the pressures of Midwestern farm life. Due to financial difficulties, they had to sell their old farmhouse and the adjoining land to make ends meet. Much of the unfolding story revolves around the conflicting views of the prairie as exemplified by Howard, who wistfully admires the "majesty" and "breadth" of the surrounding landscape, and Grant, who views the land as a site of unrelenting drudgery (45). Rather than simply dismissing Howard's perspective as obtuse and empirically unsound, the story engages both perspectives dialogically.

When Howard encounters the beauty of the countryside, it transports him backwards to his childhood. But the narrative stops short of depict-

---

77. Following the established critical practice, I use Garland's original 1891 spelling of the story, "Up the Coulee," even though in later editions he changed it to "Up the Coolly."

ing Wisconsin as a bucolic paradise by recognizing that people work the land. Garland presents an idyllic, as opposed to a pastoral, account of rural life by depicting agricultural labor rather than casting this region as one unburdened by work.[78] Farming, in this idyllic sense, remains "idealized and sublimated" nonetheless; the barley may be reaped, but the hardship of harvesting goes unnoted, at least initially.[79] Howard extends this idyllic mode by repeatedly comparing the surrounding landscapes to the paintings of Jean-François Millet, known for his exalted portrayals of laboring French peasants in works like *The Gleaners* (1857). Garland pairs a conventional mode of nostalgic emplotment with a conservative ideological impulse: the protagonist, weary of the frenetic and atomized life of the city, returns to his idyllic homeland, where he yearns to immerse himself in the community and natural beauty of the country. Howard's abstract reflections inspire him to restore his physical childhood home as though it had remained untouched by time.

The discrepancy between Howard's perceptions and the cynical resignation of his brother Grant becomes acutely apparent when Howard marches out to help Grant bale hay. Before reaching his brother and the other farmhands, he pauses to admire "the shaven slopes of the hill" and the animals feeding upon them and concludes that "there was something immemorial in the sunny slopes dotted with red and brown and gray cattle" (*Main*, 60). Time again stands still for Howard, as he indulges in the aesthetic and nostalgic pleasures of the countryside. His contentment diminishes after realizing that Grant ignores it all and recognizing the farmers cannot share in his appreciation of the landscape. His distance from his brother is further accentuated when Grant finds his clothing ostentatious. Donning what he refers to as his working "regimentals," Howard is admonished for wearing this expensive clothing in the fields (61). This rebuke triggers a series of invidious comparisons, leading to his dismissal. Grant cannot fathom that people in New York "lay around . . . and smoke and wear good clothes and toady to millionaires" while "the country's goin' to hell" (62).

Instead of embracing Grant's perspective, Garland rallies around Howard's evolving nostalgia. He escapes Grant's indictments and the "mental unrest of a great city" when he stumbles upon "an old road which he used to travel when a boy" (63). Following this road to its end, Howard finds his old boyhood house occupied by German immigrants. He imme-

---

78. For the account of the idyllic mode I draw upon, see Bakhtin, *Dialogic*, 226, and for a distillation of Garland's and regionalism's engagement with producerism, see Glazener, *Reading*, 189–228.

79. Bakhtin, *Dialogic*, 227.

diately becomes overwhelmed by a "swarm of memories," feeling "sick to the heart" as he yearns "to be a boy again" (65). The emotional force of this experience affects him so greatly that "he was like a man from whom all motives had been withdrawn" (65). This moment recalls nostalgia's manifestation as a mental disease, as described in an 1896 medical treatise as "an affective state" that leads to immobility and "a sluggishness of mind" as "a patient suffering from nostalgia thinks only of his country or home."[80]

In these final exchanges between the two brothers, Garland imagines nostalgia as an affect and mode of emplotment capable of solidifying political commitments in the name of restoring the past. Although momentarily incapacitating, Howard's episode of reverie preserves his individualism and stimulates his newfound desire "to see his mother back in the old home, with the fireplace restored" (65). This anagnorisis prompts him to restore his boyhood home and his family's financial security in the process. Howard becomes closer to Grant even as their differences remain apparent. Grant remains fixed in place and morosely obsessed with his brother's previous unwillingness to support their family economically. He cannot escape his condition, caught within a "great tragic poem," while Howard's "memories of harvest-moons, of melon-feasts, and of clear, cold winter nights" strengthen his resolve to return his family to their old home (76–77).

Grant struggles to envision an alternative to the present economically and socially unjust relations of production; he and his neighbors are "discontented, and yet hardly daring to acknowledge it" or willing to call for change (75). Garland concludes the story with the two brothers speechlessly starring at one another:

> The two men stood there, face to face, hands clasped, the one fair-skinned, full-lipped, handsome in his neat suit; the other tragic, sombre in his softened mood, his large, long, rugged Scotch face bronzed with sun and scarred with wrinkles that had histories, like sabre-cuts on a veteran, the record of his battles. (87)

Separated by a semicolon, they fall just short of achieving a complete reconciliation.[81] They share the same space but at first glance appear temporally nonsynchronous. Donning a fashionable suit, Howard occu-

---

80. Ribot, "Pathological Pleasures and Pains," 185.
81. Lutz astutely attends to this critical passage as well. But for him, this is a moment of ambivalence and abeyance rather than the foregrounding of a dialectic. See Lutz, *Cosmopolitan*, 68.

pies the ephemeral and constantly changing present temporality of modernity, but Grant figures as a racialized bronzed Scotchman who becomes the bearer of "histories." This dichotomy is not an easy one to resolve. While this passage could be read as a fundamentally and indisputably ambiguous one that endorses neither Howard's nor Grant's point of view, Garland is not presenting the reader with a choice but with a dialectic.[82] The semicolon in this passage functions as a copula as much as it punctuates their separation. Howard, the story's only character initially capable of aesthetic appreciation, suffers from a momentary lack of historical consciousness; Grant's face, by contrast, is noticeably scarred. His scar, as this trope often does, functions as a form of *mnemotechnics* by marking him with the kind of history denied to his brother. These histories do not fix him temporally, but they become recognizable to his brother Howard, heralding a call for action in the present. Their temporalities converge and the allochronism that frames the first part of the story ends. Grant emerges at this moment as a living repository of memory, a welcomed antidote to Howard's persistent forgetfulness of rural toil. Rather than dividing them, this moment bonds them together.

Garland examines the transformative potential of nostalgia and its relationship to the constitution of a people in much of his work, especially in the literary criticism appearing in *Crumbling Idols* (1894).[83] He addresses the matter directly in an essay he composed for *The Arena* magazine. Part journalism and part commentary, this article discusses the features of Henry George's Single Tax movement. Those who supported the Single Tax, or replacing all taxation with a flat property tax to dissuade land speculation, flocked to the People's Party, and much of Garland's thoughts on George bear the marks of his Midwestern Populism. He begins this essay, as so many proponents of Populism did, by recalling how "a group of some fifty odd men" gathered "on the second and third days of July, 1776" to compose the Declaration of Independence.[84] Its promises, he believes, never came to fruition, and people stand "equal only among themselves in their heritage of shame and despair" (160). Garland levels a strong case in favor of George's

---

82. See Foote, *Regional*, 51–56.

83. In this collection, Garland repeatedly looks to preceding artists and writers for inspiration even while simultaneously chiding any writer who remains too entranced by the past. He aspires to a balance: his artistic idols may be crumbling, but they ruinously haunt the present nonetheless.

84. Garland, "A New Declaration of Rights," 157. Hereafter cited parenthetically as "Declaration."

principles, but he especially emphasizes the regional diversity of the group of delegates attending the Single Tax convention in New York City. He reveled in the "picturesque" assembly of "broadhatted men from California, Texas, Virginia and Dakota" who stood alongside "slender young clerks and artisans from Boston, Chicago, Minneapolis, and Memphis" (158). He provides one of the most direct accounts of the people as a voluntary alliance of exploited workers from every quarter of the country. As distinct individuals committed to voluntary association, they are not to be confused with "some personification of a crowd" (169). The crowd or the masses, for him, is the favored political subject of the socialists, the Nationalists, and anarchists. The people, on the other hand, are men and women committed to "the fraternal, spontaneous, unconscious co-operation of individualism" over the "paternalism of a government liable to corruption and tyranny" (184). This shared love and nostalgia for Jefferson, rebranded as "our first great singletaxer," fosters the spirit of individualism and "voluntary service and co-operation" necessary for the Single Tax movement and, by extension, Populism to thrive (182).

Garland's impressionistic portrayal of Howard's and Grant's varying perspectives, as well as his own recounting of the signing of the Declaration of Independence, synthesize his aesthetics with his politics. He embraced Véron's disregard for "the realistic theory" that "reduces the artist to the condition of a mere copyist," and he called for a more individual or impressionistic art in place of realism or naturalism.[85] Véron's imperative that art impressionistically depict multiple and relative points of view guides Garland's idea of *veritism*. He stressed that what distinguished veritism from both "spectacular" and more imitative forms of art was that it would "deal with the people and their home dramas, their loves and their ambitions."[86] The veritist should capture "the deepening of social contrasts" by recording the "drama" of "a great heterogeneous, shifting, brave population." (*Crumbling*, 15). Like Véron, he despised the naturalists for treating common people condescendingly as scientific objects of study, unable to escape "the hereditary transmission of the vices that spring from ignorance, disease, chronic suffering, or ceaseless strife against misery."[87] The veritist regards these same subjects as actors and potential producers of literature in their own right. "The common man," Garland assures his readers, "is again moving in intellectual

---

85. Véron, *Aesthetics*, xxiii.
86. Garland, *Crumbling Idols*, 25. Hereafter cited parenthetically as *Crumbling*.
87. Véron, *Aesthetics*, 359.

unrest" (*Crumbling*, 141). His aesthetics brings about new equivalences to imagine a people gathering together in a new literary center such as Chicago from "Indiana, Illinois, Iowa, Wisconsin, Kentucky, and Ohio" ("Declaration," 119). As "Whitman announced it," this vision of American literature will not "come from homes of great wealth" but "from the average American home, in the city as well as in the country" (*Crumbling*, 143).

These people are fundamentally united by a common set of sentiments, and their attachment to home ranks as their most vital bond. He eschews the past, but only when it serves as an idol of conservative reverence for "the aristocratic and the old" (*Crumbling*, 140). Nostalgia in Garland's fiction is not synonymous with tradition; it is a way for the common people and the writer who depicts them to register a wrong that needs redressing. Véron, moreover, describes the mental process of artistic creation and aesthetic experience in terms resonant with nostalgia. He likens it to a "hallucination" that "call[s] up, from the stores of the memory, such recollections as may be useful in the development of the desired impression; next by a process of quasi-spontaneous fusion, to combine these into one unique result."[88] Aesthetics, for both Garland and Véron, refers to a set of sensory experiences in which the memory comingles with the imagination in a partially involuntary manner. Spontaneity, for Garland, lies at the heart of his aesthetic and political philosophy, and nostalgia or the creative reappropriation of memory drives this force.[89] It does not bring about an aesthetic revolution as much as it does a fiction of reform. Rather than rendering sensible a previously unperceived and oppressed part of society, nostalgia creates the potential for bringing average people together to fashion a new collective political subject. The short story is well suited to this task, as a democratic form capable of being inexpensively disseminated and read by those with limited leisure time. Its rise is linked to the industrial forces that Garland seeks to transform. Highlighting the social contrasts and the economic deprivation of the rural Midwest, his Populist fiction follows the mold of Populist organizations that used the instruments of business and industry to achieve their own ends.

---

88. Ibid., 376–77.

89. Garland and Véron alike borrow their theory of spontaneity from the romantics. And it is a political and poetic concept that modernist writers would continue to explore in their work. For an extensive treatment of spontaneity's genealogy and place in discussions of literature and politics, see Nickels, *The Poetry of the Possible*, 1–45.

Howard's nostalgic impressions do more than exemplify his own personal perspective or illuminate the inequities that plague the American countryside. His wistful longing for the past creates a community of "coming citizens" consistent with the aims of veritism (*Crumbling*, 26). In addition to committing individual impressions to the page, the veritist had an obligation to bring these individuals into communion with one another. Hutcheson Macaulay Posnett, a Classics and English professor whom Garland cites favorably in *Crumbling Idols*, argued writers ought to compose works of fiction that seek to "reconcile" rather than "take sides with either the individual or the social spirit."[90] By using nostalgia to expand "sympathy beyond self," Garland envisioned how a people could emerge.[91] He knew that if the Populists wished to succeed electorally, they must accomplish a nearly insurmountable task: they had to fuse various and at times rival political organizations and factions and establish ties between different regions in the nation.

"Up the Coulee" constructs this idea of the people by uniting more than just Howard's urban and Grant's rural interests. When Howard encounters the German woman now occupying his old home, his display of emotion brought on by his homesickness bridges their language gap as she responds to him by uttering "some sentences in German whose general meaning was sympathy" (*Main*, 64). Throughout the rest of the story, nostalgia consistently works in this way. During a social gathering, Howard and some local farmers listen to "old tunes" and folk music that produce "a thousand associated memories" (77). The songs bring everyone together, prompting Howard's realization "of the infinite tragedy of these lives which the world loves to call peaceful and pastoral" (78). These epiphanies stimulate the emergence of a class or laboring consciousness by revealing to Howard and the reader "that the struggle for a place to stand on this planet was eating the heart and soul out of men and women in the city, just as in the country" (80). By sharing his fantasy of a remote agrarian past with these farmers, Howard becomes aware that "suffering" is the "universal" condition of the laboring poor (81).

Other stories appearing in *Main-Travelled Roads* reconcile sectional antagonisms to draw new lines of opposition to the wealthy elite. In "Return of the Private," the charged political disputes that divided the North and South are supplanted by innocuous regional or cultural differences. Making no mention of the debate over slavery or popular sov-

---

90. Posnett, *Comparative Literature*, 371.
91. Ibid., 373.

ereignty, the characters just humorously contrast the regional differences between Northern and Southern wildlife and livestock. Private Edward Smith, the story's protagonist, undergoes this alteration in sectional sentiments. He resents fighting "for an idea" that compelled him to leave his family on their mortgaged farm "while the millionaire sent his money to England" (120). Upon returning home, he must now face "a still more hazardous future" than the "Southern march" he previously embarked upon (129). The narrative highlights the economic differences dividing the rural Midwestern farmer from the wealthy New York millionaire to render the political rivalry between the South and the Midwest negligible. Garland devises his own narrative of reconstruction moored to a nostalgic mode of emplotment, one stressing that the economic similarities between the poor whites in the Midwest and the South extend back into the past. It is precisely this kind of imaginary past and regional similarity that the 1890s Populists drew upon to forge their political alliances between these regions.

Yet even Garland's understanding of the people excluded segments of the economically disenfranchised. His desire for post–Civil War reconciliation comes with the urge to forget the legacy of slavery. The oblique reference to slavery as an incidental "idea" in "The Return of the Private" is used to suggest that the Civil War pitted poor whites against one another in the name of a dubious cause. Even though he believed blacks had a right to property, Garland states, "I do not assert [the black] should be equal in political power, or equal socially, or equal in wealth" ("Declaration," 179). He only wants to grant them an "equality of opportunity," so that when he falters, "he will see that his failure lies with himself" ("Declaration," 179). When Grant complains about his destitution in "Up the Coulee," he laments that "this cattle-raisin' and butter-makin' makes a nigger of a man" (*Main*, 76). The creation of a Populist political subject often compelled poor whites to differentiate themselves from poor blacks racially just as much from millionaires economically. Still other groups had no place in a whitewashed Populism. Garland's Midwestern landscape is completely devoid of American Indians, even though several violent conflicts broke out between U.S. forces and tribes in the Midwest throughout the latter quarter of the nineteenth century. Nostalgia creates certain social bonds only by abandoning others through a process that Nicholas Dames aptly deems nostalgia's "forms of forgetting."[92] Garland's and most white Populist writing indulged in racist repression, and it is

---

92. Dames, *Amnesiac*, 7.

this side of Populist nostalgia that Pauline Hopkins exposes as a way to excogitate a people of her own.

BLASTING THE PAST IN CONTENDING FORCES

Early in her writing and performance career Hopkins put the power of homesickness on display.[93] Before turning her attention to prose, she composed a musical drama entitled *Peculiar Sam, or The Underground Railroad* (1879).[94] Generally well received by audiences, it follows the fate of a group of slaves who flee Mississippi for Canada after learning that their master will force Virginia, or "Jinny," to marry their overseer. Jinny initiates the escape, lamenting that she will have "to leave the place where I was born," because she will not consent to "this so-called marriage"[95] Sam, the man she really wants to marry, and his family and close friends decide to join her. As they head toward their first waypoint, Jinny breaks out into a solo of the song "Home, Sweet Home." She explains that even "though we leave it in darkness and sorrow, it is still our home."[96] Later they all break out into song when they "bids good-bye to de sunny Souf" for good, bellowing the lines to "Old Kentucky Home."[97] The South may have been the site of their oppression, but their attachment to their birthplace defines them as a people. Hopkins's musical, fashioned after the minstrel play, has a satirical edge. Their love of the South ironically alludes to the nostalgic white fantasy of a plantation populated with grateful and complacent slaves. But Hopkins reminds her auditors that African-Americans had as much right to claim the South as their home as their white counterparts.

Two decades after she wrote *Peculiar Sam*, Hopkins revisited the ambivalent place of nostalgia in African-American culture and politics in *Contending Forces: Romance of Negro Life North and South*. Written in the wake of Populism's collapse and at a tumultuous time in black politics, it exposes the prejudicial shortcomings of Populism. It also imagines how an African-American and Pan-African idea of the people could take shape. She did not join the Black Populist cause and instead maintains "with

---

93. Hopkins was a singer in addition to a writer.
94. For an account of the play's performance and reception, see Brooks, *Bodies in Dissent*, 287–89.
95. Hopkins, *Peculiar Sam*, 104.
96. Ibid., 108.
97. Ibid., 118.

all the heated discussions of tariff reform, the parity of gold and silver, the hoarding of giant sums of money by trusts and combinations, still the Negro question will not 'down'; it is the most important, the mightiest in the land."[98] The novel foregrounds this problem when its most radical character declares, "The power of the almighty dollar which deadens men's hearts to the sufferings of their brothers" drives *"the contending forces that are dooming this race to despair"* (256). The eponymous contending forces in the novel are neither narrowly racial nor economic inequalities but refer to the conflict between them.[99] I thus argue that Hopkins used *Contending Forces* as an opportunity to participate not only in discussions surrounding the future of black politics but also in the wider milieu of Populist politics in the United States.

If the political category of *the people* is an empty one supplemented by "identities created on the basis of either relations of substitution or relations of combination" or "between equivalence and difference," then Hopkins identifies race, region, and economics as obstacles to any successful syntagmatic or paradigmatic structuring of populism.[100] In response to the racist undercurrents that plagued a political unification between whites and blacks from the start, Hopkins embraces the language of bloodlines to develop her form of mutualism. Regional and economic differences are aligned though a sense of interconnectedness or *interlocalism* that allows individuals to remain tied to their particular localities but with an awareness of a larger global and social totality. Hopkins's execution of the historical romance brings about this vision of interlocally connected black people. Sexually compromised women and their children who usually meet tragic ends instead find themselves romantically wed by the end of her narrative. Fortunes and homes lost are also restored, as characters—especially the women—act as representative historical actors. Within Hopkins's historical romance, nostalgia assumes several opposing modal forms from its incarnation as the desire for the restoration of slavery in the South to the homesickness associated

---

98. Hopkins, *Contending Forces*, 87–88. Hereafter cited parenthetically as *Contending*.

99. While readers of Hopkins once questioned the literary merits of her work, a number of books and essays now studiously grapple with her writing. For work on her engagement with Pan-African ideology, see Brooks, *Bodies*, 287–325, and Gaines, *Uplifting the Race*, 433–55. For scholarship on the interrelation among motherhood, bloodlines, and political alienation in her novels, see Bergman, *Motherless Child in the Novels of Pauline Hopkins*, 34–65; Gillman, *Blood Talk*, 40–43; and Leslie W. Lewis, *Telling Narratives*, 88–99. And for a reading that attends to the roles imperialism and sexual violence brutally play in Hopkins's work, see Carby, *Reconstructing Womanhood*, 128–62.

100. Laclau, *Populist*, 221.

with a diasporic longing for a transoceanic African community. Her handling of nostalgia differentiates her work from Garland's. While the latter saw the affect as essential to forging populist bonds, the first portion of Hopkins's romance enumerates the various ways it stifles the growth of a collective black political subject. Homesickness and nostalgic desires must be sated or resolved for her idea of the people to emerge.

Early in *Contending Forces,* Hopkins probes the fissures in Pan-African political solidarity when she provides a sketch of a mulatto slave-owning family in Bermuda. As his family's patriarch, Charles Montfort, prepares to relocate his assets and family to South Carolina, his concerns about the future of his property conflict with the emotions expressed by the slaves on the island enjoying their Sunday, or the day "in all tropical climes" where "the slave forgot his bonds" (24). During their respite, they dance to "the strange monotonous music of drums without tune" that recalled their ancestral "wild African life which haunted them in dreamland" (26). These diasporic visions betray an indirect homesickness for the continent where they or their parents or grandparents had once lived. Montfort does not participate, displaying instead a proleptic nostalgia for the island he will soon leave behind: "never before had he appreciated his home so much as now, when he contrasted it with the comparative bareness of the new spot he had chosen" (30). Though willing to relocate and embrace his American residency, he never feels more British than when he turns his back on Bermuda to pursue his fortune in the South. The island remains a space of unrealized mutualism. The social acceptability of racial mixing coupled with the imminent prohibition of slavery herald the rise of a new, less racially divided political subjectivity.

Hopkins uses Charles's arrival in the southern United States to level a startling but veracious indictment of the bonds underlying white Southern populism. His nominal African heritage and his wife's and children's complexion put them all at risk. Even wealth cannot straddle the color line. His extravagant riches elicit envy among the whites, especially Anson Pollock, who covets his wife, Grace. Here Hopkins's historical romance performs its genre's cultural work: it stages a cultural and political conflict in the past. As Montfort registers his dislocation through his ongoing homesickness "for the picture of his last Sunday in Bermuda," Pollack uses racial prejudice to manipulate the interests of the white working class (48). Even characters whose "sympathy was more than half enlisted" on the side of the Montforts can be persuaded with whiskey and cigars to unify against anyone with a slightly darker complexion

(55). These divisions, while situated in an antebellum historical moment, better reflect the political landscape of the post-Reconstruction South dominated by a Democratic Party emboldened by white supremacist ideology.[101] Enmity directed toward Hopkins's archetypal tragic mulatto, Grace, consolidates the Southern whites into a single constituency. They must deprive both her and her husband of their elevated economic position. Falsely claiming to suppress an impending slave revolt, Pollock and his vigilante "committee on public safety" seize Montfort's property and shoot him dead (70). Sexually threatened and probably raped, Grace mysteriously disappears and eventually dies. The young Montfort sons ultimately part ways: Charles flees to Britain with a mineralogist who pities him, while Jesse eventually escapes to Boston.

After foregrounding the divisions within Pan-Africanism and Populism, *Contending Forces* identifies the obstacles to creating a black people and then imagines how to overcome them. Nostalgia, as a structure of feeling, hinders and amplifies the social bonds required for a new form of black populism to take shape. Discord among black politicians could be traced back to the Reconstruction Era, when state Republican legislators voted unanimously on civil rights issues but parted ways on economic matters.[102] These divisions shaped the interests of activist groups and organizations from the Union League to the Colored Farmers' Alliance to the Universal Negro Improvement Association. Hopkins treats many of these constituencies in *Contending Forces* in the form of representative characters. She also registers a significant silence: black women. As many readers of *Contending Forces* note, the discussion of racial politics "is largely a masculine discourse."[103] Even though Hopkins subverted "the dominant gender conventions of her day," the political positions her male characters channel is a critical feature of her engagement with the state of black mutualism and Black Populism at the turn of the century.[104] Her consideration of these rival viewpoints unfolds within a series of chapters on the American Colored League of Boston, as they address

---

101. While Black Populists deftly exploited divisions within the white Southern political establishment to fuse the interests of the Colored Alliance with those of the white People's Party, the whites who shared their economic interests largely turned against them in the end. See Postel, *Populist*, 195–203.

102. Well-educated, free-born mulatto representatives ensured the defeat of "a variety of bills designed to protect farm and plantation laborers against eviction, fraud, and extra-economic coercion" during the Reconstruction Era. Hahn, *A Nation under Our Feet*, 261.

103. Tate, *Domestic Allegories of Political Desire*, 161. Also see Yarborough, introduction to *Contending Forces*.

104. Ibid., 165.

how to quell the "sectional prejudice . . . fostered by the Southern whites among the Negroes to stifle natural feelings of brotherly love among" them (*Contending*, 181). They hold deliberations in response to news of a lynching in the South. Southern blacks want their Northern counterparts to join them in bringing in the group of vigilantes who killed a black man for allegedly raping a white woman. Mired by internal ideological divisions, each of the members of the League's executive council represents a different major iteration of black politics at the turn of the century.

The most reprobate among the council's members is John P. Langley, an attorney and black descendent of Pollock. Langley's behavior reveals how racial solidarity can clash with some of the League's members' own electoral ambitions. He succumbs to the temptations of machine politics after conferring with Herbert Clapp, a white political operative. Clapp wants to avoid civil discord and implores Langley to assuage the passions of his fellow members. Clapp upholds the ideology of prostration, insisting "the South has rights as well as you" and that "*white* men" have already suffered too much (232). He appeals to the myth of reconciliation and a longing for an imagined era of white antebellum unity. "All sections," he declares, "must be satisfied, and if you love your country as you should, you will be willing to sacrifice a little for the good of the whole" (233). Langley retorts by parroting the interests of his people, but he converts these grievances into his own political capital. After learning the Boston Republicans will name him as the next city solicitor, he stops questioning Clapp's interests. Langley, who can aptly shape populist sentiment, represents the danger a vanguard can pose to the interests of a popular political movement. Rather than challenging the dominant structures of white power, Langley's self-interested tactics serve them.

When the Colored League debates how it should respond to the lynching, Langley is already in Clapp's pocket. He finds what at first may seem like an unlikely ally: Dr. Andrew Lewis. Lewis, who runs a college in the South resembling the Tuskegee Institute, champions a conciliatory line. He is a mulatto who entrusts the future of his race to the nostalgia displayed by white Americans for the legacy of Jeffersonian Democracy. "There would be no greater joy in life," Lewis maintains, than for them to witness their "poetic dream of superiority to all other governments realized in the 'land of the free and the home of the brave'" (242). Few rally to Lewis's position, which echoes the sentiments expressed by Booker T. Washington. He accepts the underlying premises behind the ideology of the prostrate South by lamenting "the stigma under which the Southern white labored," believing they would benevolently permit freed blacks to pursue their "general advance ... buried from public notice" (242–43). The narrative decries his views as a "delusive hope," and few members of the executive committee embrace his strategy, even though it suits his ambitions (243).

During the course of the general meeting of the Colored League, Hopkins scrutinizes an altogether different kind of black political subject: the hypermasculine black revolutionary. After Langley pleads with the crowd "to leave the punishment of criminals, the suppression of mob violence, with the national government," Luke Sawyer rises out of the crowd (252). Described as "a tall, gaunt man of very black complexion" who "in a sonorous bass voice uttered the solemn protest of Patrick Henry, so famous in history," he exclaims, "Gentlemen may cry 'Peace! Peace!' but there is no peace!" (254). Hopkins showers this figure with unrestrained praise, expressing a nostalgic longing for a transformative political history that nevertheless remains inaccessible to African-Americans. "He might have been a Cromwell, a Robespierre, a Lincoln," she opines, but such men "leave their own characteristics engraved upon the pages of ... history" only "when white" (255). Here Hopkins recognizes one of the largest barriers to the Black Populist movement that the People's Party of the Midwest and the South did not face: the ability to reanimate a Jeffersonian radical republican tradition.

Contending Forces establishes that blacks cannot indulge in this kind of revolutionary nostalgia: the color line here is as temporal as it is spatial. In her short sketch of William Wells Brown's accomplishments written for the *Colored American Magazine*, Hopkins unreservedly praises him but wonders whether his and his abolitionists' legacies can be reclaimed at the turn of the century. "How many of us today," she asks at the end of her essay, "can occupy and fill their vacant places? Not alone *occupy*, but *fill* them. Alas! How few, when we consider our advantages."[105] Hopkins commandeers Brown's history as a usable past just as Sawyer aligns himself with Patrick Henry, but there is something quixotic about this kind of historical nostalgia because it does not sow the seeds of a coming revolution. Sawyer, whose actual first name is Lycurgus, named after the militaristic reformer of Sparta in ancient Greece, embodies a revolutionary potential that can never be realized in the context of the postbellum United States.

---

105. Hopkins, *Daughter of the Revolution*, 39.

The ineffectuality of revolutionary nostalgia is further underscored when Judge Weston, the chair of the Colored League, recalls how "forty years ago, when as a young man I sat at the feet of Sumner, Phillips, Garrison, Pillsbury, Charles Lenox Remond, Nell, Robert Morris, Fred Douglas and all the mighty host of anti-slavery fathers, we thought that with the abolishment of slavery the black man's destiny would be accomplished, and fixed beyond a peradventure" (244). There is a distinct sense that the revolutionary nostalgia drawn upon by previous black writers and political figures can no longer serve the exigencies of black politics at the end of the nineteenth century. This sentiment is echoed by Hopkins's contemporary, Charles Chesnutt, who not only critiqued Southern plantation nostalgia through *The Conjure Woman* (1899) tales but also took aim at the "ideal past" in *The Marrow of Tradition* (1901), a novel revolving around the racial unrest in Wilmington, North Carolina, in 1898.[106] Chesnutt, much like Hopkins, realizes that nostalgic appropriations of the nation's past only secured "the sympathy of the North for the white South" and served "to alienate it from the colored people."[107] Both Hopkins and Chesnutt establish why a fusion of white and Black Populism could never be fully realized and testify to the distinct political evolutions of both movements. The latter necessarily remained estranged from the national mythology of the former.

Having outlined the appeasing position of Lewis, the opportunism of Langley, and the radicalism of Sawyer, Hopkins suggests nostalgia can animate an ideology of concession. This results in the perpetual oppression of the black population in the South and stalls the growth of black political power in the North. She uses the chapters devoted to the Colored League to introduce one tantalizing political alternative in the form of Will Smith, the descendant of Jesse Montfort. In keeping with the novel's phenotypical identification of various political positions, Smith exhibits the right kind of parentage. He is descended from a distinguished English lineage and free, educated black stock. Smith recuperates the nostalgia for the abolitionist era to favor a tactics of agitation over appeasement or insurrection. He insists their objectives will be reached only "by the formation of public opinion," adding that "brute force will not accomplish anything" (272). "As the anti-slavery apostles wept everywhere," he implores his auditors, "preaching the word fifty years before emancipation, *so must we do to-day*" (272). Smith's views resemble those

---

106. Chesnutt, *The Marrow of Tradition*, 214.
107. Ibid., 228.

of Populist figures such as George Washington Murray, a black South Carolinian Congressman who built the Colored Alliance in the South. He campaigned tirelessly to alter public opinion in the South and across the rest of the nation in the hopes of improving the lot of black farmers and laborers through the electoral system. He and other Alliancemen spoke out against poll taxes and other legal injustices, but they strongly disapproved of militant resistance.[108] They execrated the corruption of machine politics, and they saw themselves as carrying forward the work begun by the abolitionists and the Radical Republicans who preceded them.[109]

Smith's conciliatory and tactically savvy oration, though emotionally moving, is deflated by the reaction of those in attendance: "slowly they dispersed to their homes, filled with thoughts that burn but cannot be spoken" (273). The meeting yields no lasting political results, as those who rallied together leave with feelings of resignation, not commitment. Smith, who stands out as one of the text's most laudable figures, remains ineffectual. His recollection of the abolitionists produces melancholy, not nostalgia: one can mourn the loss of this tradition more than long for its recovery. By his own admission, Smith's schemes will not win his people social equality, because it cannot "be gained by pushing" society to accept mixed marriages (264). And he will not win political rights either in the short term. They remain exiles not only in their own nation but also from their own political tradition.

Even though the novel favors Smith's political tactics over the views expressed by the other members, *Contending Forces* does not accept his resigned view of social equality. It returns to the overarching domestic plot to imagine a mutualism committed to social equality less tethered to the nation. A series of women form a network that crosses space and time to unite its characters and their representative political positions into a collective political subject. The roles these women play vary, from Ma Smith, who runs a boarding house where blacks of various regional and ethnic backgrounds meet, to Sappho Clark, whose own past stiches together several localities. Marriage, true to many typical historical romances, performs a reconciliatory function, but the cultural syntheses are realized through an intellectual exchange between spouses instead of being allegorically embodied in the form of children.

Ma Smith, like her deceased husband, belongs to the uneducated but laborious "masses of the Negro race" (83). She must raise her children

---

108. See Ali, *Lion's*, 124–33.
109. See ibid., 113–49.

and pay off her home's mortgage as a widower without a steady stream of income. She opens up her house to boarders and proves an able manager and a savvy businesswoman. Successfully securing an education for her daughter and her son, she is not exceptional but representative of "so many families of color" who "manage to live as well as they do and to educate their children and give them a few of the refinements of living . . . so common among the whites, but supposed to be beyond the reach of a race just released from a degrading bondage" (86). Hopkins foregrounds her commitment to racial amalgamation or social equality; she claims that the nation must "allow for the infusion of white blood" (87). Although this plea for racial integration is couched in pseudo-biological terms, the novel envisions that social and political equality will be achieved within domestic spaces. Ma Smith's boarding house defies the simple division-of-separate-spheres ideology. It is as much a public as it is a private space, welcoming strangers and fostering political discussions within its walls. Her home operates as a hub within a larger network of relations. Run by the Montfort descendants and embracing Southern transplants, such as Sappho, it brings a number of localities into constellation within one another, including Bermuda, Boston, Britain, New Orleans, and North Carolina.

Ma Smith's boarding house allows its inhabitants and visitors to imagine a different kind of community. This community cannot be said to be strictly national, as its tendrils extend to points in the Caribbean and across the Atlantic. The social bonds forged in her home cannot be completely collapsed into the idea of a Black Atlantic, but nor are they entirely divorced from it. Hopkins is not invested in embracing "processes of cultural mutation and restless (dis)continuity" to overcome racial and national discourse.[110] She recognizes that "the themes of nationality, exile, and cultural affiliation accentuate the inescapable fragmentation and differentiation of the black subject," but she wants to draw new lines of affiliation as much as lines of antagonism.[111] She remains committed to what Paul Gilroy condemns as "those romantic conceptions of 'race,' 'people,' and 'nation.'"[112] She repossesses "the curse of homelessness" but in the service of reconstructing a people.[113] *Contending Forces* assumes a diasporic character, but it moves away from

---

110. Gilroy, *Black*, 2.
111. Ibid., 35.
112. Ibid., 34.
113. Ibid., 111.

a "diasporic identity" that is "permanently in flux."[114] Indeterminacy and forced migration are not sites of liberation for the characters of *Contending Forces*. Hopkins enlists the romance to create a people defined as much by their shared connections as by their own local affiliations. She opens a gap between the transnational content of her romance peopled with characters that constantly traverse continents and oceans and the form that fixes these same characters into place and time. Coextensive with the break between content and form is the affective disposition of the characters: they want to cease moving.[115] Only a faithfully executed romance promises this emotional resolution, and Hopkins delivers on this pledge. In the final chapters, she introduces tropes of redemption, renewal, reunion, and resurrection to bring about the closure her characters and presumably her readers crave. These classical romantic devices create a sense of social totality and dramatize the historical changes necessary for the realization of a people.[116]

The novel's nostalgic and retrospective framing of the various family lines draws together these estranged relations, but this affect figures both negatively and positively. It sustains the "deadly antagonism of the South" that Lewis and the other reformers must confront, but it also motivates them to restore their homes and families (*Contending*, 288). White Populism thrived off an insatiable nostalgia. By perpetually appealing to the lost tradition of Jefferson, it united urban and rural laborers. For Hopkins, on the other hand, nostalgia must either be evacuated or satisfied. Southern nostalgia and the Jim Crow laws it sanctions undermine "the large class of colored citizens who embody within themselves the highest development of American citizenship" (*Contending*, 289). Neither revolution nor reform will address this problem because, as Will declares during a dinner at Boston's Canterbury Club, "constitutional equity is a fiction," and its "amendments are dead letters; the ballot-box is nil" (297). Only through a transformation of culture and an amalgamation of the races will blacks eventually be able to enjoy their rights of citizenship fully and articulate themselves as a people.

Sappho Clark, a mysterious woman who conceals her status as a single mother, lies at the center of the romance's project of cultural and

---

114. Chow, *The Protestant Ethnic and the Spirit of Capitalism*, 130. For another critique of cosmopolitanism in sympathy with Chow's, see Cheah, "Given Culture."

115. Here I found Chow's account of the "affective dissonance" between theoretical writings on diaspora and autobiographies written by diasporic subjects instructive. See Chow, *Protestant*, 135. The former too often remains deaf to the emotional suffering wrought by forced migration and the fragmentation of community.

116. See Lukács, *Historical*, 332–50.

political reconstruction. Raped by a state senator from New Orleans, she bears the weight of a traumatic history. Unaware that she changed her name to Sappho, Luke Sawyer declaims her story to the American Colored League, believing that this "poor, ruined, half-crazed creature" died giving birth to her son (260). This story conforms to the conventions of the tragic mulatto narrative only to dispel them. Sappho lives and has secretly brought her son to Boston. After Langley exposes her, she returns with her son to New Orleans and leaves Will Smith—who had fallen in love with her—heartbroken. Her departure initiates a stylistic shift in the text toward Catholic imagery. The romance stages its discussions of politics in Protestant Boston with its exaltation of individualism and protest. New Orleans, on the other hand, is fully immersed in Catholicism. Mrs. Willis, the leader of a Boston sewing circle, voices the orthodox Catholic stance on the nature of virginity in a discussion with Sappho. Lois Brown notes that Hopkins's understanding of what entails "the preservation, loss, or reclamation of virtue clearly echoes the Catholic idea that virginity is a multifaceted state of being, one that exists in the flesh, spirit, and flesh and spirit."[117] According to these theological tenets, Sappho cannot lose her virginity as the result of a sexual assault because it violated her free will. Catholicism, consequently, insulates her from a broader set of prejudicial attitudes toward female purity and rape. Her return to the convent, for Brown, signals her transformation from "a woman traumatized by sexual scandal into one imagined as a holy mother and blessed virgin."[118] The convent is an alternative to the Northern reform movements that did not always provide blacks with the kind of liberation promised to them.

Hopkins's use of Catholic tropes also supports her broader reinvention of populist black politics. When Will returns from his studies in Europe to New Orleans, where he joins his sister Dora and her now-husband Arthur Lewis, he dreams of a choir in a cathedral singing "*Christe eleison, Kyrie eleison*" and then "the glad strains of *Gloria*" (*Contending*, 386). Shortly after these chants, he sees what he first believes to be the Virgin Mary and Child but instead turns out to be a vision of Sappho and her son Alphonse. Uncannily, he attends Easter Mass at the convent where, after he hears the same sequence of chants, he spots Alphonse in the congregation and eventually reunites with Sappho. While Hopkins's use of Marian iconography underscores Sappho's innocence, her emphasis on the *Kyrie eleison* is also intertextually inter-

---

117. Lois Brown, *Pauline Elizabeth Hopkins*, 206.
118. Ibid., 217.

connected with her political project. During the Lenten season, *Gloria* disappears from the Mass, and only the *Kyrie* is chanted; its return during the Easter Sunday ceremony signifies Christ's resurrection. Its pairing with *Gloria* accentuates Hopkins's Easter conceit: she repeatedly describes Sappho's reappearance as a metaphorical resurrection.[119] The *Kyrie*, though, reinforces the populist and interlocal dimensions of this romance. It is an ancient chant, one that likely predates Christianity with possible Egyptian roots.[120] It has always been one of the most popular litanies, translated out of Greek into a wide array of vernacular languages and incorporated into a number of other sacred and secular songs.[121] Its close association with the laity and its rumored North African roots draw out the less hierarchal and more polyvocal facets of the Roman Catholic Church. Hopkins reinforces these associations by moving Will's vision from a cathedral to its realization in one of the few African-American convents in the nation. Throughout this sequence of events, the convent emerges as a collective and matriarchal entity able to welcome a single mother of a child of mixed-race descent in ways Sappho could not be accepted in the reform circles in Boston.

Hopkins structures this moment of mutualism around the affect of nostalgia and within a broader network of distinct localities. Sappho's return and Will's rediscovery of her satisfy their nostalgia on its two different modal levels. Unable to make a home in the North, she finds that even in the face of the legal brutality of the Jim Crow South, "the convent will be a home for [her] always" (351). The sisters of the convent thus transform her forced exodus from Boston into a homecoming. Will remains fixated upon the past until he finally settles in New Orleans with Sappho, "delighted with all he saw and heard in the peaceful, happy home, the refuge of his love" (397). These multiple homecomings result in the hyperbolic realization of "a fairy tale of love and chivalry such as we read of only in books" (398). Hopkins's fidelity to this romantic mode of emplotment gives her novel its radical quality: she provides her black characters with the kind of narrative

---

119. I am grateful to Matthew Lewis Sutton of St. John's Univeristy, who assisted with this reading, for sharing his scholarly understanding of *Gloria* and the Easter Mass with me.

120. Many conjectured that the *Kyrie eleison* was a "pre-Christian" translation of a prayer originally "addressed in the Egyptian Mysteries to the Sun-God Ra, asking him to shine upon his people with his beneficent and life-giving ray." Leadbeater, *The Science of the Sacraments*, 102.

121. See Spinks, *The Place of Christ in Liturgical Prayer*, 179–84.

usually denied to them. Their marriage coincides with the restoration of the Montfort family fortune, bringing that "romantic history" to a close (374). These romantic plots converge in New Orleans, where Easter "is something to dream of, and defies description" (391). Counter to conventional expectations, freedom and racial solidarity are realized far downriver. The most ambitious reformers in the novel who first appeared in Boston—Will, his sister Dora, and her husband Arthur—now all devote themselves to racial uplift in New Orleans, united with Sappho and poorer and less cultured blacks.

The novel consequently does not end in exile, even though it concludes with Will and Sappho bound for Britain to visit that branch of the Montfort family. Instead, their nostalgia has been resolved and the contending forces dispelled, as they have found their place in a New Orleans connected to a web of other regions across North America and Europe. This interlocalism is synchronic and diachronic. The present ties between the Montforts lace together New Orleans, Boston, Canada, and England. Ma Smith's geographical ties exist in the present and project backward, and Sappho's interconnectedness with Catholicism unearths the long durée of populism in the form of a beloved litany. She envisions a people connected through shared family genealogies that bear a direct relation to localities across the globe. As Hopkins writes of Toussaint L'Ouverture in one of her essays for the *Colored American Magazine*, he crowned "Hayti . . . with the cap of liberty," but his deeds and the collective actions of his comrades are "interesting to the Negroes of the United States; brothers in blood, though speaking different languages, we should clasp our hands in friendship when we look back upon our past."[122]

---

122. Hopkins, *Daughter of the Revolution*, 21.

CHAPTER 4

LEFT NOSTALGIA
REVOLUTIONARY AESTHETICS IN THE RADICAL NOVEL

*L*UCY PARSONS waited three days before delivering her first substantive address to the inaugural convention of the Industrial Workers of the World (IWW) on June 29, 1905. A former editor and contributor to the *Alarm* newspaper and the widower of one of the five men sentenced to death for the Haymarket bombing in 1886, she provided the group that eventually became known as the Wobblies with a greater sense of historical purpose. When she finally took the podium, Parsons used her time to defend the rights of laboring women before imploring her auditors to answer the call of revolutionary socialism. She did not want the IWW to emulate the American Federation of Labor (AFL), an organization that protected only its own craftsmen and had become complicit with the wage suppression of non-AFL laborers. Parsons knew the IWW faced daunting odds. She listed the weapons that capital had at its behest: "First it has money. Then it has legislative tools. Then it has its judiciary; it has its army and its navy; it has its guns; it has armories; and last, it has the gallows."[1] But if anyone should find their resolve faltering, she urged them to recall the Chicago anarchists who nineteen years ago were hanged "for daring to raise their voices against the iniquities of the age in which we live."[2] She remembered how, on the day of her husband's execution, their detractors jubilantly sent telegrams proclaim-

---

1. Lucy Parsons, "Speeches at the Founding Convention of the Industrial Workers of the World," 80.
2. Ibid., 84.

ing the death of anarchism. Their prognostications were wrong: these Chicago "miscreants" had become martyrs, and their brand of radicalism proved resilient.[3] If the IWW could reclaim their revolutionary spirit, Parsons maintained, they would herald a "new era" of labor "when capitalism will be a thing of the past, and the new industrial republic, the commonwealth of labor, shall be in operation."[4] After she uttered that final line of her speech, the audience erupted into thunderous applause.[5]

The Wobblies were not alone in relying on figures like Lucy Parsons to provide them with a nostalgic connection to the radical past. Although many turn-of-the-century radicals looked forward to the future, they also practiced forms of historical recovery. In the wake of the Great Strike of 1877, which began when Baltimore and Ohio Railroad Company employees demanded better wages and working conditions, interest in alternatives to the United States' brand of republican capitalism reached unparalleled heights. New labor organizations were founded and radical political associations cropped up across the United States. These groups remained polymorphous, frustrating organizations that hoped to unify them into a single labor movement. Appeals to reason proved insufficient; they resorted to seizing upon the temporal and spatial nostalgia so familiar to immigrant wage workers and itinerant laborers. In the turn-of-the-century writing composed by radical intellectuals, labor organizers, and politically committed novelists, the longing to recover estranged histories and places assumed a particular affective form that I call *left nostalgia*.

I derive my understanding of left nostalgia from Walter Benjamin's idea of left-wing melancholy. He associates the phenomenon with Weimar Germany's Activist and New Objectivist lyrical poets, especially the work of Erich Kästner.[6] In the name of politically resigned middle-

---

3. Ibid.
4. Ibid., 85.
5. For a historical account of the reaction to Parsons's speech at the founding convention of the Industrial Workers of the World, see Ashbaugh, *Lucy Parsons*, 217–19.
6. The term "New Objectivity," or *Neue Sachlichkeit*, is associated with a period in German history when many artists, architects, museum curators, and writers rejected expressionism and its attendant political idealism. The movement lacked aesthetic coherence in many respects, but its students generally extolled less sanguine, realist, and naturalist art forms. After the German economy rapidly deteriorated in 1929 and fascist propaganda began to saturate popular culture, these poets treated right-wing political doctrine ironically rather than combating it directly. Revolution and artistic commitment, for many of these artists, belonged to a romantic or impracticable past inaccessible to the Germany of the 1930s. See Gay, *Weimar Culture*, 119–45.

class pragmatism, Benjamin charged, these poets abandoned revolutionary socialism by entombing it. "Political struggle," in their literary work, transforms "from a compulsory decision into an object of pleasure, from a means of production into an article of consumption."[7] Indulging in a "mimicry of the proletariat," they sounded romantic dirges that lamented the loss of revolution to supplant it with a shallow leftist intellectual culture that adhered "not to schools but to fashions" of radical thought.[8] Further extending Benjamin's conceptualization of this affect, Wendy Brown succinctly describes left melancholia as "a condition produced by an attachment to a notion of progress in which opportunities missed or political formations lost are experienced as permanent and unrecoverable."[9] Brown and Benjamin fault left melancholia for its undialectical engagement with history, as it fails to account for how past events can ignite present insurrectionary moments. Left nostalgia, conversely, looks backward but does not fixate on an object or political cause lost to a previous epoch. It reanimates the revolutionary past to serve the exigencies of the present. This process is one of mutual transformation—as accounts of past events are repeatedly revised any time they are mobilized for the present. Left nostalgia, for this reason, cannot be conflated with tradition; the latter relies on a grand narrative of historical continuity that can conform to a variety of narrative modalities, including republican romanticism, Whiggish progressivism, and consensus liberalism. Nostalgic historiography imagines the present set adrift from linear time; it establishes a direct link between the present and an estranged past. Parting ways with Marxist orthodoxy, it rejects the science of history and materialist determinism and instead aestheticizes the past by embracing anachronism and counterfactual possibility.

As with other political and literary movements explored in *Novel Nostalgias*, the radical writers examined in this chapter directed their nostalgic sentiments toward the U.S. Revolutionary and the Early National Eras. Their yearning to recapture these events, however, assumed a distinctly leftist hue by using them to uncover a transhistorical political subject—the laboring class—and its accompanying spirit, which could be reanimated only by a desire to return to previous moments of revolutionary possibility. In other words, their understanding of history retained a Marxist and Hegelian historical subject but without the accompanying teleological assurance of its predetermined

---

7. Benjamin, "Left-Wing Melancholy," 425.
8. Ibid., 424.
9. Wendy Brown, *Politics Out of History*, 168–69.

ascendency. Accordingly, they had additional events of their own to commemorate and exhume. The French Revolution, the revolutions of 1848, the Paris Commune of 1871, the Great Strike of 1877, and the Haymarket Affair of 1886 all dominated their historical imagination. This international parade of lost historical opportunities for dramatic economic and political change speaks volumes about the aims of left nostalgia. Unlike many of the previous incarnations of nostalgia explored in this book, left nostalgia did not ultimately express itself through the language of nationalism. It assumed an international form. Anarchists despised the state and its legal institutions for legislating and enforcing political and economic oppression. Socialists, though not opposed to the modern nation-state in principle, believed in practice it legitimated wage theft and protected the interests of capital. Left nostalgia incited the political imaginations of the broader populace by recasting their agitation as an effort to rehabilitate the revolutions of the past. This analeptic outlook provided a space for comparing the ethics and politics of gradual socialist reform to violent insurrection. Essayists addressed these issues directly, but radical novels and their aesthetics of social realism created the most fecund environment for imagining acts unthinkable within normative republican and liberal discourse.

This chapter focuses on two popular novels that nostalgically explored two different revolutionary paths: Upton Sinclair's *The Jungle* (1906) and Frank Harris's *The Bomb* (1908).[10] I single out these two novels in particular because they enlist left nostalgia to imagine two different political ends. Radical novels written at the turn of the century often gravitated toward socialism or anarchism as well as toward either reform or revolution. *The Jungle*, because of its ability to appeal to reform-minded progressives, became the more popular of the two and is representative

---

10. I should address two omissions from this chapter: Theodore Dreiser and Jack London. As a card-carrying member of the Communist Party, Dreiser would seem crucial to the development of radical fiction in the early twentieth century. It is perhaps for this reason, however, that Dreiser's work conforms more readily to orthodox Marxist historiography, promoting a "love of change" and expressing a general hostility toward anything remotely nostalgic in his fiction. Dreiser, "Change," 21. London, a devotee of Sinclair and a committed socialist, also stands out as an important radical literary figure. He wrestled with forms of nostalgia in his novels, especially *Burning Daylight* (1910), which celebrates a return to Jeffersonian agrarianism. But nostalgia, in his work, more often than not is an object of critique rather than an affect capable of animating a revolution. By examining Sinclair's and Harris's fiction, my aim is not to displace Dreiser or London but to broaden our understanding of how nineteenth-century iterations of nostalgia shaped the fictional and political landscape of the early twentieth century.

of much of the socialist literature of the era that sought to transform existing legal and political institutions through grassroots organizing. *The Jungle* in particular redirects pastoral and immigrant nostalgias to combat the aesthetically enchanting power of industrial wonder. This affective tension, which the novel's protagonist Jurgis Rudkus feels keenly, fuels the rise of a socialist party. *The Bomb,* by contrast, offers us a more marginal but equally representative account of incendiary radicalism. Harris's now-forgotten novel dramatically insists upon the necessity of violent revolt. Here a left nostalgia for previous revolutions places an infinite demand upon the radical agitator to put aside ethics to bring about an end to the injustices of the state. Despite their differences, both novels also establish what literary characteristics bound the radical literature of this era together. They share their naturalist contemporaries' skepticism toward liberal individualism, but they part ways with those narratives resigned to the insurmountable determinism of social, biological, and economic forces. They instead imagine a collective subject affectively driven by left nostalgia capable of dramatically altering the political status quo. By focusing on the work of Sinclair and Harris, then, I establish both the political and literary range of left nostalgia and redirect this period of U.S. literary history away from naturalism toward a body of radical writers who commanded national and international attention at this same cultural moment.[11]

---

11. In the early decades of the twentieth century, many viewed American literature through the lens of Granville Hicks, who defined the American novel as one of social protest. London and Sinclair figured prominently, but as authors of the emerging proletarian novel rather than as naturalists or muckrakers. Writers closely associated with what Hicks saw as the genteel tradition of Howells and James were discussed but not accorded a central place in his literary history. See Hicks, *The Great Tradition*. Lionel Trilling and his successors sidelined these radical writers to focus instead on American literary realism. The "ferment of realism" figured as the antecedent to Cold-War consensus liberalism. Berthoff, *The Ferment of Realism,* 1. Studies performed by New Americanist literary scholars treated this liberal narrative skeptically but left it somewhat intact (though what once looked like consensus became seen as disciplinary coercion). Michael Denning's *Mechanic Accents* stands out as one of the notable exceptions to this trend by recovering the once-maligned working-class dime novel, which found "a wide resonance in the 1880s and 1890s." Denning, *Mechanic Accents,* 153. By stressing the importance of the radical novel in turn-of-the-century U.S. literature, this chapter further develops a literary and cultural history examined most recently in Castronovo, *Beautiful,* Streeby, *Radical Sensations,* and Zimmerman, *Panic!*

RADICAL HISTORIOGRAPHIES

Cheap paper prices drove an unprecedented rise in the number of radical publications across the nation at the end of the nineteenth century.[12] These newspapers and magazines engaged in lively debates over new social theories and championed their own canons of literary, economic, and political works.[13] Many of the short articles appearing in these publications anxiously anticipated the revolution to come. *The Coming Nation,* an enormously popular socialist weekly edited by J. A. Wayland and published by the Ruskin commune in Tennessee, frequently included a poem about the socialist future written by H. C. Goodrich that shared the publication's namesake.[14] "The Coming Nation" begins with the following lines: "Down in the fast on-coming years / We see a glimmering light; / At last it comes, dispelling fears."[15] Poems like this one reflected the radical community's faith in Marx's dialectic of history. After the Great Strike of 1877, skirmishes between capital and labor only intensified, financial panics repeatedly jolted the national economy, and the law disregarded workers' interests while expanding the rights of corporate personhood. These events convinced many socialists and anarchists that the age of capital had reached its nadir. Radical publications railed against the capitalist press and published illustrations of wealth disparity. In a bar graph entitled "Cold Facts," *The Coming Nation* observed that the richest 9 percent controlled "71 percent of the

---

12. For two of the best bibliographies of radical periodicals and newspapers published in the United States, see Conlin, *The American Radical Press,* and Longa, *Anarchist Periodicals in English Published in the United States (1835–1955).*

13. It should be noted that there were several distinct strands of socialist and anarchist thought circulating throughout the late nineteenth and early twentieth centuries. By no means do I wish to suggest that this body of work can be treated monolithically, but I am interested in outlining their shared rhetorical and intellectual appropriation of past revolutionary events that they nostalgically sought to recover. Numerous histories of the radical left of note have been produced. For one of the now-classic accounts of U.S. Marxism, see Paul Buhle, *Marxism in the United States.* For an excellent recent study of the subject, see Kazin, *American Dreamers.*

14. J. A. Wayland later left *The Coming Nation* to found *The Appeal to Reason,* a newspaper that counted Upton Sinclair among its contributors. For more on Wayland's colorful career as a radical editor and publisher, see Shore, *Talkin' Socialism.* For a brief account of *The Coming Nation*'s importance, see Paul Buhle, "The Appeal to Reason and New Appeal," 50–52, and Mari Jo Buhle, "Socialist Women, Progressive Women, Coming Nation," 448.

15. H. C. Goodrich, "The Coming Nation," *The Coming Nation* (Tennessee City, TN), November 9, 1895, lines 1–3.

nation's wealth."[16] Many believed this wealth disparity would lead to a revolution. The chains of the past would be shed, and workers could embrace "with joy the coming years."[17]

As much as anarchists and socialists anticipated the world to come, embracing the future also meant looking backward. In their introduction to the inaugural March 1906 issue of *Mother Earth*, Emma Goldman and Max Baginski gazed back to the past. They wistfully recalled the era of Washington, Jefferson, and Paine, who imagined the United States as a land teeming with political and economic possibilities. Their appraisal of this moment assumes an elegiac tone when they acknowledge that the same people who fled "arbitrary and despotic lands" soon began to prey upon others by becoming "dependent on possessions, on wealth, on power."[18] Goldman and Baginski were not alone in casting Jefferson and Paine as the fallen forefathers of U.S. anarchism and socialism. These radical assessments of the nation's history coincided with the dramatic shift in historical studies. Founded just two years before the eruption of the Haymarket Affair, the American Historical Association (AHA) professionalized history as a discipline. The AHA called for, as its first president Andrew D. White claimed, the "rewriting of history from the American point of view."[19] These grand surveys of the American march of civilization left little room for anarchist and more militantly socialist appraisals of history, even as progressive historians, such as Frederick Jackson Turner, found ways of integrating Populist and liberal reform movements into their work.[20] Goldman and her contemporaries knew that their struggle was also an intellectual one, affirming *The Coming Nation*'s claim that "Rockefeller-Stanford-Carnegie educational institutions" produced only "surface-seekers and gilders of men's consciences."[21] Goldman redefined the United States' most important

---

16. "Cold Facts," *The Coming Nation* (Tennessee City, TN), November 8, 1895.

17. H. C. Goodrich, "The Coming Nation," *The Coming Nation* (Tennessee City, TN), November 9, 1895, line 16.

18. Goldman and Baginski, "Mother Earth," 3.

19. Andrew White, "On Studies in General History and the History of Civilization," 67. For more on the formation of the AHA, see Higham, *History*, and Haskell, *The Emergence of Professional Social Science*, 168–77. An account of the social sciences' hostility toward forms of radicalism can be found in Ross, *The Origins of American Social Science*, 98–141.

20. Turner's pathbreaking *The Rise of the New West, 1819–1829* (1906) responded to Populist sentiments by examining the political and economic underpinnings of U.S. history in relation to western expansion.

21. "Social Reform and the Need of It," *The Coming Nation* (Tennessee City, TN), November 9, 1895.

contribution to political thought. For historians of the 1880s and 1890s, the Constitution and its attendant laws figured as the towering achievements of the American republic and as an extension of western European jurisprudence and political theory. Anarchists and socialists, by contrast, saw the Constitution as a betrayal of democracy. As historians assigned a diminishing importance to the U.S. Revolution, anarchists and socialists insisted on reviving this revolutionary moment.

Goldman and her contemporaries celebrated the democratic will of the people unmediated by any legal apparatus. They produced a history of this power that required a different historiography and temporality. If constitutionalism and the common law tradition revered precedent to create a seamless continuity between the present and past, then the radical attitude toward the past adopted a historiography of estrangement. Histories, when they follow a cyclical or linear grand narrative, strive for diachronic continuity. Even the jeremiad sustains an image of history as a chain of successive events; the perils of decline bring with them opportunities for a contiguous restoration to previous exaltation. These narratives are sites of libidinal investment, as Louis Althusser and Fredric Jameson observe, where an individual can "imagine his or her lived relationship to transpersonal realities such as the social structure or the collective logic of History."[22] Anarchists and socialists writing at the fin de siècle lacked the Althusserian and psychoanalytic vocabulary to describe the complex relationship between capitalist ideology and grand histories, such as those called for by the AHA, but they knew their Marx well enough to recognize a connection existed. When they revisited the history of the U.S. Revolution, they reminded their readers of a revolution's power to upend historical master narratives. Revolutionary movements erupted as crises; they displayed the characteristics of Benjamin's flashing image of historical possibility and a capacity for historical disruption. For Goldman and her contemporaries, however, "articulating the past" did not consist of "approaching a memory as it flashes up in a moment of danger."[23] Their memories belonged to a perpetual past that determinist and constitutionalist narratives had usurped from them. They longed to return to these moments to connect them directly to the present, as though all radical revolutions could occupy the same synchronic moment.

Radicals celebrated the U.S. Revolution before Goldman did, but her writing was far more influential and infused with left nostalgia.

---

22. Jameson, *Political*, 30.
23. Benjamin, "On the Concept of History," 391.

Like many members of the immigrant left, she meditates on the connection between national and historical estrangement. Writing about the violent acts of particular anarchists, she notes they had either the experiences of "most young Russian immigrants" or were raised as the children of these immigrants.[24] The nation's major newspapers and periodicals seized upon these details to frame anarchism as a foreign threat. Goldman conversely insists they felt "disinherited" not from their natal homes but from their belief "in the mythical liberty of America."[25] They had yearned to secure a livelihood in a place that should have emancipated them from the fetters of oppression, but they instead discovered that few opportunities and liberties were accorded to the working poor. Although she distances herself from Leon Czolgosz, the man who assassinated William McKinley, she sympathizes with him. The son of Polish immigrants, he grew up in the United States and "faithfully honored the Nation's dead" every Decoration Day and Fourth of July.[26] He daringly imagined "a new and glorious dawn" rising out of the United States' revolutionary past.[27] He wanted to "fight for his country and die for her liberty" but realized that "he belonged to . . . no country."[28] His actions emanated from an insuppressible wish to make good on the U.S. Revolution's aims.

Goldman did not wish to cast aside this nostalgia for the principles of the American Revolution as a false ideology. The Spirit of '76, for her, was not to be commemorated but recommenced. Other anarchists and socialists shared her views. Voltairine de Cleyre, the prolific Michigan-born individualist anarchist, decried "the cheapest sort of patriotism" that perpetrated "shameless falsification of all acts of rebellion, to put the government in the right and the rebels in the wrong."[29] De Cleyre chided those who extolled Jefferson as a founder instead of as a revolutionary. Writing for the *Firebrand*, Henry Addis noted that on every Fourth of July, ironically the same orators who "sound the praises of rebels and subverters of the social order" of the eighteenth century also "condemn the revolutionists of today."[30] The renowned socialist

---

24. Goldman, *Anarchism and Other Essays*, 91.
25. Ibid.
26. Ibid., 89.
27. Ibid., 90.
28. Ibid., 89–90.
29. De Cleyre, "Anarchism and American Traditions," 94–95.
30. Henry Addis, "Fourth of July: The Spirit of '76," *Firebrand* (Portland, OR), June 27, 1897.

Frederick Krafft, however, traced this contradiction back to the inaugural moment of revolt in an essay written for school children in *The Young Socialist*. "The wealthy of this country worked the people up" to revolution, he argued, but Paine could be solely credited for asserting the rights of all men.[31] The revolutionary era of the 1770s and 1780s left at least two contrary legacies: the assertion of the universal rights of man and the countervailing installation of an oligarchy. It was not the case, as de Cleyre lamented, that "the desire for material ease long ago vanquished the spirit of '76," but that these radical essayists realized that Paine's ambitions differed markedly from those of Washington and Adams.[32] Even as they always saw the U.S. Revolution as one entangled with moneyed interests, de Cleyre's radical compatriots shared her hope that they might "see a resurrection of that proud spirit" of republican radicals.

They reconciled the historical contradiction of the U.S. Revolution by associating its libratory promise with the Declaration of Independence and the moment when "the rights of property triumphed" with the U.S. Constitution.[33] Addressing his young readers, Krafft encouraged "every boy and girl" to "read the Declaration of Independence and the Constitution of the United States . . . , so that they will know what this government should be and what it is not."[34] The criticisms leveled at the Constitution have their roots in various strands of both socialist and anarchist thought. Socialists saw the U.S. Constitution as a document that largely protected the interests of capital, and many suspected that the framers designed it to protect the economic interests of merchants and property owners. Anarchists drew on the theories of Proudhon, Bakunin, and Kropotkin to decry any kind of state on the grounds that even in representative government "there is *necessarily* alienation of a part of the liberty and of the means of the citizen."[35] Whether they embraced Proudhon's mutualism or Kropotkin's notion of social solidarity, anarchists insisted on creating an egalitarian society freed from state oppression and enriched by self-directed mutual aid. But despite their intellectual differences, radicals of every stripe rallied around the Declaration of Independence, because it proved the people possessed a mass political agency they could exercise. They referred to

---

31. Krafft, "History of Our Country for Boys and Girls: Fourteenth Chapter," 5.
32. De Cleyre, "Anarchism and American Traditions," 97.
33. Lucy Parsons, "A Piece of History," 15.
34. Krafft, "History of Our Country for Boys and Girls: Fifteenth Chapter," 5.
35. Proudhon, *General Idea of the Revolution in the Nineteenth Century*, 113.

this form of agitation as direct action, distinguishing it from indirect action relying on the use of the ballot or the sagacity of the law.[36]

The socialist agitator Daniel De Leon challenged conservative and liberal accounts of the U.S. revolutionaries. He consented that many of them were burgeoning capitalists, but he insisted that before the drafting of the Constitution they opposed the concentration of wealth. To make his point, he apparently invented a quote attributed to James Madison: "A republic cannot stand upon bayonets, and when that day comes, when the wealth of the nation will be in the hands of a few, then we must . . . readjust the laws of the nation to the changed conditions."[37] De Leon understood the rhetorical power of a left nostalgia that could transform a conservative revolution into a radical one—even if that meant imaginatively manufacturing a new historical record. Figures like Goldman and De Leon despised patriotism because they felt that the unthinking adulation of the Founders made the masses forget they were first and foremost revolutionaries. *The Alarm* did its part to remind readers of the revolutionary drive behind the Declaration by routinely printing a full, two-page announcement entitled "To the Workingmen of America." Opening with an excerpt from the Declaration of Independence that provided "the justification for armed resistance by our forefathers," it begged the question, "Do not the necessities of our present time compel us to reassert their declaration?"[38] Exhibiting a left nostalgia for these past moments and appropriating them as their own, they came to terms with the nature of revolution. "Anarchism is not," Goldman declared, "a theory of the future to be realized through

---

36. See de Cleyre, "Direct Action," 274–75.

37. De Leon, "Fourth Day," 95. De Leon probably created this quote to suit his own rhetorical aims. For the last century, references abound to this statement, but there do not appear to be any citations of the phrase before De Leon's speech. The quote is generally out of character with Madison's political leanings, including his concerns about mob rule and aversion toward the redistribution of wealth. During the secret debates of the 1787 Constitutional Convention, he argued for the creation of a Senate composed solely of property owners based on this rationale: "The government we mean to erect is intended to last for ages. The landed interest, at present, is prevalent; but, in process of time . . . will not the landed interest be overbalanced in future elections, and unless wisely provided against, what will become of your government? . . . Landholders ought to have a share in the government, to support these invaluable interests, and to balance and check the other. They ought to be so constituted as to protect the minority of the opulent against the majority." Madison, "Notes of the Secret Debates of the Federal Convention of 1787," 449–50.

38. "To the Workingmen of America," *The Alarm* (Chicago), October 4, 1884.

divine inspiration." Revolution does not rise out of a mystical messianic moment but is a vital, imaginative force "constantly creating new conditions."[39] Only direct action secured universal suffrage, for "if not for the spirit of rebellion, of the defiance on the part of the American revolutionary fathers, their posterity would still wear the King's coat."[40] Conservative historians buried the U.S. Revolution under their universal histories of western republicanism while their progressive counterparts saw it as the product of a series of determining economic and social forces. Radical writers, conversely, understood it as a manifestation of collective agency. Imagining a better future began, in part, by reclaiming the revolutionary past.

Left nostalgia for past demonstrations of direct action extended beyond the U.S. Revolution. Parsons recaptured the insurrectionary sprit of slave revolts, as her own understanding of historical dispossession emerged out of her experience as a former slave and as an African-American living under Jim Crow laws. In an essay directly addressing other blacks, she observed how the practice of sharecropping meant African-American farmers "till the soils for another to enjoy."[41] This estrangement and yearning to find a home within the nation led her to celebrate radical abolitionism. Parsons grouped poor blacks and whites together into one oppressed laboring class.[42] Debs also claimed abolitionism as a radical cause to quell the racial divisiveness that plagued the socialists, accusing anyone who held racist beliefs of lacking "the true spirit of the slavery-destroying revolutionary movement."[43] John Brown—not Harriet Beecher Stowe or William Lloyd Garrison—

---

39. Goldman, *Anarchism*, 63.
40. Ibid., 65.
41. Lucy Parsons, "The Negro," 55.
42. See Lucy Parsons, "On the 'Harmony' Between Capital and Labor, Or, the Robber and the Robbed," and "Slavery," *The Alarm* (Chicago), December 6, 1884.
43. Debs, "The Negro and the Class Struggle," 260. Debs preached the importance of class solidarity even as he celebrated the accomplishments of antislavery activists, stressing that "the workers of the world, mainly through organized effort, are becoming conscious of their interests as a class, totally regardless of color, creed, or sex, and in time they will unite and act together upon a common basis of equality" and the Manufacturers' Association. Eugene Debs, "Debs On the Color Question," *Appeal to Reason* (Kansas City, MO), July 4, 1903. Charles H. Vail expressed similar sentiments; see Vail, "The Negro Problem." Debs was sometimes criticized for not adequately addressing the racial discord that plagued his party's ranks. One of the most notoriously racist pamphlets issued under the auspices of a Socialist Labor Party newspaper was Kate Richards O'Hare's *"Nigger" Equality*, which advocated segregation on the basis that blacks were unfairly given better land to till than white southerners. See O'Hare, *"Nigger" Equality*.

received widespread praise for his role in waging a war against slavery.[44] De Cleyre and Goldman revered his raid as an example of direct action, crediting him and his band of revolutionaries for ending the "trade in the flesh of the black man" (Goldman, 66). The Northern and Southern sections bore the stains of hypocrisy: the North ended slavery but only to safeguard the interests of federalism and capitalism, and the South fought the encroachment of federalism but only to preserve slavery. John Brown, however, led a revolt against the violence perpetrated by all the states against plantation and wage slaves alike. Rescuing him from historical infamy, they established how "the direct acts of the forerunners of social change, whether they be of a peaceful or warlike nature" arouse "the conscience of the mass."[45] This was as true of the acts of Brown as it was of the labor movements after the Civil War.

These radicals sutured the causes of the U.S. Revolution and Brown's raid to the fabric of international socialism and anarchism. The Paris Commune of 1871 became a powerful political image, one that haunted or inspired many Americans during and after the Great Strike of 1877. As essential as the Civil War was to ending slavery, 1877 more than 1861 loomed large in the radical political imagination. The financial unrest of 1873 and the controversy surrounding the presidential election of 1876 set the stage for what would become an important year in the history of the U.S. labor movement. Emboldened by their majority in the House of Representatives, the Democratic Party violently suppressed the black and Republican vote in 1876. They failed to elect their candidate to the White House, but Rutherford B. Hayes won the election by a single electoral vote. In order to bring an end to what wound up being a Constitutional crisis, the Republicans withdrew troops from the South, ending Reconstruction and setting the stage for the rise of Jim Crow. Hayes also relied heavily on the support of Democratic businessmen, including Thomas A. Scott, the president of the Pennsylvania Railroad Company. Scott would eventually exercise considerable influence over Hayes when the time came for him to quell the strikes brought on by the railroad unions. Radical Republicanism was dead, but what came to be known as the Compromise of 1877 laid the groundwork for a different kind of American civil war, one between labor and capital.

Before the Panic of 1873 and the events of 1877, socialist and anarchist clubs struggled to gain a foothold in the United States. In a self-

---

44. John Brown also played an enormously central role in structuring the political rhetoric of the antebellum era. See Caleb Smith, *The Oracle and the Curse*.

45. De Cleyre, "Direct Action," 279.

promotional screed, Allan Pinkerton saw 1877 as the moment when U.S. radicals almost brought "the horrors of the Paris Commune" to North American soil.[46] Before the employees of the Baltimore and Ohio Railroad went on strike for better wages, Americans had witnessed very few major labor events. What made the B&O strike so terrifying was the speed with which it spread across the country, momentarily shutting down the nation's entire railroad infrastructure. Most major American newspapers covered the strike in a manner that must have pleased Pinkerton. They reported how local militiamen sympathized with the workers and deserted their posts, just as units belonging to the French National Guard had joined rebel forces in Paris. These articles left nothing to the imagination, conjuring up the terrors of the Paris Commune.[47] These sensational reports bore little resemblance to most of the labor activity on the ground, but they provided a pretext for repressive federal military intervention. In St. Louis, however, a number of labor organizations started holding meetings in Schuler's Hall where they consciously formed a commune and issued a manifesto before all being arrested.[48] And a similar Chicago Commune also emerged before the authorities brought its activities to a premature end. In both the popular and radical imaginations, the events of 1877 were forever intertwined with the Paris Commune. For the former, the strikes stoked fears of irrational mobs and justified the rapid expansions of private and public police forces; for the latter, the Commune and the 1877 strikes represented important chapters in an international history of direct action.

In the radical press, these events provoked a left nostalgia, stimulating a radical international imagination. The red and black flags belonged to no single nation but to a global fraternity of workers and rebels. When one workingman heard the former United States minister to France besmirching French socialism, he reportedly led his crowd of auditors in two chants to silence the retired diplomat: "Three cheers for the Paris Commune!" and "Vive la Commune!"[49] Recollections of the Haymarket Affair stirred likeminded feelings. May Day, a day signifying left nostalgia

---

46. Pinkerton, *Strikers, Communists, Tramps, and Detectives*, 79.

47. A representative sample of articles appearing in July of 1877 include "Insurrection! A Day and Night of Blood and Horror at Pittsburg," *New York Herald*, July 23, 1877; "The Mob: Pittsburg the Scene of Wild, Horrible Rioting, Approaching the Days of the Commune," *The Inter-Ocean* (Chicago), July 23, 1877; and "The Great Strike: Is It to Be the Red Flag of the Commune?," *Augusta Chronicle* (Augusta, GA), July 26, 1877.

48. See "Leaders of the Commune Arrested, *New York Tribune*," July 28, 1877; Paul M. Buhle, *Marxism in the United States*, 39; and Bellesiles, *1877*, 249.

49. "The Black Flag," *The Alarm* (Chicago), November 29, 1884.

for a limitless number of past radical actions, commemorated the fallen Chicago anarchists. The memorializing of their martyrdom in May and on November 11, the date of their execution, had global significance. The editors of *The Alarm* reminded their readers that Haymarket was just one part of a larger set of "teachings of history" that demonstrated how revolutions, "once inaugurated, are accomplished with a rapidity and resistless momentum," as was the case with the U.S. Revolution, various Italian insurrections, "the fall of the court of Louis XVI" in France, and the Haymarket Affair.[50]

The estrangement that leftists felt from their country manifested itself as a longing for an international history and political association. These feelings recast national revolutions as key steps toward the global emancipation of the working class. This nineteenth-century radical periodical and intellectual culture gave birth to the leftist literature of the early decades of the twentieth century. These novels, exemplified by the work of Sinclair and Harris, recognize the tremendous revolutionary power of left nostalgia. Longing for lost times and places, the protagonists of *The Jungle* and *The Bomb* realize that the working class has no country. They abandon the search for a new nation and instead gravitate toward what Mary Marcy called, in the pages of *The International Socialist Review*, the "real fatherland" represented by "the red flag, which means universal brotherhood of the workers of the world in their fight to abolish the profit system."[51]

OVERCOMING INDUSTRIAL WONDER IN *THE JUNGLE*

Writing for the esteemed *Bookman* magazine in 1914, Sinclair Lewis triumphantly proclaimed, "the pure individualism of Wharton and James and Howells is out of the trend."[52] He believed readers were now gravitating toward novels that "provided a complete criticism of life today and in them one finds back of all the individual's actions a lowering background of People—people with clenched fists."[53] Lewis outlined a canon of radicals that included still familiar names, such as Theodore Dreiser and Jack London, and now largely forgotten ones, such as Will

---

50. Lizzie M. Swank, "Our Memorial Day," *The Alarm* (Chicago), June 16, 1888.
51. Marcy, "The Real Fatherland," 178.
52. Sinclair Lewis, "The Passing of Capitalism," 280.
53. Ibid.

Levington Comfort and Susan Glaspell. He did not affix a generic label to this body of literature, but he characterized it as politically committed naturalism or a variation of social realism that rejected determinism and individualism. Reviewers affirmed Lewis's conspectus by registering socialist sympathies in many of the major works of late nineteenth-century and early twentieth-century U.S. literature. Other commentators saw the movement as a transatlantic one, locating correlative motifs in work by Henrik Ibsen, George Bernard Shaw, Leo Tolstoy, H. G. Wells, and Emilé Zola.[54] This socialist spirit in U.S. literature reached its apogee when Ernest Poole, the author of the widely read socialist novel *The Harbor* (1915), won the first Pulitzer Prize for fiction in 1918. But this socialist turn in U.S. fiction was short lived. The October Revolution of 1917 spurred a cultural backlash against socialism in the United States, and these writers quickly fell out favor with general readers and literary critics.

Over two decades after Lewis's essay first appeared in print, V. L. Parrington, in an addendum to the incomplete third volume of his *Main Currents in American Thought* (1930), differentiated these left-leaning writers from their naturalist predecessors. He derisively referred to their work as the problem novels of the early twentieth century, which embarked upon a "diversion from naturalism."[55] Naturalist writers depicted social, economic, and political forces with gritty realism and amoral objectivity, but problem novels naively expressed confidence in human agency and participated in "the glorification of propaganda."[56] When not disparaged as failed attempts at naturalist fiction, these novels were often lumped together with the muckraking journalism of Ray Stannard Baker and Ida M. Tarbell. The intellectual climate of the Cold War continued to stifle any effort to take these writers seriously.[57] These critical predispositions deprived this body of literature of its imaginative form and content, equating it with reportage or denigrating it as sophomoric naturalism.

---

54. See "The Literature of Anarchism."
55. Parrington, *The Main Currents of American Thought*, 346.
56. Ibid., 347.
57. This generation's characteristic aversion toward dissenting literature is best expressed by Trilling in his famous essay "Reality in America." See Trilling, *The Liberal Imagination*, 15–32. In his 1956 literary history of the U.S. radical novel, Walter B. Rideout registers this shift in literary taste: "because the crises of the fifties are not the crises of the thirties, we now find it conveniently easy to laugh at the efforts of the literary Marxists." Rideout, *The Radical Novel in the United States*, 2. Rideout underscores Sinclair's cultural importance but insists he "has never been a great creative novelist." Rideout, *Radical*, 38.

Lewis's canon did not presage the "passing of capitalism" but instead described a brief—even if an explosive—period of popularly embraced radical literary production.[58]

The most influential and successful of these novels was Sinclair's *The Jungle*. An astounding commercial success, it became associated with the passage of the 1906 Pure Food and Drug Act. Billed by Sinclair as the *Uncle Tom's Cabin* of his generation, *The Jungle* became an object of similar critical scorn. Sinclair's contemporaries condemned the book for its factual inaccuracies and for being one of many "socialist tracts" written "in the guise of fiction."[59] This indictment shaped the future reception of Sinclair's work when it received mention at all.[60] Recent commentators continue to struggle with *The Jungle*'s status as a novel. Its tone, sentimentality, and didacticism pose obstacles to engaging it seriously. Taking up the novel in strictly pedagogical terms, instructors debate whether they can "teach the good without tripping on the aesthetically bumpy ground where art seems uncomfortably close to propaganda."[61] Largely absent from these discussions is any acknowledgement of Sinclair's aesthetics, an omission justified by Sinclair's own insistence on characterizing his work as both journalism and propaganda.[62] Cecelia Tichi rightly observes that "no muckraker text was plumbed for its cultural symbol" or for its "types of ambiguity."[63]

---

58. Sinclair Lewis, "The Passing of Capitalism," 280.

59. "Recent Fiction," 570.

60. Very little serious literary criticism on *The Jungle* can be found prior to the 1980s. Those who did mention the novel deplored its form and downplayed its political efficacy. In a study of popular fiction published in 1950 and continually reprinted until the early 1960s, James David Hart represented the view of many of his scholarly contemporaries when he dismissed *The Jungle* for its naturalist excesses and muckraking diatribes. Devoting scant attention to the novel, Hart concludes: "Though Sinclair wanted to change the public mind, he succeeded mainly in turning its stomach." Hart, *The Popular Book*, 220.

61. Castronovo, "Teaching the Good," 168. Here Castronovo accounts for the more widely held anxieties about teaching Sinclair. In the introduction to his edited version of *The Jungle*, he addresses the thorny issue of Sinclair's aesthetics by noting that Sinclair's "most famous novel sought to counteract what he saw as the ruling class's lock upon aesthetic representation." Castronovo, introduction to *The Jungle*, xxi.

62. Those who have engaged Sinclair's novel as a work of literature generally view it through the lenses of naturalism or ecocriticism. Some key examples include Dickstein, *A Mirror in the Roadway*, 41–50; Rosendale, "In Search of Left Ecology's Useable Past"; and Tavernier-Courbin, "*The Call of the Wild* and *The Jungle*."

63. Tichi, "Exposé and Excess," 823. Even when Morris Dickstein sympathetically attends to its literary features, he concedes that "Sinclair's method is too journalistic to make *The Jungle* a great city novel." Dickstein, *Mirror*, 44.

This critical legacy clashes with *The Jungle*'s and other politically committed turn-of-the-century novels' celebration of aesthetic experience as a phenomenon that could impede or foster the development of a radical political consciousness. Sinclair's Packingtown, the meatpacking district of Chicago, is an artistically loaded space where characters become overwhelmed by the magnitude of industrialization and find a modicum of *gemütlichkeit* in musical expression. Radical novels generally affirmed an inherent bond between art and politics, as documented by those who studied the sociological dimensions of revolutions. "A revolution is not productive of results until it has sunk into the soul of the multitude," Gustave Le Bon observed, further maintaining that only aesthetic and cultural experiences "unchained the passions confined by the bonds of ages."[64] Accordingly, the protagonists of these novels appear predisposed for revolutionary activity when they exhibit, as Blair Carrhart does in Isaac Kahn Friedman's *By Bread Alone* (1901), a strong desire to "read Shakespeare" and other literary works when they should "have been studying philosophy" or more practical subjects.[65] Similarly, Avis Everhard in London's dystopic *The Iron Heel* (1915) employs a form of subterfuge that she describes as the creation of "a new art."[66] For this group of writers, art could reinforce or dismantle the structures of feeling that made radical political transformation unthinkable.

Demanding a new kind of novel and "Socialism in America!," *The Jungle* ambitiously calls for an aesthetic and political transformation rather than for a reform of the meatpacking industry.[67] Deploying the conventions of American literary realism and naturalism, it rebels against the scientific verisimilitude of naturalism and against the fundamental legal and economic institutions of the United States. This revolt is not predicated on ratiocination but on feeling. As an author committed to reclaiming Stowe's sentimental power, Sinclair generated "new impulses for men to thrill to, new perils for them to overcome, new sacrifices for them to make, new joys for them to experience."[68] In *The Jungle*, I argue, two opposing sentiments embody the challenges to and possibilities of radical political transformation: industrial wonder and left nostalgia. Packingtown, for Sinclair's characters, presents itself as a place of boundless wonder that suppresses the alienation elicited by

---

64. Le Bon, *The Psychology of Revolution*, 24.
65. Friedman, *By Bread Alone*, 3.
66. London, *The Iron Heel*, 275.
67. Sinclair, *The Jungle*, 328. Hereafter cited parenthetically as *Jungle*.
68. Sinclair, *Mammonart*, 10.

industrial labor. Wonder, in *The Jungle*, has the capacity to keep workers in a state of perpetual enchantment where neither the future nor the past can be imagined. Only nostalgia, or the immigrant's recollection of the homeland lost in space and in time, can break the spell of this wonder. This left nostalgia constructs a collective home in the world, consisting of "a national, or rather international, system for the providing of the material needs of men" (*Jungle*, 323). To outline *The Jungle*'s revolutionary aesthetic project, I revisit Sinclair's propagandistic theory of art, clarify wonder's role in sustaining the fantasies of industrial capitalism, and establish how left nostalgia forges bonds of solidarity among workers in the novel.

In a set of serialized essays that he later self-published as a collection in 1924 under the title of *Mammonart*, Sinclair outlined his own theory of art and took aim at Harvard's Irving Babbit and other conservative literary critics committed to creating a reactionary tradition of American literature. Like Lewis, Sinclair proposed his own rival canon of "rebel artists, who have failed to serve their masters."[69] Throughout *Mammonart* he infamously refers to his own novels and every work of art as propaganda, asserting that it all produces "ideas of truth and desirable behavior" that serve the interests of a particular economic class.[70] Although he defined propaganda as the "effort directed systematically toward the gaining of support for an opinion or course of action," Sinclair's elastic understanding of it vexed both sympathetic and skeptical readers.[71] Propaganda, by his account, is synonymous with an orthodox Marxist understanding of ideology insofar as he insists art can reproduce the relations of production. When Sinclair asserts that art can alter these relations by "*modifying other personalities, inciting them to changes of feeling, belief and action,*" he ascribes a different meaning to propaganda.[72] Theodor Adorno usefully distinguishes between "committed" and "tendentious" art, but Sinclair's understanding of propaganda straddles this distinction. Like committed art, Sinclair's art-as-propaganda works "at the level of fundamental attitudes," but it does not contain an "inherently ambiguous" content.[73] He unequivocally champions socialism in *The Jungle*, but socialism is not broken down tendentiously into a set of precisely articulated principles. It is instead described as a state of "human existence"

---

69. Ibid., 8.
70. Ibid., 10.
71. Ibid., 10a.
72. Ibid., 10.
73. Adorno, "Commitment," 180.

allowing for "the free development of every personality, unrestricted by laws save those of its own being" (*Jungle*, 319).

Written fifteen years before *Mammonart*, *The Jungle* executed many of Sinclair's aesthetic principles in practice before he critically defined them. It established his reputation as a muckraker, but it is hardly a piece of descriptive journalism. This lengthy novel contains a strong narrative arc that follows Jurgis Rudkus, a Lithuanian émigré, as he struggles to adapt to his new surroundings in Chicago. After he and his extended family move to the city, they all secure employment in the meatpacking industry. As Sinclair meticulously describes their working conditions, he explores Jurgis's emerging political consciousness from a pliant meatpacker into a socialist revolutionary. By taking his readers upon this psychological journey, Sinclair examines both the artistry of capitulation and the aesthetics of antagonism.

The creation of consensual exploitation is an art in *The Jungle*. When Jurgis and his wife Ona encounter Packingtown for the first time, they do not recoil in horror at its sight. Looking down upon the mass of buildings and through the miasma, they discover that "all the sordid suggestions of the place were gone—in the twilight it was a vision of power" (31). They become intoxicated by the slaughterhouse's force: "it seemed a dream of wonder, with its tale of human energy, of things being done, of employment for thousands upon thousands of men, of opportunity and freedom, of life and love and joy" (31). Their experience is at once both in keeping and out of step with nineteenth-century and early-twentieth-century portrayals of industrialization. On the one hand, factories often opened their doors to visitors who would be awestruck by the scale of the facilities and the workforce. These buildings towered as modern marvels and testaments to the infinite potential of engineering and industrial mass labor. Workers experienced these factories in starkly different terms. Jurgis's perception of Packingtown conforms more to a visitor's than to a typical laborer's impression of the factory. These buildings, as one mill worker testified, did not represent progress but "a constant race from morning to night after this machinery."[74] The historian David E. Nye argues that both responses contributed to the development of what he refers to as the "industrial sublime," which "combined the abstraction of a man-made landscape with the dynamism of moving machinery and powerful forces" to shock and awe the viewer.[75]

---

74. Howard, "Testimony of Robert S. Howard," 25.
75. Nye, *American Technological Sublime*, 126.

Jurgis and Ona, however, do not fear the sight of Packingtown even before "all the sordid suggestions of the place were gone"; they reverentially gaze upon the stockyards below and anticipate the pleasures of working among a mass of human beings (31). Their reaction to the vastness of Packingtown lacks that "degree of horror," terror, or fear essential to any sublime experience, as both Burke and Kant understood it.[76] Even George Santayana, who emphasized the ecstasy of the sublime more so than Burke or Kant, conceded that "subdued and objectified terror is what is commonly regarded as the essence of the sublime."[77] Having just strolled past dilapidated houses and inhaled "a ghastly odor," Jurgis and Ona could hardly deem the Packingtown landscape beautiful either (*Jungle*, 30). Rather than experiencing the beautiful or the sublime, they experience an extraordinary sense of wonder.

Wonder may be only a diminutive derivation of the sublime, akin to what Burke deems the "inferior effects" of "admiration, reverence, and respect."[78] But wonder possesses its own distinct set of aesthetic properties that can produce, like the sublime, a range of ancillary affects, including awe and reverence. In the seventeenth and eighteenth centuries, Philip Fisher maintains, wonder shed its purely theological meaning to denote a particular encounter with "the unusual" that "leads to pleasure rather than fear."[79] It is "a sudden experience of an extraordinary object that produces delight."[80] Wondrous events make one cognizant of the finitude of the self in the presence of boundless power, but, unlike experiences of the sublime, they do not threaten the subject with annihilation. Instead the subject becomes aware, as Kant explains, that one's "connection with that world . . . is not merely contingent . . . but universal and necessary."[81] While the sublime remains impenetrable to reason, the wondrous can be known, can inspire curiosity, and can be integrated with the subject.

That Jurgis and his family, when they first visit the stockyard grounds, experience wonder defies expectation. Sinclair acknowledges as much when he notes that "our friends were not poetical," so the sight of thousands of cattle being slaughtered by hundreds of overworked men

---

76. Burke, *A Philosophical Inquiry into the Origin of our Ideas of the Sublime and the Beautiful*, 53.
77. Santayana, *The Sense of Beauty*, 147.
78. Burke, *Philosophical*, 53.
79. Philip Fisher, *Wonder, the Rainbow, and the Aesthetics of Rare Experience*, 48.
80. Ibid., 55.
81. Kant, *Critique of Practical Reason*, 269.

"suggested to them no metaphors of human destiny" but evoked only "the wonderful efficiency of it all" (34). This panorama of slaughter spurs Sinclair's own philosophical meditation surrounding "the hog-squeal of the universe" (37). This cosmic hog-squeal, which oxymoronically bears elements of both the comic and the sublime, functions as a conceit for the way industrial production sacrifices the individual for the sake of profit. But for Jurgis, this bloody drama of mass production unfolds "like a wonderful poem to him" (38). What could be a sublime experience of terror and foreboding instead becomes an awesome opportunity to join a mass army of industrial workers. Sinclair's simile aptly represents the power of industrial wonderment: like poetry, it describes an act of creative possibility that exceeds the limitations of the self.[82]

Sinclair's treatment of wonder moves beyond the realm of straightforward didacticism to wrestle with the structures of feeling that make laborers willing participants in the industrial process. His account of Jurgis's industrial wonderment clashes with the Marxian account of alienation: the condition of the propertyless worker who must sell his labor as a commodity. As the laborer becomes devalued, the products of labor—things—correspondingly increase in value. Wage workers thus become alienated from their labor, because, as they produce more efficiently and efficaciously, the less valuable their service becomes. Industrial technology compounds this process of alienation by further accelerating the working process. In an 1887 landmark study edited by George E. McNeill, *The Labor Movement: The Problem of To-Day*, the Knights of Labor maintain that "the steam, electricity, chemistry and productive machinery are competitors, and not co-operators" with the wage workers, as "the conditions of his employment are debasing, and not elevating."[83] Marx puts a finer aesthetic point on alienation when he insists that labor "produces . . . deformity for the worker."[84] The worker cannot be the subject that appreciates either beauty or the sublime; he or she is instead an object of sublimity that recedes into the industrial background.

Wonder structures Jurgis's wider apprehension and engagement with the world. After becoming apprised of the way the managers accelerate

---

82. Sinclair's alignment of poetry with the wonder of industrial production mobilizes the Aristotelian idea of *poïesis* to denote production or activities directed at realizing an external end, including craftwork, poetry, and rhetoric.
83. McNeill, *The Labor Movement: The Problem of To-Day*, 455.
84. Marx, *Economic and Philosophical Manuscripts*, 124.

the production line, he marvels "at their speed and power as if they had been wonderful machines" (56). Even after joining the line, "he rather enjoyed it" and could not believe that the other "men *hated* their work" (57). His wonderment hardens him against the union organizing in the plant, so he "had no sympathy with such ideas as this—he could do the work himself, and so could the rest of them, he declared, if they were good for anything" (58). Sinclair underscores that many laborers took "an interest in the work they did" even though "they had no share in it," and this realization "was wonderful, when one came to think of it" (199). Through wonder, Jurgis and many of his fellow workers cathect with the abstract boundlessness of laissez faire economics, depriving them of the ability to feel empathy for their fellow laborers. It prevents them from perceiving the injustices that surround them. Even after Jurgis sustains an injury of his own, he continues to experience the wondrous power of "an unseen hand" that drags him to a fertilizer plant, where he continues to labor in deplorable conditions (126). Industrial wonder's close association with the unseen hand of capitalism represents an agency capable of transcending the limitations of the self and the body. The trope of the wonderful "unseen hand" surfaces later in the novel in the form of the judge and politician Pat "Growler" Callahan, who serves as a metonym for machine politics "whereby the packers held down the people of the district" (152). In *The Jungle*, capitalism works not by appealing to an individual's self-interest or through a disenchantment of the world, as Sinclair's contemporary Max Weber argued, but through a process of derationalization, transforming scientific and managerial processes into awesome modern marvels.[85] Capitalism, for Sinclair, creates willing disciples by recasting instances of pedestrian exploitation as opportunities to experience capitalist transcendence.

The power of wonder, along with its attendant promises of boundless production and limitless consumption, rests upon its ability to shape the way subjects perceive their world. The problem of economic exploitation in *The Jungle* is aesthetic as much as it is political in character. Antagonism becomes possible when subjects see their world differently; this realization requires an aesthetic revolution. The countervailing force that eventually enables Jurgis to break the spell of industrial wonder is left nostalgia. Sinclair introduces the dialectical dynamic between wonder and nostalgia in the novel's first chapter, which revolves around Jurgis's and Ona's *veselija*, the traditional Lithuanian wedding feast, held

---

85. See Weber, "Science as a Vocation."

in the back room of a saloon. The newlyweds are overwhelmed, and Ona looks upon her surroundings with "fearful eyes of wonder" (10). A small orchestra transforms the saloon into "a fairy place, a wonderland, a little corner of the high mansions of the sky" (8). As a ceremony that weds them as much to each other as to the reproduction of the relations of production, their wedding and reception elicit a wondrous anticipation further amplified by the sounds of Tamoszius Kuszleika's violin and accompanying orchestra. Prolepsis gives way to analepsis when the musicians play "passionate and rebellious" music that Sinclair explains "is their music, music of home" (10).

These folk songs exemplify the agrarian communitarian principles evoked by the *veselija*, a ceremony whereby all attendees contribute financially to the celebration. Immigrant nostalgia for Lithuania counterbalances the wonder of marriage, and the older guests dance and dress in a manner "reminiscent in some detail of home" (13). While wonderment atomizes the individual participants by drawing our attention to the emotional states of particular characters, nostalgia fosters collective cohesion among the people by emphasizing how generations of Lithuanians celebrated together. This movement from monadic wonder to communal nostalgia culminates with the *acziavimas*, an approximately four-hour dance where all "the guests form a great ring . . . in a circle" (15). Every man may also dance with the bride, honoring a custom that, in a carnivalesque fashion, momentarily upsets the normative expectations for marriage. The chapter's conclusion portends both the threat capitalism poses to these Lithuanian laborers and the threat nostalgia for these earlier communal bonds poses to capitalism. Many of the attendees cannot afford to contribute their fair share because their wages remain so low, but their stubborn commitment to this tradition is framed as an act of defiance. "The *veselija* has come down to them from a far-off time," Sinclair explains, which enables them to "break [their] chains" before returning to their toil and living "upon the memory" of this ceremony for the rest of their lives (16). To threaten this tradition would be to unleash this rebellious spirit, supplanting an immigrant nostalgia that assuages the wrongs these laborers endure with a left nostalgia that would redress them. Marija briefly experiences this loss and a concomitant desire to restore the community that industrial capitalism gradually destroyed, discovering her "state of wonderful exaltation . . . was leaving" (16–17).

Wonder loses its hold on Jurgis only after his son Antanas dies. The circumstances surrounding Antanas's passing resemble the deaths of young children featured in many other sentimental and naturalist novels. Some measure of sympathy is elicited in the characters, Aniele and Marija, who mourn his death. Antanas's fate has a naturalist, predestined quality insofar as it is the necessary outcome of living in the depraved environment of Packingtown. But the book radically departs from these conventions when it tracks the "peculiar way" Jurgis reacts to the death of his son (202). With his wife and all of his children dead, he renounces his obligations to the remaining members of his extended family and his circle of friends. He chases an archetypal nineteenth-century masculine fantasy by assuming the life of a tramp, free from any domestic obligations. After he leaves Chicago for the countryside, "a thought that had been lurking within him, unspoken, unrecognized, leaped into sudden life" (202). He no longer harbors a reverence for the power of industry, and he decides "to be free, to tear off his shackles, to rise up and fight" (203). Here Sinclair foregrounds the classic dyadic tension between the pastoral and the metropolitan. While Populist writers, such as Garland, debunked the facile depictions of rural America as a harmonious and prelapsarian space, Sinclair adapts this conventional symbolism to his own ends. In some measure, Jurgis's life in the country provides him with an asylum, mimicking the quintessential narrative of American republicanism harkening back to Crèvecoeur. "He was a free man now, a buccaneer," and this freedom allows Jurgis to rediscover "his lost youthful vigor, his joy and power that he had mourned and forgotten!" (207).

As a tramp, Jurgis learns to reject what Packingtown taught him to desire, but his story of individualist liberation soon gives way to a communal one. It is not the freedom from women or children that chiefly arouses his political consciousness; it is the nostalgia he feels for his agrarian past that prompts him "to think of himself nowadays" (206). The Midwestern plains remind him of his past life in Eastern Europe. When he smells the countryside, "his heart beat wildly—he was out in the country again!" (203). This moment of return makes him aware of his estrangement from his natal community. He realizes that "for three long years he had never seen a country sight nor heard a country sound," and he rejoices at the thought of finally taking a bath and immersing himself all the way into the water for the first time "since he left Lithuania" (203–4). The attraction of Lithuania arises from its communal transparency in contrast with the fractured and ambiguous relations among the people in the city. Finitude and regression transform the previously deemed infinite wonders of the city into sublime terrors. Jurgis finds himself "venturing even to dream" of a future where he might no longer stink of fertilizer and live the life of a wage slave (205). This nostalgic episode functions as the radical fulcrum of the novel, as he resolves at this moment "to battle with the world" (207). Alternatives to the industrial life he knew in Chicago now become imaginable.

The aesthetic revolution of this novel, however, occurs at the moment it abandons the liberal form and content of the picaresque. After spending time back in Chicago moving from one job to the next, Jurgis stumbles upon a political rally. He initially dismisses the protestors but finds himself seduced by a "young and beautiful" woman who "called him 'comrade'" (285). From this moment, his centrality to the narrative diminishes and the nostalgia permeating the text becomes less individual and more communal in orientation. It is this moment in the novel that generations of critics have chided, because it shifts focus away from Jurgis as an individual to his place within the revolutionary multitude. Far from a failure, this shift represents a generic rupture and an invention of a new revolutionary novel finely calibrated to make its readers sensible of a state of fundamental inequalities. Listening to a charismatic orator, Jurgis becomes overpowered by this new dominant voice, which then assumes control of *The Jungle*. The speaker describes the ceaseless "seeking and striving and yearning" of the working masses and situates this struggle diachronically within "a movement beginning in the far-off past" (291). This gesture backward exemplifies left nostalgia—memories of the past no longer simply haunt the present as "old ghosts beckoning" to the individuals who harbor them but instead become sutured to the present (279). What at first emerges as "a dream of resistance" in the minds and hearts of the working masses "in a flash . . . becomes an act!" (291). This nostalgic yearning to restore the spirit of resistance to the present heralds a sublime revolution "of presences of awe and terror" that renders Jurgis "a mere man no longer" as "all his old hopes and longings" returned to him (291–92). Left nostalgia, in this moment and others, is expressed as a longing to recover a past that throws the self-legitimating narrative of capitalism into a state of crisis. This legitimation crisis in *The Jungle* overturns naturalist mimesis, a genre buttressing the economic status quo with narratives of social Darwinism and other iterations of determinism. At the moment *The Jungle* configures a new "visibility of a common world," it realizes its revolutionary promise, to the chagrin of many reviewers.[86] Sinclair's art-as-propaganda is made manifest: his novel no

---

86. Rancière, *Dissensus*, 167.

longer calls upon its readers to decipher it symptomatically. It boldly announces its revolutionary telos to render it democratically accessible. "To a Socialist," Sinclair instructs his readers directly, "the victory of his class was his victory" (297).

The novel's final chapters oscillate from political speeches back to Jurgis's home life, which "reminded him of his old happiness," but this nostalgia now drives his desire to take "a plunge into the Socialist movement" (313). His and other workers' unabated wishes to recover the happiness of the past compel them to "Organize! Organize! Organize!" in the hope of creating a better future (327). This unifying imperative allows Sinclair to take aim at the vestiges of the bourgeois novel, decrying the "Individualism" that demanded workers "obey the orders of a steel magnate" (308). Marriage under capitalism, in the words of the agitator Nicholas Schliemann, only protected "the predatory man's exploitation of the sex-pleasure" (315). This radical dismantlement of the dominant cultural and economic institutions of the early twentieth century creates new "wonders to be discovered" no longer tethered to industrial exploitation (313). Sinclair finally challenges his readers to abandon their generic expectations; his novel does not end in marriage or in death. It ends with the sense of a beginning that calls upon its readers to embrace a "radical Democracy left without a lie with which to cover its nakedness!" (328). Celebrating this ending means rallying around Sinclair's aesthetic revolution and a radically different American novel.

THE INFINITELY DEMANDING POLITICS OF *THE BOMB*

In the third volume of *Contemporary Portraits* (1920), Frank Harris hails Upton Sinclair as a great American novelist, declaring *The Jungle* "very nearly a masterpiece" but with a few glaring blemishes.[87] One of his main indictments of *The Jungle* stands wholly at odds with those who had condemned its propagandistic qualities. Harris wishes Sinclair had worked the novel's ending "up to crescendo to flaming revolt."[88] When leveling this criticism, he may have had in mind his own radical novel, *The Bomb*, which revolves around the Haymarket Affair. Although it did not find as large an audience as *The Jungle*, *The Bomb* secured a prominent place in

---

87. Frank Harris, *Contemporary Portraits*, 15.
88. Ibid.

the radical literary canons promoted by various socialist and anarchist periodicals across the United States and Europe. Sinclair, though expressing dissatisfaction with Harris's later work, included a chapter from *The Bomb* in his edited collection, *The Cry for Justice: An Anthology of the Literature of Social Protest* (1915).[89] This excerpt concluded the section "Revolt" and appeared alongside work by Shelley, Emerson, Whitman, Marx, Ibsen, and Sinclair himself. Harris's appearance in this anthology elevated his standing in the United States' radical literary scene. Despite spending the better part of his early literary career in Britain and publishing *The Bomb* first in London, Harris earned an important place as a radical American author. In a laudatory review of his work for *The Nation*, J. W. Krutch insisted Harris succeeded "by virtue" of his "American 'push.'"[90]

The Bomb offers a salient meditation on insurrectionary violence, reproducing with some measure of fidelity the sentiments of important anarchist thinkers, including Johann Most, Georges Sorel, and Mikhail Bakunin. Harris's left nostalgia for the era of the Chicago anarchists is matched only by the nostalgia the novel's characters express for the actions of their revolutionary predecessors. It imagines a form of international radicalism that calls for armed revolt rather than for a change in electoral representation. Like *The Jungle*, it dismantles the novel's classically liberal subject, but it also challenges its readers to embrace bloodshed. Harris's novel on the Haymarket Affair examines an iteration of anarchism that places an infinite political demand upon the novel's protagonist, who feels compelled to throw a bomb in defiance of the state. The revolution depicted in *The Bomb* rejects all the institutions of the state, from the law to marriage. Unlike *The Jungle*, *The Bomb* never dwells on a folk or immigrant nostalgia for the past or the traditions of Europe, even as it largely describes the lives of émigrés. Harris's characters long to recover lost moments of possibility—those rare episodes when a democratic community may have come into being.

Left nostalgia in *The Bomb*, I argue, foments radical violence through a longing to recapture the spirit of previous uprisings. The aims of these bombers are absolute: all barriers to the creation of this democratic community must be eliminated. At the epicenter of this explosive ultimatum lies the Jacobin tradition that, in the words of Robespierre, identifies terror as "an emanation of virtue" when it is "a consequence of the general

---

89. See Sinclair, *The Cry for Justice*, 281.
90. Krutch, "The Case of Frank Harris," 19.

principle of democracy."[91] This incarnation of left nostalgia horrified nineteenth-century literary luminaries on both sides of the Atlantic—Howells, James, Eliot, and Arnold—and the liberal intellectuals of the vital center who followed them.[92] Twenty-first-century left intellectuals still debate of the efficacy and ethicality of the views expressed by radicals, such as Most in 1884, who insisted "the importance of explosives as an instrument for carrying out revolutions orientated to social justice is obvious."[93] What makes *The Bomb* a perilous read, then, is not the possibility that it may negate "a potential world of different choices," as Castronovo astutely observes of *A Hazard of New Fortunes*, but that it affirms that violence is the only answer to state repression.[94]

The Bomb delivers this revolutionary imperative by transforming the *bildungsroman* into an impressionistic form that nostalgically and anachronistically fosters working-class solidarity. As his political consciousness develops, Harris's protagonist, Rudolph Schnaubelt, questions the legitimacy of the law and abandons his bourgeois pursuit of a wife for the sake of the anarchist cause. Schnaubelt surrenders himself to a form of anarchism that is less about unrestrained freedom than about what the political philosopher Simon Critchley calls "infinite responsibility"—

---

91. Robespierre, "On the Principles of Political Morality That Should Guide the National Convention in the Domestic Administration of the Republic," 115.

92. *The Bomb* has attracted only marginal attention in recent years despite its relative importance to the literary culture of the early twentieth century. The last major literary critic to write about Harris substantially was Everett Carter, who, at the beginning of his career, wrote an essay about the Haymarket Affair in American literature. Carter, "The Haymarket Affair in Literature." He recognizes its importance, noting that it represents the event more exhaustively than either Howells in *A Hazard of New Fortunes* or Robert Herrick in *Memoirs of an American Citizen*. Carter expresses little admiration for Harris's craft, but he recognizes the novel's importance. Writing in the immediate aftermath of the Sacco and Vanzetti trial, Carter rebuffs the modernist dictum of art's for art's sake, insisting that "literature—good literature as well as cheap and sentimental literature—inevitably comes out of the crucible of a national injustice," as illustrated "by the literary reaction to the hanging of four anarchists after a bomb exploded in Haymarket Square." Carter, "Haymarket," 270. The rise of consensus liberalism, however, did not create a welcoming intellectual environment for Harris's work, and it has attracted very few readers since the 1930s.

93. Most, *Science of Revolutionary Warfare*, 1. Žižek urges the left in the twenty-first century to stop wishing for "a decaffeinated revolution, or a revolution which does not smell of revolution" by rehabilitating the transformative power of revolutionary terror. Žižek, *In Defense of Lost Causes*, 158. Violence under these circumstances may be as necessary as it is permissible. Judith Butler and Simon Critchley forcefully repudiate state and revolutionary violence, hoping to imagine "another vision of the future than that which perpetuates violence in the name of denying it." Butler, *Precarious Life*, 18.

94. Castronovo, *Beautiful*, 105.

the duty of the ethical subject to rectify the political injustices suffered by others ahead of one's own self-interests.[95] Whereas left nostalgia in *The Jungle* affectively broke the spell of wonder, in *The Bomb* it becomes a gateway to the revolutionary sublime. Out of his nostalgia for the libratory promises of past revolutions, Schnaubelt throws a bomb at a crowd of policemen, sacrificing his own ethical integrity out of a limitless political responsibility to social and economic justice.

Harris never considered himself an anarchist, even though he flirted with more moderate forms of socialism throughout his adult life. He led an important literary career that spanned several nations and two continents.[96] In London, he worked as a journalist and eventually as the editor of the *Fortnightly Review* and the *Saturday Evening News*. During his editorship of these two periodicals, he befriended and championed the work of George Bernard Shaw and H. G. Wells. His conversations with Shaw and Wells led him to adopt many of the principles of Fabianism—though it is not clear whether he actively participated in the activities of Sidney and Beatrice Webb's socialist reform society. After the First World War, he returned to the United States, where he eventually became a naturalized citizen. In the 1920s, he served as the editor of the American edition of the highly respected *Pearson's Magazine*, where he could continue to promote his brand of moderate socialism.[97]

Written under the radical influence of Shaw and Wells, *The Bomb* established Harris as a novelist in his own right, even if its rendering of nineteenth-century anarchism misses the mark.[98] His interest in the

---

95. Critchley, *Infinitely Demanding*, 93.

96. Harris was born in Galway, Ireland, the son of a Welsh naval officer. After attending a boarding school in Wales for part of his childhood, he ran away to the United States, where he worked as a laborer on a series of jobs until he eventually wound up attending law school at the University of Kansas. His interest in the law sustained him only so long, and he eventually returned to the European continent, where he sought out an academic education in Germany and France before settling in London for a period of time.

97. Harris remained a central fixture of the American and British literary scene until the Second World War, earning him the attention of a few biographers. One of the earliest portraits of Harris came in the form of a 1917 pamphlet by a respected literary critic, Temple Scott. Scott, who wrote prolifically about a wide range of writers from Swift to Poe, deemed Harris a "genius" whose "literary gifts have been undervalued because he has always written as a radical." Scott, *Frank Harris*, 2. The first major biography of Harris appeared in 1931, which declared *The Bomb* "a masterpiece of realism." Tobin and Gertz, *Frank Harris*, 151. A year after *Frank Harris* appeared on bookshelves, Farrar & Reinhart published another biography of him. See Kingsmill, *Frank Harris*. Harris continued to inspire occasional scholarly monographs until the early 1980s.

98. David Weir correctly faults Harris for creating a "historically anomalous" combina-

events of the Haymarket Affair stemmed from a progressive journalistic impulse to get the story right. He travelled to Chicago to gather evidence and review court records and decided to write a novel instead of a journalistic piece based on his findings. First published in London in 1908, *The Bomb* succeeded commercially and even garnered positive reviews in a number of august literary venues despite being banned in parts of the country.[99] Expressing reservations about its anarchist and socialist themes, the *Times Literary Supplement* nevertheless lauded Harris for displaying "a real power of realistic narrative" that "undoubtedly keeps the reader at grips with the story and the characters."[100] Its success in Britain helped Harris secure a U.S. publisher in 1909, Mitchel Kennerley, who published a number of other radical novels. Reviewers in the United States did not receive the novel as warmly as their British counterparts. The *New York Times* railed Harris for not possessing "the story-telling gift in the first place, and, in the second, writ[ing] fiction with a prentice hand."[101] Another review appearing in many regional newspapers bemoaned that while *The Bomb* might pass as "a good piece of newspaper work," it "is not much of a novel."[102] These reviews betrayed their disgust with Harris's politics and his candid treatment of sexuality. The novel, however, earned an entirely different reputation in the radical press. Writing for *Mother Earth*, Alexander Berkman excitedly praised Harris for sympathetically capturing "the spirit of human revolt culminating in the tragedy of the Haymarket . . . with convincing reality."[103] Many in the radical literary community in the United States echoed Berkman's verdict.[104] As late as the 1920s, subsequent publishers of *The Bomb* continued to market it in politically progressive and radical

---

tion of socialism, anarchism, and syndicalism that misrepresents the underlying philosophical principles of these movements. Weir, *Anarchy and Culture*, 111. But this feature of his novel is consistent with other forms of left nostalgia insofar as Goldman and De Leon also radically fused forms of eighteenth-century republicanism (e.g., their appraisals of Paine and Madison) to nineteenth-century anarchism and socialism to narrate their revolutionary histories.

99. Harris was the victim of some politically motivated criticism that resulted in the banning of his first novel by the Birmingham Library. See Tobin and Gertz, *Frank Harris*, 155.
100. Lancaster, Review of *The Bomb*, 446.
101. "The Haymarket Tragedy," *New York Times*, February 27, 1909.
102. "Haymarket Tragedy in Fiction," *Springfield Republican* (Springfield, MA), February 28, 1909.
103. Berkman, "Review of *The Bomb*," 19.
104. Lucy Parsons was the significant exception to this rule. She resented the way Harris depicted her husband as an obtuse radical thinker.

publications, as evidenced by an advertisement that appeared in an issue of *The Crisis*, which billed it as a "realistic novel of the Chicago riots . . . very significant today."[105]

Harris prefaces his novel by declaring that "the jubilation of the capitalistic press" expressed over the execution of the Haymarket anarchists must be counterbalanced by a more sympathetic account of the incident and the events preceding it.[106] What follows this opening observation is a meditation on historiography. He must contend with a corrupted archive filled with reports "from American newspapers [that] were bitterly one-sided" except for those by labor leaders, who provided "little islets of facts" among "the sea of lies" (5). A number of nineteenth-century histories of the affair and the trial would have been available to Harris, but these accounts made no pretense of neutrality even if they claimed objectivity. They celebrated the verdict and the sentencing for demonstrating that the country "is capable of protecting itself from the insidious assaults of enemies who seek its destruction under guises calculated to conceal the criminal."[107] Those who sympathized with the defendants repudiated any act of revolutionary violence and instead chastised the legal proceedings for convicting eight men for a crime the court acknowledged they did not directly commit.[108] These exponents speculated that, as "the real author is still unknown," the bomber could have "belonged to the Pinkertons or to some other source of *agents provocateurs*" employed by the government to provide a pretext for a "CONTRIVED . . . JUDICIAL ASSASSINATION of the accused."[109] Harris wanted to exonerate the men convicted, but he also went a step further by offering a justification for the bombing.

He labels his book "a history" but concedes "there are no facts to go upon" (*Bomb*, 6). Memory and affection for the deeds of his subjects, he insists, will produce a narrative far more true than any empirically based study of the newspaper accounts and the trial documents. The factual accounts are themselves delusions, or fictions bearing trumped-up subtitles such as "Seven Dangling Nooses for the Dynamite Fiends."[110] It is not that "everything is a fiction," but that his novel can become a new way of what

---

105. "Books Worth Reading," 190.
106. Harris, *The Bomb*, 5. Hereafter cited parenthetically as *Bomb*.
107. *Anarchy at an End*, 124.
108. They were ultimately convicted of provoking the attack because the prosecution could not definitively connect any of them to the act itself.
109. Leon Lewis, *The Facts Concerning the Eight Condemned Leaders*, 14.
110. *Anarchy at an End*, 1.

Rancière describes as "connecting the presentation of facts and forms of intelligibility."[111] Where the dominant history sees only senseless evil, Harris wants the Haymarket Affair to render visible the violence of capital and to "remind the reader of the value of sympathy with ideas which he perhaps dislikes" (*Bomb*, 6). Although the foreword is not overtly nostalgic, it laments that the Haymarket Affair has become estranged not just from America's national memory but from the international community's consciousness as well. The novel keeps the story of the Haymarket Affair alive, reading more like a hagiography than apologia.

Becoming more demonstratively nostalgic, the opening chapters reproduce the retrospective architecture of the foreword. The entire narrative is a testimony told from the perspective of Schnaubelt, one of the suspects allegedly responsible for the Haymarket bombing who managed to elude the authorities and flee the country. Schnaubelt, on the verge of dying from consumption in a state of exile in Switzerland, records his fond recollections of Louis Lingg—a "born rebel" that he believes was "the greatest man that ever lived" (9). He freely admits that he has forgotten many of the trivial details associated with the Haymarket Affair but insists that "memory is in itself an artist" capable of rendering a far more faithful portrait of what "happened long ago" (10). Even though Lingg instructed him not to dwell on the past, Schnaubelt yearns to return to a time when he could inhabit the same space as his fallen idol. In contrast, he expresses very little love for his hometown of Lindau. Schnaubelt suffers from a type of nostalgia markedly different from the nostalgia chiefly associated with homesickness. It instead reflects a sentiment best expressed by James Creelman, who insisted in 1908 that "Radicalism was suffering from moral nostalgia."[112] They longed for those moments in the late nineteenth century when leaders, such as Powderly and Bryan, remained ideologically faithful and commanded large crowds of auditors. Schnaubelt similarly yearns for the time when Lingg "spoke with strange authority, and with a still nobler spirit than Caesar's" to the laborers of Chicago (142). But he also experiences a curious nostalgia for the time in his life when "America" still "seemed to call" him (15). He can no longer harbor the hope that he might find justice and equality in the United States but wishes he could experience that anticipatory promise again.

Schnaubelt recalls when he first arrived in New York as an educated member of the German middle class with an unwavering faith in his self-

---

111. Rancière, *Politics*, 38.
112. Creelman, "Mr. Bryan Explained," 364.

reliance. Falling into a state of abject poverty, he slowly loses his faith in liberal individualism. Through the beneficence of others, he secures temporary employment as a day laborer and construction worker. Unlike Horatio Alger's lionized Ragged Dick, who climbs the social ladder with the aid of economically superior benefactors, Schnaubelt receives help only from fellow members of the working class: a day laborer offers him a place to sleep, a fellow German émigré puts him in touch with a newspaper interested in publishing his writing, and an Irish sex worker rescues him from the hands of the police. He nevertheless celebrates his individual pluck until he participates in the construction of the Brooklyn Bridge. He vividly describes the horrors of working at great depths and the physical strain of the decompression process—an experience that tempts him to revel in his own resolve until he watches a fellow worker die excruciatingly from the bends. At this moment, Schnaubelt "was recalled to thinking life . . . by seeing a huge Swiss workman fall down one morning as if he were trying to tie his arms and legs in knots" (39). He then collapses, "bathed in blood" (40). This man's death convinces him to assume greater political responsibility for the fate of his laboring comrades. He begins writing for Dr. Goldschmidt, a socialist newspaper editor in New York. Pitching a story to him, he learns that he "had gone a long way in thought during [his] year in New York" after realizing that "now Plato and his Republic sounded ridiculous" to him (51). Schnaubelt abandons the tenets of the liberal education he acquired in Bismarck's Germany and embraces socialism, followed by anarchism. He adopts the view that "humanity was separated into two camps—the 'Haves' and the 'Have-nots'" (66).

Schnaubelt relocates to Chicago, where much of the novel explores the working conditions of the Chicago industries and the radical intellectual culture nourished by *The Alarm* and *Arbeiter-Zeitung* newspapers. Harris describes the conversations that take place at meetings of the Chicago Lehr and Wehr Verein, a radical teaching club, facilitated by the anarchists. During these discussions, Schnaubelt's voice recedes into the background to open a space for a host of radical orators to level indictments of the state. No facet of government is spared from their critique, as they cite the innumerable ways it protects business interests ahead of the rights of its people. Lingg, whom Schnaubelt finds especially persuasive, sarcastically declaims that while the French have begun regulating the use of lead, "the democratic American Government pays no attention to such matters; the health of workingmen doesn't concern it" (100). These fulminations culminate with a larger dismal of American jurisprudence. At the end of a wide-ranging conversation on Socrates' vision of republican laws as "faint reflections of the eternal, divine laws which . . . should be obeyed," Lingg objurgates the notion that any law could be written to protect the weak from the strong (139). "Laws are made for the protection of property," he declares. "They are made by the strong in their own interest; the wolf wants to be assured peaceable enjoyment of his 'kill'"(141). Although stripped of any philosophical complexity, this statement colorfully expresses the widely held anarchist view of the state as "the economic master of its servants."[113] The wrong wrought by capitalist exploitation cannot be readdressed through a lawsuit or reform; revolution is the only viable course of action for Lingg.

Lingg's forceful repudiation of the law, however, cannot fully legitimate the instigation of violent revolution. This revolution becomes imaginable, for Schnaubelt and others, when tethered to a broader left nostalgia for past revolutions. As in the writing by de Cleyre, Goldman, Parsons, and Most, Harris's cast of anarchists revive the "spirit of the American revolution" (*Bomb*, 152). The Declaration of Independence, a document representing direct action unmitigated by the state, figures prominently in the thinking of Lingg. He underscores this point at the close of the novel when the Haymarket anarchists stand trial for their alleged involvement in the bombing. The judge overseeing their case reminds them that any resistance of the law is a crime, but Lingg rebukes him in court. "Our Declaration of Independence," Lingg avows, "is a higher authority than Judge Gary, and it asserts that resistance to tyranny, to unlawful authority, is right" (282). The state forfeited its claim to the Declaration when it permitted policemen to beat an assembly of peaceful protesters for exercising their freedom of speech. They nevertheless feel estranged from the Declaration, acknowledging "that native-born Americans would claim for themselves rights and privileges which they would not accord to foreigners" (65). As immigrants unable to lay a nationalist claim on the U.S. Revolution, Harris's anarchists place it in an international context. Lingg notes that "ever since the French Revolution there has been an approach towards equality" (103). He brings this spirit back by provocatively asking, "Why should there not be another revolution, and a similar approach towards equality . . . ?" (104).[114] For the anarchists in *The Bomb*, what matters

---

113. Goldman, *Anarchism*, 65.

114. Harris parts ways with political theorists such as Burke and later, Arendt, who insisted on drawing a clear delineation between the U.S. Revolution and the European revolutions that followed it. Arendt insists the U.S. Revolution sought only to establish

most was the U.S. revolutionaries' expression of equality through direct action: they declared their independence from a state as equals. For Lingg and Schnaubelt, the American and French Revolutions did not fail; the republics that followed them did.

Lingg and Schnaubelt adopt a philosophical position resembling Critchley's theory of anarchist ethics, which places an infinite demand upon the subject to put the interests of the politically disenfranchised before the subject's own. He characterizes the ethical subject as "a split subject" because it can never meet its ethical expectations.[115] This subject has an obligation to promote "the cultivation of the other's freedom" ahead of one's own self-interests.[116] Affect, as much as reason, drives the subject to redirect the desire for personal liberation toward fulfilling its infinite responsibility to others, so that through a process of sublimation the subject experiences "satisfaction without repression."[117] For Critchley, this process is necessarily "committed to non-violence."[118] Lingg and Schnaubelt believe they have a limitless duty to ensure the political "dreams of to-day are the realities of tomorrow," but they conclude that violence cannot be avoided (*Bomb*, 192). In *The Bomb*, the fissure dividing the ethical subject grows out of the regrettable need for revolutionary violence—an act that requires Schnaubelt to make ethical compromises for the sake of politics.

Harris's anarchist contemporaries shared Critchley's aversion to the killing of other human beings, but they saw no other way to achieve their political aims. Nonviolent protest and lobbies for reform proved ineffectual, and they could not tolerate the senseless and ceaseless murder of their fellow laborers and activists at the hands of the police and the Pinkertons. Even the incendiary Most, who wrote bomb-making instruction manuals, expressed reservations over violence. He repudiated the "ugly caricature" of the anarchist as a figure holding "a dagger in one hand, a torch in the other, and all his pockets brimful with dynamite-bombs."[119] He maintains that "the anarchists are no blood-hounds" and have "no lust for murder," but "they carry on a revolutionary agitation,

---

liberty and freedom; it did not stand for social equality. This distinction allows her to differentiate the U.S. Revolution from the European revolutions of 1789 and 1848. See *Revolution*, 37–78.

115. Critchley, *Infinitely*, 63.
116. Ibid., 93.
117. Ibid., 71.
118. Ibid., 147.
119. Most, *The Social Monster*, 1.

because they know that the power of a privileged class has never yet been broken by peaceable means."[120] Synthesizing the views of Proudhon and Kautsky, Georges Sorel acknowledges the infinite or sublime ethical obligation to liberate the proletariat. Only a war waged by the proletariat "bound to end in their triumph or enslavement" will elicit this "sentiment of sublimity."[121] For Sorel, however, this ethical sublimity is specifically expressed "with *violence enlightened by the idea of the general strike*."[122]

To justify violent revolt, Harris emphasizes that love, not revenge, motivates Schnaubelt to take up the bomb. Lingg emerges as an attractive figure in no small part because of "his infinite kindness of nature," a man who "was singularly considerate and sympathetic to every form of weakness" (*Bomb*, 187). This quality attracts Schnaubelt, who abandons his romantic partner Elise after Lingg "smiled at [him] with loving-kindness in the deep eyes" (173). When he travels on a small boat with Lingg and his partner Ida—who both do not believe in the institution of marriage—to test some pipe bombs, a love triangle is cemented. They "hope there will be no bomb-throwing needed," but doing so would be an act of love: a moral sacrifice inspired by Lingg's own boundless concern for the general welfare of the working class (170). Schnaubelt conveys his "loving gratitude to him," but his commitment to political violence chiefly emanates from the "wild exhilaration" of knowing that he would give "more than [Lingg] expected" (173). His love for Elise becomes sublimated. He "triumphed over [his] passion," redirecting it toward his revolutionary commitments (197). His rechanneled passions are further facilitated by his left nostalgia. Both before and during the bombing, Schnaubelt remains acutely aware that "Tom Paine, who was the leading spirit of the American revolution; he said that the English race would never be humanized till they had learned in England what war was" (152).

By putting a bomb into the hands of his protagonist, Harris compels his readers to bear witness to Schnaubelt's violent act. After his comrades and fellow immigrant workers are subjected to several waves of police brutality, Schnaubelt and Lingg conclude that violence is a politically necessary response. While *The Bomb* employs the language of melodrama, it examines the rationale behind Schnaubelt's decision to throw a bomb at the Chicago police with psychological complexity. After Albert Parsons delivers a speech, which Harris unfairly characterizes as "clap-

---

120. Ibid., 10.
121. Sorel, *Reflections on Violence*, 210.
122. Ibid., 251.

trap" for advocating reform, the police begin beating the crowd (230). Schnaubelt throws the bomb, and the explosion sends him to the ground. "Men were thrown down in front of me," he recalls, and "I heard groans and cries, and shrieks behind me" (232). Lingg tries to prevent him from examining his surroundings closely, whisking him away from the crowd. When Schnaubelt snatches glimpses of his act, he does not experience elation but feels "sickened" by the sight of "a great pit" formed by the explosion around which lay "pieces of men, in every direction" (233). Although confident in the righteousness of his actions, he cannot celebrate the death of the policemen he killed. He accepts the trauma he must endure as part of his infinite obligation to his fellow workers.

Harris establishes how left nostalgia for the Paris Commune, the French Revolution, and the American Revolution propelled Lingg and Schnaubelt to revolt against the state, and their actions now assume a legacy of their own. Harris does not romanticize the destruction wrought by the bomb, but he praises Lingg's and Schnaubelt's ethical and political commitments. Lingg takes his own life, and Schnaubelt never returns to Elise despite his love for her. The latter remains in a state of exile in Europe and longs to return to Chicago, lamenting that "I was almost completely cut off from the American world" (292). Harris uses the trial to memorialize the men wrongly convicted, noting how Albert and Lucy Parsons made entreaties "to the American people, based on the Declaration of Independence" (297). Although the general public initially reviles the Haymarket anarchists, the trial and the hangings are eventually remembered as examples of "judicial murder" (298). Schnaubelt feels vindicated, knowing that "the bomb thrown in the Haymarket put an end to the bludgeoning and pistolling of unarmed men and women by the police" (326). The monument erected in the memory of the police near the Haymarket was eventually removed because "somehow or other it was generally understood that the police were not the heroes of the occasion" (327). Similar reversals occurred during the course of the French Revolution, and Schnaubelt nears the end of his life feeling confident that his actions will be nostalgically revered "by the destitute and the dispossessed for whom we gave our lives" (329).

The concluding sentiment of *The Bomb* is further borne out in its immediate publication history. In every instance of its reissuing, the novel provided a new generation of radicals with a past to return to nostalgically. Harris's portrayal of the vibrant radical intellectual culture of 1880s Chicago was one that the Wobblies of the early twentieth century would revere and the Marxists of the 1920s and 1930s would reinvent. Perhaps sensing the ongoing potency of *The Bomb*, the editors at the University of Chicago Press recruited a reformed radical, John Dos Passos, to write a preface to their 1963 edition of *The Bomb* aimed at dispelling any sensations of left nostalgia the book might elicit. Writing as a Goldwater Republican, Dos Passos repurposed the novel as an object lesson in the dangers of memorializing the radical past. Noting that "critics have complained of historical inaccuracies," he implores anyone reading it to regard "the notion that society could be shocked into justice and charity by the blowing up of a few policemen" as "delusions relegated to the psychiatric ward."[123] Only a few years after Dos Passos wrote these words, the events of 1968 created a receptive atmosphere to books like the one Harris wrote. In their political manifesto, the Weather Underground claimed the Haymarket martyrs as their forebears, noting that "from this struggle, people all around the world commemorate May Day."[124] And the most recent edition of *The Bomb* includes a celebratory afterward by the prominent anarchist John Zerzan, one of the key figures associated with the black bloc tactics implemented during the 1999 World Trade Organization protests in Seattle. Although embarking upon two different political projects, the left nostalgia and radical internationalism found in *The Jungle* and *The Bomb* remained resilient throughout the twentieth century.

---

123. Dos Passos, introduction to *The Bomb*, iii.
124. Weather Underground Organization, *Prairie Fire*, 82.

CHAPTER 5

COSMOPOLITAN NOSTALGIA IN L. FRANK BAUM'S OZ AND HENRY JAMES'S AMERICA

THE PRECEDING CHAPTERS of this book enumerate the versatile uses of nostalgia during the second half of the nineteenth century. In the 1850s, it registered the absence of a shared sense of national belonging that would become an essential part of Reconstruction-Era culture. During these decades nostalgia amplified racial and regional antagonisms. This affect then became a facet of the literary and movement culture that began in the 1870s and extended into the early twentieth century. While proponents of American literary realism amassed prestige for their craft and sought to cultivate cultural consensus in their work, writing infused with nostalgia stoked the flames of political discord.[1] Cast as both a reactionary and radical feeling, it expressed alienated nationalisms and new non-national political visions. The meaning of nostalgia began changing in the early decades of the twentieth century. Its standing as a mental illness gradually diminished even as it continued to denote both homesickness and the yearning to reclaim a lost past. Reports of homesick soldiers still circulated during the Spanish-American War, but the physician S. Weir Mitchell contended in 1914 that "nostalgia" is "a disorder we rarely see nowadays."[2] Instead of disappearing from the popular vernacular, it began to represent a mass-produced feeling for a simpler

---

1. For an account of how practitioners of American literary realism cultivated its cultural and intellectual distinction, see Barrish, *American Literary Realism, Critical Theory, and Intellectual Prestige*, 16–47.
2. S. Weir Mitchell, "The Medical Department in the Civil War," 1449.

time that generated social cohesiveness even as Goldman, Sinclair, and Harris still enlisted it to engender political dissent. This final chapter argues that this new iteration of nostalgia paradoxically coincided with its role in turn-of-the-century discussions of cosmopolitanism.

Turn-of-the-century essayists regarded nostalgia as an Anglo-Saxon attribute in debates surrounding the future of U.S. imperialism. When U.S. soldiers at war in Cuba and the Philippines described their battle trauma in terms of homesickness, newspaper reports instructed their readers to see this condition as indicative of their unflagging loyalty. They would never go native because when abroad, they could think only of returning home. Wanderlust and nostalgia had often been deemed opposing sentiments, but now they increasingly worked in tandem with one another.[3] As long as Americans abroad remembered that there was no place like home, they could travel and engage in imperial pursuits without risking cultural contamination. When Americans appeared as reluctant travelers with strong affections for home, nostalgia could legitimate U.S. military action and global commercial activity in the name of cosmopolitanism: they engaged the wider world not because they wanted to do so, but because they felt ethically obligated to protect the liberties and free markets of strangers.

What I call *cosmopolitan nostalgia* in this chapter became fully realized in turn-of-the-century literary works. After sketching out the state of nineteenth-century and early-twentieth-century cosmopolitan discourse, this chapter turns to work by L. Frank Baum and Henry James that shaped and reflected upon the changing character of nostalgia and its relationship to cosmopolitanism at the beginning of the twentieth century. Baum and James may very well seem, at first glance, like an odd couple. The fact that their work reached very different audiences, though, establishes how nostalgia intersected with cosmopolitanism within a wide cultural context. Baum's *The Wonderful Wizard of Oz* (1900)—though pitched toward children—quickly became a popular sensation among readers of all ages, and his fantasy novel also clearly emerged out of a broader literary culture. James's "The Jolly Corner" (1908) and *The American Scene* (1905–06; 1907) seize upon this same phenomenon of cosmopolitan nostalgia but in a manner that indicts its place in the mass culture that fed the commercial success of Baum's work. For these reasons, reading Baum and James in tandem provides us

---

3. Nostalgia, especially when associated with the goal of restoring a lost home or past, is generally seen as incompatible with cosmopolitanism. See Boym, *Future*, 41–48; Lasch, *True*, 114–15; and Posnock, *Color and Culture*, 46 and 90–91.

with a much more complete picture of cosmopolitanism and nostalgia at the turn of the century in ways that presage the career of both terms in the twentieth century.

The Wonderful Wizard of Oz's treatment of Kansas and Dorothy Gale revises the conventions of American literary naturalism and the imperial romance to construct a logic of cosmopolitan and nostalgic desire. This desire—or rather Dorothy's efforts to dispel it with the aim of returning home—justifies her fantastical acts of imperial intervention within the affairs of Oz. Both of the works I examine by James explore the dynamics of returning to the United States from Europe after an extended period of self-imposed exile. "The Jolly Corner" explores the intersubjective dynamics of nostalgia and its relationship to cosmopolitanism. *The American Scene* translates these individual experiences into a sociological critique of cosmopolitan nostalgia. Even as Sinclair and Harris continued to believe in nostalgia's capacity for social transformation, James saw how this affect could generate social consensus by translating it into a consumer, as opposed to a political, desire. The cosmopolitan nostalgia engineered by what James deems the "hotel-spirit" transforms this affect into a marketable commodity. Here he anticipates the rise of a dominant form of twentieth-century nostalgia: one used by advertisers to sell products tied to childhood memories. Absorbed by consumer culture, nostalgia possessed a seductive power that could be manufactured profitably on a mass scale. This chapter shifts the discussion on late-nineteenth-century imperialism to establish that a close association emerged between U.S. interventionism and the discourse of cosmopolitanism.

COSMOPOLITANISM BEFORE THE GREAT WAR

In the 1890s before the publication of Baum's *Wonderful Wizard of Oz* and James's *American Scene*, interest in cosmopolitanism flourished in the United States as the country rose to global economic and military power. Cosmopolitanism was then, as it remains now, a protean concept.[4] The word conjured up a range of images, from Kant's vision of a world federation of independent republics striving for perpetual peace

---

4. For accounts of cosmopolitan discourse in the 1890s and the early twentieth century, see Berman, *Modernist Fiction*, 28–53, Cadle, *The Mediating Nation*, and Peyser, *Utopia and Cosmopolis*. For comprehensive surveys of contemporary work on cosmopolitanism, see Amanda Anderson, "Cosmopolitanism, Universalism, and the Divided Legacies of Modernity," 265–89, and Lutz, *Cosmopolitan*, 49–58.

to a privileged traveling citizen of the world. More often than not it was used loosely to denote a sentiment synonymous with wanderlust, a set of ethical obligations to strangers, or an appreciation for cultural diversity. By engaging rather than occupying the wider world, the sentiment and ethos of cosmopolitanism conflicted with the raw imperial ambitions of the McKinley and Roosevelt administrations.[5] At the same time, expansionism sustained the popular and clinical fascination with the countervailing phenomenon of nostalgia. U.S. doctors remained intensely interested in the pathology of nostalgia, finding evidence of epidemics of it among the soldiers who fought in the Spanish-American War.[6] Reports of widespread nostalgia among soldiers serving in Cuba and the Philippines so captured the popular imagination that poets made it a subject of their verse.[7] Psychologists maintained that since nostalgia was an adverse reaction to "the strange and untried," it undermined the migratory impulse to venture out into the world. Many physicians argued that nostalgia frequently afflicted "Americans of Anglo-Saxon stock," so that to suffer from nostalgia marked one as truly American.[8] Cosmopolitanism and nostalgia therefore were two powerful but antithetical reactions to empire building.

Optimism spurred by rapid advances in science and technology reached a delirious high and anticipated greater global economic interdependence, modeled at various World's Expositions, even as domestic producers still reaped the benefits of trade protectionism. "Our planet," wrote Grant Allen, "is daily shrinking—and also expanding. Shrinking as regards distances, and the time taken to traverse them; expanding as regards to the number of nations, races, creeds, and moral codes which the average citizen now begins to cognize or to come in contact with."[9] By the end of the nineteenth century, cosmopolitanism was no longer an abstract ideal but an existing cultural experience. Excitement about this and other societal changes lent itself to further meditations on cosmopolitanism in both a systemic and an individual form.

---

5. Figures as diverse as Andrew Carnegie, William James, and American Peace Society president Edward Atkinson opposed imperialism in the name of internationalism. For an excellent account of how James and other pragmatists wrestled with Kant's work on cosmopolitanism, see Bartel, "Kant's Narrative of Hope in the Gilded Age."

6. There is a wealth of medical and newspaper accounts of nostalgia, especially concerning the Spanish-American War. For one of the most authoritative reports on wartime nostalgia, see Senn, *Medico-surgical Aspects of the Spanish American War*.

7. See, for example, Carr, "Nostalgia," and Rand and Rand, *Random Rimes*.

8. Kline, "The Migratory Impulse v. Love of Home," 79, 76.

9. Allen, "Novels without a Purpose," 228.

As a world system, cosmopolitanism often went hand in hand with capitalism. "The bourgeoisie," Karl Marx and Friedrich Engels famously declared in 1848, "has through its exploitation of the world market given a cosmopolitan character to production and consumption in every country."[10] Free-trade advocates, in fact, insisted on the intrinsic cosmopolitan character of laissez-faire economics, and some suggested that economic interdependence would forestall armed conflict.[11] These views reflected those of Kant, who contended that nation-states brought together by the "spirit of commerce" would find waging war against one another economically disadvantageous.[12] In the years bracketing the war with Spain and the U.S. occupations of Cuba and the Philippines, cosmopolitanism or internationalism became the rallying cry of many antiwar and anti-imperialist politicians, business leaders, and thinkers.[13] Once again Kant's cosmopolitanism had come back from the dead. For instance, Paul S. Reinsch, a political scientist at the University of Wisconsin, channeled Kant by insisting that "concrete and practical" cosmopolitan institutions "be created in order that international action may become real," both to prevent conflict and to facilitate trade among nation-states.[14]

When it bore less-institutional connotations, cosmopolitanism signified a general "sentiment which embraces the whole human race" and the individual cosmopolitan or "citizen of the universe."[15] In the late nineteenth century, people could assume this cosmopolitan identity far more easily from the comfort of their homes by paging through worldly periodicals than they could by traveling around the globe. This understanding of cosmopolitanism, rooted in stoicism, could be applied either approvingly to the privileged elite or derisively to unwanted immigrants.

---

10. Marx and Engels, *Communist Manifesto*, 39. Antonio Gramsci, who further developed the Marxist charge against cosmopolitanism, continues to inform the scholarship, best exemplified in Timothy Brennan's work, that condemns cosmopolitanism for its associations with class privilege and economic exploitation. See Gramsci, *Selections from the Prison Notebooks*, 17–18, and Timothy Brennan, *At Home in the World*.

11. See Elliott, "Ethics of the Tariff Controversy."

12. Kant, "Perpetual Peace," 114.

13. William James wrote one of the more cogent critiques of war for the Association of International Conciliation more than a decade after hostilities had broken out between the United States and Spain; it was later reprinted by *McClure's Magazine* and *Popular Science Monthly*. See James, "The Moral Equivalent of War."

14. Reinsch, "International Administrative Law and National Sovereignty," 17. See also Reinsch, *World Politics at the End of the Nineteenth Century, as Influenced by the Oriental Situation*.

15. Lalor, "Cosmopolitanism," 674.

Jessica Berman describes how periodicals like the *Cosmopolitan* cultivated a privileged sensibility in their readers by catering to their "wanderlust and desire for exotica."[16] This cosmopolitanism also turned inward by stimulating "the local color boom after the Civil War," which put unfamiliar sections of the nation on display for metropolitan readers.[17] Many feared, however, that such a sensibility, coupled with loose immigration policies, would corrupt the national character, for "the cosmopolitanism of a nation made up of fragments of nations of diverse origin, diverse languages and literatures, and diverse and often hostile histories of triumphs and defeats . . . might react disastrously in a great national crisis."[18] Partly to counter these claims, the *Cosmopolitan* and other self-styled national magazines sought "to perpetuate cosmopolitanism as an enlightened national identity."[19] Other writers, following the *Cosmopolitan*'s lead, maintained that "the best cosmopolitan, undoubtedly, is the man of patriotism who visits other countries."[20] Americans, all agreed, must somehow shed their sectional divisiveness and become citizens of the world while remaining loyal patriots.[21]

Into the debate entered Pierre de Coubertin, the principal founder of the International Olympic Committee, who proposed that a proper cosmopolitan or internationalist spirit "should be the state of mind of those who love their country above all, who seek to draw to it the friendship of foreigners by professing for the countries of those foreigners an intelligent and enlightened sympathy."[22] Partly on this basis, he hoped that New York would hold the third Olympic Games, so that "the distinctly cosmopolitan character" of his "enterprise" would be manifest.[23] Coubertin believed not only that patriotism and cosmopolitanism must be congenial sentiments but also that U.S. citizens had realized this spirit more fully than any other people. Indeed, many saw "Americanization" and "cosmopolitan" as one and the same.[24] This sensibility took an ethical turn by implying that every individual had a moral obligation to humanity

---

16. Berman, *Modernist Fiction*, 30.
17. Lutz, *Cosmopolitan*, 12.
18. Atchison, *Un-American Immigration*, 137.
19. Berman, *Modernist Fiction*, 32.
20. Shaw, "Baron Pierre de Courbertin," 435.
21. Martha Nussbaum, more recently, spurred a similar debate about the compatibility between patriotism and cosmopolitanism. See Nussbaum, "Patriotism and Cosmopolitanism."
22. De Coubertin, "Does Cosmopolitan Life Lead to International Friendliness?," 434.
23. De Coubertin, "The Meeting of the Olympian Games," 803.
24. Pillsbury, "The Present Political Outlook," 55.

in toto. Many turn-of-the-century educators reminded their readers that "the perfection, and, above all, the moralization of humanity, was in Kant a cosmopolitan ideal."[25] Arthur Ernest Davies, a professor of philosophy at Ohio State University, felt so confident in the triumph of cosmopolitan ethics that he declared "the morality of the modern man . . . decidedly cosmopolitan."[26]

That cosmopolitanism could be embraced by many of its proponents only if it incorporated an essential sense of U.S. nationality points to a larger dynamic between the universal and the particular that was intrinsic to the concept. Cosmopolitanism necessarily shares a "reciprocal relation to the particular."[27] Exploring this reciprocal relationship, the new cosmopolitans of the late-twentieth and early-twenty-first centuries elevated the place of the particular by insisting on a contingency of cosmopolitanisms, not a universal cosmopolitanism. An expansive lexicon of adjectives describing its iterations took shape: Kwame Anthony Appiah's "rooted cosmopolitanism," Homi K. Bhabha's "vernacular cosmopolitanism," James Clifford's "discrepant cosmopolitanism," and Bruce Robbins's situated or "actually existing cosmopolitanism" are some of the more widely cited.[28] But these formulations have little in common with how cosmopolitanism was assimilated to U.S. nationalism a century ago. During the second half of the nineteenth century, "the notion of the universal . . . remain[ed] contained within, or at least constrained by, particular experiences of the local."[29] The local in this instance often meant national, as best evinced by the *Cosmopolitan*'s commitment to a nationalism enlightened by cosmopolitanism. *The Wonderful Wizard of Oz* negotiates the relationship between the local and global but in an entirely different manner, through the evocation of a decidedly anticosmopolitan sentiment: nostalgia.

WHEN DOROTHY BECAME HISTORY

After reading *The Wonderful Wizard of Oz* or watching Metro-Goldwyn-Mayer's (MGM) 1939 adaptation of it, one may well wonder why Dorothy

---

25. Misawa, *Modern Educators and Their Ideals*, 144.
26. Davies, *The Moral Life*, 171.
27. Posnock, *Color and Culture*, 21.
28. See Appiah, *The Ethics of Identity*, 213–72; Bhabha, "Unsatisfied," 191–207; Clifford, *Routes*, 17–46; and Robbins, "Actually Existing Cosmopolitanism," 1–19.
29. Berman, *Modernist Fiction*, 36.

would ever wish to leave Oz. For those who would question her desire, Baum provides a pointed, albeit humorous, answer. When the Scarecrow confesses to Dorothy just hours after befriending her that he "cannot understand why you should wish to leave this beautiful country and go back to the dry, gray place you call Kansas," she simply replies, "That is because you have no brains."[30] Her response has not stopped commentators from finding fault with her desire to return home. Seeing Kansas as "hell," Salman Rushdie insists that such a radical story of escape cannot possibly end on such a reactionary note; instead, he argues, in her heart "Oz finally became home" for Dorothy.[31] Still, her desire—her nostalgia, or homesickness—can hardly be dismissed when it animates one of the most powerful and culturally significant ideas imagined in Oz. And what is Oz's big idea?

To answer this question, only the outcomes of Dorothy's visit to Oz need to be recounted: she celebrates the differences of strangers, liberates oppressed peoples from the arbitrary rule of what amount to petty regional warlords, and deposes an ineffectual dictator to install a federation of peoples ruled by the Scarecrow. No mere escapist tale, this is Immanuel Kant's bedtime story about the "wild and fanciful" idea of cosmopolitanism.[32] Yet, paradoxically, this idea is realized in *The Wonderful Wizard of Oz* through its disavowal—as a consequence of the nostalgic desire to return to and remain at home.

Vexing countless readers of *The Wonderful Wizard of Oz*, Baum—who explored the world at home by repeatedly visiting the World's Columbian Exposition of 1893 while residing in Chicago—had written a fantasy that imagined how cosmopolitan and nostalgic desire could work in antagonistic tension with one another.[33] I argue that Baum does not so much reconcile nostalgia with cosmopolitanism as depict Dorothy's nostalgia for Kansas as the desire that compels her to develop a cosmopolitan ethics only as a means to return home. But this psychic fantasy of cosmopolitan nostalgia inevitably compromises her engagement with strangers, transforming her ethics into an illiberal form of internationalist

---

30. Baum, *The Wonderful Wizard of Oz*, 44. Hereafter cited parenthetically as *WW*.

31. Rushdie, *The Wizard of Oz*, 57.

32. Kant, "Idea for a Universal History with a Cosmopolitan Purpose," 47. To describe cosmopolitanism, Kant uses the adjective *schwärmerisch*, literally "rapturous" or "wildly enthusiastic" but also connoting the *fantastic* or *fanciful*, as most translators have suggested Kant uses it in this essay.

33. For Baum's interest in the World's Columbian Exposition, see Katharine M. L. Rogers, *Frank Baum*, 45–64, and Schwartz, *Finding Oz*, 224–25.

expansionism. By entwining these incompatible phenomena, Baum creates a lasting metaphor for U.S. foreign policy: Dorothy as the reluctant traveler who selflessly intervenes in the affairs of strangers with the intention of returning home instead of remaining abroad.

What I offer is a case for reading *The Wonderful Wizard of Oz* in its larger literary and cultural context by establishing how this seemingly innocuous children's story yielded one of the more resilient metaphors for U.S. interventionism in the twentieth and twenty-first centuries.[34] I hope to extend the conversation in U.S. literary studies on empire to include fictional genres beyond the imperial romance. Narratives of imperialism usually call to mind the romance genre because it both preserves and contains vanishing cultures as it incorporates them.[35] The story is a familiar one: Native Americans, Filipinos, and Puerto Ricans are merely the barbaric predecessors of Europeans or Anglo-Americans, and as those peoples assimilate or disappear, the imperial romance archives their dying ways of life. Baum's fantasy works differently, imagining difference as something that cannot be assimilated but instead can be appreciated and engaged. Through cosmopolitan nostalgia Baum's fairy tale participates in and also departs from larger conversations about internationalism that were transacted in period magazines like the *Cosmopolitan* and that still are in contemporary work on global feeling and cosmopolitan ethics.

What does Dorothy want? The answer to this question seems straightforward, but only if her desires are not compared to those of her naturalist contemporaries, like Stephen Crane's Maggie or Theodore Dreiser's Carrie. Desire figures as prominently in *The Wonderful Wizard of Oz* as it does in turn-of-the-century U.S. culture at large. Current literary critics continue to see desire as animating naturalist narratives and depriving their protagonists of agency. Of particular interest to students of this literature is what Thorstein Veblen famously referred to as "conspicuous consumption." The drive to consume informed the master narrative of the late nineteenth century, so that, following Walter Benn Michaels's powerful account, critics often understand the logic of naturalism and the desires of the period to have been "made available by consumer

---

34. I am not interested in producing another allegorical reading—as compelling as such readings often are—of *The Wonderful Wizard of Oz*. For allegorical interpretations of Baum, see Erisman, "L. Frank Baum and the Progressive Dilemma"; Littlefield, "*The Wizard of Oz*"; and Ritter, "Silver Slippers and a Golden Cap."

35. For the relationship between romance and imperialism, see Glazener, *Reading*, 147–88; Hebard, "Romantic Sovereignty"; and Kaplan, *The Anarchy of Empire*, 92–120.

capitalism" in homologous terms.[36] Michaels insists that we read all turn-of-the-century literature as complicit with the aims of consumer culture, because in some measure all these texts reproduce the drive to consume, regardless of their authors' stated aims. Naturalist novels can never escape the biological or economic determinism that they seek to indict. Subsequent literary critics have left the central assumptions of Michaels's account largely unchallenged even while amending or supplementing parts of it.[37]

But what happens when desire—or the protagonist who falls victim to desire—is taken out of context, out of the cultural moment? *The Wonderful Wizard of Oz* explores this question by transporting us out of the realm of naturalism and into the fantasy of cosmopolitan nostalgia. Although a cyclone removes Dorothy from her context, we might concur with Stuart Culver's claim that the book indulges in "consumer desire" even as it seemingly performs "a conventional criticism of the commodity fetish."[38] Such accounts of Baum's narrative rely heavily on comparisons between passages from *The Wonderful Wizard of Oz* and *The Art of Decorating Dry Goods Windows and Interiors*, published in the same year. This work, which Baum wrote as a window dresser for Marshall Fields, certainly contains sections that resonate with his more celebrated book. Notably, his theorization of "the harmony of color" calls to mind the color-coded regions of Oz, and the mechanical special effects he describes how to develop resemble those employed by the Wizard in the Emerald City.[39] The parallels between the two texts, as well as Baum's own attempt to mass-produce Oz-related commodities, from sequels to the original book to musical adaptations of the fairy tale, have led readers to attribute to him an "astute exploitation of the intersection between the fantastic and modern commodity culture."[40] Indeed, Oz did become for Baum "an advertisement for a trademark" in a manner that prefigured the way that the large production studios of the 1930s, like MGM and Disney, used their renditions of fairy tales for market-branding purposes.[41] But these readings overlook dimensions of Baum's story that complicate its relationship to turn-of-the-century consumer

---

36. Michaels, *The Gold Standard and the Logic of Naturalism*, 19.
37. See, for example, Fleissner, *Women, Compulsion, Modernity*, and Margolis, *The Public Life of Privacy in Nineteenth-Century American Literature*.
38. Culver, "What Manikins Want," 98.
39. Baum, *Art of Decorating Dry Goods Windows and Interiors*, 22.
40. Kim, "Strategic Credulity," 218.
41. Zipes, *Happily Ever After*, 87.

culture. While *The Wonderful Wizard of Oz* is complicit with the rise of capitalism and an industry invested in the mass production of fairy tales, its inventive use of nostalgic desire does not serve merely as an object lesson in conspicuous consumption.

One of the more remarkable aspects of the book is that when it opens Dorothy desires nothing. Unlike the cinematic Dorothy of *The Wizard of Oz*, Baum's Dorothy does not wish to leave Kansas for somewhere over the rainbow. Instead, she would appear to live a life of contentment and even joy, which prompts Aunt Em to look "at the little girl with wonder that she could find anything to laugh at" (*WW*, 10). Baum offers us few clues as to why or how Dorothy finds happiness in dreary Kansas, but we can assume that he uses her disposition to make her legible as an archetypal heroine. Not even Aunt Em or Uncle Henry, though downtrodden and overworked, longs for a better life. The family consumes almost nothing; they live lives of conspicuous destitution. Not only are they determined by their context, but also they also welcome it.

Only when the cyclone takes Dorothy out of this context and deposits her in Oz does she express a desire. Soon after learning that she has unwittingly killed the wicked Witch of the East, Dorothy realizes that she may never see Kansas again. She begins "to sob," and her "tears seemed to grieve the kind-hearted Munchkins, for they immediately took out their handkerchiefs and began to weep also" (23). This sentimental moment has a twofold significance. First, it signals Dorothy's first, and only intense, experience of desire; as we soon discover, her "anxious" wish "to get back to [her] Aunt and Uncle" propels the narrative (23). Second, through her explosion of tears she manipulates the Munchkins into assisting her. This moment is the first of several instances in which her emotions grant her affective mastery over others.

Yet Dorothy's nostalgia also produces a kind of self-control that becomes a central formal and discursive feature of the text. Inasmuch as she denies herself the pleasures that Oz has to offer, determined to return home, she is emblematic not of Veblen's conspicuous consumption but of Max Weber's ascetic rationalism. Weber provided capitalism with a logic of self-denial that rationalized both productivity and the acquisition of commodities for the sole purpose of acquiring them. Within this logic, wealth is "bad ethically only in so far as it is a temptation to idleness and sinful enjoyment of life."[42] In *The Wonderful Wizard of Oz*, Weberian asceticism sustains the illusion that Dorothy's meddling in the affairs of

---

42. Weber, *The Protestant Ethic and the Spirit of Capitalism*, 163.

Oz is entirely disinterested. Just as asceticism makes the accumulation of wealth look like virtuous self-denial, the asceticism associated with nostalgia in Baum's book gives expansionism the appearance of ethical cosmopolitan disinterestedness. For Dorothy, now a de facto witch herself, Oz becomes a possession. There is every reason to believe that it, and the Emerald City specifically, could provide her with ceaseless amusement and liberation from the toils of farm life in Kansas. Nostalgia compels Dorothy to resist such temptations by preventing her from becoming satisfied with her circumstances. After freeing the Winkies, for example, she and her companions "found everything they needed to make them comfortable," until she "thought of Aunt Em" and declared that she must "get back to Kansas" (164–65).

Explaining that her uncle will need her help on the farm, she forgoes the beauties of Oz and elects to pursue the "righteous life" of labor.[43] Dorothy's practice of ascetic rationalism and her nostalgic display undermine the pleasures of the imagination itself. Indulging her fantasies is the ultimate temptation that she must overcome. That Baum portrays Dorothy favorably for suppressing her imagination seems peculiar in a book "written solely to pleasure children of today" (WW, 3). Nevertheless, the narrative abandons the goal stated in its preface by challenging its readers to embrace the quotidian world of labor over the extraordinary Oz. To a degree, Baum eliminates this contradiction in subsequent tales of Oz by providing Dorothy with a new home there. Her permanent departure from Kansas in *The Emerald City of Oz* (1910), however, means that Oz and its imaginative promise will "entirely disappear from the knowledge of the rest of the world."[44] Celebrating the end of his creation, Baum insists that his readers "have no right to feel grieved" and should instead embrace their own world, humdrum though it may be.[45] It is no wonder that Baum's contemporaries suspected that he "did not believe" in the fanciful power of fairy tales and that he could not "conceal" his skepticism of them.[46]

Thus, nostalgia in *The Wonderful Wizard of Oz* is both the disease and the antidote that animates the narrative. Even though Dorothy is immersed in a world of imaginative possibility, her nostalgia dictates that she must return to the world as it is—Kansas. But her homesickness, which winds up driving her out of Oz, also occasions her foray into its

---

43. Ibid., 157.
44. Baum, *The Emerald City of Oz*, 294.
45. Ibid., 295.
46. "Fairy Tales," *New York Times*, May 11, 1919.

various regions. This contradictory quality of nostalgia in Baum's fairy tale explains why he devotes so little ink to a portrayal of the home to which Dorothy desperately wishes to return. Her home, so "sun blistered" that "the rains [had] washed" the paint away, is a blank canvas (WW, 10). The desire to return to the American home partly lies in its vacuousness, which can be filled or supplemented by any number of possible imaginary but unrealizable homes. But the ultimate aim of Dorothy's adventure in Oz—to return home—bears a formal significance greater than its compatibility with Weber's conceptualization of asceticism. Dorothy's nostalgia persuades her that she has always wanted to be at home, when it was her very removal to Oz that produced both her sense of loss and her desire. That this desire develops incrementally only makes us less mindful that Baum never provides us with an adequate account of her home.

The final chapter, "Home Again," for instance, is less than half a page long, and in it we learn that Dorothy has really returned to a "new farm-house" rather than to her old home, which remains in Munchkin Country (259). What is significant about her false restoration is less the realization that, to quote Thomas Wolfe, she "can't go home again" than that she has desired it even though "there is no place like home" to which to return (WW, 44). This fantasy produces an imaginary tale that dramatizes a child's resolution to resist the enticements of the imagination. Having been forced to imagine Oz against her will, Dorothy behaves as though such a utopian possibility never existed.[47] Here Baum's fantasy and the typical imperial romance part ways. As Amy Kaplan argues, such romances envisioned Americans traveling "out into the world without bearing the foreign into the home," in part by suggesting that those who executed these imperialist exploits would remain abroad.[48] Few late-nineteenth-century romances illustrate this argument better or contrast more starkly with *The Wonderful Wizard of Oz* than Richard Harding Davis's *Soldiers of Fortune* (1897). At the center of this tale of U.S. interventionism in Latin America is a cast of characters defined by their exile from the United States. Unlike Dorothy, when one of these characters recalls his home in the United States by reciting the lines "For there's no place like home, Sweet Home," he does so knowing that he will remain abroad, where he can continue to advance U.S. culture and foreign policy.[49] Davis establishes in his romance that "Americanness and a con-

---

47. For readings of Oz's utopian character, see Barrett, "From Wonderland to Wasteland"; Nathanson, *Over the Rainbow*; and Zipes, *When Dreams Came True*.
48. Kaplan, *The Anarchy of Empire*, 11.
49. Richard Harding Davis, *Soldiers of Fortune*, 88.

nection to home and tradition cease to be placebound."[50] *The Wonderful Wizard of Oz*, on the other hand, imagines not only that Americanness is bound to a particular place but also that imperialist exploits can appear virtuous only insofar as the subject desires to return home.

Does Dorothy's nostalgic desire have a telos? The answer to this question lies in the relationship between her nostalgia and Baum's engagement with turn-of-the-century discussions of cosmopolitanism. To see how Dorothy's nostalgia has cosmopolitan consequences, it helps to consider Slavoj Žižek's work on the psychodynamics of fantasy. By inventing a Kansas worth fighting for, Dorothy's nostalgia exemplifies "the radically intersubjective character of fantasy."[51] That fantasy always entails an exploration of "the subject's relation to his/her Other," and this process shapes the subject's identity through "the dialectical connection between recognition of desire and desire for recognition."[52] This dialectic of desire explains how the subject's object of fantasy turns out to be what others desire from him or her; fantasy "provide[s] an answer to 'What does society want from me?'"[53] Žižek's description of fantasy's radical intersubjectivity has its corollary in cosmopolitan ethics. Appiah, whose work has shaped the philosophical discussion of cosmopolitanism for twenty years, maintains that "ethical obligation" is also a product of intersubjective interaction.[54] A cosmopolitan ethics emerges from a subject's engagement with strangers, and, like the radical intersubjectivity of fantasy, this engagement helps determine the subject's identity.

Dorothy cares only to return to Kansas, but the realization of this nostalgic desire immediately requires her to care about the desires of those around her; she must ask not what Oz can do for her but what she can do for Oz. This consciousness first awakens in her when the Munchkins thank her for killing the wicked Witch of the East and "setting" them "free from bondage" (*WW*, 19). She cannot understand how she can have "killed anything," but after being celebrated as the Munchkins' liberator, she starts to wonder in what other ways "an innocent, harmless little girl" might assist them (*WW*, 19). Converting the question Dorothy asks of herself from "What do I want?" into "What do *others* want from me?," *The Wonderful Wizard of Oz* creates a matrix of desire that compels

---

50. Murphy, *Hemispheric*, 143.
51. Žižek, *The Plague of Fantasies*, 9.
52. Ibid., 8.
53. Ibid., 9.
54. Appiah, *The Ethics of Identity*, 236.

her to develop her own cosmopolitan ethics.[55] Her ethics soon veers off course, however, from the type of cosmopolitanism Appiah defends to a form of "ruthless cosmopolitanism."[56] While by no means intrinsic to all cosmopolitanisms, Dorothy's ethics functions as a rationale for intervening in the affairs of Oz after she discovers that it "has failed to measure up to the levels of good practice that merit recognition as civilized."[57] Below I examine how the intersubjective fantasy at work in Baum's fairy tale teaches readers "how to desire" interventionism in cosmopolitanism's name.[58]

Dorothy's steadfast commitment to Kansas does not, I should emphasize, contain or constrain cosmopolitanism in the text; it renders cosmopolitanism undesirable as an end in itself. Dorothy learns about Oz only to keep it at arm's length from home. She develops a cosmopolitan ethics without ever truly becoming a cosmopolitan in the elitist sense of the word; in contrast to the interlopers usually found in local-color writing, who appear "more cosmopolitan than the locals," Dorothy clings to her provincial and incorruptible attachment to Kansas as though it were a virtue.[59] In the process, the book shuttles between the systemic and the individual senses of the cosmopolitan.

Dorothy's own ethical way of relating to strangers rationalizes a particular cosmopolitan categorical imperative. Her ethos develops early in the book. On arriving in Oz, she learns from the Munchkins that "Oz has never been civilized," which explains why "witches and wizards" still exist within its borders (*WW*, 22). This revelation immediately grants Dorothy social superiority despite her youth. While Kansas inhabits the temporal realm of the civilized, Oz is stuck in a more primitive state. In an imperial romance Dorothy would incorporate this archaic culture into a larger diachronic narrative. In Baum's book she learns to embrace and to tolerate uncivilized strangeness even though her nostalgia for Kansas puts her at odds with the wonders of Oz. By admitting their primitiveness, the Munchkins establish the pretext for Dorothy's involvement in their affairs as an enterprise equally committed to liberating oppressed peoples and to expelling the wonderment that has made

---

55. Žižek, *The Plague of Fantasies*, 9.
56. Appiah, *The Ethics of Identity*, 220.
57. Gilroy, *Postcolonial Melancholia*, 60. Without leveling an invective at all forms of cosmopolitanism, Gilroy finds that Western military interventions often have been conducted in the name of cosmopolitanism and humanitarianism.
58. Žižek, *The Plague of Fantasies*, 7.
59. Lutz, *Cosmopolitan*, 80.

their enslavement possible. Dorothy's first victory against the world of wonder occurs, in fact, when she kills one of the two wicked witches. While the Munchkins adamantly believe that Dorothy is a "noble Sorceress," her sorcery can be easily explained by the effects of the cyclone (19). By ridding Munchkin Country of the Witch of the East's despotism with her house, Dorothy uncannily supplants the strange with the homely. This moment resembles what Kaplan calls the "Manifest Domesticity" of the nineteenth century, whereby the domestic sphere became "a more potent agent for national expansion" and U.S. imperialism than overtly masculine Machtpolitik.[60] But Dorothy's domesticity has a distinctly cosmopolitan character. Rather than expel the foreign or seek to convert the uncivilized, she embraces strangers in an effort to create a more pluralistic world. She renders the strange familiar and tolerable but not, at least initially, the same. Her nostalgia prevents her from going native in a world of strangers. The book continually stresses the alien character of Oz by describing it as "a strange and beautiful country" and its inhabitants as "a strange people" (WW, 188). Oz's citizens also repeatedly label Dorothy a stranger, as they do the Scarecrow, the Tin Woodman, and the Cowardly Lion after they have left their respective regions. When they first arrive at the Emerald City, for example, the "Guardian of the Gates" announces the arrival of "strangers" (124). When Dorothy and her party head out to destroy the Witch of the West, the Witch commands her legions of bees to "go to the strangers and sting them to death!" (145). And when Dorothy goes to find Glinda, the good Witch of the South, a soldier in the Emerald City warns her that she must travel to the realm of the Quadlings, "a race of queer men who do not like strangers to cross their country" (215). In a land full of both wonder and isolated cultures, Oz's own inhabitants seem strange to one another. Dorothy emerges as the one person capable of bringing these discrete populations into contact with one another. We learn early in the story that she "did not feel nearly as bad as you might think a little girl would who had been suddenly whisked away from her own country and set down in the midst of a strange land" (31). Paradoxically, her wish to return home forces her to take an interest in the welfare of others, and she becomes an exemplary citizen of the world who develops an ethics according to which "we have obligations to strangers."[61]

Dorothy's nascent understanding of cosmopolitan ethics is shaped by several examples of both how and how not to treat strangers. Both wicked

---

60. Kaplan, *The Anarchy of Empire*, 29.
61. Appiah, *Cosmopolitanism*, 153.

witches enforce anticosmopolitan policies by prohibiting the Munchkins and the Winkies from traveling outside their regions. The witches also refuse to leave their dominions, whereas Dorothy freely travels from place to place. The evil witches practice an absolute hostility by naming enemies strangers and waging perpetual war on them.

Baum further casts the witches' wickedness in anticosmopolitan terms by implicitly equating goodness with hospitality. Indeed, many inhabitants of Oz open their homes to Dorothy and her companions. Nearly every group of new people she encounters offers them food and shelter, from Boq the Munchkin to the green people of the Emerald City, who encourage her to make herself "perfectly at home" (*WW*, 126). These inhabitants of Oz honor a version of Kant's cosmopolitan maxim of universal hospitality, or "the right of a stranger not to be treated with hostility when he arrives on someone else's territory."[62]

By making herself "perfectly at home," Dorothy exercises an increasingly interventionist cosmopolitanism. Though imperial conquest and cosmopolitanism are often incompatible with each other, liberating peoples arbitrarily oppressed by a despot in the name of cosmopolitanism may be permissible. Kant's stipulation that "the Civil Constitution of Every State shall be Republican" and not despotic potentially sanctions interventionism aimed at cultivating the political conditions necessary for a perpetual peace congenial to cosmopolitanism.[63] Dorothy's interventionism occurs most obviously when she invades the country of the Winkies. Stemming solely from her desire to be sent "back to Kansas," her decision is morally unambiguous, because the Witch of the West has enslaved these people (*WW*, 129). Liberal tolerance here encompasses a universalism that imposes Dorothy's understanding of justice on the inhabitants of Oz. Her behavior and Baum's tale generally illustrate the often necessary relationship among discourses of tolerance, cosmopolitanism, and interventionism. The witches' intolerable intolerance of strangers justifies Dorothy's assertion of cosmopolitan superiority.

Predictably, the Winkies embrace Dorothy and her companions as liberators and willingly serve her, "delighted to do all in their power for [her], who had set them free from bondage" (160). They in turn find themselves "no longer prisoners in a strange land" (155). Thus Dorothy spends "a few happy days at the Yellow Castle," where the Wicked Witch once lived, and begins to feel almost at home in Winkie Country (162). Similar events occur when Dorothy liberates some mice from a bellicose

---

62. Kant, "Perpetual Peace," 105.
63. Ibid., 99.

tiger and when the Cowardly Lion kills a tyrannical spider in a country that at first seems "disagreeable" but that later he can conceive no "pleasanter home" than (239–40). Traveling to strange locales and talking to strangers make these places feel just like home.

There would be almost nothing questionable about Dorothy's pursuits if she did not replace malevolent dictators with benevolent ones. When Dorothy arrives in Oz, the Wizard purportedly rules the entire land, but he proves a weak leader, incapable of founding a federation of integrated nations overseen by a central power. By contrast, Dorothy makes this dream a reality by eliminating the two witches who stand in its way. While her actions answer the wishes of the Winkies and the Munchkins, the realization of their desires also becomes the fulfillment of Dorothy's and her companions' wishes. For all practical purposes, the Munchkins consider Dorothy their new sovereign sorceress, and we learn of the Tin Woodman's hope to return to Winkie Country: "The Winkies were very kind to me, and wanted me to rule over them after the Wicked Witch died. I am fond of the Winkies, and if I could get back again to the country of the West I should like nothing better than to rule over them forever" (255). The Tin Woodman's rationale for returning to the Winkies to rule them because they "were very kind" to him risks overstepping the bounds of cosmopolitan hospitality.

While the Tin Woodman's desire to preside over the Winkies could be well intentioned, the Cowardly Lion's decision to return to Quadling Country, where he will rule as "the King of Beasts," is unambiguously self-serving (237). Baum depicts the animals as "holding a meeting" to decide democratically who should rid the jungle of the spider (240). The Cowardly Lion agrees to do it, but only on the condition that the other animals "bow down" and "obey" him (241). As though such a condition were in no way coercive, they "gladly" assent (241). In other words, one of the principal fantasies at work in the text is that the Cowardly Lion, the Tin Woodman, and Dorothy are innocent narcissists, believing that what they desire is what others desire of them. Here the book reveals, in spite of itself, a slippage between global feeling and global ruling that twenty-first-century theorists of cosmopolitanism, like Robbins, caution against.

The Scarecrow's succession to the throne of Oz serves as the supreme embodiment of a new world order. Before the Wizard leaves via hot-air balloon, he crowns the Scarecrow "ruler of the Emerald City" (212). As he begins to appreciate the power he has inherited, the Scarecrow recounts his rags-to-riches story by recalling that "a short time ago I was up on a pole in a farmer's cornfield" (212). While his ascension to authority both seems benevolent and is laughably entertaining, his professed humility typifies what Theodor W. Adorno describes as the "great little man" rhetorical device: tyrants and fascist speakers often portray themselves to their auditors as "both weak and strong: weak insofar as each member of the crowd is conceived of being capable of identifying himself with the leader . . . ; strong insofar as he represents" collective power.[64] The Scarecrow may be the most powerful person in Oz, but he also wears clothes that "every man wore in this country" (WW, 36). This commonman topos allows the master to appear as a savior. The Scarecrow answers this messianic calling as the "wonderful . . . ruler" of Oz and reminds Glinda, the Witch of the South, and Dorothy that "Oz has made me its ruler and the people like me" (255). By using this rhetorical device, the Scarecrow draws on the American master narrative of upward social mobility. We cannot forget, however, that behind this straw man stands Dorothy, who "lifted" him "off the pole" like a puppet (37). Remarking that he "might have passed [his] whole life in the farmer's cornfield," the Scarecrow acknowledges his debt, for Dorothy has the ultimate power to pull his strings (257). She and her companions transform Oz into a confederation of what O. Henry famously called "banana republics" in *Cabbages and Kings*.[65]

By establishing these benevolent puppet dictatorships, Dorothy brings about a perpetual peace, but at the expense of several of the prerequisite articles that Kant outlines. Nevertheless, her cosmopolitanism remains perfectly consistent with capitalist cosmopolitanism, which subjects the globe to its rule in the name of making it feel like home and creates the semblance of change in order to leave the original power structures unaltered. Oz may no longer have wicked witches, but it remains a land ruled by dictators. Dorothy must talk to strangers in Oz not because she really loves them but because she means to ensure that the rest of Oz will leave her alone in Kansas. That the provincial and the cosmopolitan become one is best captured by the fact that the Emerald City and Kansas both occupy the geographic centers of their maps. Baum implies that the journey to the center and the periphery are and must be one and the same. Dorothy, in other words, became one of the twentieth century's most beloved heroines because she embodies and defines a U.S. cosmopolitan archetype: she is as innocent as she is reluctant to leave home. Like

---

64. Adorno, *The Psychological Technique of Martin Luther Thomas' Radio Addresses*, 19.
65. O. Henry, *Cabbages and Kings*, 132.

Alden Pyle from Graham Greene's *Quiet American*, one of her fictional twentieth-century successors, Dorothy ostensibly wants "to do good, not to any individual person, but to a country, a continent, a world," even though she knows that she "should have stayed at home."[66]

Her nostalgic reluctance invariably returns us to Dorothy's local connection to Kansas. "What's the matter with Kansas?"—most of us now associate this question with Thomas Frank's book on contemporary politics, but it was first posed by William Allen White in an attack on the burgeoning Populist movement in 1896.[67] White adamantly maintained that Kansas was losing "in population and wealth" at a far greater rate than the rest of the country.[68] He faulted the Populists for these declines, reasoning that they had rendered Kansas less hospitable by their political agitation. With his state losing thousands of inhabitants yearly, White would have found no humor in the Scarecrow's remark that "it is fortunate for Kansas" that Dorothy has the brains to return home, because otherwise the state "would have no people at all" (45). White's column reveals that in the 1890s Kansas barely registered in the national consciousness. More than a century later, however, Frank's book attests that Kansas occupies a central place in the national imagination. With the rise of the "culture of the middle," we have come to regard this state as one of the great custodians of U.S. identity.[69] Kansas is part of a heartland that, in the minds of those who live on the coasts of the United States, never has to grow up.

What made perceptions of Kansas shift? The explanation has a lot to do with what Baum conveys in his fairy tale's most memorable phrase, "There is no place like home" (44). Citing Ernst Bloch's belief that the utopian home "is not a place we actually know or have known," Jack Zipes argues that Baum's Kansas functions as a utopia only insofar as it embodies a promise that can never be fulfilled.[70] A gray and empty Kansas cannot serve as a utopia, but Kansas "could become" every bit as colorful and populous as Oz.[71] Nostalgia could set in motion this metamorphosis by transforming the "long since dully experienced environment" of the

---

66. Greene, *The Quiet American*, 13, 16.
67. See Frank, *What's the Matter with Kansas?*
68. William Allen White, "What's the Matter with Kansas?," 196.
69. For the rise of the "culture of the middle," see Hegeman, *Patterns for America*, 126–57.
70. Zipes, *Fairy Tale as Myth/Myth as Fairy Tale*, 127.
71. Ibid., 128.

habitual home into something "itself colorful, in fact utopian."[72] In *The Wonderful Wizard of Oz*, however, homesickness moves in an opposite direction. Far from imagined in more colorful terms, Kansas continues to be as dull as ever, while Dorothy does everything in her power to make Oz less colorful and less wonderful on her journey home. Utopia in Baum's fairy tale is a noplace marked less as an "enduring indeterminacy" than as an enduring immutability.[73] Perhaps only coincidentally, the story's textual history followed a similar course. The word *wonderful* soon disappeared from the titles of the film and theatrical adaptations of the book, and in the 1939 MGM film Oz ceased to be an actual place and became instead a dream populated by nearly the same cast as in Kansas. The more the world changes, the more Kansas must stay the same.

Herein lies *The Wonderful Wizard of Oz*'s lasting cultural importance. As arguably the most popular American fairy tale ever written, it reimagines the Protestant work ethic for a coming global era as one in which provincialism is always longed for and international intervention is always motivated by the selfless love of liberty for all. For this reason, we should not be at all surprised to discover that Henry M. Littlefield begins his paradigmatic Populist reading of *The Wonderful Wizard of Oz* with an anecdote illustrative of "Churchill's nostalgia" for the fairy tale.[74] Littlefield mentions how Churchill loved to recall that his Australian and British World War II brigades sang songs from *The Wizard of Oz* as they campaigned across North Africa and then Europe. For Littlefield, the former prime minister's nostalgia "is only one symptom of the world-wide delight found in an American fairytale."[75] But an anecdote about soldiers waging war against a xenophobic dictator to the tune of "We're off to see the Wizard, the wonderful Wizard of Oz" grows in significance when we realize that U.S. policy makers, political scientists, and journalists have repeatedly used *The Wonderful Wizard of Oz* to elucidate the rationale behind many major conflicts of the twentieth and twenty-first centuries.[76] First published

---

72. Bloch, *Principle of Hope*, 373.
73. Bloch, "Can Hope Be Disappointed?," 341.
74. Littlefield, "The Wizard of Oz," 47.
75. Ibid.
76. In addition to describing World War II, *The Wizard of Oz* often served as a metaphor for the Cold War and the regional conflicts it spurred. Moscow frequently played the part of the Wizard, though sometimes the Wizard stood in for other nemeses to U.S. power or even for a weak United Nations. See, for example, "The Atom and the Iron Curtain," *Los Angeles Times*, October 10, 1948; Albert Bermel, "A Fit Instrument of Survival," *New York Times*, August 4, 1948; Gaddis, *We Now Know*, 257–59, 280; Hindy, "The Kremlin

in the wake of the Spanish-American War, when the United States began to emerge as a global power, Baum's fairy tale achieved its current popularity during the Korean War era, when the MGM film adaptation began to appear widely on television.[77] Baum's tale flexed its muscle again in a 2006 episode of *Frontline* when the reporter Michael Gordon described how the second Iraq War was often characterized by members of the Bush administration "as the ding-dong-the-witch-is-dead school of regime change: We go in, we kill the wicked witch, the munchkins jump up, they're grateful, and then we get in the hot-air balloon and we're out of there."[78] Few if any imperial romances—or any literary texts, for that matter—published so long ago are so frequently cited to rationalize contemporary U.S. geopolitical decisions. While turn-of-the-century romances of U.S. imperialism have long since faded from popular memory, *The Wonderful Wizard of Oz*'s persistence establishes that the United States can expand ceaselessly outward so long as the journey always remains homeward bound.

HENRY JAMES'S FATAL NOSTALGIA

As commentators have repeatedly demonstrated, James's prose is thoroughly saturated with cosmopolitan tropes.[79] While he meditated on cosmopolitanism at various moments throughout his entire career, his most extended exploration of the phenomenon of nostalgia unfolds in prose he composed toward the end of his life. After briefly returning to the United States in the early twentieth century, he wrote *The American Scene* and some short fiction based on his homecoming. In the writing produced during the final years of his life, Beverly Haviland avers, James "tried to explain and to illustrate in various ways just what was at stake for the culture if the sense of the past, such as had sustained him in his life and works, were to be lost."[80] Despite his desire to preserve features of the American past, I argue, James remained wary of nostalgia.

Watchers Were Dazzled by Oz"; and Leen, "Caught in Traffic," *Washington Post*, February 18, 1990.

77. Zipes, *Fairy Tale as Myth*, 122.

78. Gordon, "The Lost Year in Iraq."

79. Many studies reflect on cosmopolitan tropes in James. See, for example, Agathocleous, *Urban Realism and the Cosmopolitan Imagination in the Nineteenth Century*, 133–44; Berman, *Modernist Fiction*; Peyser, *Utopia*, 135–68; and Tinter, *The Cosmopolitan World of Henry James*.

80. Haviland, *Henry James's Last Romance*, 2.

Even as his contemporaries Sinclair and Harris enkindled the radical political imagination with nostalgia, James noted how historical sites like Washington Irving's birthplace reinvented and commercialized the past for a modern museum-going public. This commercialized nostalgia, for James, was not a form of antimodernism but a product of modernity and cosmopolitanism. Yet he cannot entirely disparage it as an aesthetic category because, unlike the sublime or the beautiful, it still bears a democratic promise even in its commercialized form. Nostalgia, like its cousin kitsch, is art's bad democratic conscience.[81]

While *The Wonderful Wizard of Oz* justifies U.S. imperialism by generating a fantasy of isolationism though cosmopolitan nostalgia, James castigates this same affective dynamic for stymieing the development of a global consciousness in the United States. Incanting the hotel-spirit, Americans can travel throughout their country and the world with their home in tow. The two crucial pieces from James's fourth phase that best represent his skepticism toward nostalgia are his short story "The Jolly Corner" and *The American Scene*. In "The Jolly Corner," he casts nostalgia as a psychologically dysfunctional affect that transforms the past into both an idyllic and a commercial object. He levels one of the earliest liberal indictments of what Arendt would later describe as the "nostalgia for a still intact past" for being a dangerously reactionary emotion.[82] Indulging in nostalgia threatens this tale's protagonist with annihilation. *The American Scene* moves beyond the realm of psychology and into the domain of culture; it is in this crucial travelogue that James fully explores the perils and possibilities associated with the mass-produced nostalgia of historical homes, art museums, and hotel culture.

The plot of "The Jolly Corner" is deceptively simple: the American expatriate and thoroughly Europeanized aesthete Spencer Brydon returns to New York to tend to his two inherited properties. While exploring the vacant rooms of his childhood home, the jolly corner, he encounters and eventually rejects his ghostly alter ego haunting the premises. He realizes that he never could be this person, and he recoils from this visage in horror and into the arms of his childhood confidant

---

81. Adorno makes this claim about kitsch, but the formulation is placed most succinctly by Richard Leppert in his analysis of his views of mass-produced art. See Adorno, *Essays on Music*, 364 and 501–5. My association between Adorno's account of kitsch and the cultural and aesthetic qualities of nostalgia is somewhat anticipated by Austin. See Austin, *Nostalgia*, 124.

82. Arendt, *Origins of Totalitarianism*, ix.

Alice Staverton. Around this straightforward gothic plot, James weaves what he describes in "The Art of Fiction" as a "huge spider-web of the finest silken threads" that capture "the very atmosphere of the mind."[83] He limns with meticulous detail Brydon's shifting mental state as he first pursues and then rejects his apparitional doppelganger. Assuming the grotesque form of a man with two missing fingers and a face that Brydon finds "too hideous as *his*," this figure remains inscrutable.[84] Commentators have fleshed out the possible identities of this spectral self, diversely representing capitalist success, closeted homosexuality, or the narcissistic rejection of any cohesive self.[85] Pairing "The Beast in the Jungle" with "The Figure in the Carpet," critics attend to its intricate formal properties as much as its psychological content. As Lee Clark Mitchell suggests, "the story may well be said to thematize figuration itself" insofar as the ghostly presence represents a floating signifier or another type of semiotic detachment.[86] Space and time further confound the reader in this story, as they do throughout much of James's later fiction: Brydon loses himself on the fourth floor of his old apartment and time accelerates when he learns "he had taken hours for minutes" (515). All of this disorientation, however, is oriented around a curious flirtation with nostalgia. He wishes to know what remaining in New York would "have made" of him (500). This unwavering curiosity creates the pretext for a critique of the psychology of nostalgia.

Much like Dorothy's dull and gray Kansas farmhouse, Brydon's ancestral home is only a collection of unfurnished "great blank rooms" (496). It embodied "the ugly things of his far-away youth," driving him away from the United States to find refuge in cosmopolitan Europe (492). He fears that if he had remained in New York, he may "have discovered his genius in time really to start some new variety of awful architectural hare and run it till it burrowed a gold-mine" (495). New York embodies all of the virtues championed by American commercialism; this metropolis would have transformed him into the robber baron that his life in Europe forestalled. Unlike Dorothy, he resists the call to return to this industrial and commercial utopia. These empty rooms signify the absence of Brydon's nostalgia. He may feel estranged from his childhood past,

---

83. James, "Art of Fiction," 580.
84. James, "The Jolly Corner," 519. Hereafter cited parenthetically.
85. Representative readings of these approaches to the "The Jolly Corner" include the following: on queer reading, see Savoy, "The Queer Subject of 'The Jolly Corner,'" and on Brydon's narcissism, see Claggett, "Narcissism and the Conditions of Self-Knowledge in James's 'The Jolly Corner.'"
86. Lee Clark Mitchell, "'Ghostlier Demarcations, Keener Sounds,'" 223.

but this sense of alienation does not initially produce a longing for his past, instead eliciting a "deep abjection" associated with the shame he feels for leaving his home (516). Indeed, the language of psychoanalysis remains a useful one for arriving at an understanding of James's examination of nostalgia and the threat it poses. Linda Zwinger, channeling the work of Julia Kristeva, astutely recognizes that Brydon's abjection occurs because he cannot "face the possibility that this figure [his alter ego] in fact conjures *him*" and occupies a space that he cannot fully possess.[87] But his sense of abjection also results from a lost feeling—a lack or an absence that must be supplemented in a narrative structured around homecoming. Brydon is aware that indulging in nostalgia to fill his empty rooms with the phantasms of the past comes with the threat of recovering his lost, commercially driven self. Restoring his lost past or home may require him to annihilate the present.

His cosmopolitanism fails to inoculate him against the threat nostalgia poses. His experiences in Europe coupled with his memories of a New York skyline before the development of the skyscraper compel him to long for the city's lost architectural features. His desire to preserve the jolly corner stems from his aversion toward the "dishonored and disfigured" modern buildings encroaching upon the "westward reaches" of the neighborhood (495). His "sentimental" attachment to this building, based more on his love of old architecture than upon its association with his childhood, renders him vulnerable to feelings expressed by Alice Staverton (497). Alice, much more than Brydon, expresses an unrestrained nostalgia for the old city. She lives in a small house to which "she had subtly managed to cling through her almost unbroken New York career" (493). Her home serves as an archive guarding against "the awful modern crush" in which her maid tends to a collection of souvenirs: she "dusted her relics and trimmed her lamps and polished her silver" (494).

Alice displays a compulsive drive to supplant living memory with an archival record of it. As Jacques Derrida reminds us, the idea of the archive can trace its etymological roots back to the "Greek *arkheion*: initially a house, a domicile, an address, the residence of the superior magistrates."[88] Like these ancient magistrates, Staverton protects the documents, or relics in this case, from the ravages of time. Yet her efforts render the city's forgetfulness permissible, so long as she preserves what writers from Wesley Washington Pasko to Edith Wharton deemed "Old

---

87. Zwinger, "'*Treat* me your subject,'" 9.
88. Derrida, *Archive Fever*, 2.

New York."⁸⁹ Like the Derridean notions of archive and hypomnesia, her surname—Staverton—evokes this double bind. *To stave* can mean "to destroy" or "to break to pieces," but it can also mean "to renew" (as in to repair the staves of a cask or bucket), "to repel," and "to ward off."⁹⁰ Her historical preservation "incites forgetfulness" even as it "assures the possibility of memorization, of repetition, of reproduction, or of reimpression."⁹¹ As James explains, she provided Brydon with a hermetically sealed place populated with "memories and histories into which he could enter" (494). Brydon and Staverton shared "communities of knowledge . . . of presences of the other age," and her preservation of this epoch allowed him to embrace "the freedom of a wanderer" (494). His cosmopolitanism and expatriation permitted the forgetting of his past home, because he always had a house arrested in time—an archive—to visit.

Once he finds himself both figuratively and physically back in his home and in the presence of Staverton, Brydon gradually expresses an interest in what he left behind. His desire to revisit the past emerges less from his own feelings of nostalgia than out of a desire to share Staverton's "yearning look" (497). She yearns both for the past the jolly corner represents and for the counterfactual future it could have spun. After Brydon confides to her that he suspects "a strange *alter ego*" lies "deep down somewhere within me," Staverton confesses that she can imagine this personage from a parallel universe (501). "Twice over" she has "seen him in a dream," she divulges, believing that she knows what Brydon, the faithful American, may have become (502). He desperately wants to know what "the wretch" is like—a sentiment that denotes not nostalgia but the affect's absence (503). He yearns to experience a feeling that he impulsively rejected. He "followed strange paths and worshipped strange gods" that he suspects have "not been edifying" (501). Nostalgia for Kansas made Dorothy's cosmopolitan exploits permissible, but Brydon's lack of nostalgia impelled him to see the world without any promise of seeing his home again. Having returned to New York, he longs to establish an affective attachment to it and to imagine what remaining at home may have done to him.

Shalyn Claggett argues that Brydon's incessant desire to know his alternate self points to his underlying narcissism. Brydon certainly

---

89. *Old New York* was the title of the magazine on the city's history that Pasko edited. See Pasko, "Editor's Note," 64.

90. See "stave, v.," *OED Online*, September 2014, Oxford University Press, http://www.oed.com/view/Entry/189393 (accessed September 12, 2014).

91. Derrida, *Archive Fever*, 11.

appears self-absorbed, admitting he "was leading . . . a selfish frivolous scandalous life" in Europe (501). Freudian narcissism shares some psychical similarities to nostalgia insofar as it may attach itself to "what the self was."[92] But his obsession with himself gradually morphs into a larger preoccupation with New York's past. This component of Brydon's psychoaffective state registers a sense of loss or nostalgic dispossession as much as it may point to a sense of narcissistic self-possession. Initially, the drive to see himself as he might have been is expressed as pure curiosity.[93] Working as a form of cerebral perambulation, Brydon's curiosity in his alter ego inspires behavior normally associated with a feeling he does not experience: nostalgia. In some measure, he displays what the early-twentieth-century art critic Charles S. Ricketts deems the "intellectual nostalgia" found in the art of Delacroix or Rossetti, which he describes as a state of being "haunted by the regret for splendid things" or "the beauty of faded" palaces from the past.[94] James's contemporaries often saw this kind of intellectual nostalgia as a product of travel. Anna Alexander Rogers, for example, insists in an essay published in 1911 that only the cosmopolitan in self-imposed "exile" can fully experience a "passionate nostalgia" for the "Stars and Stripes" or the tune of "'Dixie,' played on a mandolin and a guitar."[95] Periodicals and books throughout the opening decade of this new century had begun exploring a nostalgia for nostalgia's sake, or as Dorothy Canfield writes of her characters in "The House with the Woodbine," they experienced a "nostalgia for they knew not what" as their memories "soon faded into a child's hazy vision of a half-remembered past."[96]

Nurturing his curiosity, Brydon exhibits the classic psychological symptoms associated with nostalgia. He becomes swept up into a grand hallucination initially brought on by his own volition. Projecting "straight over the bristling line of hard unconscious heads and into the other, the real, the waiting life," he enters the jolly corner beguiled by "the slow opening bars of some rich music" of his past (504). The

---

92. Claggett, "Narcissism," 192.
93. Posnock situates William James's and Henry James's contending views of curiosity in relation to its longer history, from antiquity's love of pure curiosity to Augustine's denouncement of it as "ocular desire" to Francis Bacon's insistence that curiosity serve empirical ends lest it devolve into speculative theory. Posnock, *The Trial of Curiosity*, 37. While he does not address "The Jolly Corner" specifically, Posnock insists that in all his work Henry James indulges in pure inquisitiveness, which "is simultaneously autotelic, purposeless, and profitable." Posnock, *The Trial of Curiosity*, 43.
94. Ricketts, *The Art of Prado*, 140.
95. Anna Alexander Rogers, "What We Put Up With," 113–14.
96. Canfield, "The House with the Woodbine," 345.

synesthesia produced by this nostalgic immersion scrambles his senses, throwing him into a trancelike state. "His *alter ego* 'walked'" about the premises, he imagines, while Brydon remains motionless for a time, hoping to "waylay him and meet him" (505). His wish reaches its fulfillment in a moment punctuated by anamorphosis. As he gazes upon this "spectral yet human" figure, he measures his current relative worth against the person he could have become. This process of evaluation requires him to place himself at another remove as, for a moment, he imagines watching himself "gape at his other self" (519). This anamorphic act, what Jacques Lacan would characterize as a moment when "*I see myself seeing myself*" has the potential to affirm the subject's existence, yet "by reducing itself solely to this certainty of being a subject it becomes active annihilation."[97] Here my reading resembles those that have approached the tale as an inversion of the myth of Narcissus (Brydon survives only by rejecting his other self) or as a story about abjection. But the object of Brydon's abjection is nostalgia, a sentiment he "neither gives up nor assumes."[98] As a consequence, he does not reject his counterfactual self but instead collapses: "His head went round; he was going; he had gone" (520).

The encounter leaves him "abysmally passive" even as he relishes the knowledge that almost brought about his death (520). As we witnessed in previous literary works, Brydon's flirtation with nostalgia is an aesthetic occasion, one marked by beauty and a potential—albeit unrealized—shift in genre. In a story structured around an understated romance between Brydon and Staverton, the former's realization of what he may have become could have developed into a tragic peripeteia. His overriding curiosity, however, prevents him from fully surrendering himself to this emotion. James succeeds in establishing its danger nonetheless. By returning to a state of estrangement from his past, Brydon saves his life and consummates the romance. Divided into three parts, the story remains only a shadow of a tripartite tragedy; the tragic haunts but does not overwhelm Brydon. Whereas in many of the previous texts we have encountered, moments of nostalgia create aesthetic and political possibility, "The Jolly Corner" condemns nostalgia as a fatal, reactionary affect.

James's critique of nostalgia in "The Jolly Corner" is, then, twofold. On the one hand, states of nostalgia are synonymous with those of abjection. The longing to recover a lost past and home alters this lost object beyond recognition, dredging "a deep well of memory that is unapproach-

---

97. Lacan, *The Four Fundamental Concepts of Psychoanalysis*, 81.
98. Kristeva, *Powers of Horror*, 15.

able and intimate."⁹⁹ As much as James shares his protagonist's abhorrence of modern architecture and embraces "values other than the beastly rent-values," he returns nostalgia to its pathological origins (497). When sought out for its own sake and experience, nostalgia promotes emotional lability and self-destruction in a manner that echoes the antebellum descriptions of the disease discussed in the introduction and first chapter of this book. James understands nostalgia's subtle perniciousness. Far from challenging the status quo, it can work in tandem with cosmopolitanism and commercialism. The story concludes with Staverton assuring Brydon that his doppelganger "isn't—no, he isn't—*you!*" (525). He can only escape the horror wrought by his apparitional self by embracing her, the person who "accepted" the ghost and cannot "disown him" (524). She serves as the custodian of this past and the counterfactual timeline that a nostalgia for it might produce. She remembers, repeats, and revisits it, so he can avoid bearing this burden. Nostalgia in "The Jolly Corner" cannot transport the United States back to a golden age of architecture, but it can wreak mental anguish instead.

Serialized three years before "The Jolly Corner," *The American Scene* is not confined to the solipsism of a single expatriate. Previous commentators have unpacked this text's wealth of social content and untangled its complex form, noting James's ambivalent attitudes toward immigrants, observations on the rise of modernity, uses of the urban picturesque, and meditations on historical consciousness.¹⁰⁰ While any serious engagement with *The American Scene* necessarily wanders into these rich areas of analysis, my reading is interested in their relevance to James's understanding of nostalgia's cultural and aesthetic significance in the early twentieth century. At the time James wrote his travelogue, attitudes toward art and its place in popular culture began shifting. Progressive art collectors, intellectuals, and social reformers wanted to democratize art history, believing that everyone had a right to appreciate the beautiful and the past. Art museums and historical sites became increasingly important civic institutions. Those involved with maintaining these organizations engaged the work of John Ruskin, who stressed that architecture, like all

---

99. Ibid., 6.
100. Excellent studies of *The American Scene* abound, but representative scholarship on these areas of inquiry include Blair, *Henry James and Writing of Race and Nation*, 158–210; Buelens, "Possessing the American Scene"; Burrows, *A Familiar Strangeness*, 71–79; Cameron, *Thinking in Henry James*, 1–31; Susan Griffin, *The Historical Eye*, 91–148; Haviland, *Henry James's Last Romance*, 49–162; Kendall Johnson, *Henry James and the Visual*, 155–88; and Rawlings, *Henry James and the Abuse of the Past*, 26–32.

forms of art, could realize its greatness only "in becoming memorial or monumental."[101] Although he had many adherents, curators and connoisseurs imagined a more democratic Ruskin. They wanted to make masterworks of craft more widely accessible to direct industry by reproducing versions of this art for mass consumption.[102]

James critiques this Progressive-Era historical consciousness when he tours a series of historical homes and art museums in *The American Scene*. He describes the effect two presidential homes have upon him: the cottage where James Garfield perished, lying among the chain of towns dotting the New Jersey shoreline, and Ulysses S. Grant's home sitting on the Upper East Side. Their surrounding environments define his reception of both homes. The Jersey Shore and the accompanying "condition" it exemplifies "connote" commercial monstrosity, an unearned cultural confidence, and shallow appearances.[103] Everything drifts on the surface "with too little history about them for dignity of ruin" (10). The old hotels and gambling houses evoke a sense of the past, but they cannot generate the sensations of the sublime associated with ruins that exude an epic sense of time measured in ages punctuated by cataclysms. James instead feels the absence of historicity on the New Jersey shoreline. These buildings lack both historical content and aesthetic form. They are diminutive figures that he labels "pathetic," an aesthetic category that may assume but often falls short of the sublime (9).[104] For James, the pathetic is a mitigating phenomenon, as these homes trigger minor, easily consumable sensations of wistfulness rather than awe, admiration, or mourning. These "modest structures," he explains, had "exactly the effect of objects diminished by recession into space—as if to symbolize the rapidity of their recession into time" (11). Both Garfield's home and Grant's in New York represent the fetishization of the past, unable to produce a national tradition. James revises the role of the collection as exemplified by Staverton's residence in "The Jolly Corner." Although her home permits forgetfulness by preserving the past, these historical sites function as objects unto themselves or as tourist destinations awaiting consumable acquisition rather than as memorials of recollection.

The presidential homes initiate the guiding split between James's formally complex nostalgia and the vacuous conventionalism of the

---

101. Ruskin, *Seven Lamps of Architecture*, 165.
102. See Trask, *Things American*, 8–12 and 119–21.
103. James, *The American Scene*, 9. Hereafter cited parenthetically.
104. See Schiller, "On the Pathetic."

commercial versions of the feeling. The former is closely associated with homesickness or the memories of places James once actually inhabited. Like the protagonist of "The Jolly Corner," he experiences a sense of alienation in the city of his childhood, New York. Everywhere he finds evidence of "new landmarks crushing the old quite as violent children stamp on snails and caterpillars" (63). Recoiling from the presence of these buildings and the immigrant population, he concludes "there was no escape . . . but into the past" (68). He returns to his childhood, which teems with aesthetic complexity and "intrinsic beauty": "There, I repeat, was the delicacy, there the mystery, there the wonder, in especial, of the unquenchable intensity of the impressions received in childhood" (69). He laments that the city leveled his birthplace to the ground and failed to erect a "commemorative mural tablet," replacing his quaint home with one of the emissaries of the "fifty-floored conspiracy against the very idea of the ancient graces" complicit with "the common fund of mere economic convenience" (71). Modern architecture represents a threat to the livelihood of James's nostalgia and artistic values. It also jeopardizes the nation's historical consciousness because old buildings are often razed to create space for "a row of sky-scrapers yielding rents" (214).

These concerns assume additional urgency when he reflects upon the nation's literary past. He visits two prominent literary sites: Washington Irving's home and the House of the Seven Gables site in Salem. Both draw out the competing iterations of nostalgia explored by James. When he first approaches Sunnyside, James embraces a romantic past with conservative undertones. What may just be a "very childish experience" of the surrounding countryside evokes "the general iridescence of a past of Indian summers hanging about mild ghosts half asleep, in hammocks, over still milder novels" (116). For a moment, he embarks upon Rip Van Winkle's parasomniac journey in reverse. His direct allusion to Irving's short story on the historical disjuncture and continuity precipitated by the U.S. Revolutionary War foregrounds his jarring return to the present when he visits the grounds of the author's home. Here finds "the little American literary past" under assault by "modernity" as "the place is inevitably, to-day, but a qualified Sleepy Hollow—the Sleepy Hollow of the author's charming imagination was, as I take it, off somewhere in the hills, or in some dreamland of old autumns, happily unprofanable now" (117). Even as James rallies around Irving's conservative vision of a pastoral North America, he does so diminutively. The United States possesses an aborted literary tradition. Still "little" or in its infancy, the crushing power of modernity overwhelms it in view of the Irving house in the form of highways and scattered early motor cars.

Far more unnerving is the way the historic home has been preserved. "Modernity," James explains, "with its terrible power of working its will, of abounding in its sense, of gilding its toy—modernity, with its pockets full of money and its conscience full of virtue, its heart really full of tenderness, has seated itself there under pretext of guarding the shrine" (117). Rather than leaving the home intact and permitting it to live through the passage of time, curators have embalmed it with corridors dedicated to Irving's biography and his historical period. James finds this feature of the home appalling for two reasons. On the one hand, it falsifies the nation's attitude toward art by encouraging visitors to forget that the United States often "refused sustenance" to its writers (118). Similarly, this tourist appendage exaggerates U.S. literature's larger global significance by casting the nation's "earlier 'intellectual activity' into a vague golden perspective, a haze as of some unbroken spell of the same Indian summer" imagined by James moments earlier (118). This kind of nostalgia corrupts the content of history to stifle the literary imagination and ambitions of the present. He portrays the area surrounding Sleepy Hollow not as a knowable community but as an ephemeral one unmoored from history.

He airs a similar grievance concerning the House of the Seven Gables site. Here the anticipated sublimity of the "Witch House" flounders into an "anti-climax," displaying a "brief and provisional" character that barely inspires his curiosity (199). He winces at the placard posted outside the entrance, a feature of many nineteenth-century historic sites and houses designed to lure in visitors. James refuses to enter what had become one of the nation's most modernly designed tourist attractions. In a study written several decades after *The American Scene* for the American Association of Museums, Laurence Vail Coleman praised the Gables venue for pioneering the concept of the museum resort. The structures on the premises served as seasonal tourist lodgings and included a dining house and an antique store.[105] Some curators considered such accommodations to be "too commercial for historic house museums," but Coleman saw these adaptations as essential to their preservation.[106] These features prompt James to lump the museum grounds in with "the smoky modernism" encroaching upon "the small original Hawthornesque world" of old

---

105. See Coleman, *Historic House Museums*, 102–3.
106. Ibid., 101.

Salem (200). He embraces Hawthorne's less commercially viable birthplace, where he and the home's simple guide both silently cast aside the House of the Seven Gables as merely "the idea of the admirable book" rendered "dead as a low acquaintance" by the vivacity of Hawthorne's novel (201). For James, Hawthorne's sparsely adorned and unfrequented home nurtures a blank but creative nostalgia. It stimulates his imagination and allows him to pursue a series of subjects concerning genius, generational change, and literary inspiration. The presidential homes, Irving's birthplace, and the House of the Seven Gables site all deprive nostalgia of its varied iterations of spatial and temporal displacement.

Later in the twentieth century, two iconic intellectual studies described the phenomenon James grappled with in Salem. Daniel J. Boorstin argued that tourist sites like those visited by James participated in the "diluted, contrived, prefabricated" creation of "pseudo-events" that shut down an active engagement with the past to install an official tradition complicit with the dominant values of the present.[107] And Umberto Eco observed that such historical homes produced a kitschy past that supplanted historical consciousness with an ethos of consumption. Historically preserved homes, such as Henry Flagler's house in Palm Beach, Florida, synthesize the United States' enchantment with "futuristic planning" with the nation's expressions of "nostalgic remorse."[108] Nostalgia of this kind can be easily satisfied any time one visits a record shop and browses the racks (or now the "Classic Hits" page on an online music store) for a musical representative of a particular decade. What Eco describes as nostalgia is exactly the kind of twentieth-century nostalgia that James perceives at these historical sites. He also encounters it among the Newport elite who harbor "nostalgia, however exquisite" for their golden years as tourists in Paris that he finds "sterile, for they appear to have left no seed" (166). Paris is not a living city for them; it's a metonym for a place fixed in time. This emerging form of nostalgia always synchronically historicizes art, fashioning an image of the past organized around a consensus. It departs from the Populist, socialist, anarchist, and even sectionalist nostalgias that aestheticized and reconstructed a contested past. The content of James's nostalgia for the United States' literary past differs from that of the left nostalgia of Goldman, Harris, Parsons, and Sinclair, but the form of his feeling is almost indistinguishable.

---

107. Boorstin, *The Image*, 79.
108. Eco, *Travels in Hyperreality*, 10.

He, however, did not anticipate Boorstin's and Eco's concerns about commercialized art's creation of false or simulated experiences. What he found most appalling was the way this emerging form of nostalgia deprived U.S. art and architecture of beauty and rendered them monotonous. This kind of design "disengages differences" to render the artwork reproducible on a mass scale (138). James confronts the commercial and industrial "abolition of *forms*" or artworks emptied of their "reference to their past, present or future possibility" (22). Susan Griffin argues that James grappled with these formal changes by channeling Ruskin's idea of functionalism. When viewing either landscapes or architecture, he fears that consumption for its own sake has become the ruling principle of U.S. aesthetics.[109] This "destructive gaze of consumerism" obliterates time and space, signaling a decline of civilization that eludes James's own narrative prowess.[110] Tonally, *The American Scene* sounds notes of declension, but the aesthetics of modernity operate apart from diachronic narratives of ascent or descent. Architecture brought to life by "the cold breath of Wall Street" exists only in the present, "squaring itself between an absent future and an absent past as solidly as it can" (121). This empty and homogeneous time cannot nourish a developed American "æsthetic law" that takes "up the references" to a long past (263). A work of art loses its value when unmoored from its historical relations. This point becomes especially clear to him when he visits the Metropolitan Museum of Art (MET). Even though the art museum moved in a democratically accessible direction, its collections took art out of context. James could not help but notice "there was money in the air, ever so much money—that was, grossly expressed" (143). Wealth's unceasing power undermines the aesthetics of what James would deem, if put in their proper relation, artistic masterpieces. Instead, art instrumentally serves an indexical role in the MET: its presence is a quantified measure of the nation's economic and cultural capital but little more.

The American Scene revisits the intersubjective dynamics of "The Jolly Corner" to alter them slightly. The "restless analyst" inhabits the perspective, though not the position, of Brydon's alter ego: he immerses himself in a nation fully modernized and enraptured with the money power or the "whole theory of life" in the United States (176). In lieu of the counterfactual specter of commercialism that frightens Brydon, the ghost haunt-

---

109. See also Agnew, "The Consuming Vision of Henry James."
110. Susan Griffin, *The Historical Eye*, 95.

ing *The American Scene* is the possibility of returning nostalgically to a time before "the cottages have all turned" into villas and skyscrapers—to a moment when "the history of its beauty" had yet to run its course (158). James answers his own question "of whether some ghost of that were recoverable" in the negative (159). In place of this sentiment resides a mass-produced and cosmopolitan iteration of nostalgia that permeates *The Wonderful Wizard of Oz*. But while Baum's vision of cosmopolitan nostalgia relies on a logic of self-denial, James observes how it can work in tandem with consumer self-indulgence in the form of the hotel-spirit.

The hotel was an American invention, and one that aimed to create a cosmopolitan space. A. K. Sandoval-Strausz argues that "it makes sense to see Kant's theoretical efforts and hotel builders' architectural endeavors as manifestations of the same cosmopolitan impulse."[111] Toward the end of the nineteenth century, the imperial hotel took shape in the United States and eventually spread around the world. Buoyed by the surge in Gilded Age wealth, travel for pleasure became more commonplace and acceptable. Tourism and the expansion of railway infrastructure stimulated the growth of more hotels designed as destinations unto themselves with a wide array of new amenities. These large resorts first cropped up across the West and in southern locales like parts of Florida. They marketed their locations as places where visitors could experience the exotic while having the luxury of retreating back into the space of the familiar. Domestic tourism facilitated westward imperialism in a way that would be reproduced internationally. American hotels abroad hosted U.S. diplomatic envoys and businessmen, enabling the United States to spread its influence throughout parts of South America, the Caribbean, and other parts of the globe. Investors and builders in other countries emulated these resorts, so that "colonialism had made the American hotel the global standard for commercial hospitality."[112] The imperial hotel nurtured two usually opposing sentiments: wanderlust and the nostalgia for home.

James associates the hotel-spirit with the monotonous drive of commercialism that standardizes an image of American culture. It expresses "a social, indeed positively an æsthetic ideal, and making it so, at this supreme pitch, a synonym for civilization, for the capture of conceived manners themselves" (79). Ostensibly, the hotel conforms to the Progressive impulse behind the democratization of taste, introducing its guests

---

111. Sandoval-Strausz, *Hotel*, 314.
112. Ibid., 123.

to a range of architectural forms. At the Charleston hotel, for example, James encounters design features that convey "a certain romantic grandeur of scale, the scale positively of 'Latin' construction" (298). But it only simulates these artistic styles, ripping them out of their historical context to create a false sense of luxury. They manufacture desires for art and luxury that their customers believe to be their own. "The hotel was leading," James asserts when it comes to landscaping and gardening, "not following—imposing the standard, not submitting to it" (327). Those who succumb to the intoxicating luster of the hotel experience "a gilded yearning" for more worldly goods (329).

Nostalgia animates these intertwined desires even as the hotel promises to bring this affect to a satisfying end. The hotel sates the tourist's homesickness through a process of reverse mimeticism: hotels do not resemble the homes of their guests but instead instruct them how to make their homes more like hotels. He arrives at this realization in Florida, where he finds all the resorts and homes of Palm Beach imbibing the hotel-spirit by striving to realize "the ideal form of the final home" (330). Florida, for James, is the best embodiment of this phenomenon. There "the hotel-spirit" is "in sole *articulate* possession" of everything in that state where nature can only momentarily deprive "it of supremacy" (325–26). Only at this fleeting moment, when James ventures beyond the enclosures of the Palm Beach resort community, does he witness a Northern woman in a state of "thin nostalgic sadness" for the Florida untouched by development, but even this emotional display is calibrated "for the right felicity . . . of having succeeded in straying a little" (331). James realizes that nostalgia, even for nature, could be the product of turn-of-the-century consumer culture.

Drawing out the mutually constitutive sentiments of wanderlust and nostalgia, the hotel is a feat of social engineering. James marvels at its capacity for attracting a beautifully pluralistic crowd of various social types into its public space only to transform them into a harmonious whole. In the Waldorf-Astoria, he observers "hundreds and hundreds of people in circulation" who gradually find their way around the "storied labyrinth the very firesides and pathways of home" (81). Here the homelike is effortlessly wed to an aesthetics that evokes both "a Mohammedan mosque," "an easy Versailles," and "Oriental opulence" (80–81). Yet the heterogeneity of forms and people, unlike in those moments when James betrays his xenophobic attitude toward newly arriving immigrants, "was a social order in positively stable equilibrium" (81). Through its force the hotel-spirit homogenizes and molds what he deems the plasticity of

U.S. culture and its people. "Distinct as you are," James assures, "you are not even definite, and it would be terrible not to be able to suppose that you are as yet but an instalment [sic], a current number, like that of the morning paper, a specimen of a type in course of serialization" (300). The uniqueness of the people who embrace the hotel-spirit is thus offset by their place within a perpetual serial of types; they will remain, no matter how ostensibly idiosyncratic, part of a set. Overseen by the "consummate management above," this "paradise peopled with unmistakable American shapes . . . melted together and left one uncertain which of them one was, at a given turn of the maze" (81). Under the complete control of the hotel staff, they cease being the subjects of luxury and become objects of the hotel's own eclectic collection of personages. James does not present the hotel as an exalted example of consensus and social stability but as a "cage" where "the whole housed populace move as in mild and consenting suspicion of its captured and governed state, its having to consent to inordinate fusion as the price of what it seemed pleased to regard as inordinate luxury" (325). Yet the desire to feel at home in this lavish world overrides any discomfort or suspicion; they will acquiesce without dissent.

Even as the hotel breaks down social barriers and compromises the separation between the private and public spheres by creating a space of hospitality and spectacle, its democratic reach remains limited. James acknowledges that hotels assiduously maintain two conditions for admittance: one must pay a "high pecuniary tax" and "be presumably 'respectable'" (79). He marvels at "the apparently deep-seated inaptitude of the negro race at large for any alertness of personal service" when a "negro porter" plunges his bag into the mud (312). Certain subjects may only serve the hotel where they must suffer the indignities of the guests who demand a flawless execution of their duties. In this instance, even James abides by the expectations the hotel sets for him. But this particular encounter illuminates the false democracy engendered by the hotel-spirit and its attendant service economy. The hotel denies entrance to many, but it gladly nurtures the desires of everyone. These spaces reproduce art and architecture on a mass scale, but instead of introducing their guests to the power of aesthetics, they redirect them toward "the ordinate *desire for taste*" (328). It is this desire and the love of opulence that everyone in the United States and especially in Florida enjoys. They may never achieve it, but they will live and die by its ideal. As a model home, the hotel becomes the telos of U.S. consumption and, by extension, of American society. Instead of despising those who enjoy the hotel's ornate hospitality, the American populace will cling to the hope that they will be able to purchase their way into its hallowed chambers.

James thus gives us a glimpse of one of the futures of nostalgia, one that redirects its democratic accessibility to serve the needs of consumption. As in *The Wonderful Wizard of Oz*, nostalgia supports the nation's imperial efforts, but in this case by generating affection for the hotel as "a synonym for civilization" (79). James recognizes hotels "facilitated expansionism" and "became advance outposts for overseas empires."[113] At the same time, he attested to the way the hotel-spirit worked in concert with other phenomena associated with the culture of Progressivism, from the historic homesite to the MET, to produce consensus within the nation. In both Baum's and James's work, nostalgia assumes a different character—one that no longer necessarily animates antagonisms, but one that suppresses them. Its life as an antagonistic affect that expressed a sense of estrangement from home, nevertheless, did not end at the dawn of the new century. Its potency as a political sentiment would be felt again at various moments in the many decades that followed.

---

113. Sandoval-Strausz, *Hotel*, 119.

EPILOGUE

"TAKING THE COUNTRY BACK" IN THE TWENTY-FIRST CENTURY

*I*N AN ICONIC SCENE from the first season of Matthew Weiner's *Mad Men* (2007), adman Don Draper makes a pitch to a group of Kodak executives in a dimly lit conference room. Charged with developing an advertising campaign for a slide projector called "the wheel," he concedes that technology might move merchandise but insists "there's the rare occasion when the public can be engaged on a level beyond flash if they have a sentimental bond with the product."[1] Customers, he assures his clients, can form "a deeper bond with the product" when it appeals to a "delicate but potent" sensation: "nostalgia."[2] Draper renames the device "the carousel," as he cycles through a series of canned photos of his own wife and children that project a narrative of the perfect Cold War family that we know to be a fiction. His marriage is doomed, slowly decaying in a Westchester suburb. Yet, as TV reviewer Jenny Diski maintains, Weiner introduces his viewers to a world that is far from hell. It seduces audiences with a "false nostalgia" for the "urban and suburban America" of the 1950s and 1960s.[3] It sins against synchrony: unlike the work of Richard Yates or Billy Wilder, Weiner's television series views this period "only retrospectively."[4] Revolting or revolutionary, *Mad Men* brings the twenty-first century back full circle to the nineteenth century—back to an affect

---

1. "The Wheel."
2. Ibid.
3. Diski, "Unfaithful," 74.
4. Ibid. My phrasing here is a play on Haviland, "The Sin of Synecdoche."

that always rings false and is equal parts art and artifice. Produced in the opening decades of the twenty-first century, an era not unlike that of the Gilded Age, fraught with economic turmoil, the early seasons of *Mad Men* simultaneously reproduce and challenge its audience's desire to long for an economically and culturally stable past.

As exemplified by *Mad Men*, twenty-first-century TV serials, films, and novels abound with meditations on nostalgia that also occasionally chart its storied genealogy.[5] But the fascination with and indulgence in the kind of mass-produced nostalgia anticipated by Henry James only captures one state of nostalgia in recent years. As in the nineteenth century, it is a formidable and pervasive feeling mobilized by competing political interests. In the wake of the 2008 election and during a period of protracted economic decline, two protest groups organized themselves around rival nostalgias: the Tea Party and the Occupy Movement. At the same time, the last two decades have also witnessed the rise of a powerful paradigm of legal interpretation—textualism or originalism—that aspires to recover "how the text of the Constitution was originally understood."[6] I conclude by reflecting upon how forms of nineteenth-century nostalgia residually continue to imagine alternative political and legal possibilities from positions of temporal and spatial estrangement. The imperative to take the country or the Constitution back, one of the mantras of twenty-first-century politics, abides by a nostalgic narrative logic not unlike those examined throughout *Novel Nostalgias*.

A populist incarnation of neoliberalism, the Tea Party movement gained traction in response to the passage of the Troubled Asset Relief Program as well as the Great Recession. Several competing organizations claim to best represent the group, but they all rally around two interconnected ideas: freedom and the "need . . . to take our country back."[7] The idea of freedom remains somewhat elusive in this body of writing, defined negatively against centralized government, as best expressed by

---

5. Seemingly lowbrow TV serials, such as *Terminator: The Sarah Connor Chronicles* (2008–9) and *Revolutions* (2012–13), and critically exalted films, such as *Children of Men* (2006), indulge in nostalgia for our present moment, when late capitalism could continue to sustain its illusion of ceaseless abundance and neoliberal progress. A wide range of apocalyptic novels have also hit the shelves that trade in various nostalgic tropes, including Peter Heller's *The Dog Stars* (2012), Cormac McCarthy's *The Road* (2007), and Karen Thompson Walker's *The Age of Miracles* (2013). Recent fiction that addresses the idea of nostalgia directly includes Patricia Hampl's *The Florist's Daughter* (2009) and Nicole Krauss's *The History of Love* (2006).

6. Scalia, "Common-Law Courts in a Civil-Law System," 112.

7. Meckler and Martin, *Tea Party Patriots*, 15.

the FreedomWorks's declaration, "Government Fails. Freedom Works."[8] The shared presumption is that at some unspecified moment in the past, freedom existed and was then lost, so the Tea Party must work to restore "a government that once existed to protect our rights to life, liberty, and the pursuit of happiness."[9] The rhetorical cleverness of these statements, however, resides with their ambiguity. As understood by both Melville in *Israel Potter* and Baum in *The Wonderful Wizard of Oz*, nostalgia works best when its object—the home—remains a blank canvas for the reader to paint his or her own picture. But like their nineteenth-century predecessors, members of the Tea Party repeatedly return to the Founders. Unlike in the literature of the People's Party of a century ago, though, the Founders speak with one voice in Tea Party tracts. Jefferson is often quoted alongside excerpts from the *Federalist Papers*, as though he completely subscribed to the principles outlined by Madison, Hamilton, and Jay. Similar to the People's Party, they also imagine a people by romancing the events of the U.S. Revolution and the Boston Tea Party.

Writing on behalf of the Tea Party, Mark Meckler and Jenny Beth Martin frame their objectives in terms of what must be done "to return America to the free-market greatness that took us from the Jamestown settlement to the great pioneer migrations to the West, through the industrial revolution."[10] This familiar account of exceptionalism curiously reaches back to Jamestown, rather than to Plymouth and the *Mayflower*, to indulge in nostalgia for a founding narrative whitewashed of slavery, Indian removal, the Civil War, class strife, and xenophobia. Indeed, the same nineteenth century that teemed with the very antagonisms examined in my book emerges in this body of literature as a time when the nation remained on the right track until the fateful year of 1913. For them, this year stands out as the moment when their America was taken away from them by the imposition of a national income tax, which permitted a tyrannically centralized federal government to emerge. As their detractors assert, "one of the distinctive features of the modern American right has been nostalgia for the late 19th century, with its minimal taxation, absence of regulation and reliance on faith-based charity rather than government social programs."[11]

The economic uncertainties that stimulated the rise of the Tea Party also drove the left-leaning Occupy Wall Street movement, which first

---

8. FreedomWorks, "About Us."
9. Meckler and Martin, *Tea Party Patriots*, 13.
10. Ibid., 45–46.
11. Paul Krugman, "Gilded Once More," *New York Times*, April 27, 2007.

established itself in Zuccotti Park on September 17, 2011. They initially trafficked in rhetorical vagaries, but intellectuals within and outside the academy rushed to theorize this manifestation of direct action. As in the nineteenth century, they too returned to the United States' Revolutionary Era but largely confined their hero worship to Thomas Paine, reprinting some of his writing alongside their own treatises.[12] Much like the socialists and anarchists that came before them, they embraced a left nostalgia for a long history of past and present international revolutionary movements. First looking to the Arab Spring for inspiration, they soon appealed to the legacy of the labor movement.

Their yearning for past revolutions and mass movements earned them the ridicule of conservative commentators for displaying nostalgic naïveté. Matthew Continetti of *The Weekly Standard* vented his exasperation over "that slight dizziness" one feels when coming into contact with "the clouds of left-wing nostalgia in New York City and Washington."[13] Continetti contends that "the very notion of a backward-looking left is laughable," because since "the French Revolution, the left has been the party of progress, riding the wave of history to that distant shore where man will cast off the chains of society."[14] My reading of Goldman, Parsons, Sinclair, and Harris, however, established that even for them a better future could become visible only when refracted through the prism of the past. In his sympathetic but still critical history of Occupy, Todd Gitlin similarly observes that they identified "Emma Goldman and Peter Kropotkin" as their predecessors and saw themselves as restoring the revolutionary spirit behind a broad range of movements "from the Industrial Workers of the World to the Spanish anarchists, from SNCC to the Black Panthers, the Cuban revolution to the Vietnamese resistance, [and] from Gandhi to King."[15] Gitlin too places them within this leftist revolutionary framework and suggests they also championed "the right to assemble," as the Anti-Federalists did.[16] Unlike Continetti, he recognizes the creative potential—even if sometimes flawed character—of Occupy's left nostalgia. "They were neither Marxists . . . nor anarchists," Gitlin explains, but "they talked about dual power," demanding a "participatory democratic system—in

---

12. See Blumenkranz et al., *Occupy!*
13. Continetti, "The Reactionary Left."
14. Ibid.
15. Gitlin, *Occupy Nation*, 137–38.
16. Ibid., 243.

the economy, in the political system."[17] In other words, their left nostalgia led them neither to found a new political party nor to commit acts of revolutionary violence, but the hope of recovering the spirit of these lost revolutionary moments nevertheless animated their solidarity with one another and their sense of history.

The political antagonisms and attendant possibilities wrought by these two movements repeat—albeit with important differences—many of the nineteenth-century nostalgic tropes and ideas examined throughout my book. Yet one of the most powerful manifestations of nostalgia in the twenty-first century is also one of its most brilliantly subtle: the nostalgic hermeneutics of Justice Antonin Scalia and his fellow practitioners of textualism. While members of the Tea Party have praised the virtues of strict constructionism, defined loosely as the effort to restore the original meaning of the Constitution as the framers intended it, Scalia takes considerable care to differentiate himself from what he sees as the simple-mindedness of this type of interpretation. He stresses that a good textualist—and therefore a good judge, in his estimation—knows "it is the *law* that governs, not the intent of the lawgiver."[18] Dismissing the idea of "Living Constitutionalism," he avers that every judge ought to attempt to recover "the original meaning of the text."[19]

When Scalia excoriates those who read for intent or in light of the differences between the Constitution's cultural moment and ours, a literary critic cannot help but hear the echoes of New Criticism. Not surprisingly, Scalia quotes T. S. Eliot favorably when he admonishes "literary critics who forget they are dealing with a text."[20] Yet we know Eliot was preceded by a generation of literary commentators, Sinclair Lewis and Upton Sinclair among them, who read well beyond the confines of the text. Scalia would certainly bristle at the implication that he harbors nostalgia of any kind, even though the underlying logic behind originalism is a nostalgic one. Deeming "the notion of a Living Constitution . . . pretty new," Scalia dismisses any suggestion that courts have long adapted the Constitution to suit changing circumstances, from the *Marbury v. Madison* (1803) decision forward.[21] While I will not provide a comprehensive account of Scalia's legal hermeneutics, there is good reason to regard his particular kind of originalism as

---

17. Ibid., 133.
18. Scalia, "Common-Law Courts," 92.
19. Ibid., 118.
20. Scalia and Garner, *Reading Law*, 9.
21. Ibid., 405.

a recent innovation.²² Its ability to appeal to conservative populists, moreover, stems from the sense that the law no longer makes them feel at home in the United States. Scalia cites the *Dred Scott* decision as an example of a proto-Living Constitutionalism in practice, but he directly associates this interpretive paradigm with the Warren Court. The conservative disregard for this Court, which expanded and protected the civil rights of individuals in a nearly unprecedented way, hits the same notes white Southerners did in the nineteenth century who resented the Radical Republican policies of Reconstruction. The parallels are imperfect, to be sure, but their resonances illustrate how nostalgia still transforms lines of political antagonism into structures of feeling.

These early-twenty-first-century nostalgias, though, also return us to where this epilogue began: the era represented in *Mad Men*. While the U.S. Revolutionary period remains a playground for contending nostalgias, the 1950s are almost equally contested historical terrain now. For the right, it is a decade representative of American exceptionalism and economic and military supremacy before the tumult of the 1960s. For liberals, it is a decade pregnant with recoverable possibilities: union power was strong, the welfare state was robust, and Earl Warren presided over a progressive court. These appropriations necessarily require certain qualifications. Depending on the ideological flavor of the nostalgia expressed, one must either downplay the power of the federal government or deemphasize the institutionalized race and gender inequality of the time. It is difficult not to find the nostalgia for the 1950s displayed in contemporary political discourse and in *Mad Man* alike troubling, but my book demonstrates how nostalgia can imagine rather than just arrest sweeping political changes. In the United States, radical political possibility often begins with the realization that there really is no place like home.

---

22. What early nineteenth-century jurists understood as originalism was a matter of debate. See Slauter, *State as a Work of Art*, 19–26.

BIBLIOGRAPHY

Adorno, Theodor. "Commitment." Translated by Francis McDonagh. In *Aesthetics and Politics*, edited by Ronald Taylor, 177–95. London: Verso, 1977.

———. *Essays on Music*. Edited by Richard Leppert. Translated by Susan H. Gillespie. Berkeley: University of California Press, 2002.

———. *The Psychological Technique of Martin Luther Thomas' Radio Addresses*. Stanford, CA: Stanford University Press, 2000.

———. *Quasi una Fantasia: Essays on Modern Music*. Translated by Rodney Livingstone. London: Verso, 1992.

"An Account of the *Cachexia Africana*." *The Medical and Physical Journal* 2 (1799): 171–73.

Agacinski, Sylviane. *Time Passing: Modernity and Nostalgia*. Translated by Jody Gladding. New York: Columbia University Press, 2003.

Agamben, Giorgio. *Homo Sacer: Sovereign Power and Bare Life*. Translated by Daniel Heller-Roazen. Stanford, CA: Stanford University Press, 1998.

———. *The State of Exception*. Translated by Kevin Attell. Chicago: University of Chicago Press, 2005.

Agathocleous, Tanya. *Urban Realism and the Cosmopolitan Imagination in the Nineteenth Century*. Cambridge: Cambridge University Press, 2011.

Agnew, Christopher. "The Consuming Vision of Henry James." In *The Culture of Consumption: Critical Essays in American History 1880–1980*, edited by Richard Wightman Fox and T. J. Jackson Lears, 65–100. New York: Pantheon, 1983.

Ahrens, Gale, ed. *Lucy Parsons: Freedom, Equality, and Solidarity. Writings and Speeches, 1878–1937*. Chicago: Charles H. Kerr Publishing Company, 2004.

Ali, Omar H. *In the Lion's Mouth: Black Populism in the New South, 1886–1900*. Jackson: University Press of Mississippi, 2010.

Allen, Grant. "Novels without a Purpose." *North American Review*, August 1896, 223–35.

A. M. P. "Stanzas: Progress." *Knickerbocker Magazine*, May 1848, 397–98.

Anarchy at an End: Lives, Trial, and Conviction of the Eight Chicago Anarchists. Chicago: G. S. Baldwin, 1886.

Anderson, Amanda. "Cosmopolitanism, Universalism, and the Divided Legacies of Modernity." In Cheah and Robbins, 265–89.

Anderson, Benedict. *Imagined Communities: Reflections on the Origin and Spread of Nationalism*. 3rd ed. New York: Verso, 2006.

Anderson, David. "Dying of Nostalgia: Homesickness in the Union Army during the Civil War." *Civil War History* 56 (2010): 247–82.

Anderson, Donald Lee, and Tryggve Anderson. "Nostalgia and Malingering in the Military during the Civil War." *Perspectives in Biology and Medicine* 28 (1984): 156–66.

Andrews, Sidney. *The South Since the War: As Shown by Fourteen Weeks of Travel and Observation in Georgia and the Carolinas*. Boston: Ticknor and Fields, 1866.

Appiah, Kwame Anthony. *Cosmopolitanism: Ethics in a World of Strangers*. New York: W. W. Norton, 2006.

———. *The Ethics of Identity*. Princeton, NJ: Princeton University Press, 2005.

Appleby, Joyce. *Liberalism and Republicanism in the Historical Imagination*. Cambridge, MA: Harvard University Press, 1992.

Arac, Jonathan. *The Emergence of American Literary Narrative*. Cambridge, MA: Harvard University Press, 2005.

Aranda, José E. Jr. "Contradictory Impulses: María Amparo Ruiz de Burton, Resistance Theory, and the Politics of Chicano/a Studies." In *No More Separate Spheres!: A Next Wave American Studies Reader*, edited by Cathy N. Davidson and Jessamyn Hatcher, 121–48. Durham, NC: Duke University Press, 2002.

Arendt, Hannah. *On Revolution*. New York: Penguin, 2006.

———. *The Origins of Totalitarianism*. New York: Harcourt, 1966.

Armstrong, Nancy. "Why Daughters Die: The Racial Logic of American Sentimentalism." *The Yale Journal of Criticism* 7, no. 2 (1994): 1–24.

Ashbaugh, Carolyn. *Lucy Parsons: American Revolutionary*. Chicago: Charles H. Kerr Publishing Company, 1976.

Atchison, Rena Michaels. *Un-American Immigration: Its Present Effects and Future Perils*. Chicago: Kerr, 1894.

Austin, Linda M. *Nostalgia in Transition, 1780–1917*. Charlottesville: University of Virginia Press, 2007.

Ayers, Edward L. *What Caused the Civil War?: Reflections on the South and Southern History*. New York: W. W. Norton, 2005.

Badiou, Alain. *Metapolitics*. Translated by Jason Baker. London: Verso, 2005.

Baker, Bruce E. *What Reconstruction Meant: Historical Memory in the American South*. Charlottesville: University of Virginia Press, 2007.

Bakhtin, Mikhail M. *The Dialogic Imagination*. Translated by Caryl Emerson and Michael Holquist. Austin: University of Texas Press, 1981.

Barnes, Elizabeth. *States of Sympathy: Seduction and Democracy in the American Novel*. New York: Columbia University Press, 1997.

Barrett, Laura. "From Wonderland to Wasteland: *The Wonderful Wizard of Oz, The Great Gatsby*, and the New American Fairy Tale." *Papers on Language and Literature* 42 (2006): 150–80.

Barrish, Philip. *American Literary Realism, Critical Theory, and Intellectual Prestige, 1880–1995*. Cambridge: Cambridge University Press, 2001.

Bartel, Kim. "Kant's Narrative of Hope in the Gilded Age." *American Literary History* 19 (2007): 661—88.

Bartholow, Roberts. "Chapter First." In *Sanitary Memoirs of the War of Rebellion*, vol. 1, 3–41. New York: United States Sanitary Commission, 1867.

Baum, L. Frank. *The Art of Decorating Dry Goods Windows and Interiors: A Complete Manual of Window Trimming, Designed as an Educator in All the Details of the Art, According to the Best Accepted Methods, and Treating Fully Every Important Subject*. Chicago: Show Window Publishing, 1900.

———. *The Emerald City of Oz*. Chicago: Reilly and Britton, 1910.

———. *The Wonderful Wizard of Oz*. Edited by Susan Wolstenholme. New York: Oxford University Press, 1997.

Bell, Michael Davitt. *The Problem of American Realism: Studies in the Cultural History of a Literary Idea*. Chicago: University of Chicago Press, 1993.

Bellamy, Edward. *Looking Backward, 2000–1887*. Edited by Alex MacDonald. Ontario: Broadview, 2003.

Bellesiles, Michael A. *1877: America's Year of Living Violently*. New York: New Press, 2010.

Belnap, Jeffrey, and Raul Fernández, eds. *Jose Marti's "Our America": From National to Hemispheric Cultural Studies*. Durham, NC: Duke University Press, 1998.

Benjamin, Walter. "Left-Wing Melancholy." Translated by Ben Brewster. In *Walter Benjamin: Selected Writings*, vol. 2, edited by Michael W. Jennings, Howard Eiland, and Gary Smith, 423–27. Cambridge, MA: Harvard University Press, 1999.

———. "On the Concept of History." Translated by Harry Zohn. In *Walter Benjamin: Selected Writings*, vol. 4, edited by Howard Eiland and Michael W. Jennings, 389–400. Cambridge, MA: Harvard University Press, 2003.

Bergman, Jill. *Motherless Child in the Novels of Pauline Hopkins*. Baton Rouge: Louisiana State University Press, 2012.

Berkman, Alexander. Review of *The Bomb* by Frank Harris. *Mother Earth*, March 1909, 15–20.

Berlant, Lauren. *The Anatomy of National Fantasy: Hawthorne, Utopia and Everyday Life*. Chicago: University of Chicago Press, 1991.

———. *Cruel Optimism*. Durham, NC: Duke University Press, 2011.

Berman, Jessica. *Modernist Fiction, Cosmopolitanism, and the Politics of Community*. Cambridge: Cambridge University Press, 2001.

Bernath, Michael. *Confederate Minds: The Struggle for Intellectual Independence in the Civil War South*. Chapel Hill: University of North Carolina Press, 2010.

Berthoff, Warner. *The Ferment of Realism: American Literature 1884–1919*. Cambridge: Cambridge University Press, 1965.

Bhabha, Homi K. *The Location of Culture*. New York: Routledge, 1991.

———. "Unsatisfied: Notes on Vernacular Cosmopolitanism." In *Text and Nation: Cross-disciplinary Essays on Cultural and National Identities*, edited by Laura García-Moreno and Peter C. Pfeiffer, 191–207. Columbia, SC: Camden House, 1996.

Blair, Sara. *Henry James and the Writing of Race and Nation*. New York: Cambridge University Press, 1996.

Blight, David W. *Race and Reunion: The Civil War in American Memory*. Cambridge, MA: Harvard University Press, 2001.

Bloch, Ernst. "Can Hope Be Disappointed?" In *Literary Essays*, translated by Andrew Joron et al., 339–45. Stanford, CA: Stanford University Press, 1998.

———. *The Principle of Hope*. Translated by Neville Plaice, Stephen Plaice, and Paul Knight, 3 vols. Cambridge, MA: The Massachusetts Institute of Technology Press, 1986.

Blumenkranz, Carla, et al., eds. *Occupy!: Scenes from Occupied America*. New York: Verso, 2011.

"Books Worth Reading." *The Crisis*, August 1921, 190.

Boorstin, Daniel J. *The Image: A Guide to Pseudo-Events in America*. New York: Harper & Row, 1961.

Bost, Suzanne. "West Meets East: Nineteenth-Century Southern Dialogues on Mixture, Race, Gender, and Nation." *Mississippi Quarterly* 56 (2003): 647–56.

Boym, Svetlana. *The Future of Nostalgia*. New York: Basic Books, 2001.

Bramen, Carrie Tirado. *The Uses of Variety: Modern Americanism and the Quest for National Distinctiveness*. Cambridge, MA: Harvard University Press, 2000.

Brennan, Teresa. *The Transmission of Affect*. Ithaca: Cornell University Press, 2004.

Brennan, Timothy. *At Home in the World: Cosmopolitanism Now*. Cambridge, MA: Harvard University Press, 1997.

Brodhead, Richard. *Cultures of Letters: Scenes of Reading and Writing in Nineteenth-Century America*. Chicago: University of Chicago Press, 1993.

Brooks, Daphne A. *Bodies in Dissent: Spectacular Performances of Race and Freedom, 1850–1910*. Durham, NC: Duke University Press, 2006.

Brown, Bill. "The Popular, the Populist, and the Populace—Locating Hamlin Garland in the Politics of Culture." *Arizona Quarterly* 50, no. 3 (1994): 89–110.

Brown, Gillian. *Domestic Individualism: Imagining Self in Nineteenth-Century America*. Berkeley: University of California Press, 1990.

Brown, Lois. *Pauline Elizabeth Hopkins: Black Daughter of the Revolution*. Chapel Hill: University of North Carolina Press, 2008.

Brown, Wendy. *Politics Out of History*. Princeton, NJ: Princeton University Press, 2001.

Brown, William Wells. *Clotel: or, The President's Daughter: A Narrative of Slave Life in the United States*. Edited by Robert S. Levine. Boston: Bedford/St. Martin's, 2000.

———. *Clotelle: or, The Colored Heroine*. In *Clotel: or, The President's Daughter: A Narrative of Slave Life in the United States*, edited by Robert S. Levine, 309–27. Boston: Bedford/St. Martin's, 2000.

———. *Narrative of William W. Brown, A Fugitive Slave*. In *William Wells Brown: A Reader*, edited by Ezra Greenspan, 5-61. Athens: University of Georgia Press, 2008.

Brusky, Sarah. "Beyond the Ending of Maternal Absence in *A New-England Tale*, *The Wide, Wide, World*, and *St. Elmo*." *ESQ* 46 (2000): 149–76.

Bryan, William Jennings. *The First Battle: A Story of the Campaign of 1896*. Chicago: W. B. Conkey, 1896.

Buck, Solon J. *The Agrarian Crusade: A Chronicle of the Farmer in Politics*. New Haven, CT: Yale University Press, 1920.

Bucknill, John Charles, and Daniel H. Tuke. *A Manual of Psychological Medicine*. New York: Hafner Publishing Company, 1968.

Buel, Alex W. "Hungarian Independence." In *Appendix to the Congressional Globe*. 31st Cong., 1st Sess. (1850), 143–48.

Buelens, Gert. "Possessing the American Scene: Race and Vulgarity, Seduction and Judgment." In *Enacting History in Henry James*, edited by Gert Buelens, 166–92. Cambridge: Cambridge University Press, 1997.

Buell, Lawrence. *New England Literary Culture: From Revolution through Renaissance*. Cambridge: Cambridge University Press, 1986.

Buhle, Mari Jo. "*Socialist Woman, Progressive Woman, Coming Nation*." In Conlin, 442–49.

Buhle, Paul M. "*The Appeal to Reason* and *New Appeal*." In Conlin, 50–59.

———. *Marxism in the United States: Remapping the History of the American Left*. London: Verso, 1987.

Burke, Edmund. *A Philosophical Inquiry into the Origin of our Ideas of the Sublime and the Beautiful*. Oxford: Oxford University Press, 1990.

Burnham, Michelle. *Captivity and Sentiment: Cultural Exchange in American Literature, 1682–1861*. Hanover, NH: Dartmouth College Press, 1997.

Burrows, Stuart. *A Familiar Strangeness: American Fiction and the Language of Photography, 1839–1945*. Athens: University of Georgia Press, 2010.

Burton, Robert. *The Anatomy of Melancholy*. Vol. 1. New York: W. J. Widdleton, 1870.

Butler, Judith. *Precarious Life: The Powers of Mourning and Violence*. London: Verso, 2004.

Cadle, Nathaniel. *The Mediating Nation: Late American Realism, Globalization, and the Progressive State*. Chapel Hill: University of North Carolina Press, 2014.

Cahill, Edward. *Liberty of the Imagination: Aesthetic Theory, Literary Form, and Politics in the Early United States*. Philadelphia: University of Pennsylvania Press, 2012.

Cameron, Sharon. *Thinking in Henry James*. Chicago: University of Chicago Press, 1991.

Canfield, Dorothy. "The House with the Woodbine." *Munsey's Magazine*, June 1907, 345–50.

Carby, Hazel V. *Reconstructing Womanhood: The Emergence of the Afro-American Woman Novelist*. New York: Oxford University Press, 1987.

Carey, Matthew Jr., ed. *The Democratic Speaker's Hand-Book*. Cincinnati, OH: Miami Print and Publishing Co., 1868.

Carr, Robert V. "Nostalgia." *Overland Monthly and Out West Magazine*, December 1901, 410.

Carter, Everett. "The Haymarket Affair in Literature." *American Quarterly* 2 (1950): 270–78.

Cass, Lewis. "Diplomatic Relations with Austria." In *Appendix to the Congressional Globe*. 31st Cong., 1st Sess. (1850), 54–58.

Castiglia, Christopher. *Bound and Determined: Captivity, Culture-Crossing, and White Womanhood from Mary Rowlandson to Patty Hearst*. Chicago: University of Chicago Press, 1996.

———. *Interior States: Institutional Consciousness and the Inner Life of Democracy in the Antebellum United States*. Durham, NC: Duke University Press, 2008.

Castronovo, Russ. *Beautiful Democracy: Aesthetics and Anarchy in a Global Era*. Chicago: University of Chicago Press, 2007.

———. *Fathering the Nation: American Genealogies of Slavery and Freedom*. Berkeley: University of California Press, 1995.

———. Introduction to *The Jungle*, by Upton Sinclair, vii–xxv. Edited by Russ Castronovo. Oxford: Oxford University Press, 2010.

———. "Teaching the Good." *Journal of Narrative Theory* 41(2011): 167–74.

Cheah, Pheng. "Given Culture: Rethinking Cosmopolitical Freedom in Transnationalism." In Cheah and Robbins, 290–328.

Cheah, Pheng, and Bruce Robbins, eds. *Cosmopolitics: Thinking and Feeling beyond the Nation*. Minneapolis: University of Minnesota Press, 1998.

Cheng, Anne Anlin. *The Melancholy of Race*. New York: Oxford University Press, 2000.

Chesnutt, Charles. *The Marrow of Tradition*. Edited by Eric Sundquist. New York: Penguin, 1993.

Child, Lydia Maria. *A Romance of the Republic*. Boston: Ticknor and Fields, 1867.

Chow, Rey. *The Protestant Ethnic and the Spirit of Capitalism*. New York: Columbia University Press, 2002.

"Chronic Rebellion." *Advocate of Peace*, September/October 1868, 119–22.

Claggett, Shalyn. "Narcissism and the Conditions of Self-Knowledge in James's 'The Jolly Corner.'" *Henry James Review* 26 (2005): 189–200.

Clemens, Jeremiah. "Resolutions Regarding Slavery." In *Appendix to the Congressional Globe*. 31st Cong., 1st Sess. (1850), 52–54.

Clifford, James. *Routes: Travel and Translation in the Late Twentieth Century*. Cambridge, MA: Harvard University Press, 1997.

Coleman, Laurence Vail. *Historic House Museums*. Washington, DC: American Association of Museums, 1933.

Conlin, Joseph R., ed. *The American Radical Press, 1880–1960*. 2 vols. Westport, CT: Greenwood Press, 1974.

Continetti, Matthew. "The Reactionary Left." *The Weekly Standard*, Nov 11, 2011. http://www.weeklystandard.com/articles/reactionary-left_604180.html.

Cox, Samuel S. "Miscegenation or Amalgamation. Fate of the Freedman." Washington, DC: Constitutional Union, 1864.

———. "The Nation's Hope in the Democracy—Historic Lessons for Civil War." Washington, DC: L. Towers & Co., 1864.

Creelman, James. "Mr. Bryan Explained." *Pearson's Magazine*, April 1908, 343–64.

Critchley, Simon. *Infinitely Demanding: Ethics of Commitment, Politics of Resistance*. London: Verso, 2007.

Culver, Stuart. "What Manikins Want: *The Wonderful Wizard of Oz* and The Art of Decorating Dry Goods Windows." *Representations* 21 (1988): 97–116.

Dames, Nicholas. *Amnesiac Selves: Nostalgia, Forgetting, and British Fiction, 1810–1870*. New York: Oxford University Press, 2001.

Darwin, Erasmus. *Zoonomia; or, the Laws of Organic Life*. Vol. 2. London: J. Johnson, 1796.

Davies, Arthur Ernest. *The Moral Life: A Study in Genetic Ethics*. Baltimore, MD: Review Publishing, 1909.

Davis, Fred. *Yearning for Yesterday: A Sociology of Nostalgia*. New York: The Free Press, 1979.

Davis, Richard Harding. *Soldiers of Fortune*. New York: Scribner, 1911.

Dean, Eric T. *Shook over Hell: Post-Traumatic Stress, Vietnam, and the Civil War*. Cambridge, MA: Harvard University Press, 1997.

Debs, Eugene V. "The Negro and the Class Struggle." *The International Socialist Review* 4 (1903): 257–60.

De Cleyre, Voltairine. "Anarchism and American Traditions." In Presley and Sartwell, 91–102.

———. "Direct Action." In Presley and Sartwell, 273–86.

De Coubertin, Pierre. "Does Cosmopolitan Life Lead to International Friendliness?" *American Monthly Review of Reviews*, April 1898, 429–34.

———. "The Meeting of the Olympian Games." *North American Review*, June 1900, 802–11.

De Forest, John W. *Miss Ravenel's Conversion from Secession to Loyalty*. New York: Penguin, 2000.

Dekker, George. *The American Historical Romance*. Cambridge: Cambridge University Press, 1987.

de la Luz Montes, Amelia María. "María Amparo Ruiz de Burton Negotiates American Literary Politics and Culture." In *Challenging Boundaries: Gender and Periodization*, edited by Joyce W. Warren and Margaret Dickie, 202–25. Athens: University of Georgia Press, 2000.

De Leon, Daniel. "Fourth Day." In *Proceedings of the Tenth National Convention of the Socialist Labor Party*, 93–97. New York: New York Labor News Company, 1901.

Deleuze, Gilles. *The Logic of Sense*. Edited by Constantin V. Boundas. Translated by Mark Lester. New York: Columbia University Press, 1990.

Dennett, John Richard. "The South as It Is: XXXIV." *The Nation*, April 5, 1866, 431–33.

Denning, Michael. *Mechanic Accents: Dime Novels and Working-Class Culture in America*. Rev. ed. London: Verso, 1998.

Derrida, Jacques. *Archive Fever: A Freudian Impression*. Translated by Eric Prenowitz. Chicago: University of Chicago Press, 1995.

———. *Dissemination*. Translated by Barbara Johnson. Chicago: University of Chicago Press, 1981.

Dickstein, Morris. *A Mirror in the Roadway: Literature and the Real World*. Princeton, NJ: Princeton University Press, 2005.

Dillon, Elizabeth Maddock. "Sentimental Aesthetics." *American Literature* 76 (2004): 495–523.

Dimock, Wai Chee. *Through Other Continents: American Literature Across Deep Time*. Princeton, NJ: Princeton University Press, 2006.

Diski, Jenny. "Unfaithful: The False Nostalgia of Mad Men." *Harper's Magazine*, January 2012, 74.

Dixon, Thomas. *The Clansman: An Historical Romance of the Ku Klux Klan*. New York: Doubleday, Page & Co., 1905.

Donnelly, Ignatius. *Caesar's Column: A Story of the Twentieth Century*. Chicago: F. J. Schulte & Company, 1890.

Doolen, Andy. *Territories of Empire: U.S. Writing from the Louisiana Purchase to Mexican Independence*. New York: Oxford University Press, 2014.

Dos Passos, John. Introduction to *The Bomb*, by Frank Harris, i–xxiii. Chicago: University of Chicago Press, 1963.

Dreiser, Theodore. "Change." In *Hey Rub-A-Dub-Dub: A Book of the Mystery and Wonder and Terror of Life*, 19–23. New York: Boni & Liveright, 1920.

Drexler, Michael J. and Ed White. *The Traumatic Colonel: The Founding Fathers, Slavery, and the Phantasmatic Aaron Burr*. New York: New York University Press, 2014.

duCille, Ann. *The Coupling Convention: Sex, Text, and Tradition in Black Women's Fiction*. New York: Oxford University Press, 1993.

Dunning, Nelson A. *The Farmers' Alliance History and Agricultural Digest*. Washington, DC: The Alliance Publishing Co., 1891.

Eco, Umberto. *Travels in Hyperreality: Essays*. Translated by William Weaver. New York: Harcourt Brace, 1986.

Elliott, Orrin Leslie. "Ethics of the Tariff Controversy." *Overland Monthly and Out West Magazine*, March 1894, 281–94.

Ellison, Julie. *Cato's Tears and the Making of Anglo-American Emotion*. Chicago: University of Chicago Press, 1999.

Emery, Sarah E. V. *Seven Financial Conspiracies Which Have Enslaved the American People*. Lansing, MI: Robert Smith & Co., 1887.

Erisman, Fred. "L. Frank Baum and the Progressive Dilemma." *American Quarterly* 20 (1968): 616–23.

Ernest, John. *Liberation Historiography: African-American Writers and the Challenge of History, 1894–1861*. Chapel Hill: University of North Carolina Press, 2004.

Esposito, Roberto. *Communitas: The Origin and Destiny of Community*. Translated by Timothy Campbell. Stanford, CA: Stanford University Press, 2010.

Evans, Augusta J. *St. Elmo*. New York: Grosset & Dunlap, 1894.

Fabi, M. Giulia. *Passing and the Rise of the African-American Novel*. Urbana: University of Illinois Press, 2001.

Fabian, Johannes. *Time and the Other: How Anthropology Makes Its Object*. 2nd ed. New York: Columbia University Press, 2002.

Fahs, Alice. *The Imagined Civil War: Popular Literature of the North and South*. Chapel Hill: University of North Carolina Press, 2001.

Falconer, William. *A Dissertation on the Influence of the Passions upon Disorders of the Body*. London: C. Dilly, 1788.

Farrison, William Edward. *William Wells Brown: Author and Reformer*. Chicago: University of Chicago Press, 1969.

Faust, Drew Gilpin. *The Creation of Confederate Nationalism: Ideology and Identity in the Civil War South*. Baton Rouge: Louisiana State University Press, 1988.

———. *Mothers of Invention: Women of the Slaveholding South in the American Civil War*. Chapel Hill: University of North Carolina Press, 1996.

Fern, Fanny. *Ruth Hall: A Domestic Tale of the Present Time*. Edited by Joyce Warren. New Brunswick: Rutgers University Press, 1986.

Fetterley, Judith, and Marjorie Pryse. *Writing Out of Place: Regionalism, Women, and American Literary Culture*. Urbana: University of Illinois Press, 2003.

Ficino. "Learned People and Melancholy." In *The Nature of Melancholy: From Aristotle to Kristeva*, edited by Jennifer Radden, 87–93. New York: Oxford University Press, 2000.

Fidler, William Perry. *Augusta Evans Wilson, 1835–1909: A Biography*. Birmingham: University of Alabama Press, 1951.

Fisher, Beth. "The Captive Mexicana and the Desiring Bourgeois Woman: Domesticity and Expansionism in Ruiz de Burton's *Who Would Have Thought It?*" *Legacy* 16 (1999): 59–69.

Fisher, Philip. *The Vehement Passions*. Princeton, NJ: Princeton University Press, 2002.

———. *Wonder, the Rainbow, and the Aesthetics of Rare Experiences*. Cambridge, MA: Harvard University Press, 1998.

Fleissner, Jennifer L. "Earth-Eating, Addiction, Nostalgia: Charles Chesnutt's Diasporic Regionalism." *Studies in Romanticism* 49 (2010): 313–36.

———. *Women, Compulsion, Modernity: The Moment of American Naturalism*. Chicago: University of Chicago Press, 2004.

Flower, B. O. *Lessons Learned from Other Lives*. Boston: Spectator Publishing Co., 1889.

Foner, Eric. *Reconstruction: America's Unfinished Revolution, 1863–1867*. New York: Harper & Row, 1988.

Foote, Stephanie. *Regional Fictions: Culture and Identity in Nineteenth-Century American Literature*. Madison: University of Wisconsin Press, 2001.

"A Fragment from Mexican History." *Land We Love*, October 1866, 425–28.

Frank, Thomas. *What's the Matter with Kansas? How Conservatives Won the Heart of America*. New York: Metropolitan Books, 2004.

FreedomWorks. "About Us." Last modified September 12, 2014. http://www.freedomworks.org/about/about-freedomworks.

Freud, Sigmund. "Mourning and Melancholia." In Vol. 14 of *The Standard Edition of the Complete Psychological Works of Sigmund Freud*, edited and translated by James Strachey, 243–58. London: Hogarth Press, 1957.

Friedman, Isaac Kahn. *By Bread Alone*. New York: McClure, Philips & Co., 1901

Fuller, Randall. *From Battlefields Rising: How the Civil War Transformed American Literature*. New York: Oxford University Press, 2011.

Gaddis, John Lewis. *We Now Know: Rethinking Cold War History*. Oxford: Clarendon, 1997.

Gaines, Kevin. *Uplifting the Race: Black Leadership, Politics, and Culture in the Twentieth Century*. Chapel Hill: University of North Carolina Press, 1996.

Gardner, Jared. *Master Plots: Race and the Founding of an American Literature, 1787–1845*. Baltimore: The Johns Hopkins University Press, 1998.

Garland, Hamlin. *Crumbling Idols: Twelve Essays on Art Dealing Chiefly with Literature, Painting, and the Drama*. Edited by Jane Johnson. Cambridge, MA: Harvard University Press, 1960.

———. *Main-Travelled Roads*. Lincoln: University of Nebraska Press, 1995.

———. "A New Declaration of Rights." *The Arena*, January 1891, 157–84.

Gay, Peter. *Weimer Culture: The Outsider as Insider*. New York: W. W. Norton, 2001.

Gildersleeve, Basil L. "A Southerner in the Peloponnesian War." *Atlantic Monthly*, September 1897, 330–42.

Giles, Paul. *Virtual Americas: Transnational Fictions and the Transatlantic Imaginary*. Durham, NC: Duke University Press, 2002.

Gillman, Susan. *Blood Talk: American Race Melodrama and the Culture of the Occult*. Chicago: University of Chicago Press, 2003.

Gilmore, Paul. *Aesthetic Materialism: Electricity and American Romanticism*. Stanford, CA: Stanford University Press, 2008.

Gilroy, Paul. *The Black Atlantic: Modernity and the Double Consciousness*. Cambridge, MA: Harvard University Press, 1993.

———. *Postcolonial Melancholia*. New York: Columbia University Press, 2005.

Gitlin, Todd. *Occupy Nation: The Roots, the Spirit, and the Promise of Occupy Wall Street*. New York: HarperCollins, 2012.

Glazener, Nancy. *Reading for Realism: The History of a U.S. Literary Institution, 1850–1910*. Durham, NC: Duke University Press, 1997.

Glover, Stephen. "The Georgian Slave: Ballad." Cleveland, OH: S. Brainard & Co., 1852.

Goldman, Emma. *Anarchism and Other Essays*. 3rd ed. New York: Mother Earth Publishing Association, 1917.

Goldman, Emma, and Max Baginski. "Mother Earth." *Mother Earth*, March 1906, 1–4.

Gonzales, Manuel G. *Mexicanos: A History of Mexicans in the United States*. Bloomington: Indiana University Press, 1999.

Gonzales-Berry, Erlinda, and Chuck Tatum, eds. *Recovering the U.S. Hispanic Literary Heritage*. Vol. 2. Houston: Arte Público Press, 1993.

González, John Morán. *The Troubled Union: Expansionist Imperatives in Post-Reconstruction American Novels*. Columbus: The Ohio State University Press, 2010.

Goodwyn, Lawrence. *The Populist Moment: A Short History of the Agrarian Revolt in America*. New York: Oxford University Press, 1978.

Gordon, Michael. Interview by Michael Kirk. "The Lost Year in Iraq." *Frontline*. PBS. August 10, 2006.

Gould, Philip. *Barbaric Traffic: Commerce and Antislavery in the Eighteenth-Century Atlantic World*. Cambridge, MA: Harvard University Press, 2003.

———. *Covenant and Republic: Historical Romance and the Politics of Puritanism*. Cambridge: Cambridge University Press, 1996.

Gramsci, Antonio. *Selections from the Prison Notebooks*. Edited and translated by Quintin Hoare and Geoffrey Nowell Smith. New York: International Publishers, 1971.

Greene, Graham. *The Quiet American*. New York: Viking, 1955.

Griffin, Martin. *Ashes of the Mind: Memory in Northern Literature, 1865–1900*. Amherst: University of Massachusetts Press, 2009.

Griffin, Susan. *The Historical Eye: The Texture of the Visual in the Late James*. Boston: University Press of New England, 1991.

Guislain, Joseph. "Traité sur L'Alienation Mentale, &c." In *The Treatment of Insanity*, translated and edited by John M. Galt, 137–49. New York: Harper & Brothers, 1846.

Hahn, Steven. *A Nation under Our Feet: Black Political Struggles in the Rural South from Slavery to the Great Migration*. Cambridge, MA: Harvard University Press, 2003.

Hale, Edward Everett. "The Man without a Country." *Atlantic Monthly*, December 1863, 665–80.

Hamilton, Robert. *The Duties of a Regimental Surgeon Considered*. Vol. 1. London: J. Johnson, 1787.

Harle, Jonathan. *An Historical Essay on the State of Physick in the Old and New Testament, and the Apocryphal Interval*. London: Richard Ford, 1729.

Harris, Frank. *The Bomb*. New York: Mitchell Kennerley, 1909.

———. *Contemporary Portraits*. Vol. 3. New York: Frank Harris, 1920.

Harris, Susan K. *Nineteenth-Century American Women's Novels: Interpretative Strategies*. Cambridge: Cambridge University Press, 1990.

Harrison, Gabriel. *John Howard Payne, Dramatist, Poet, Actor, and Author of Home, Sweet Home! His Life and Writings*. Rev. ed. Philadelphia: J. P. Lippincott & Co., 1885.

Hart, James David. *The Popular Book: A History of America's Literary Taste*. New York: Oxford University Press, 1950.

Harte, Bret. "The Argonauts of '49." In *The Luck of Roaring Camp and Other Writings*, 229–49. New York: Penguin, 2001.

Hartman, Saidiya V. *Scenes of Subjection: Terror, Slavery, and Self-Making in Nineteenth-Century America*. New York: Oxford University Press, 1997.

Haskell, Thomas L. *The Emergence of Professional Social Science: The American Social Science Association and the Nineteenth-Century Crisis of Authority*. 2nd ed. Baltimore: The Johns Hopkins University Press, 2000.

Haviland, Beverly. *Henry James's Last Romance: Making Sense of the Past and the American Scene*. Cambridge: Cambridge University Press, 1997.

———. "The Sin of Synecdoche: Hawthorne's Allegory Against Symbolism in 'Rappaccini's Daughter.'" *Texas Studies in Literature and Language* 29 (1987): 278–301.

Hebard, Andrew. "Romantic Sovereignty: Popular Romances and the American Imperial State in the Philippines." *American Quarterly* 57 (2005): 805–30.

Hegeman, Susan. *Patterns for America: Modernism and the Concept of Culture*. Princeton, NJ: Princeton University Press, 1999.

Hendler, Glenn. *Public Sentiments: Structures of Feeling in Nineteenth-Century Literature*. Chapel Hill: University of North Carolina Press, 2001.

Hentz, Caroline Lee. *The Planter's Northern Bride*. 2 vols. Philadelphia: A. Hart, Late Carey and Hart, 1854.

Herr, Cheryl Temple. *Critical Regionalism and Cultural Studies: From Ireland to the American Midwest*. Gainesville: University Press of Florida, 1996.

Hicks, Granville. *The Great Tradition: An Interpretation of American Literature since the Civil War*. New York: Macmillan, 1933.

Higgins, Brian, and Hershel Parker, eds. *Herman Melville: The Contemporary Reviews*. New York: Cambridge University Press, 1995.

"High Noon of the Empire." *The Overland Monthly and Out West Magazine*, July 1868, 21–28.

Higham, John. *History: Professional Scholarship in America*. Baltimore: Johns Hopkins University Press, 1989.

Hindy, Steve. "The Kremlin Watchers Were Dazzled by Oz." *Newsday*, October 17, 1991, 123.

Hobsbawm, Eric. "Introduction: Inventing Tradition." In *The Invention of Tradition*, edited by Eric Hobsbawm and Terence Ranger, 1–14. Cambridge: Cambridge University Press, 1983.

Hofer, Johannes. *Medical Dissertation on Nostalgia by Johannes Hofer, 1688*. Translated by Carolyn Kiser Anspach. *Bulletin of the History of Medicine* 2 (1934): 376–91.

Hofstadter, Richard. *Anti-Intellectualism in American Life*. New York: Vintage, 1962.

———. *The Age of Reform*. New York: Vintage, 1955.

"Home Sickness." *The Ladies' Pearl*, April 1842, 223.

Homestead, Melissa. *American Women Authors and Literary Property, 1822–1869*. Cambridge: Cambridge University Press, 2005.

Hopkins, Pauline E. *Contending Forces: A Romance Illustrative of Negro Life North and South*. New York: Oxford University Press, 1986.

———. *Daughter of the Revolution: The Major Nonfiction Works of Pauline E. Hopkins*. Edited by Ira Dworkin. New Brunswick, NJ: Rutgers University Press, 2007.

———. *Peculiar Sam, or The Underground Railroad*. In *The Roots of African-American Drama: An Anthology of Plays, 1858–1938*, edited by Leo Hamalian and James V. Hatch, 100–23. Detroit: Wayne State University Press, 1991.

Horner, Jonah. *On Health; What Preserves, What Destorys, and What Restores It*. London: Ward & Co., 1858.

Hough, Rev. J. W. *Our Country's Mission, or the Present Suffering of the Nation Justified by Future Glory*. Burlington, VT: Free Press, 1864.

Howard, Robert S. "Testimony of Robert S. Howard." In *Labor and Capital in the Gilded Age*, edited by John A. Garraty, 22–26. Boston: Little, Brown and Company, 1968.

Howe, Irving. "Reganism: The Spirit of the Times." In *Selected Writings 1950–1990*, 410–23. New York: Harcourt, 1990.

Howells, William Dean. *Criticism and Fiction*. New York: Harper & Brothers, 1891.

———. *A Hazard of New Fortunes*. New York: Penguin, 2001.

———. Introduction to *Main-Travelled Roads*, by Hamlin Garland, 1–4. Lincoln: University of Nebraska Press, 1995.

Hutcheson, Francis. *An Inquiry into the Original of Our Ideas of Beauty and Virtue in Two Treatises*. Edited by Wolfgang Leidhold. Indianapolis: Liberty Fund, 2004.

Hyde, Carrie. "Outcast Patriotism: The Dilemma of Negative Instruction in 'The Man without a Country.'" *ELH* 77 (2010): 915–39.

Irving, Washington. "The Broken Heart." In *The Works of Washington Irving*, 87–93. Vol. 2. Rev ed. New York: George P. Putnam, 1850.

Jacobs, Margaret D. "Mixed Bloods, Mestizas, and Pintos: Race, Gender, and Claims to Whiteness in Helen Hunt Jackson's *Ramona* and Maria Amparo Ruiz de Burton's *Who Would Have Thought It?*" *Western American Literature* 36 (2001): 212–31.

James, Henry. *The American Scene*. New York: Penguin, 1994.

———. "The Art of Fiction." In *Henry James: Major Stories & Essays*, 572–93. New York: Library of America, 1999.

———. "The Jolly Corner." In *Henry James: Major Stories & Essays*, 491–525. New York: Library of America, 1999.

James, Jennifer. "Civil War Wounds: William Wells Brown, Violence, and the Domestic Narrative." *African American Review* 39 (2005): 39–54.

James, William. "The Moral Equivalent of War." In *The Writings of William James: A Comprehensive Edition*, edited by John J. McDermott, 660–71. New York: Random House, 1967.

Jameson, Fredric. *The Political Unconsciousness: Narrative as Socially Symbolic Act*. Ithaca: Cornell University Press, 1981.

———. *Postmodernism, or, the Cultural Logic of Late Capitalism*. Durham, NC: Duke University Press, 1991.

Johns, Gillian. "'Moral Authority,' History, and the Case of Canonization: William Wells Brown's *Clotel* and *Clotelle*." In *Multiculturalism: Roots and Realities*, edited by C. James Trotman, 218–37. Bloomington: Indiana University Press, 2002.

Johnson, Bradley. "Dueling Sentiments: Responses to Patriarchal Violence in Augusta Jane Evans' *St. Elmo*." *Southern Literary Journal* 33 (2001): 14–29.

Johnson, Kendall. *Henry James and the Visual*. Cambridge: Cambridge University Press, 2007.

Joseph, Philip. *American Literary Regionalism in a Global Age*. Baton Rouge: Louisiana State University Press, 2007.

Kammen, Michael. *Mystic Chords of Memory: The Transformation of Tradition in American Culture*. Vintage: Random House, 1991.

Kant, Immanuel. *Anthropology from a Pragmatic Point of View*. Translated by Mary J. Gregor. The Hague, Netherlands: Martinus Nijhoff, 1974.

———. *Critique of the Power of Judgment*. Edited by Paul Guyer. Translated by Paul Guyer and Eric Matthews. Cambridge: Cambridge University Press, 2000.

———. *Critique of Practical Reason*. Translated by Paul Guyer. In *Practical Philosophy*, edited by Mary J. Gregor, 133–271. Cambridge: Cambridge University Press, 1996.

———. "Idea for a Universal History with a Cosmopolitan Purpose." In *Political Writings*, edited by H. S. Reiss, translated by H. B. Nisbet, 2nd ed., 41–53. Cambridge: Cambridge University Press, 1991.

———. "Perpetual Peace: A Philosophical Sketch." Translated by H. B. Nisbet. In *Political Writings*, edited by H. S. Reiss. 2nd ed., 93–130. Cambridge: Cambridge University Press, 1991.

Kaplan, Amy. *The Anarchy of Empire in the Making of U.S. Culture*. Cambridge, MA: Harvard University Press, 2002.

———. *The Social Construction of American Realism*. Chicago: University of Chicago Press, 1992.

Kazin, Michael. *American Dreamers: How the Left Changed a Nation*. New York: Alfred A. Knopf, 2011.

Kim, Helen M. "Strategic Credulity: Oz as Mass Cultural Parable." *Cultural Critique* 33 (1996): 213–33.

Kingsmill, Hugh. *Frank Harris*. New York: Farrar & Reinhart, 1932.

Kline, Linus W. "The Migratory Impulse vs. Love of Home." *American Journal of Psychology* 10 (1898): 1–81.

Krafft, Frederick. "History of Our Country for Boys and Girls: Fourteenth Chapter." *The Little Socialist Magazine*, April 1910, 5.

———. "History of Our Country for Boys and Girls: Fifteenth Chapter." *The Little Socialist Magazine*, May 1910, 5.

Kristeva, Julia. *Powers of Horror: An Essay on Abjection*. New York: Columbia University Press, 1982.

Krutch, J. W. "The Case of Frank Harris." *The Nation*, July 5, 1922, 19–20.

Lacan, Jacques. *Écrits*. Translated by Bruce Fink. New York: W. W. Norton, 2006.

———. *The Four Fundamental Concepts of Psychoanalysis*. Translated by Alan Sheridan. New York: W. W. Norton, 1981.

Laclau, Ernesto. *On Populist Reason*. London: Verso, 2005.

Lalor, John J., ed. "Cosmopolitanism." In *Cyclopedia of Political Science, Political Economy, and of the Political History of the United States*, vol. 1, 674. New York: Merrill, 1893.

Lancaster, William Joseph Cosens. Review of *The Bomb*. *Times Literary Supplement*, December 3, 1908, 446.

"The Land We Love." *The Land We Love*, July 1866, 12.

Lasch, Christopher. *The True and Only Heaven: Progress and Its Critics*. New York: W. W. Norton, 1991.

Laurie, Bruce. *Artisans into Workers: Labor in Nineteenth-Century America*. Urbana: University of Illinois Press, 1997.

Leadbeater, Charles Webster. *The Science of the Sacraments*. London: St. Alban Press, 1920.

Lears, T. J. Jackson. *No Place of Grace: Antimodernism and the Transformation of American Culture, 1880—1920*. Chicago: University of Chicago Press, 1983.

Le Bon, Gustave. *The Psychology of Revolution*. London: T. Fisher Unwin, 1913.

Lewis, Leon. *The Facts Concerning the Eight Condemned Leaders*. Greenport, NY: Leon Lewis, 1887.

Lewis, Leslie W. *Telling Narratives: Secrets in African American Literature*. Urbana: University of Illinois Press, 2007.

Lewis, Sinclair. "The Passing of Capitalism." *The Bookman; A Review of Books and Life*, November 1914, 280–86.

Leys, Ruth. "The Turn to Affect: A Critique." *Critical Inquiry* 37 (2011): 434–72.

Lilley, James D. *Common Things: Romance and the Aesthetics of Belonging in Atlantic Modernity*. New York: Fordham University Press, 2014.

"The Limits of Obedience to Acts of Government." *The Old Guard*, October 1868, 721–28.

Lincoln, Abraham. "Address to the Young Men's Lyceum of Springfield, Illinois." In *Abraham Lincoln: Speeches and Writings, 1832–1852*, edited by Don E. Fehrenbacher, 28–36. New York: Library of America, 1989.

Lippard, George. *Legends of Mexico*. Philadelphia: T. B. Peterson, 1847.

"The Literature of Anarchism." *Liberty*, May 1887, 3.

Littlefield, Henry M. "The Wizard of Oz: Parable on Populism." *American Quarterly* 16 (1964): 47–58.

Locke, John. *An Essay Concerning Human Understanding*. New York: E. P. Dutton and Co., 1910.

———. *Two Treatises of Government and A Letter Concerning Toleration*. Edited by Ian Shapiro. New Haven, CT: Yale University Press, 2003.

Loewen, James W., and Edward H. Sebesta, eds. *The Confederate and Neo-Confederate Reader: The "Great Truth" about the "Lost Cause."* Oxford, MS: University of Mississippi Press, 2010.

London, Jack. *The Iron Heel*. New York: Review of Reviews, 1917.

Longa, Ernesto A. *Anarchist Periodicals in English Published in the United States (1835–1955): An Annotated Guide*. Lanham, MD: Scarecrow Press, 2010.

Loughran, Trish. *The Republic in Print: Print Culture in the Age of U.S. Nation Building, 1770-1870*. New York: Columbia University Press, 2007.

Lott, Eric. *Love and Theft: Blackface Minstrelsy and the American Working Class*. New York: Oxford University Press, 1993.

Löwy, Malcolm, and Robert Sayre. *Romanticism against the Tide of Modernity*. Translated by Catherine Porter. Durham, NC: Duke University Press, 2001.

Luis-Brown, David. *Waves of Decolonization: Discourses of Race and Hemispheric Citizenship in Cuba, Mexico, and the United States*. Durham, NC: Duke University Press, 2008.

Lukács, Georg. *The Historical Novel*. Lincoln: University of Nebraska Press, 1983.

Lutz, Tom. *Cosmopolitan Vistas: American Literary Regionalism and Literary Value*. Ithaca, NY: Cornell University Press, 2004.

Madam Tell. "Heart Loneliness." *Michigan Farmer*, August 6, 1859, 262.

Madison, James. "Notes of the Secret Debates of the Federal Convention of 1787." *The Debates in the Several State Conventions of the Adoption of the Federal Constitution*, vol. 1, 2nd ed., edited by Jonathan Elliot, 389–479. Washington, DC: Jonathan Elliot, 1836.

Marcy, Mary. "The Real Fatherland." *The International Socialist Review* 15 (1914): 177–78.

Margolis, Stacey. *The Public Life of Privacy in Nineteenth-Century American Literature*. Durham, NC: Duke University Press, 2005.

Martinez, James Michael. *Carpetbaggers, Cavalry, and the Ku Klux Klan*. Lanham, MD: Rowman & Littlefield, 2007.

Marx, Karl. *Economic and Philosophical Manuscripts*. In *Karl Marx: Early Writings*, 63–219. Translated by T. B. Bottomore. New York: McGraw-Hill, 1963.

———. *The Eighteenth Brumaire of Louis Bonaparte*. New York: International Publishers, 1963.

Marx, Karl, and Federick Engels. *The Communist Manifesto: A Modern Edition*. London: Verso, 1998.

Massumi, Brian. *Parables for the Virtual: Movement, Affect, Sensation*. Durham, NC: Duke University Press, 2002.

Matt, Susan J. *Homesickness: An American History*. New York: Oxford University Press, 2011.

Matthiessen, F. O. *American Renaissance: Art and Expression in the Age of Emerson and Whitman*. New York: Oxford University Press, 1941.

McGerr, Michael. *A Fierce Discontent: The Rise and Fall of the Progressive Movement in America, 1870–1920*. New York: Oxford University Press, 2003.

McGill, Meredith. *American Literature and the Culture of Reprinting, 1834–1853*. Philadelphia: University of Pennsylvania Press, 2003.

McMath, Robert C. Jr. *American Populism: A Social History, 1877–1898*. New York: Hill and Wang, 1992.

McNeill, George E., ed. *The Labor Movement: The Problem of To-Day*. Boston: A. M. Bridgman & Co., 1887.

McPherson, Tara. *Reconstructing Dixie: Race, Gender, and Nostalgia in Imagined South*. Durham, NC: Duke University Press, 2003.

Meckler, Mark, and Jenny Beth Martin. *Tea Party Patriots: The Second American Revolution*. New York: Henry Holt and Company, 2012.

Melville, Herman. "Hawthorne and His Mosses." In *American Literature, American Culture*, edited by Gordon Hunter, 92–102. New York: Oxford University Press, 1999.

———. *Israel Potter: His Fifty Years of Exile*. Edited by Harrison Hayford et al. Evanston, IL: Northwestern University Press, 1982.

———. "Israel Potter; Or, Fifty Years of Exile. A Fourth of July Story." *Putnam's Monthly*, July 1854, 66–75.

Merish, Lori. *Sentimental Materialism: Gender, Commodity Culture, and Nineteenth-Century American Literature*. Durham, NC: Duke University Press, 2000.

Michaels, Walter Benn. *The Gold Standard and the Logic of Naturalism*. Berkeley: University of California Press, 1987.

Misawa, Tadasu. *Modern Educators and Their Ideals*. New York: Appleton, 1909.

Mississippi Secession Convention. "A Declaration of the Immediate Causes Which Induce and Justify the Secession of the State of Mississippi from the Federal Union." In Loewen and Sebesta, 127–29.

Mitchell, Lee Clark. "'Ghostlier Demarcations, Keener Sounds': Scare Quotes in 'The Jolly Corner.'" *Henry James Review* 28 (2007): 223–31.

Mitchell, S. Weir. "The Medical Department in the Civil War." *Journal of the American Medical Association* 62 (1914): 1445–50.

Montgomery, James. "The Voyage of the Blind." In *The Poetical Works of James Montgomery*, vol. 3, 261–70. Boston: Little, Brown & Co., 1858.

Most, Johann. *Science of Revolutionary Warfare*. El Dorado, AR: Desert Publications, 1978.

———. *The Social Monster: A Paper on Communism and Anarchism*. New York: Bernhard & Schenck, 1890.

Mott, Frank Luther. *Golden Multitudes: The Story of Best Sellers in the United States*. New York: Macmillan Co., 1947.

Mouffe, Chantal. *The Return of the Political*. 2nd. ed. London: Verso, 2005.

Murison, Justine. *The Politics of Anxiety in Nineteenth-Century American Literature*. Cambridge: Cambridge University Press, 2011.

Murphy, Gretchen. *Hemispheric Imaginings: The Monroe Doctrine and Narratives of U.S. Empire*. Durham, NC: Duke University Press, 2005.

Nabers, Deak. "The Problem of Revolution in the Age of Slavery: *Clotel*, Fiction, and the Government of Man." *Representations* 91 (2005): 84–108.

Nathanson, Paul. *Over the Rainbow: "The Wizard of Oz" as a Secular Myth of America*. Albany: State University of New York Press, 1991.

"National People's Party Platform." In *A Populist Reader: Selections from the Works of American Populist Leaders*, edited by George Brown Tindall, 90–96. New York: Harper & Row, 1966.

"The New South: What It Is Doing, and What It Wants." *Putnam's Magazine*, April 1870, 458–64.

Ngai, Sianne. *Ugly Feelings*. Cambridge, MA: Harvard University Press, 2002.

Nickels, Joel. *The Poetry of the Possible: Spontaneity, Modernism, and the Multitude*. Minneapolis: University of Minnesota Press, 2012.

Nordhoff, Charles. *The Cotton States in the Spring and Summer of 1875*. New York: D. Appleton & Company, 1876.

"Nostalgia, or Home Sickness." *The Boston Medical and Surgical Journal*, August 2, 1848, 9–10.

"Novels: Their Meaning and Their Mission." *Putnam's Monthly*, October 1854, 389–96.

Nussbaum, Martha. "Patriotism and Cosmopolitanism." In *For Love of Country: Debating the Limits of Patriotism*, edited by Joshua Cohen, 3–17. Boston: Beacon, 1996.

Nye, David E. *American Technological Sublime*. Cambridge, MA: The Massachusetts Institute of Technology Press, 1994.

O'Hare, Kate Richards. *"Nigger" Equality*. St. Louis: Ripsaw, 1912.

O. Henry. *Cabbages and Kings*. New York: Burt, 1904.

"The Old and the New South." *The International Review*, March 1876, 209–23.

Olmsted, Frederick Law. *A Journey in the Seaboard Slave States*. New York: Dix & Edwards, 1856.

Onuf, Peter S. "Federalism, Republicanism, and the Origins of American Sectionalism." In *All Over the Map: Rethinking American Regions*, edited by Edward L. Ayers et al., 11–37. Baltimore: The Johns Hopkins University Press, 1996.

Pancoast, Henry S. *An Introduction to American Literature*. New York: Henry Holt and Company, 1898.

Parrington, Vernon Louis. *Main Currents in American Thought: An Interpretation of American Literature from the Beginnings to 1920*. 3 vols. New York: Harcourt, Brace and Company, 1930.

Parsons, Frank. "The Philosophy of Mutualism." *The Arena*, May 1894, 783–815.

Parsons, Lucy. "The Negro: Let Him Leave Politics to the Politician and Prayers to the Preacher." In Ahrens, 54–56.

———. "On the 'Harmony' Between Capital and Labor, Or, the Robber and the Robbed." In Ahrens, 39–40.

———. "A Piece of History." *The Rebel*, October 20, 1895, 15.

———. "Speeches at the Founding Convention of the Industrial Workers of the World." In Ahrens, 77–85.

Pasko, Wesley Washington. "Editor's Note." *Old New York*, August 1889, 64.

Payne, John Howard. *Clari; or, The Maid of Milan*. New York: Samuel French Publisher, 1857.

———. "Home, Sweet Home." Boston: Lee and Shepard, 1882.

Peyser, Thomas. *Utopia and Cosmopolis: Globalization in the Era of American Literary Realism*. Durham, NC: Duke University Press, 1998.

Pike, James Shepherd. *The Prostrate State: South Carolina under Negro Government*. New York: D. Appleton and Company, 1874.

Pillsbury, Arthur J. "The Present Political Outlook: I. The Republican View." *Overland Monthly and Out West Magazine*, July 1898, 53–57.

Pinkerton, Allan. *Strikers, Communists, Tramps, and Detectives*. New York: G. W. Carleton & Co., 1878.

Pita, Beatrice. "Engendering Critique: Race, Class, and Gender in Ruiz de Burton and Martí." In Belnap and Fernández, 129–44.

Pizer, Donald. *Hamlin Garland's Early Work and Career*. Berkeley: University of California Press, 1960.

Pollack, Norman. *The Populist Response to Industrial America*. New York: W. W. Norton, 1966.

Porter, Edward J. "The Loved of Other Years." *Graham's Magazine*, August 1851, 99.

Posnett, Hutcheson Macaulay. *Comparative Literature*. New York: D. Appleton and Company, 1896.

Posnock, Ross. *Color and Culture: Black Writers and the Making of the Modern Intellectual*. Cambridge, MA: Harvard University Press, 2000.

———. *The Trial of Curiosity: Henry James, William James, and the Challenge of Modernity*. New York: Oxford University Press, 1991.

Postel, Charles. *The Populist Vision*. New York: Oxford University Press, 2007.

Powderly, Terence. *Thirty Years of Labor: 1859–1889*. Columbus, OH: Excelsior Publishing, 1889.

Pratt, Lloyd. *Archives of American Time: Literature and Modernity in the Nineteenth Century*. Philadelphia: University of Pennsylvania Press, 2009.

Presley, Sharon, and Crispin Sartwell, eds. *Exquisite Rebel: The Essays of Voltairine de Cleyre: Anarchist, Feminist, Genius*. Buffalo: State University of New York Press, 2005.

"Proceedings of Public Societies." *Monthly Magazine and British Register*, May 1, 1822, 336–40.

Proudhon, Pierre-Joseph. *General Idea of the Revolution in the Nineteenth Century*. Translated by John Beverley Robinson. New York: Dover, 2003.

Rancière, Jacques. *Aesthetics and Its Discontents*. Translated by Steven Corcoran. Cambridge, UK: Polity, 2009.

———. *Disagreement: Politics and Philosophy*. Translated by Julie Rose. Minneapolis: University of Minnesota Press, 1999.

———. *Dissensus: On Politics and Aesthetics*. Translated and edited by Steven Corcoran. London: Continuum, 2010.

———. *The Flesh of Words: The Politics of Writing*. Translated by Charlotte Mandell. Stanford, CA: Stanford University Press, 2004.

———. *Mute Speech: Literature, Critical Theory, and Politics*. Translated by James Swenson. New York: Columbia University Press, 2011.

———. *The Politics of Aesthetics*. Translated by Gabriel Rockhill. London: Continuum, 2004.

———. "Who Is the Subject of the Rights of Man?" *South Atlantic Quarterly* 103 (2004): 297–310.

Rand, N. W., and J. P. Rand. *Random Rimes: Medical and Miscellaneous*. 2nd ed. Boston: Clapp, 1899.

Rawlings, Peter. *Henry James and the Abuse of the Past*. London: Palgrave, 2005.

"Recent Fiction and the Critics." *Current Literature*, May 1908, 569–72.

Reid, Thomas. *Essays on the Intellectual Powers of Man*. Edited by Derek R. Brookes. University Park: Pennsylvania State University Press, 2002.

Reid-Pharr, Robert. *Conjugal Union: The Body, the House, and the Black American*. New York: Oxford University Press, 1999.

Reinsch, Paul S. "International Administrative Law and National Sovereignty." *American Journal of International Law* 3 (1909): 1–45.

———. *World Politics at the End of the Nineteenth Century, as Influenced by the Oriental Situation*. New York: Macmillan, 1902.

Reising, Russell. *Loose Ends: Closure and Crisis in the American Social Text*. Durham, NC: Duke University Press, 1996.

"Reminiscences of Mexico." *Frank Leslie's New Monthly*, July 1866, 401–8.

Renan, Ernest. "What Is a Nation?" In *Nation and Narration*, edited by Homi K. Bhabha, 8–22. New York: Routledge, 1990.

Reynolds, David S. *Walt Whitman's America: A Cultural Biography*. New York: Vintage, 1996.

Reynolds, Larry J. *European Revolutions and the American Literary Renaissance.* New Haven, CT: Yale University Press, 1988.

Ribot, Théodule-Armand. "Pathological Pleasures and Pains," *The Monist,* January 1896, 174–87.

Ricketts, Charles S. *The Art of Prado.* Boston: L. C. Page & Company, 1907.

Rideout, Walter B. *The Radical Novel in the United States, 1900–1954: Some Interrelations of Literature and Society.* Cambridge, MA: Harvard University Press, 1956.

Ritter, Gretchen. "Silver Slippers and a Golden Cap: L. Frank Baum's *The Wonderful Wizard of Oz* and Historical Memory in American Politics." *Journal of American Studies* 31 (1997): 171–202.

Rivera, John-Michael. *The Emergence of Mexican America: Recovering Stories of Mexican Peoplehood in U.S. Culture.* New York: New York University Press, 2006.

Robbins, Bruce. "Actually Existing Cosmopolitanism." In Cheah and Robbins, 1–19.

——. "Espionage as Vocation: Raymond Williams's Loyalties." In *Intellectuals: Aesthetics, Politics, and Academics,* edited by Bruce Robbins, 273–90. Minneapolis: University of Minnesota Press, 1990.

Robespierre, Maximilien. "On the Principles of Political Morality That Should Guide the National Convention in the Domestic Administration of the Republic." Translated by John Howe. In *Virtue and Terror,* edited by Jean Ducange, 108–25. London: Verso, 2007.

Rodríguez, Manuel M. Martín. "Textual and Land Reclamations: The Critical Reception of Early Chicana/o Literature." In Gonzales-Berry and Tatum, 40–58.

Rogers, Anna Alexander. "What We Put Up With." In *Why American Marriages Fail and Other Papers,* 111–47. Boston: Houghton Mifflin, 1909.

Rogers, Katharine M. *L. Frank Baum, Creator of Oz.* New York: St. Martin's, 2002.

Rogin, Michael Paul. *Subversive Genealogy: The Politics and Art of Herman Melville.* Berkeley: University of California Press, 1985.

Rohrbach, Augusta. *Truth Stranger Than Fiction: Race, Realism, and the U.S. Literary Marketplace.* New York: Palgrave, 2002.

Romero, Lora. *Home Fronts: Domesticity and Its Critics in the Antebellum United States.* Durham, NC: Duke University Press, 1997.

Rosaldo, Renato. *Culture and Truth: The Remaking of Social Analysis.* 2nd ed. Boston: Beacon Press, 1993.

Rosen, George. "Nostalgia: A 'Forgotten' Psychological Disorder." *Clio Medica* 10 (1975): 29–51.

Rosendale, Steven. "In Search of Left Ecology's Usable Past: *The Jungle,* Social Change, and the Class Character of Environmental Impairment." In *The Greening of Literary Scholarship: Literature, Theory, and the Environment,* edited by Steven Rosendale, 59–76. Iowa City: University of Iowa Press, 2002.

Ross, Dorothy. *The Origins of American Social Science.* Cambridge: Cambridge University Press, 1991.

Rowlandson, Mary. *A True History of the Captivity and Restoration of Mrs. Mary Rowlandson.* Edited by Amy Schrager Lang. In *Journeys in New Worlds: Early American Women's Narratives,* edited by William L. Andrews, 11–65. Madison: University of Wisconsin Press, 1990.

Ruiz de Burton, María Amparo. *Who Would Have Thought It?* Edited by Rosaura Sánchez and Beatrice Pita. Houston: Arte Público Press, 1995.

Rush, Benjamin. *Medical Inquiries and Observations upon the Diseases of the Mind*. Philadelphia: Kimber & Richardson, 1812.

Rushdie, Salman. *The Wizard of Oz*. London: British Film Institute, 1992.

Ruskin, John. *Seven Lamps of Architecture*. New York: John Wiley & Sons, 1889.

Russell, David. "A Southern Patriot's Sacrifice: Patriarchal Repositioning in Augusta Evans's *St. Elmo*." *Southern Studies* 12, nos. 1–2 (2005): 47–62.

Sala, George Augustus. "Form-Sickness." In *Under the Sun: Essays Mainly Written in Hot Countries*, 18–33. London: Tinsley Brothers, 1872.

Saldívar, José David. "Nuestra América's Borders: Remapping American Cultural Studies." In Belnap and Fernández, 145–75.

Sampson, Marmaduke B. *Slavery in the United States: A Letter to the Hon. Daniel Webster*. London: S. Highly, 1845.

Samuels, Shirley. *Facing America: Iconography and the Civil War*. New York: Oxford University Press, 2004.

———. *Romances of the Republic: Women, the Family, and Violence in the Literature of the Early American Nation*. New York: Oxford University Press, 1996.

Sánchez, María Carla. "Whiteness Invisible: Early Mexican American Writing and the Color of Literary History." In *Passing: Identity and Interpretation in Sexuality, Race, and Religion*, edited by María Carla Sánchez and Linda Schlossberg, 64–91. New York: New York University Press, 2001.

Sánchez, Rosaura. "Dismantling the Colossus: Martí and Ruiz de Burton on the Formulation of Anglo América." In Belnap and Fernández, 115–28.

Sánchez, Rosaura, and Beatrice Pita. "María Amparo Ruiz de Burton and the Power of Her Pen." In *Latina Legacies: Identity, Biography, and Community*, edited by Vicki L. Ruiz and Virginia Sanchez Korrol, 72–83. New York: Oxford University Press, 2005.

Sandoval-Strausz, A. K. *Hotel: An American History*. New Haven, CT: Yale University Press, 2007.

Santayana, George. *The Sense of Beauty: Being the Outline of Aesthetic Theory*. New York: Charles Scribner's Sons, 1895.

Savoy, Eric. "The Queer Subject of 'The Jolly Corner.'" *Henry James Review* 20 (1999): 1–21.

Scalia, Antonin. "Common-Law Courts in a Civil-Law System: The Role of the United States Federal Courts in Interpreting the Constitution and Laws." Lecture for Tanner Lectures on Human Values, Princeton University, Princeton, NJ. March 8–9, 1995.

Scalia, Antonin, and Bryan A. Garner. *Reading Law: The Interpretation of Legal Texts*. St. Paul, MN: Thomson/West, 2012.

Schiller, Friedrich. *On the Aesthetic Education of Man*. Translated by Elizabeth M. Wilkinson and L. A. Willoughby. Oxford: Oxford University Press, 1967.

———. "On the Pathetic." Translated by Daniel O. Dahlstorm. In *Essays: Friedrich Schiller*, edited by Walter Hinderer and Daniel O. Dahlstorm, 45–69. New York: Continuum, 2005.

Schlesinger, Arthur M. Jr. *The Vital Center: The Politics of Freedom*. New Brunswick, NJ: Transaction, 1998.

Schoolman, Martha. *Abolitionist Geographies*. Minneapolis: University of Minnesota Press, 2014.

Schreiner, Hermann L. "Take Me Home." In *Confederate Songs*, 2–5. Savannah: John C. Schreiner & Sons, 1866.

Schwartz, Evan I. *Finding Oz: How L. Frank Baum Discovered the Great American Story*. Boston: Houghton Mifflin, 2009.

Schweninger, Lee. "*Clotel* and the Historicity of the Anecdote." *MELUS* 24.1 (1999): 21–36.

Scott, Temple. *Frank Harris, the Man of To-day and To-morrow*. New York: n.p., 1917.

Seltzer, Mark. *Henry James and the Art of Power*. Ithaca, NY: Cornell University Press, 1984.

Senn, Nicholas. *Medico-surgical Aspects of the Spanish American War*. Chicago: American Medical Association Press, 1900.

Shaw, Albert. "Baron Pierre de Coubertin." *American Monthly Review of Reviews*, April 1898, 435–38.

Shore, Elliot. *Talkin' Socialism: J. A. Wayland and the Role of the Press in Radicalism, 1890–1912*. Lawrence: University of Kansas Press, 1988.

Silyn Roberts, Siân. *Gothic Subjects: The Transformation of American Individualism in American Fiction, 1790–1861*. Philadelphia: University of Pennsylvania Press, 2014.

Sinclair, Upton. *The Jungle*. Edited by Clare Virginia Eby. New York: W. W. Norton, 2003.

———. *Mammonart: An Essay on Economic Interpretation*. Pasadena: n.p., 1924.

Sinclair, Upton, ed. *The Cry for Justice: An Anthology of the Literature of Social Protest*. Philadelphia: John C. Wilson Company, 1915.

Sizer, Lyde Cullen. *The Political Work of Northern Women Writers and the Civil War, 1850–1872*. Chapel Hill: University of North Carolina Press, 2000.

Slauter, Eric. *The State as a Work of Art: The Cultural Origins of the Constitution*. Chicago: University of Chicago Press, 2009.

Smith, Adam. *The Theory of Moral Sentiments*. London: A. Millar, 1759.

Smith, Caleb. *The Oracle and the Curse: A Poetics of Justice from the Revolution to the Civil War*. Cambridge, MA: Harvard University Press, 2013.

Smith, Henry Nash. *Virgin Land: The American West as Symbol and Myth*. Cambridge, MA: Harvard University Press, 1950.

Sofer, Naomi Z. *Making the "America of Art": Cultural Nationalism and Nineteenth-Century Women Writers*. Columbus: The Ohio State University Press, 2005.

Sommer, Doris. *Foundational Fictions: The National Romances of Latin America*. Berkeley: University of California Press, 1991.

Sorel, Georges. *Reflections on Violence*. Edited by Jeremy Jennings. Translated by Thomas Ernest Hulme and Jeremy Jennings. Cambridge: Cambridge University Press, 1999.

South Carolina Secession Convention. "The Address of the People of South Carolina, Assembled in Convention, To the People of the Slaveholding States of the United States 1861. In Loewan and Sebesta, 118–26.

"Southern Reconstruction." *Lippincott's Magazine*, February 1869, 222–27.

"Southern Reconstruction." *Methodist Quarterly Review*, July 1870, 379–97.

Spinks, Bryan D. *The Place of Christ in Liturgical Prayer: Trinity, Christology, and Liturgical Theology*. Collegeville, MN: Liturgical Press, 2008.

Staples, Alice. "Mother, Home and Heaven." *The Union Literary Magazine*, March 1869, 4–6.

Stern, Julia. *The Plight of Feeling: Sympathy and Dissent in the Early American Novel*. Chicago: University of Chicago Press, 1997.

Stewart, Dugald. *Elements of the Philosophy of the Human Mind.* Vol. 1. Boston: Little, Brown, and Co., 1854.

Stowe, Harriet Beecher. *Dred: A Tale of the Great Dismal Swamp.* Edited by Robert S. Levine. Chapel Hill: University of North Carolina Press, 2006.

Streeby, Shelley. *American Sensations: Class, Empire, and the Production of Popular Culture.* Berkeley: University of California Press, 2002.

———. *Radical Sensations: World Movements, Violence, and Visual Culture.* Durham, NC: Duke University Press, 2013.

Tate, Claudia. *Domestic Allegories of Political Desire: The Black Heroine's Text at the Turn of the Century.* New York: Oxford University Press, 1996.

Tavernier-Courbin, Jacqueline. "*The Call of the Wild* and *The Jungle*: Jack London's and Upton Sinclair's Animal and Human Jungles." In *The Cambridge Companion to American Realism and Naturalism*, edited by Donald Pizer, 236–62. Cambridge: Cambridge University Press, 1995.

Tawil, Ezra. *The Making of Racial Sentiment: Slavery and the Birth of the Frontier Romance.* Cambridge: Cambridge University Press, 2006.

Taylor, Lewis. "The 'Carpet-Baggers' and 'State Rights.'" *The Independent*, September 19, 1872, 1.

Tennenhouse, Leonard. *The Importance of Feeling English: American Literature and the British Diaspora, 1750–1850.* Princeton, NJ: Princeton University Press, 2007.

Thrailkill, Jane F. *Affecting Fictions: Mind, Body, and Emotion in American Literary Realism.* Cambridge, MA: Harvard University Press, 2007.

Tichi, Cecelia. "Exposé and Excess." *American Literature History* 15 (2003): 822–29.

Tinnemeyer, Andrea. *Identity Politics of the Captivity Narrative after 1848.* Lincoln: University of Nebraska Press, 2006.

Tintner, Adeline R. *The Cosmopolitan World of Henry James: An Intertextual Study.* Baton Rouge: Louisiana State University Press, 1991.

"To the Author of the *Lounger*." *The Lounger*, December, 23 1786, 300–11.

Tobin, A. I., and Elmer Gertz. *Frank Harris: A Study in Black and White.* Chicago: Madelaine Mendelsohn, 1931.

Tompkins, Jane. *Sensational Designs: The Cultural Work of American Fiction, 1790–1860.* New York: Oxford University Press, 1985.

Tourgée, Albion W. *A Fool's Errand: A Novel of the South during Reconstruction.* New York: Fords, Howard & Hubert, 1879.

Trachtenberg, Alan. *The Incorporation of America: Culture and Society in the Gilded Age.* New York: Hill and Wang, 1982.

Trask, Jeffrey. *Things American: Art Museums and Civic Culture in the Progressive Era.* Philadelphia: University of Pennsylvania Press, 2012.

Trescot, W. H. "Oration Delivered Before the South Carolina Historical Society." *Russell's Magazine*, July 1859, 289–307.

Trilling, Lionel. *The Liberal Imagination.* Garden City, NY: Anchor, 1953.

Turner, Frederick Jackson. *The Rise of the New West, 1819–1829.* New York: Harper & Brothers, 1906.

Tyler, Royall. *The Algerine Captive, or, the Life and Adventures of Doctor Updike Underhill.* New York: Modern Library, 2002.

Unger, Irwin. *Populism: Nostalgic or Progressive?* Chicago: Rand McNally, 1964.

Upham, Thomas Cogswell. *Abridgement of Mental Philosophy.* New York: Harper & Brothers, 1861.

Vail, Charles H. "The Negro Problem." *International Socialist Review* 1 (1901): 464–70.

Véron, Eugène. *Aesthetics.* Translated by W. H. Armstrong. London: Chapman & Hall, 1879.

Vidal, Gore. *Imperial America: Reflections on the United States of Amnesia.* New York: Avalon, 2005.

Voigt, Lisa. *Writing Captivity in the Early Modern Atlantic: Circulations of Knowledge and Authority in the Iberian and English Imperial Worlds.* Chapel Hill: University of North Carolina Press, 2009.

Wallace, William Ross. "The Mounds of America." *Graham's Magazine*, December 1851, 327.

Warren, Kenneth W. *Black and White Strangers: Race and American Literary Realism.* Chicago: University of Chicago Press, 1993.

Watson, Thomas E. *The Life and Speeches of Thomas E. Watson.* Nashville: Thomas E. Watson, 1906.

Watts, Edward. *An American Colony: Regionalism and the Roots of Midwestern Culture.* Columbus: Ohio State University Press, 2002.

Weather Underground Organization. *Prairie Fire: The Politics of Revolutionary Anti-Imperialism.* San Francisco: Communications Co., 1974.

Weber, Max. *The Protestant Ethic and the Spirit of Capitalism.* Translated by Talcott Parsons. New York: Scribner, 1958.

———. "Science as a Vocation." In *From Max Weber: Essays in Sociology*, edited and translated by H. H. Gerth and C. Wright Mills, 129–56. New York: Oxford University Press, 1946.

Weir, David. *Anarchy and Culture: The Aesthetic Politics of Modernism.* Amherst: University of Massachusetts Press, 1997.

Werman, David. "Normal and Pathological Nostalgia." *Journal of American Psychoanalytic Association* 25 (1977): 387–98.

Wertheimer, Eric. *Imagined Empires: Incas, Aztecs, and the New World of American Literature, 1771–1876.* New York: Cambridge University Press, 1999.

Wexler, Laura. *Tender Violence: Domestic Visions in an Age of U.S. Imperialism.* Chapel Hill: University of North Carolina Press, 2000.

"What to Do with the South." *Every Saturday*, April 22, 1871, 362.

"The Wheel." *Mad Men.* First broadcast October 18, 2007, by AMC. Directed by Matthew Weiner and written by Matthew Weiner and Robin Veith.

White, Andrew D. "On Studies in General History and the History of Civilization." In *Papers of the American Historical Association*, vol. 1, 49–72. New York: G. P. Putnam, 1885.

White, Ed. *The Backcountry and the City: Colonization and Conflict in Early America.* Minneapolis: University of Minnesota Press, 2005.

White, Hayden. *Metahistory: The Historical Imagination in Nineteenth-Century Europe.* Baltimore: The Johns Hopkins University Press, 1973.

White, William Allen. "What's the Matter with Kansas?" In *A Populist Reader: Selections from the Works of American Populist Leaders*, edited by George Brown Tindall, 192–99. New York: Harper and Row, 1966.

Whitman, Walt. "Democratic Vistas." In *The Collected Writings of Walt Whitman: Prose Works 1892*, vol. 2, edited by Floyd Stovall, 361–426. New York: New York University Press, 1964.

Widmer, Edward L. *Young America: The Flowering of Democracy in New York City*. New York: Oxford University Press, 1999.

Wildschut, Tim, et al. "Nostalgia: Content, Triggers, Functions." *Journal of Personality and Social Psychology* 91 (2006): 975–92.

Wilentz, Sean. *The Rise of American Democracy: Jefferson to Lincoln*. New York: W. W. Norton, 2005.

Williams, Albert. "Modern Types of Gold and Silver Miners." *Engineering Magazine*, October 1891, 48–62.

Williams, David. *Bitterly Divided: The South's Inner Civil War*. New York: New Press, 2008.

Williams, Raymond. *The Country and the City*. Oxford: Oxford University Press, 1973.

Wilson, Edmund. *Patriotic Gore: Studies in the Literature of the American Civil War*. New York: Farrar, Straus and Giroux, 1962.

Wilson, Ivy G. *Specters of Democracy: Blackness and the Aesthetics of Politics in the Antebellum U.S.* New York: Oxford University Press, 2011.

Wood, Gordon. *The Radicalism of the American Revolution*. New York: Vintage, 1993.

Yarborough, Richard. Introduction to *Contending Forces: A Romance Illustrative of Negro Life North and South*, by Pauline E. Hopkins, i–xlviii. New York: Oxford University Press, 1986.

Young, Elizabeth. *Disarming the Nation: Women's Writing and the American Civil War*. Chicago: University of Chicago Press, 1999.

"Zaragoza." *The Penny Magazine*, September 13, 1845, 353–55.

Zimmerman, David A. *Panic!: Markets, Crises, and Crowds in American Fiction*. Chapel Hill: University of North Carolina Press, 2006.

Zipes, Jack. *Fairy Tale as Myth/Myth as Fairy Tale*. Lexington: University Press of Kentucky, 1994.

———. *Happily Ever After: Fairy Tales, Children, and the Culture Industry*. New York: Routledge, 1997.

———. *When Dreams Came True: Classical Fairy Tales and Their Tradition*. 2nd ed. New York: Routledge, 2007.

Žižek, Slavoj. *In Defense of Lost Causes*. London: Verso, 2008.

———. *Looking Awry: An Introduction to Jacques Lacan through Popular Culture*. Cambridge, MA: The Massachusetts Institute of Technology Press, 1991.

———. *The Plague of Fantasies*. London: Verso, 1997.

Zwinger, Lynda. "'Treat me your subject': Henry James's 'The Jolly Corner' and I." *Henry James Review* 29 (2008): 1–15.

INDEX

Abolitionism, 19, 22, 33, 41, 58, 70, 126–28, 145. *See also* American Colonization Society; slavery; specific abolitionist writers

Adorno, Theodor, 15n69, 152, 191, 195n81

Aesthetics, 12–20, 110–11, 137, 150–60, 202–3, 206–9; as commitment 110, 128, 135n6, 148–50, 151–53, 160–63; and common sense (*sensus communis*), 6, 7–8, 9, 17; Rancière's theory of (*see also* Rancière, Jacques), 5–6, 17–20, 44, 65–66, 86–95, 165–66; veritist (*see also* Garland, Hamlin; Véron, Eugene), 98, 111n70, 111n71, 111–12, 115–19. *See also* Kant; Schiller; sublime; wonder

Affect theory, 4, 15n70, 15–16, 16n71, 135–36, 161, 169. *See also under* nostalgia

Africa (and Africans), 42, 43, 109, 123, 132, 193; black Atlantic, 39n49, 123, 129; Pan-Africanism, 121–22, 123, 124. *See also under* nostalgia. *See also* African-Americans; slavery

African-Americans, 11, 121, 145; citizenship and, 22, 39–40; literature and, 5, 33, 37–50, 68; politics and, 121, 124–25 *See also under* nostalgia; populism. *See also* Africa; slavery

Agacinski, Sylviane, 14n60

Agamben, Giorgio, 17–18n81, 52–53, 53n80

Agrarianism, 24, 97, 99, 101, 103, 109, 111, 137n10; revolutionary, 105, 157. *See also* People's Party; populism

Alarm, The, 134, 144–45, 147–48, 167

Aldrich, Thomas Bailey, 69

Ali, Omar H., 99n10, 128

American Colonization Society, 43, 45

American Historical Association (AHA), 140–41

American Renaissance, 28, 35n35

American Revolution. *See* U.S. Revolution

Anarchism (and anarchists), 19–20, 22, 24–25, 106, 117, 134–48, 161–72, 205, 214; ethics and, 169–70. *See also* Haymarket Affair; specific anarchist writers

Anderson, Amanda, 175n4

Anderson, Benedict, 33–34n26. *See also* nationalism

Anderson, David, 66

Anderson, Donald Lee and Tryggve Anderson, 16

Appiah, Kwame Anthony, 179, 186–87

Appleby, Joyce, 57n94

Arac, Jonathan, 64n7

Aranda, Jr., José E., 94n107

Arena, The, 2, 102, 116,

Arendt, Hannah, 14n61, 52–53, 53n80, 57, 168–69n114, 195

Armstrong, Nancy, 48n69

Asceticism (capitalist), 183–85, 193, 207. *See also* capitalism; consumerism

Austin, Linda M., 8n25, 13, 17n76, 195n81

Ayers, Edward L., 36

Badiou, Alain, 20n89, 53n80

Baginski, Max, 140

Bakhtin, Mikhail M., 84, 114

Barnes, Elizabeth, 78

Bartel, Kim, 176n5

Baum, Lyman Frank: *The Art of Decorating Dry Goods Windows and Interiors,* 182–83; *The Emerald City of Oz,* 184; *The Wonderful Wizard of Oz,* 25, 174–75, 179–94, 213

Bell, Michael Davitt, 100n11

Bellamy, Edward, 98, 108, 110

Benjamin, Walter, 34n26, 135–36, 141

Berkman, Alexander, 164

Berlant, Lauren, 16n71, 29

Berman, Jessica, 175n4, 178, 194n79

Bermuda, 123, 129

Berthoff, Warner, 4n14, 138n11

Bhabha, Homi K., 91n100, 179

Biopolitics, 17–18n81, 20n89, 52–53, 53n80, 66, 83, 124

Blacks. *See* African; African-American; slavery

Blair, Sara, 201n100

Blight, David W., 64, 67n22

Bloch, Ernst, 192–93

Boorstin, Daniel J., 205

Bourdieu, Pierre, 16

Boym, Svetlana, 15, 174n3

Bramen, Carrie Tirado, 64n7, 85

Brennan, Teresa, 15n70

Brennan, Timothy, 177n10

Brodhead, Richard, 64n7, 100n11, 110, 110n66

Brooks, Daphne A., 121n94, 122n99

Brown, Bill, 111n71

Brown, Gillian, 92n106

Brown, Wendy, 136

Brown, William Wells, 22, 33, 37, 58, 126; *Clotel: or, The President's Daughter;* 4, 21, 22, 29–30, 32, 37–50, 55–57, 59; *Clotelle: or, The Colored Heroine* 30, 50; *My Southern Home,* 50; *Narrative,* 51

Bryan, William Jennings, 108, 166

Buchannan, James, 27–28, 37

Bucknill, John Charles, 32n18, 56

Buelens, Gert, 201n100

Buell, Lawrence, 54–55n88

Buhle, Mari Jo, 139n14

Buhle, Paul M., 139n13, 139n14, 147n48

Burke, Edmund, 16, 154, 168n114

Burnham, Michelle, 58, 86n85

Burr, Aaron (and Burr Conspiracy), 61

Burrows, Stuart, 201n100

Burton, Robert, 11n44

Butler, Judith, 162n93

Cahill, Edward, 4n13

Calhoun, John C., 35

California, 92, 94

Cameron, Sharon, 201n100

Capitalism, 13, 143, 152, 156–58, 181–83, 196, 206; corruption of, 101; development of, 111n70, 141, 183, 212; globalization and, 176–77, 191; marriage contract and, 160; opposition to, 135, 137–39, 144–45, 148–50, 159, 166–68, 213–14; slavery and, 146. *See also* consumerism; liberalism

Captivity narrative, 52, 58, 84, 86–90, 92, 94

Caribbean, 33, 129, 133, 174, 176–77, 207, 214

Carter, Everett, 162n92

Cass, Lewis, 35

Castiglia, Christopher, 4n13, 86

Castronovo, Russ, 4n13, 13, 51, 59n97, 138n11, 150, 150n61, 162

Catholicism, 89–90, 131–33

Cheah, Pheng, 130n114

Cheng, Anne Anlin, 3, 3n12

Chesnutt, Charles, 68, 127

Chicago, Illinois, 117, 118, 134–35, 147, 151–60, 164–67, 171–72, 180

Child, Lydia Maria, 74

Chow, Rey, 130, 130n115

Christianity (and scripture), 47, 51, 75, 89. *See also* asceticism; Catholicism

Civil War (U.S.), 2, 90, 146, 213; 1848 European revolutions and, 35–36; cultural consequences of, 21, 28–29, 66, 72–73, 86, 98, 178; medical history and, 2, 16, 173; Northern nationalism and, 61–63; race and, 30, 38, 50; reconciliation romances of, 64–65, 73–74; soldiers' experience of, 66–67, 81n71, 93–94, 113, 119–21; Southern experience of (*see also* Confederate nationalism), 5, 62–63, 72, 77–78. *See also* Reconstruction; slavery

Clifford, James, 179

Coming Nation, The, 139–40

Confederacy (Confederate States of America), 21, 62, 78, 94; secession and, 27, 29, 37, 40, 76–77

Confederate nationalism, 2, 20, 22–23, 31, 35–36, 62–65, 67–73, 75–83, 93–95

Constitution (U.S.), 27, 44, 57, 144n37, 146; Bill of Rights and, 93; originalist interpretation of (and textualist), 25–26, 212, 215–16; radical critique of, 45–46, 130, 141–46; sectionalism and, 34–35

Consumerism (and consumption), 15, 177, 207, 210; "conspicuous consumption" and, 181, 183; culture and, 175, 182–83, 202, 205–6, 208; manufacturing desire and, 25, 156, 175, 181–82, 209, 211. *See also* capitalism

Consumption. *See* consumerism

Cooke, Rose Terry, 100

Cosmopolitanism, 22, 174, 194; 1890s and early-twentieth-century discussions of, 175–9; affect and, 177, 186–87, 195, 196–201; capitalism and, 177, 191, 197, 207–10; citizen-of-the-world and, 113, 175–76, 177, 188, 198; civilization and, 85; critiques of, 130n114, 177, 187n57; ethics and, 10n40, 178–79, 180–81, 184, 187–89; hospitality and, 175, 189–90, 207–10; intersubjectivity and, 175, 186–87; interventionism and, 174–75, 177–78, 180–94; modernity and, 195–201; nationalism and, 178, 199; Olympic Games and, 178–79; theories of, 50n73, 179, 187–88, 190; world federation of nations and, 175–76, 180, 189, 191. *See also* Kant, Immanuel. *See also under* fantasy; nostalgia; print history; regionalism

Cox, Samuel S., 70–71

Crèvecoeur, J. Hector St. John, 54, 158

Critchley, Simon, 160, 162n93, 162–63, 169

Culver, Stuart, 182

Dakota Territory, 109, 117

Dames, Nicholas, 12–13, 120

Darwin, Erasmus, 7–8

Darwinism, 159. *See also* naturalism

Davis, Fred, 7

Davis, Richard Harding, 185

Dean, Eric T., 67n23

Debs, Eugene V., 24, 145, 145n43

Declaration of Independence, 22; populism and, 105–7, 116–17; race and, 43, 46; radical celebration of, 143–44, 168, 171. *See also* Constitution; Jefferson, Thomas; U.S. Revolution

De Cleyre, Voltairine, 142, 168; "Anarchism and American Traditions," 142–43; "Direct Action," 144, 146

De Coubertin, Pierre, 178

De Forest, John W., 73–74

Dekker, George, 44–45, 54n87

Delaney, Martin, 38

De Leon, Daniel, 24, 144, 144n37, 164n98

Deleuze, Gilles, 15n70

Democratic Party, 70–71, 83, 108, 124, 146

Denning, Michael, 138n11

Derrida, Jacques, 5, 5n17, 197–98

Dewey, John, 16

Dillon, Elizabeth Maddock, 17n77

Dimock, Wai Chee, 44, 65, 82

Dixon, Thomas, 70, 70n42

Domesticity, 82, 90, 124, 158, 188, 209; cult of (Republican Motherhood, private sphere), 78–79, 92–94, 128–29; manifest (Kaplan's notion of), 92, 188; race and, 128–30. *See also* sentiment

Donnelly, Ignatius, 98, 107, 108–9

Dos Passos, John, 172

Douglass, Frederick, 38, 127

Dreiser, Theodore, 137n10, 148, 181

duCille, Ann, 38n48

Eco, Umberto, 205

Economic recession, 212. *See also* financial panics

Ellison, Julie, 86n85

Emerson, Ralph Waldo, 34, 54, 65n11, 161

Empire. *See* imperialism; Spanish Empire

Engels, Frederick, 177

Ernest, John, 38n48, 40n52

Esposito, Roberto, 66, 83

Evans, Augusta J., 63n4, 65, 74, 94; *St. Elmo*, 23, 63, 63n6, 65, 66, 75–83, 84n77, 85, 95

Exceptionalism (U.S.), 41, 213, 216. *See also* imperialism; nationalism

Fabian, Johannes, 110

Fahs, Alice, 64

Fantasy, 82, 119, 182; cosmopolitanism and, 180–81; genre and, 174; imperialism and, 92, 175, 185; motifs of, 6, 157, 158; nation and, 29, 79, 195; psychology of, 180, 185, 186–87; race and, 121

Farmers' Alliance, 101, 103, 105, 128. *See also* People's Party; populism

Faust, Drew Gilpin, 72n51, 75

Fern, Fanny, 79–80

Fetterley, Judith, 100n12

Ficino, 11n44

Financial panics: in 1873, 97, 101, 139, 146; in 1893, 101, 139

Fisher, Philip, 13n56, 154

Fleissner, Jennifer L., 4n13, 11n49, 182n37

Flower, B. O., 2

Foner, Eric, 69, 70n41, 71n46, 77

Foote, Stephanie, 110, 111n71, 116n82

Founding Fathers (filiopietism), 37, 40–41, 51–52, 56–58, 59

Fourth of July, 27, 53, 58, 105, 142

Frank, Thomas, 192

Franklin, Benjamin, 56, 57–58

Free Soil Party, 35

Freeman, Mary Wilkins, 97, 100

Freud, Sigmund, 3, 199

Friedman, Isaac Kahn, 151

Frontline (PBS program), 194

Gaines, Kevin, 122n99

Gardner, Jared, 87n86

Garland, Hamlin, 21, 24, 98, 109, 123, 158; *Crumbling Idols*, 116, 117–18, 119; *Main-Travelled Roads*, 109–21; "A New Declaration of Rights," 116, 118, 120

INDEX • 245

Garrison, William Lloyd, 45, 127, 145

Gay, Peter, 135n6

Genre theory, 28–29, 65–66, 82–83, 84, 86–87, 160, 186–87. *See also* aesthetics; specific genres

George, Henry. *See* Single Tax movement

Giles, Paul, 53n82, 55

Gillman, Susan, 122n99

Gilmore, Paul, 4n13

Gilroy, Paul, 39n49, 129, 187n57

Gitlin, Todd, 214–15

Glazener, Nancy, 5, 64n7, 100n11, 114n78, 181n35

Goldman, Emma, 24, 140–42, 144–46, 164n98, 168, 174, 205, 214

Gonzales, Manuel G., 90

González, John M., 85n78, 94

Goodwyn, Lawrence, 99n9

Gothic (genre), 10n42, 196–201

Gould, Philip, 41, 87n86

Gramsci, Antonio, 177n10

Grange, the, 101

Great Strike of 1877, 135, 137, 139, 146–47, 147n47. *See also* Knights of Labor; labor; unions

Greene, Graham, 192

Griffin, Susan, 201n100, 206

Guillory, John, 16

Guislain, Joseph, 32n18

Hale, Edward Everett, 61–63

Hamilton, Alexander, 105, 213

Harris, Frank, 163n97, 163–64, 174, 175, 195, 205, 214; *The Bomb*, 24, 25, 137–38, 148, 160–72; *Contemporary Portraits*, 160–61

Harris, Susan K., 75n62

Harte, Bret, 104n36

Hartman, Saidiya V., 92n106

Haskell, Thomas L., 140n19

Haviland, Beverly, 194, 201n100, 211n4

Hawthorne, Nathaniel, 28–29, 51, 54, 203–5

Hayes, Rutherford B., 70, 146

Haymarket Affair, 140; historical memory of, 24, 134, 137, 147–48; literature and, 160–72

Hebard, Andrew, 181n35

Hegeman, Susan, 192n69

Hemispheric literary studies, 84–85, 90, 94, 185

Hendler, Glenn, 4n13

Hentz, Caroline Lee, 41

Herr, Cheryl Temple, 111n71

Hicks, Granville, 138n11

Historical romance, 84, 95; consensus-generating features, 5, 22, 29–30, 46; nationalism and, 28; race and, 38–40, 99, 122–33; theories of, 19, 28–29, 39–40, 52, 54n87, 86; U.S. literature and, 28, 40–42, 44–46, 48; *Waverly* model of, 40. *See also under* U.S. Revolution

Historical sites, 195, 202–6

Historiography, 18–19, 24, 34, 39–49, 99–100, 110–11, 135–38, 139–48, 165. *See also under* populism

Hobsbawm, Eric, 18n86

Hofer, Johannes, 6–7, 15

Hofstadter, Richard, 14n61, 99n8

"Home, Sweet Home," 1–3, 24, 67, 121, 185, 192. *See also* Payne, John Howard

Homesickness. *See* nostalgia

Homestead, Melissa, 63n4, 76

Homo sacer. *See* biopolitics

Hopkins, Pauline E., 21, 68, 98, 121; *Contending Forces*, 24, 98–99, 121–33; *Daughter of the Revolution*, 126, 133; *Peculiar Sam*, 121

Hotels, 202, 207, 208–10; "hotel-spirit," 25, 175, 195, 207–9. *See also under* imperialism; nostalgia

Howe, Irving, 14n61
Howells, William Dean, 5, 95, 100, 100n11, 111–12, 138n11, 148; *A Hazard of New Fortunes*, 162, 162n92. *See also* realism
Hutcheson, Francis, 10
Hyde, Carrie, 62n3
Hypomnēsis. *See* Derrida, Jacques

Immigration (and immigrants), 12, 17, 24–25, 66, 84, 114–15, 177; radicalism and, 135–38, 141–42, 153, 156–58, 161, 168, 170; xenophobia and, 178, 201, 203, 208
Imperialism (U.S.), 25, 92, 94, 122, 174–76, 188–89, 193–94, 195, 207–8; Central America and, 85, 90–92; hotels and, 207, 210; Latin America and, 87–88n91; opponents of, 84n78, 176n5; scholarship on, 181. *See also* Mexican-American War; regionalism; Spanish-American War; Spanish Empire
Imperial romance, 2, 181, 185–87, 194
Indians. *See* indigenous peoples
Indigenous peoples, 46, 84, 87, 88–89, 94, 120, 181; Apache nation, 83, 89–90; Aztecs, 91–92; Indian removal and, 213. *See also under* nostalgia
Irving, Washington, 49, 195, 203–5

James, Henry, 22, 25, 138n11, 148, 162, 212; *The American Scene*, 22, 25, 174, 175, 194, 195, 201–10; "The Art of Fiction," 196; "The Jolly Corner," 25, 174–75, 194, 195–201, 202–3, 206
James, William, 176n5, 177n13, 199n93
Jameson, Fredric, 14–15, 86–87, 141
Jefferson, Thomas, 61; *Notes on the State of Virginia*, 43; Populists and, 24, 97, 101–9, 111, 117, 130; race and, 125–26; radical left movements and, 137n10, 140, 142; slavery and, 37–50; Tea Party Movement and, 213. *See under* nostalgia
Jewett, Sarah Orne, 97, 100

Jews and Judaism, 11, 109; anti-Semitism and, 99n7, 109
Johns, Gillian, 50
Joseph, Philip, 100n13

Kammen, Michael, 14
Kansas, 106, 163n96, 175, 179–94
Kant, Immanuel, 16, 17, 175, 176n5, 179, 191, 207; *Anthropology from a Pragmatic Point of View*, 9; "Idea for a Universal History with a Cosmopolitan Purpose," 180; *Critique of the Power of Judgment*, 9, 17; *Critique of Practical Reason*, 154; "Perpetual Peace: A Philosophical Sketch," 177, 189
Kaplan, Amy, 4n14, 92, 100n11, 181n35, 185, 188
Kazin, Michael, 139n13
Knights of Labor, 99n9, 101, 107, 155; *Journal of the Knights of Labor*, 104, 105n42, 106. *See also* People's Party; populism; Powderly, Terence; unions
Kossuth, Lajos, 35, 47, 57
Kristeva, Julia, 197, 200
Ku Klux Klan, 23, 69–70. *See also* Dixon, Thomas; prostration

Labor: African-American, 128; labor movements, 24, 97, 106–7, 135, 146, 155, 214; "labor question," 96; southern (white working class), 77, 125–26; wage, 4, 17, 19, 101, 130, 135–36, 145, 152–60, 166–69. *See also* anarchism; Great Strike of 1877; Knights of Labor; populism; slavery; socialism; unions
Lacan, Jacques, 13n56, 200
Laclau, Ernesto, 98, 102, 107, 122. *See also* Mouffe, Chantel
Lasch, Christopher, 14, 174n3
Laurie, Bruce, 99n9
Law: black disenfranchisement and, 37, 39, 47, 70; common (Anglo-American tradition), 141; copyright, 76; Jim Crow, 130, 132, 145, 146; labor, 139; natural,

40, 44; positive (constitutional, statutory), 43; radical rejection of (*see also* anarchism), 144, 161–62, 165, 168; Reconstruction and, 70. *See also* Constitution

Lears, T. J. Jackson, 14n60

Le Bon, Gustave, 151

Lewis, Sinclair, 148–50, 152, 215

Leys, Ruth, 15n70

Liberalism, 83–85, 137, 140, 195; consensus and, 4–6, 14n61, 19, 57, 136, 138n11, 162; historiography and, 42, 57n94, 144; individualism and, 13, 117, 131, 138, 160–61, 167; literature and, 4n14, 41, 138n11, 148–49, 159; and tolerance, 180–81, 189. *See also* Locke, John; neoliberalism

Lincoln, Abraham, 34, 62, 70n42, 93, 105, 126

Lippard, George, 41

Littlefield, Henry M., 181n34, 193

Local-color writing. *See* regionalism

Locke, John, 10; *An Essay Concerning Human Understanding*, 8; *Two Treatises of Government*, 43

London, Jack, 137n10, 138n11, 148, 151

Longa, Ernesto A., 139n12

Lost Cause (ideology of), 64, 67, 71–73. *See also* Ku Klux Klan; prostration; sectionalism

Lott, Eric, 35n35, 91

L'Ouverture, Toussaint, 133

Luis-Brown, David, 85n78

Lukács, Georg, 28, 40–41, 130n116

Lutz, Tom, 64n7, 100, 111n70, 115n81, 175n4, 178, 187

Mad Men (TV series), 211–12, 216

Madison, James, 144, 144n37, 164n98, 213

Maladie du pays. *See* nostalgia

Margolis, Stacey, 182n37

Marx, Karl (and Marxism), 136, 139, 141, 161, 214; *The Communist Manifesto*, 177, 177n10; *Economic and Philosophical Manuscripts*, 155; *The Eighteenth Brumaire of Louis Bonaparte*, 28; Marxism, 99n9, 136, 137n10, 139n13, 149n57, 152, 171. *See also* anarchism; socialism

Massumi, Brian, 15n70

Matt, Susan J., 2n8, 13, 67n23

Matthiessen, F. O., 28

McGerr, Michael, 99n10

McGill, Meredith, 29

McMath Jr., Robert C., 99n10

McPherson, Tara, 70n42

Melancholy, 3, 6, 11, 15, 33, 36, 49, 128, 135–36

Melville, Herman: "Hawthorne and His Mosses," 54; "Israel Potter" (serialization in *Putnam's Monthly*), 53; *Israel Potter* (novel), 22, 29–31, 32, 51–60, 76, 213

Merish, Lori, 83–84

Mexico, 61, 87–88, 90, 91–92, 94–95. *See also* Mexican-American War; Spain; Spanish Empire

Mexican-American War, 12, 22, 29, 32, 41, 66–67, 87–88n91

Michaels, Walter Benn, 181–82

Midwest, 23, 69, 101, 104, 111–13, 109–21, 126, 192. *See also* Chicago; Dakota Territory; Kansas

Millet, Jean-François, 114

Minstrelsy (blackface), 83, 90–92, 94

Mississippi, 37n43, 50, 71, 121

Mitchell, Lee Clark, 196

Mitchell, S. Weir, 173

Most, Johann, 161, 162, 168, 169

Mother Earth, 140, 164

Mott, Frank Luther, 63n6

Mouffe, Chantal, 20n89. *See also* Laclau, Ernesto

Murison, Justine, 4n13, 10n42

Murphy, Gretchen, 85, 186

Museums, 135n6, 195, 201–2, 204, 206

Nabers, Deak, 44

"National People's Party Platform." *See under* People's Party

Nationalism, 13, 22, 137, 168, 179; black (African-American), 38; Irish, 49; literary, 28–29, 204; theory of, 5n17, 10, 33–34n26; U.S., 28–29, 35, 41, 50–51, 53–55, 58–59, 64, 85, 179. *See also* Confederate nationalism. *See also under* nostalgia

Native Americans. *See* indigenous peoples

Naturalism (literary movement), 112, 138, 149, 151, 158–59, 175; studies of, 117, 135n6, 138n11, 149, 150n62, 181–82

Neoliberalism, 212–13

New Orleans, 71, 73–74, 129, 131–33

New York, 113–14, 117, 120, 195–201, 214; cosmopolitanism and, 178; intellectual culture and, 166–67; publishing and, 23, 75, 79–80, 100, 167; regionalism and, 69, 100n11

New York Herald, 103n29, 147n47

New York Times, 98, 164, 184, 193n76, 213

Ngai, Sianne, 13, 15n70

Nickels, Joel, 118n89

Nostalgia: affective characteristics of, 1–2, 3; amnesia and, 5, 13, 120; Africans and African Americans and (dirt-eating and "negro consumption"), 11, 30, 32–33, 42–43, 121–22, 123, 126–33; children and, 33, 103, 196–97; cosmopolitanism and, 25, 174, 176, 179, 179–94; critical dismissal of, 13–14, 200, 211; democratic quality of, 11, 33–34, 103, 108; history of, 6, 12–13, 15–16, 19, 21–26; hotels and, 208; indigenous peoples and, 67; imperialism and, 15n67, 19; Jews and, 11; as a medical disorder, 6–12, 16, 32, 55–56, 81, 115, 118, 195; nationalism and, 31–37, 61–62, 67; political dimensions (general), 4–6, 19–20, 20–22, 200, 210; poverty and, 103, 104; race and, 85–86; radical (left nostalgia), 24, 135–38, 141–42, 144–45, 147–48, 151–52; 156–72, 205, 214–15; regionally specific, 67–69, 103–4, 195–201, 203, 207; rural (agrarian, pastoral), 1–3, 21, 22, 59–60, 104–5, 109–21, 156–57, 158–59, 179–80, 183–93; sailors and, 30, 32; Southern (Dixie, sectionalist), 46, 63, 68–70, 73–74, 76, 199, 205; soldiers and, 8, 67, 113, 173; spiritualism and, 81n71; women and, 11, 33, 81

Nussbaum, Martha, 178n21

Nye, David E., 153

Occupy Wall Street, 25, 212, 213–14

O'Hare, Kate Richards, 145n43

O. Henry (William Sydney Porter), 191

Olmsted, Frederick Law, 33

Onuf, Peter S., 34n26

Optic, Oliver (William Taylor Adams), 65

Overland Monthly, The, 90

Paine, Thomas, 40, 140, 143, 163–64n98, 170, 214

Pancoast, Henry S., 100n11

Paris Commune of 1871, 71n46, 137, 146–47, 171

Parker, Hershel, 53n82

Parrington, Vernon Louis, 149

Parsons, Albert, 170–71

Parsons, Frank, 102

Parsons, Lucy, 24, 135, 164n104, 168, 171, 205, 214; "The Negro," 145; "On the 'Harmony' Between Capital and Labor," 145; "A Piece of History," 143; "Speeches at the Founding Convention of the Industrial Workers of the World," 134–35

Pastoral, 77, 109–10, 114, 119, 138, 158, 203

Payne, John Howard, 1–3. *See also* "Home, Sweet Home"

INDEX • 249

People's Party (U.S. political party), 24,
    101–3, 105–9, 116, 124n101, 126, 213.
    "National People's Party Platform," 107.
    See also Donnelly, Ignatius; populism;
    Watson, Thomas

Peyser, Thomas, 175n4, 194n79

Pinkerton, Allan, 147

Pinkertons, 107, 165, 169

Pita, Beatrice, 84–85n78

Pizer, Donald, 112n73

Plantation fiction, 41–42, 64n9, 91, 93, 121,
    127

Pollack, Norman, 99n9

Populism: black 97n3, 98–99, 99n10, 101,
    121–33; historiography of, 97, 99–100;
    literature and, 24, 99, 109–33; politi-
    cal movement (U.S.), 23–24, 97–100,
    101, 102–9, 130, 192, 193, 205; theories
    of, 98, 102, 122. See also People's Party,
    regionalism

Porter, Edward J., 22, 31–32, 33

Posnett, Hutcheson Macaulay, 119

Posnock, Ross, 174n3, 179, 199n93

Postcolonialism (and postcolonial theory),
    15n67, 187n57

Postel, Charles, 99n10, 101n15, 124n101

Powderly, Terence, 101, 166. See also
    Knights of Labor

Pratt, Lloyd, 29

Print history, 34n26; antebellum era and,
    31–37; capitalism and, 165; cosmo-
    politan periodicals and, 178–79, 181;
    radical press and, 139–45, 147–48;
    Southern periodicals and (see also Con-
    federate nationalism), 72–73. See also
    publishing under New York

Progressivism, 4, 99, 181n34, 201–2, 207

Prostration (Southern ideology of), 63, 71,
    76, 78, 82, 90, 94, 125–27. See also
    Dixon, Thomas; Ku Klux Klan; Recon-
    struction

Protestant work ethic. See asceticism;
    Weber, Max

Proudhon, Pierre-Joseph, 143, 170

Pryse, Marjorie, 100n12

Psychoanalysis (and psychoanalytic theory),
    3, 13n56; 13–14n58; 15n70, 135–36,
    186–87, 197–201, 206

Race: affect, 3n12; Anglo-Saxon purity and,
    25, 70, 174, 176; as a basis of oppres-
    sion (racism), 64, 70, 84–85, 120–22,
    129, 145, 216; conflict and, 23, 67, 91,
    122–33; critical theory and, 86; mis-
    cegenation and, 44, 48, 70, 84, 86–89,
    132. See also Africa; African-American;
    indigenous peoples; slavery

Rancière, Jacques, 5–6, 19–20, 44, 98; Aes-
    thetics and Its Discontents, 5, 18–19;
    Disagreement, 17, 18n82, 86; Dissensus,
    17–18n81, 18n82, 18n85, 40, 102, 159;
    The Flesh of Words, 18, 65–66, 86; Mute
    Speech, 46; The Politics of Aesthetics,
    17n79, 18, 18n85, 39, 166; "Who Is the
    Subject of the Rights of Man?," 53n80.
    See also aesthetics

Rawlings, Peter, 201n100

Realism (American Literary), 19, 97, 112,
    151, 163n97; critical history of, 4n14;
    liberalism and, 5, 138n11; literary pres-
    tige of, 4–5, 173; regionalism and, 98,
    100n11; theories of, 117, 137, 149. See
    also Howells, William Dean

Reconstruction (U.S.), 23, 63, 66–74, 85,
    216; laws of, 23, 70; literature and, 23,
    64, 74, 76; populism and, 101, 120,
    124; race and, 50, 64n10, 66, 69–70,
    124n102, 146; Radical Republicans and,
    67–70, 76, 82, 128; Southern white
    rejection of, 62, 67, 71–73, 82–83, 84,
    91–93. See also Confederate national-
    ism; Lost Cause; prostration. See also
    under regionalism

Regionalism, 54, 59–60, 71–72, 85, 97,
    100–1, 110, 112, 114n78, 119–20; cos-
    mopolitanism and, 100, 117, 178, 187,
    191; critical regionalism, 111n71; impe-
    rialism and, 100; interlocalism and, 24,
    122, 132–33; Northeastern publishers
    and, 79–80, 100, 100n11, 109–10; race
    and, 128; Reconstruction and, 68–73,

76, 78; politics and, 23–24, 64, 91, 94–95, 99–100, 110, 117, 173. *See also under* New York

Reid, Thomas, 9

Reid-Pharr, Robert, 38

Reising, Russell, 57n91

Renan, Ernest, 5n17

Revolution, 126–27, 214; 1848 European, 28, 34–36, 46–47, 57, 137; French (1789), 49, 52, 57, 71, 137, 168–69, 171, 214; radical (anarchist, socialist), 145–48, 151, 161–62, 169–72; theories of, 57, 168–69n114. *See also* U.S. Revolution

Reynolds, David S., 97n2

Reynolds, Larry J., 35n35

Rideout, Walter B., 149n57

Robbins, Bruce, 14, 179, 190

Robespierre, Maximilien, 126, 161–62

Rogin, Michael Paul, 52

Rohrbach, Augusta, 38n46

Romance. *See* historical romance; imperial romance; sentiment

Romero, Lora, 92

Rosaldo, Renato, 15n67

Rosen, George, 8n22

Ross, Dorothy, 140n19

Rowlandson, Mary, 89

Rowson, Susanna, 36

Ruiz de Burton, María Amparo, 23, 63–66, 83–95

Rush, Benjamin, 12, 32n18

Rushdie, Salman, 180

Ruskin, John, 201–2, 206

Sala, George Augustus, 9–10

Saldívar, José David, 85n78

Samuels, Shirley, 28, 64n7

Sánchez, Rosaura, 84–85n78

Sandoval-Strausz, A. K., 207, 210

Santayana, George, 16, 154

Savoy, Eric, 196n85

Sayre, Robert, 77n68

Scalia, Antonin, 26, 215–16

Schiller, Friedrich, 17, 17n76, 202

Schlesinger, Jr. Arthur M., 14n61

Schreiner, Hermann L., 31–32

Scott, Walter, 40, 44–45

Scottish Enlightenment, 8, 9–11. *See also* common sense *under* aesthetics

Sectionalism, 19, 21–23, 27–30, 31–37, 39, 59, 64n9, 82–83, 146. *See also* Confederate nationalism; Lost Cause; prostration

Seltzer, Mark, 4n14

Sentiment (and sentimentalism), 16, 36–37, 211; familial feeling and, 78, 92; literary history and, 162n92; nation and, 10; novels and, 28, 36–37, 37–39, 41, 48, 78–79, 83–84, 150–51, 157–58; philosophy of, 17n77; race and, 48; tragic mulatto and, 37–38, 128, 130–33. *See also* domesticity; historical romance; sympathy

Silyn Roberts, Siân, 10n42

Simms, William Gilmore, 41

Sinclair, Upton, 138, 138n11, 139n14, 149n57, 174–75, 195, 205, 214, 215; *The Cry for Justice*, 161; *The Jungle*, 4, 24, 137–38, 137n10, 148–60, 161, 163, 172; *Mammonart*, 151–53

Single Tax movement, 116–17

Sizer, Lyde Cullen, 64n8

Slauter, Eric, 216n22

Slave revolts, 24, 38, 48, 61n1, 124, 145

Slavery, 33–34, 46, 50, 123; economics and, 146; Jamestown and, 46, 213; legacy of, 120, 127, 213; liberalism and, 43–44, 93; narratives of, 37–50, 52; sectional crisis and, 35, 39, 41, 91, 119, 122. *See also* abolitionism; Confederate nationalism; slave revolts

Smith, Adam, 10–11, 54n87

Smith, Caleb, 146n44

Smith, Henry Nash, 111n71

Socialism, 21, 22, 24–25, 102, 137–38, 139–47, 163–64n98, 160–64, 167, 205; Fabian, 163; internationalism, 19, 21, 24, 137, 146–48, 161, 166–69, 172; Nationalism (Bellamy's program of), 108; revolutionary, 134, 136, 153; in U.S., 139n14, 140, 149, 150–52, 167

Sofer, Naomi Z., 75n60

Sommer, Doris, 87, 89

Sorel, Georges, 161, 170

South, the. *See* Confederacy; Confederate nationalism; regionalism

South Carolina, 27–28, 35, 71n46, 123

Sovereignty, 44, 70, 177

Spain, 88–90, 92, 94, 214

Spanish-American War, 25, 173–74, 176–77, 194

Spanish Empire, 90, 92

Stern, Julia, 36

Stewart, Dugald, 8

Stowe, Harriet Beecher, 36–37, 42, 75, 93, 145, 151

Streeby, Shelley, 41n57, 138n11

Strikes (labor). *See under* unions. *See* Great Strike of 1877

Sublime, 16, 158, 159, 195, 202; industrial, 153–55; revolutionary, 163, 170. *See also* aesthetics; Kant, Immanuel

Sui Sin Far (Edith Maude Eaton), 100

Sympathy, 2, 28, 62, 78, 107; class and, 78, 80, 82, 119, 158; nationalism and, 32, 35, 178; philosophy of, 10–11, 102, 170; race and, 39, 42, 48, 67, 84–85, 127. *See also* sentiment

Tate, Claudia, 124

Tawil, Ezra, 48n69, 87n86

Tea Party Movement, 25, 212–13, 215

Tennenhouse, Leonard, 87

Thrailkill, Jane F., 4n13, 15n70

Tichi, Cecelia, 150

Tintner, Adeline R., 194n79

Tompkins, Jane, 92n106

Tourgée, Albion W., 74

Trachtenberg, Alan, 4

Tradition, 186, 202; of Chicano/a resistance, 84–85n78; of Hispanophone literature, 86–87; immigrants and, 156–57, 161; of indigenous peoples, 91n104, 92; of Jeffersonian democracy, 5, 126, 130; literature and, 28–29, 31–33, 40, 76, 82, 84–88, 138n11, 152, 203–5; race and, 39–47, 127–28; populism and, 96–99; radicalism and, 136–48, 164; sectionalism and, 65, 87; theories of, 18n86, 18–19, 57–58, 118; of U.S. Revolution (*see also* U.S. Revolution), 35–37, 39–42, 45–47, 52–60, 84

Trilling, Lionel, 138n11, 149n57

Tuke, Daniel H. *See* Bucknill, John Charles

Turner, Frederick Jackson, 99n7, 140

Tyler, Royall, 52

Unions (labor, trade), 24, 96, 101, 111, 135, 139, 156, 165, 216; American Federation of Labor (AFL), 134; International Workers of the World (IWW, Wobblies), 134–35, 171; strikes, 24, 170. *See also* Great Strike of 1877; Knights of Labor; labor; populism

U.S. Revolution, 12, 36, 55, 71, 203, 216; 1848 European revolutions and, 35–36, 46–47; blacks and, 5, 21, 37–40, 42–43, 45–49; historical romances of, 41, 45–46, 54–60; historiography and, 5, 22, 34, 45–46, 51, 58, 141; philosophy and, 52–53, 53n80, 58; populism and, 105, 213; radicalism and, 24, 136, 141–46, 148, 168–71, 214; Reconstruction and, 71; sectionalism and, 27–28, 33, 34n26, 35–36; Spirit of '76 and, 28, 35, 116, 142–43. *See also* revolution

Utopia, 99n8, 185, 196; dystopia and, 108, 151, 212n5; literature of, 97–98, 108; philosophy of, 192–93

Véron, Eugène, 112, 117–18

Vidal, Gore, 5
Voigt, Lisa, 87

Warren Court, 216
Warren, Kenneth W., 64n7
Watson, Thomas E., 105
Watts, Edward, 112n76
Weather Underground Organization, 172
Weber, Max, 156, 183–84, 185, 193
Weir, David, 163–64n98
Wertheimer, Eric, 91n104
West, the, 23, 59, 63, 68–69, 83–95, 99n7, 101, 104, 140n20, 213
Wexler, Laura, 92n106
White, Andrew D., 140
White, Ed, 61n1, 97n4
White, Hayden, 110–11
White, William Allen, 192
Whitman, Walt, 96–97, 118, 161
Widmer, Edward L., 53
Wilentz, Sean, 35
Williams, David, 63n5, 67n22

Williams, Raymond, 111n70
Wilson, Edmund, 64n7
Wilson, Ivy G., 4n13, 38, 44
Wisconsin, 109, 113–14, 118, 177
Wobblies. *See under* unions
Wonder (as an aesthetic category), 25, 138, 148, 151–57, 163, 188, 203. *See also* sublime
Wood, Gordon, 57
World's Columbian Exposition of 1893, 176, 180
World Trade Protest (Seattle, 1999), 172

Yarborough, Richard, 124n103
Young America movement, 53–54. *See also* nationalism
Young, Elizabeth, 64n7, 76

Zimmerman, David A., 138n11
Zipes, Jack, 182, 185, 192, 194
Zitkala-Ša (Gertrude Simmons Bonnin), 100
Žižek, Slavoj, 13–14n58, 162n93, 186–87

www.ingramcontent.com/pod-product-compliance
Lightning Source LLC
Chambersburg PA
CBHW030109010526
44116CB00005B/169